BLAXPLOITATION CINEMA
THE ESSENTIAL REFERENCE GUIDE

Originally published by FAB Press, April 2008
Revised second edition first published December 2020, re-printed July 2021
This second edition third pressing published February 2022

FAB Press Ltd.
2 Farleigh, Ramsden Road
Godalming, Surrey
GU7 1QE, England, U.K.

www.fabpress.com

Edited and Designed by Harvey Fenton,
with thanks to Francis Brewster for production assistance.

Front cover illustration
Montage created by Kevin Coward from American original theatrical release poster art for **Blast** (aka **The Final Comedown**, 1972), **Coffy** (1973), **Dolemite** (1975), **TNT Jackson** (1974), **Super Fly** (1972), **Shaft's Big Score!** (1972) and **Slaughter** (1972).

Back cover illustration
Adapted from the Belgian theatrical release poster for **Black Belt Jones** (1974).

Frontispiece illustration
Clean cut and all *African* American, karate champion Jim Kelly carved a niche for himself as the black Bruce Lee in films like **Black Belt Jones** (1974), **Hot Potato** (1975), and **Black Samurai** (1976). (J. Howard Collection)

Title page illustration:
Adapted from an admat created for the promotion of **Hit!** (1973).

A CIP catalogue record for this book is available from the British Library.

hardcover:
ISBN 978 1 903254 37 0

Printed in Czech Republic

BLAXPLOITATION
CINEMA

The Essential Reference Guide

Josiah Howard

A FAB PRESS PRESENTATION

Acknowledgements

First, to all the wonderful actors, actresses, directors, producers, writers, musicians and behind the scenes people who put their talent and efforts into the body of films known as blaxploitation, a great and heartfelt thank you. You not only gave new meaning to the term 'Film Noir,' you also uplifted a generation of film lovers and filmmakers and paved the way for today's black superstars to take their rightful place at the highest levels of the motion picture industry.

I am greatly indebted to the ten directors who took time out of their busy schedules to be interviewed for this book. Paul Bogart, Matt Cimber, Larry Cohen, Robert A. Endelson, Jamaa Fanaka, Jack Hill, Jonathan Kaplan, Arthur Marks, Cirio H. Santiago and Don Schain – thank you. Your comments, reminiscences and keen observations have made this book much more than it would have been otherwise. Also of great help to me was David Walker's limited-edition *BadAzz MoFo* fanzine. Filled with exclusive interviews, obscure poster art, and the writer/editor/publisher's own irreverent film reviews, Mr. Walker's hard work, dedication and appreciation of the blaxploitation film genre was a source of information that would have been difficult to find elsewhere. Also helpful were four other fanzines: Paul J. Brown's *Baad Mutha@*!#ers*; Brian Albright's *Alternative Cinema*; John Hudson's *Rewinder*; and Mason Storm's *Encyclopedia of Cinematic Trash*.

Mr. Terry Carter, thank you for your generous, patient and always uplifting correspondence.

Mr. Harvey Fenton and Mr. Francis Brewster, thank you for continuing to challenge me and for going way beyond the call of duty to make sure that this book was the best that it possibly could be.

Finally many thanks go to Gail Ann Blackmer, Artur Zebrowski, Scott Mortenson, Jed Root, Darrin Perry, Tony Alansky, Alan Hamilton, Clarence E. Gamblin, Marc Morris, Tristan Thompson, New York City Public Library, Plainfield, New Jersey Public Library, Kim's Video, NYC and Soul Images.

Arch but elegant: Tamara Dobson starred as a high-kicking undercover narcotics agent in two films, **Cleopatra Jones** (1973, *above*), and **Cleopatra Jones and the Casino of Gold** (1975). (J. Howard Collection)

Contents

The plight of returning Vietnam Veterans was explored in many blaxploitation films including **Welcome Home Brother Charles** (1975) and **The Black Six** (1973). In 1973's **Gordon's War**, Paul Winfield *(above, second from left)* lays out his plan for a battle against the drug dealers in his neighbourhood. (J. Howard Collection)

About the Book

Blaxploitation Cinema: The Essential Reference Guide came about in stops and starts. I grew up in a small, mostly African-American suburban town in New Jersey called Plainfield. Front Street, the main thoroughfare, boasted a grandly columned bank, a record shop, a 'boutique,' numerous clothing and wig stores, and two movie houses, the old but still somewhat respectable Strand and the West End's faded, partially dilapidated Liberty.

My first exposure to blaxploitation films came at the age of twelve, when my best friend's grandmother took me along with her two grandchildren on a three-day trip to New York City. Though I loved our trip to Coney Island's famed 'Astro Land,' it was our trip to 42nd Street's New Amsterdam Theater (before it was renovated and became home to *The Lion King*) that really left its mark on me. That fateful day in 1974, we took in a 'return engagement' double of *Coffy* and *Trouble Man*. The back-to-back barrage of sounds and images simply blew me away. From that point on I was hooked; I went to as many blaxploitation films as I possibly could.

As an adult my interest in blaxploitation films continued. I bought the few books that were available on the genre, kept clippings and collected memorabilia, and when the home video market took off, purchased as many films as my meagre earnings would allow. But even though I remained an interested observer and ardent fan of the films, I hesitated for many years to seriously consider putting together a book on the genre. My 'logic' was that there really weren't enough movies to fill an entire book and that, since I already thought I knew everything there was to know about the pictures, it wouldn't be a project that would hold my interest for very long. I was wrong on both counts. Reviewing, cataloguing (and often discovering) the films in this book has been both pleasurable and informative.

Neither a hard-core intellectual film theory discourse, nor a nostalgic 'celebration,' it is my hope that *Blaxploitation Cinema: The Essential Reference Guide* is, instead, an American film guidebook; a comprehensive look at the blaxploitation film genre, its players and its many creative participants.

About the Author

Josiah Howard writes on popular culture and is the author of four books. A senior contributor at Furious Cinema and The Grindhouse Cinema Database, Howard also lectures on film and has curated festivals internationally: America, Brazil, the Netherlands and the UK. His writing credits include articles for *The American Library of Congress*, *The New York Times* and *Reader's Digest*.

Author photo by Kamron Hinatsu.

Josiah Howard

Defining Blaxploitation Films

What is a blaxploitation film? What combination of elements differentiates blaxploitation films from Hollywood's many general-release action films? Is every 1970s film featuring an African American in a leading role a blaxploitation film?

To be sure, defining blaxploitation films is not an easy task. The late, great Gordon Parks Sr., director of *Shaft* – perhaps the genre's most celebrated picture – was one of several prominent directors who, taking offense at both the term 'blaxploitation' and the classification of their films as such, refused to be interviewed for this book.

For the purposes of this book blaxploitation films are defined as 1970s black-cast or black-themed films (or mainstream Hollywood pictures featuring at least one prominent African-American player in a modern-minded narrative steeped in and/or influenced by the concurrent Black Pride movement), created, developed, and most importantly, *heavily promoted* to young, inner-city, black audiences.

Adhering to this broad definition (and with a pointed refusal on my part to view the term 'blaxploitation' as in any way negative, derogatory or limited to films that deal with drugs, crime or are necessarily set in the ghetto) means that above-ground, critically-acclaimed black-cast 'prestige' pictures like *Claudine* (which actually *does* take place in the ghetto) and *Sounder*, documentary films like *Wattstax* and *Save the Children*, musicals like *Sparkle* and *Don't Play Us Cheap*, melodramas like *A Hero Ain't Nothin' But a Sandwich* and *Cornbread Earl and Me*, and comedies like *Which Way Is Up?* and *Skin Game* – all of which were given the green-light to capitalise upon (and 'exploit') the financial success and popularity of the easier to categorise, action-oriented 'blaxploitation' pictures – are also included among the book's listings.

Also covered are several grey-area films whose big budgets, top name (white) stars and/or general-interest advertising campaigns do not obscure the fact that the productions are, through their liberal use of African-American players, themes and concerns, heavily influenced by the concurrently popular blaxploitation film genre. Some of these grey-area pictures (all of which feature a black player in a contemporary-minded leading role) include comedies, e.g. *Blazing Saddles* and *Mother, Jugs & Speed*, fantasy films such as *The Angel Levine* and *The Omega Man*, exposés on miscegenation like *Cinderella Liberty* and *The Landlord*, and 'slice-of-life' dramas such as *Fingers* and *The Grasshopper*.

Along with the hundreds of blaxploitation movies made Stateside, this book also takes account of the many exclusively foreign-made films that were imported to America, often re-titled, and re-distributed as 'blaxploitation' films. Some of these pictures include *Black Fire* (Mexico), *Soul Brothers of Kung Fu* and *The Black Dragon* (both Hong Kong), *Mandinga* and *Passion Plantation* (both Italy), *Mister Deathman* (South Africa), *Slavers* (West Germany), and *Man Friday* and *Embassy* (two films from Great Britain that both retained their original titles).

What all of the films in this book have in common is that they were a part of, or directly capitalised on, the high visibility and financial success of America's one and only African-American motion picture boom.

above: Jim Kelly and Gloria Hendry in a posed publicity still taken during the making of **Black Belt Jones** (1974).

Ron O'Neal, as Priest in 1972's **Super Fly**, set trends in both fashion and hairstyles. (Soul Images)

Chapter One

What's Going On?

BLACK FILMS, 1960-1970

The 1960s proved to be a decade marked by unforeseen incident and a dramatic change in American race relations. The ongoing war in Vietnam, the assassinations of Malcolm X, Martin Luther King Jr. and the Kennedys, combined with an ever-increasing number of inner-city race riots (most notably in Watts, Detroit and Newark) intensified the growing need for tolerance and unity.

As well as advancing the causes and concerns of African Americans, the 1960s civil rights and Black Power movements – aided and abetted by popularised slogans like 'Say It Loud I'm Black and I'm Proud' and 'Black Is Beautiful' – ushered in a new era of white awareness and appreciation of African-American cultural iconography. Be it the co-opting of black hairstyles, fashion and catchphrases, or the widespread appeal of soul music and its stars, the new white familiarity with the extraneous accoutrements of black life created an outwardly unified front behind which progressive-minded films featuring black actors and/or black themes could be developed and marketed. Initiated during a decade marked by a number of other radical movements (the sexual revolution, feminism, anti-war, free speech), the liberal use of African Americans in 1960s films seemed like an inevitable, if belated, social progression.

Without question Sidney Poitier was the era's biggest black star. His roles in films like *A Patch of Blue* (1965), *In the Heat of the Night*, *To Sir with Love* and *Guess Who's Coming to Dinner* (all 1967), and *For Love of Ivy* (1968) placed him among (white) Hollywood's elite. The often-written-about downside of Poitier's accomplishment (a major *New York Times* editorial appeared under the screaming headline "Why Does White America Love Sidney Poitier So?") was that his catalogue of film characters were, for the most part, variations on a single personality type; one that never adequately addressed or displayed the frustration, disappointment and/or out-and-out-anger that was so much a part of the 1960s African-American experience.

Appealing to audiences on a level that Poitier could not was former NFL fullback Jim Brown. Though the pro football player-turned actor occupied a lower tier of stardom in the minds of white filmgoers, Brown was the contemporary black man's cinema hero, an everyman who shot, kicked and beat up people in a string of supporting roles in action films like *Rio Conchos* (1964), *The Dirty Dozen* (1967), *Ice Station Zebra* and *Dark of the Sun* (both 1968), *100 Rifles*, *Riot* and *Kenner* (all 1969). Poitier's films appealed to the white masses and the black bourgeoisie while Brown's films attracted the younger, politically inclined, black audience.

Along with Poitier's star vehicles and Brown's action pictures, the 1960s saw the release of several other popular films that featured blacks. While some appeared to offer social commentary – *The Cool World* (1963); *Nothing But a Man* (1964); and *The Learning Tree* (1969) – others (sometimes serious, sometimes salacious) 'covered' but did not comment on a number of controversial topics: miscegenation (*One Potato, Two Potato* (1964)); racism (*If He Hollers Let Him Go* and *The Story of a Three Day Pass* (both 1968)); black assimilation (*Putney Swope* (1968) and *A Change of Mind* (1969)); and black rage (*Up Tight* (1968) and *Slaves* (1969)). Films such as these appealed to an increasingly cynical and disillusioned African-American movie-going public who were impatiently awaiting the arrival of more realistic and socially aware black film characters in narratives that accurately reflected the changing times.

And the times *were* changing. A national fatigue, prompted by the bleakness of everyday news reports (growing crime, rising inflation, 'Watergate') combined with an unprecedented number of rapidly manufactured pre-fab suburban communities, resulted in a mass white exodus from America's urban centres. When African Americans moved into the spaces vacated by upwardly mobile whites (becoming the major proprietors of 'downtown' area businesses) the value of the black consumer dollar, as it related to both hard goods and the entertainment industry, took on a more prominent significance. If Hollywood wanted to keep black money rolling in, the film capital would have to seriously consider the needs and expectations of America's newest urban dwellers.

The first year of the new decade saw the release of an ambitious, pointedly modern, and carefully targeted batch of black cast and/or black themed pictures. *Halls of Anger*, *Right On!*, *...tick...tick...tick...*, and *The Liberation of L.B. Jones* (all 1970), had titles that accurately reflected the contentious, volatile and unpredictable mood of the day. Not only did African Americans flock to see Hollywood's new line of black pictures, but their presence and (financial) support also created an atmosphere of excitement and prosperity that often invigorated inner-city areas. Black interest in Hollywood's new films turned formerly abandoned 'downtown' movie houses – once considered antiquated and unsafe – into bustling entertainment venues that were not only profitable, but also 'hip'.

Operating on the premise that young African-American audiences wanted not only to examine contemporary issues, but also sometimes to escape from them, United Artists released a mid-budget multi-cast comedy called *Cotton Comes to Harlem*. In no time at all the film became the biggest grossing 'black' film to date, generating revenue of over $15.4 million, an unheard of amount in 1970. In what seemed like an instant, films featuring African Americans were shuttled from the margins and hastily moved into the motion picture industry's main arena.

A GENRE IS BORN

1970's *Cotton Comes to Harlem* was followed by 1971's *Sweet Sweetback's Baadasssss Song*. Where *Cotton* had been a major Hollywood studio release employing the varied talents of hundreds of craftsmen, jack-of-all-trades Melvin Van Peebles wrote, produced, directed, financed, scored and starred in *Sweetback*. Filmed entirely on location, Van Peebles's film cost $450,000 to make. By the end of the year it had grossed $12 million.

While *Cotton Comes to Harlem* was filled with familiar and inoffensive (though 'hip') Hollywood film characters set in a romanticised urban setting, *Sweetback* dared to present a different image, that of a bold and proud 'anti-hero' fearlessly making his way through the harsh, ugly ghetto streets.

Stark, challenging, often disturbing, the film, rated X "by an all white jury" (later edited to R) was filled with frank language, extreme violence and vividly enacted sexual situations. Though critics were divided on the merits of the picture, everyone agreed that *Sweet Sweetback's Baadasssss Song*, with its avant-garde presentation of black male anger and sexuality, set a new standard in the representation of African-American males in mainstream American cinema. As one high-profile black actor (who remained anonymous) told *Newsweek*, from this point on black audiences,

especially young ones, would no longer tolerate black pictures that featured "warmhearted, whitewashed men and women... filled with love, trust and patience." Proof that *Sweetback* fully encompassed the new militant mood of the day came with the Black Panther Party's across-the-board endorsement; *Sweet Sweetback's Baadasssss Song* was made required viewing for all Panther members.

At the same time that *Sweetback* was showing American audiences images of unrestrained defiance, revenge and ultimate victory, MGM released *Shaft*, a film adaptation of Ernest Tidyman's best selling novel. Originally intended for one of Hollywood's leading white actors (both Charlton Heston and Steve McQueen were considered), when the studio tallied up the enormous profits of *Cotton* and *Sweetback*, the film's dialogue was hastily rewritten.

Shaft was directed by *The Learning Tree*'s Gordon Parks Sr. and starred Richard Roundtree, an African-American print model and theatre actor. Articulate, intelligent and suave, John Shaft's edges were filed down so that the all-important film industry demographic (white males aged 14 to 28) could also identify with the character. A standard detective story in blackface, there were *Shaft* suits, belts, coats, beach towels, sweatshirts, aftershave and cologne. Additionally, and perhaps most importantly, the film generated a thrilling chart-topping, Oscar and Grammy winning title song 'Theme from Shaft' performed by one of the era's most popular black stars, Isaac Hayes.

Both *Sweetback* and *Shaft* brought the content, image and ideology of the 'new black films' to the masses. Equally important, both productions employed blacks in pivotal roles in front of *and* behind the cameras. But even though both pictures were targeted to young black audiences, the two films were worlds apart. *Sweetback* challenged, insulted, provoked and surpassed the expectations of its audience and introduced a new black film hero. *Shaft*, in the tradition of Hollywood's biggest box-office bonanzas, simply entertained.

Hollywood had been struggling and the studios were desperately searching for a windfall; by 1970 Columbia, Fox and, in particular, MGM – who held an infamous yard sale of celebrity props and costumes – were teetering on the verge of bankruptcy. Dwindling theatre attendance, the stronghold of television and the demise of the Hollywood 'star system' had all contributed to the collapse of tinseltown's infrastructure. Consequently, anything at all that could generate quick and ready capital was of the utmost importance. Put together on modest budgets, released with minimal fanfare, and reaping unanticipated financial rewards, Hollywood came to view 'black' films as a major part of the route out of their deepening fiscal crisis.

This iconic image from 1971's **Shaft** (also used on the film's poster art) shows that New York City detective John Shaft (Richard Roundtree) was a black film hero who was most definitely not to be messed with. (Soul Images).

COPYCATS

Following the phenomenal success of *Sweet Sweetback's Baadasssss Song* and *Shaft*, a formula for making movies was firmly set in place. Gather together a group of African-American actors, set the story in the ghetto, spice the dialogue with expletives and 'hip' lingo, throw in a mix of sex and violence and place the main characters in positions of power (or at least dominance) over whites. The result: a sure-fire hit.

1972 saw the official beginning of what *Time* magazine called "The Black Movie Boom." The inevitable sequel to *Shaft*, *Shaft's Big Score!* (actually a much better movie than its predecessor) was one of the first out of the cannon. But if MGM had hoped to corner the market for black films, they were sorely mistaken. The pictures came from everywhere and they came all at once. From the major studios (Metro Goldwyn Mayer, Warner Bros., Paramount), the independents (American International Pictures), and upstarts (Dimension, General Film Corporation, Moonstone).

Over the course of just twelve months out came *Across 110th Street, Black Mama, White Mama, Hammer, The Legend of Nigger Charley, Buck and the Preacher, Black Gunn, Slaughter, Come Back Charleston Blue, Cool Breeze, Melinda, The Limit, Top of the Heap, Trouble Man, Hit Man* and *Super Fly*, among many others.

Super Fly is the landmark film from this period. *Shaft* generalised the genre's appeal, but *Super Fly* amplified the modes of representation and took both language and clothing to the extreme. Starring theatre actor Ron O'Neal and directed by Gordon Parks Jr., the picture (which had been previewed for inner-city residents in key urban markets) was buoyed by a strong word of mouth campaign, the result of which was that in its very first week at only two New York City theatres, *Super Fly* grossed more than $1 million. Just two months later the $500,000 production had brought in $11 million more! As reported in the 4 October, 1972 edition of *Variety*, *Super Fly* did the unheard of; it knocked *The Godfather* out of the top spot to become, for a short time, the highest grossing film in America – black or white.

BLACKS PROTEST BLACK FILMS

Upon the release of *Super Fly* black moviegoers suddenly found that they belonged to one of two distinct categories: either (A) those who enjoyed the films and appreciated the fact that blacks actors were working more now than ever before, or (B) those who saw the films as violent, 'pornographic' narratives filled with negative and/or derogatory images and themes. *Super Fly* was unceremoniously placed into the latter category.

The controversy surrounding the picture, and consequently a few other films released in 1972 (in particular *Trouble Man*, *Hit Man* and Jim Brown's 'comeback' vehicle, *Slaughter*) was loud and unrelenting. The National Catholic Office was the first to condemn the film, yet their official non-support was dim in comparison to the circus-like atmosphere created by noisy black picketers who lined the streets outside of theatres carrying signs that read "Black Shame, White Profits!" and "We Are Not All Pimps and Whores!"

Concurrent with the vividly played out public opposition to the steadily growing array of black cast action movies, newspapers and magazines across the country ran lengthy, investigative articles about the ongoing discord. When several employees of American International Pictures (producers of some of the more low-end black films) reported that their cars had been firebombed, the situation moved from aggravating to dangerous.

It was in the midst of the protests surrounding *Super Fly* that *Variety* published an article in which Junius Griffin (Head of the Los Angeles chapter of NAACP – The National Association for the Advance-ment of Colored People – and a former Hollywood press agent who failed to acquire the *Super Fly* account!) combined the words 'black' and 'exploitation' and came up with 'blaxploitation,' a sensationalist phrase that forever categorised any and all black cast films released during the 1970s. "We must insist that our children are not exposed to a diet of so-called black movies that glorify black males as pimps, dope pushers, gangsters and super males with vast physical prowess but no cognitive skills," said Griffin in a 1972 interview with *Newsweek*.

Griffin's damnations were duly noted by other highly visible African Americans, including PUSH's (People United to Save Humanity) Jesse Jackson, and black television producer Tony Brown, who told *Ebony*, "The 'blaxploitation' films are a phenomenon of self-hate. Just look at the image of *Super Fly*. Going to see yourself as a drug dealer when you're oppressed is sick. Not only are blacks identifying with him, they're paying for the identification. It's sort of like a Jew paying to get into Auschwitz. Blacks who contribute to the making of these films are guilty of nothing less than treason." Yet more anti-blaxploitation sentiment came from the Washington,

Where John Shaft was a private detective trying to solve a case in Harlem, *Super Fly*'s main character, Priest, was an ostentatiously dressed (and coifed) Harlem dope dealer planning to outsmart the mob. The film was written by a black former advertising copywriter and was accompanied by a hit soundtrack album by soul artist Curtis Mayfield. "*Super Fly* would not have been half as successful as it was had it not been for that wonderful soundtrack," conceded the film's co-star Sheila Frazier in a 2002 interview included on the *BaadAsssss Cinema* documentary, and the general public agreed. In an era when albums rarely contained more than one hit, 'Super Fly', 'Freddie's Dead' and 'Pusherman' were all released as singles and became consumer favourites.

Gordon Parks Jr.'s *Super Fly* (the third super-successful black-action film *directed* by an African American) was independently financed. Like *Sweetback* before it, the start-up money came from dentists, lawyers and other successful African-American businessmen. Before the picture was even completed director Parks had several Hollywood film studios bidding for the distribution rights. Warner Bros., a shadow of its former self at the time, but still a major player, came out on top of the bidding war. But along with what would become one of the decade's most memorable motion pictures, the film studio got something it hadn't bargained for – a wave of nationwide criticism, boycotts and picketing.

D.C. based BAN (Blacks Against Narcotics), who co-opted the film's title and referred to it in vigorously promoted print material as "Super-Genocide."

In response to the public debate about the merits of blaxploitation films, many African Americans working in the genre felt compelled to speak out in defence of their participation. "It's ridiculous to imply that blacks don't know the difference between fantasy and reality and therefore will be influenced by these films in an unhealthy way," said *Shaft*'s director Gordon Parks Sr. at the time. Pam Grier (blaxploitation's only real female star) echoed the director's sentiments. She told *Time*: "There are a mass of blacks who like action films. They can't release their aggressions on Hollywood soap operas." Perhaps the most eloquent argument in favour of blaxploitation films came from *Super Fly*'s director Gordon Parks Jr. "Blacks want to be entertained just like everyone else," he told *Newsweek*, "and if they enjoy super-heroes with fast cars and fancy clothes, well, that's the American dream – *everyone's* American dream."

For a brief period at the height of the turbulent discourse an organisation called CAB (Coalition Against Blaxploitation) was formed. The group, headed by Junius Griffin, was made up of representatives of black political groups like NAACP, CORE (Congress of Racial Equality) and SCLS (the Southern Christian Leadership Conference). One of CAB's objectives was to create a separate movie rating system to alert black filmgoers to films that (in the coalition's opinion) contained derogatory and/or negative representations of African Americans. Movies that passed the test would be classified as 'Superior,' those that didn't would be labelled 'Thoroughly Objectionable'. But as ambitious and vociferous as they were, CAB was destined to have only a limited period of activity. Rife with their own inner conflict, unable to agree on terms and the direction in which the agency should proceed, the 'coalition' disbanded mere months after it was formed.

A MONSTER HE CAN'T CONTROL... HAS TAKEN OVER HIS VERY SOUL!

THE FEAR OF THE YEAR IS HERE!
DR. BLACK MR. HYDE

DR. BLACK-MR. HYDE starring BERNIE CASEY and ROSALIND CASH
Co-starring MARIE O'HENRY, JI-TU CUMBUKA, MILT KOGAN and STU GILLIAM As "SILKY"
Executive Producer MANFRED BERNHARD • Produced By CHARLES WALKER • Screenplay By LARRY LeBRON
Directed By WILLIAM CRAIN • Music By JOHNNY PATE • A DIMENSION PICTURES RELEASE • METROCOLOR

In the shadows of the public debate about blaxploitation films (which only served to make the pictures more popular than they already were) a sub-genre emerged – black-cast horror films! When 1972's *Blacula* (a take on the classic *Dracula*), starring veteran black actor William Marshall, became an audience favourite, the film was swiftly followed by a sequel, *Scream Blacula Scream*, and a string of like-minded productions. Before it was all over we had *Blackenstein*, *Dr. Black, Mr. Hyde*, *Ganja & Hess*, *J.D.'s Revenge*, *The Twilight People*, *House on Skull Mountain*, *Devil's Express*, *The Thing with Two Heads*, *Abby*, *The Beast Must Die*, *Night of the Cobra Woman*, and *Lord Shango*.

LADIES NIGHT

Judging strictly by the number of films released, 1973 proved to be blaxploitation's banner year. The boom was taking place in the context of the sexual revolution and the still-going-strong youth and drug counter culture. More importantly, the relaxing of censorship laws over the course of the previous few years had made it possible to present film images that were specifically designed to excite, tempt and titillate in a way that filmmakers had never been allowed to before. Explicit violence, obscene language, gratuitous nudity (almost always female) and a

BLOODSUCKER! Deadlier than Dracula!

"'BLACULA' IS THE MOST HORRIFYING FILM OF THE DECADE." — Count Dracula Society

SAMUEL Z. ARKOFF presents

BLACULA

An AMERICAN INTERNATIONAL Picture
WILLIAM MARSHALL · DENISE NICHOLAS · VONETTA McGEE
GORDON PINSET and THALMUS RASULALA as Gordon COLOR BY MOVIELAB PG

general attempt to top one another in terms of vulgarity and 'shock value' permeated most of the blaxploitation films released from this point on.

1973's hits included *Trick Baby* (first screened late 1972), *The Mack*, *Hell Up in Harlem*, *The Spook Who Sat by the Door*, *The Soul of Nigger Charley*, *Five on the Black Hand Side*, *Black Caesar*, *That Man Bolt*, *Gordon's War*, *Slaughter's Big Rip-Off*, *Hit!*, *Sweet Jesus Preacher Man*, *Detroit 9000*, *Black Eye*, *Savage!* and *The Slams*. Most refreshing of the new crop of films were those that featured females in the same violent, over-the-top narratives that African-American men had popularised. *Coffy* and *Cleopatra Jones*, two almost simultaneously released 'female hero' action pictures, ignited yet another blaxploitation sub-genre. *Coffy*, starring former receptionist Pam Grier, was particularly noteworthy as it seemed to deliberately mock the restrictions suggested by genre critics and the now defunct CAB. Vicious and gory, filled with shocking language, excessive nudity and lewd sexual situations, American International Pictures' *Coffy* set the highest and most provocative standard yet for an R-rated film. Not surprisingly the slim-budgeted (only $500,000) film became a blockbuster hit.

At the other end of the spectrum Warner Bros.' *Cleopatra Jones* appealed to fans of the James Bond series. The PG-rated big-budget action film starred model Tamara Dobson as a globe-trotting, karate-kicking private detective. Quick to smile, 'sophisticated' Jones never disrobed and never got into a fight unless provoked. Grier followed *Coffy* (another blaxploitation release that provoked protests and picketing) with *Foxy Brown*, *Sheba Baby* and *Friday Foster*, while Dobson reprised her role in the sequel to *Cleopatra Jones*, *Cleopatra Jones and the Casino of Gold*.

With their success measured in dollars and reactions (*Newsweek* reported that during a screening of *Foxy Brown* audiences "whooped and hollered" so loudly that the projectionist had to turn up the sound), the visually arresting 'female hero' films kept on coming. Prominent examples include: *Sugar Hill* (Marki Bey); *Lady Cocoa* (Lola Falana); *Velvet Smooth* (Johnnie Hill); *TNT Jackson* (Jean Bell); and *Emma Mae* (Jerri Hayes.) But that wasn't all. This new group of films featuring self-possessed women followed a succession of earlier movies that had showcased sisters in less fortunate circumstances. These included *The Big Doll House*, *The Big Bird Cage*, *The Hot Box*, *Women in Cages* and *The Arena*.

By 1974 blaxploitation films were a staple in urban (and select suburban) movie houses across America. As *Variety* reported in a 9 October, 1974 article, "Thanks to blaxploitation films the industry is on the verge of its highest domestic box-office results in twenty eight years." Flamboyant advertising campaigns, which included gigantic lurid posters, glossy lobby cards and handbills, and outsized, brightly coloured marquee letters and film logos, made the pictures seem omnipresent. Often featured

above: A stylish, stark and effective admat for **Gordon's War** (1973).
opposite: Model-turned-actress Tamara Dobson poses in a promotional still for **Cleopatra Jones** (1973).

in magazines, discussed in newspapers and reviewed on television, even if you never went to see a blaxploitation film, you most certainly knew that they existed.

More than three years into their popular run, blaxploitation pictures (now often presented on double bills) continued to keep America's oversized, run-down urban movie houses filled to capacity. In fact, a 20-month *Chicago Tribune* study concluded that "Black-oriented movies, the majority of whose viewers are black youth, keep the eight white-owned Chicago Loop theaters alive and in business." The study also revealed that blaxploitation films brought in a full 41% of the box-office take at the city's five largest venues. Not only did the pictures present American audiences with a new generation of formally (and informally) trained black actors and actresses, the movies were also known to showcase popular black athletes (Jim Brown, Fred Williamson, Rosey Grier), singers (Gladys Knight, Isaac Hayes, Curtis Mayfield), pin-up models (Marki Bey, Gloria Hendry, Jean Bell), and comedians (Richard Pryor, Moms Mabley, Redd Foxx).

But even the thrill of seeing contemporary African-American celebrities perform outside of their established milieu wasn't enough to obscure one broadening reality; the plots and scenarios of the pictures themselves were becoming over-familiar and shamelessly derivative. Additionally, the paltry budgets, tight schedules and inferior production values – once viewed as the incidental shortcomings of a film genre in its infancy – now became irritating distractions. As writer Ed Guerrero put it, "A uniformly low standard had been set."

1974's films included *The Black Godfather*, *The Take*, *The Education of Sonny Carson*, *Bamboo Gods & Iron Men*, *Amazing Grace*, *Super Dude* and *Three the Hard Way*, among others. That year's biggest money-makers were *Truck Turner*, starring singer-turned-actor Isaac Hayes as a don't-mess-with-me, gun-toting bounty hunter, and *Uptown Saturday Night*, a comedy that told the slapstick tale of two friends who misplace a winning lottery ticket. *Uptown Saturday Night* was directed by and starred Sidney Poitier, with a cast that included Bill Cosby, Harry Belafonte and Flip Wilson.

A NEW DAY

By 1975 blaxploitation films had entered a new and final phase of popularity. The genre's attempt to infiltrate the small screen on a weekly basis with *Get Christie Love!* starring Teresa Graves (22 episodes) and the short-lived *Shaft* TV series starring Richard Roundtree (7 episodes) had been unsuccessful. Additionally, black presence in critically acclaimed network television specials like *Brian's Song*, *Green Eyes*, *The Autobiography of Miss Jane Pittman* and later, *Roots*, seemed to significantly diminish the ongoing necessity of theatrically-released black cast films.

above: Determined: Any package given to Jim Kelly in **Black Belt Jones** (1974) will most assuredly reach its intended destination.

Even the emergence of another two blaxploitation sub genres – westerns (*Thomasine & Bushrod*, *Three Tough Guys*, *Adios Amigo*), and black cast karate films (*Black Belt Jones*, *Ebony, Ivory & Jade*, *The Dynamite Brothers*) – couldn't disguise what appeared to be the constant stirring of the same old soup.

1975's offerings included *The Black Gestapo*, *Aaron Loves Angela*, *Bucktown*, *Man Friday*, *The Candy Tangerine Man*, *Darktown Strutters* and *Deliver Us from Evil*. The standouts that year were *Mandingo*, a big-budget Dino De Laurentiis produced plantation melodrama starring popular boxer Ken Norton, *Cooley High*, a black cast answer to *American Graffiti* starring *Welcome Back Kotter*'s Lawrence Hilton-Jacobs, and *Dolemite*, the first in a series of films that starred risqué rapper/comic Rudy Ray Moore. *Abby*, a film about a woman possessed by the devil, was widely discussed, not because it was frightening, but because it seemed to borrow too much from *The Exorcist*. "Abby doesn't need a man anymore... the devil is her lover now!" screamed the ads, but when Warner Bros. (owners of *The Exorcist*) threatened to sue, American International Pictures quietly pulled the film from theatres.

Along with their growing sameness and interchangeable film titles (a full forty blaxploitation films contain the word 'black' in the title), fading black interest and consequent dwindling theatre attendance was further exacerbated by the broad appeal of a slew of concurrently released 'white-action' films like *Walking Tall* and *Mean Streets* (both 1973), *Death Wish* (1974) and *Rocky* (1976). Mirroring blaxploitation's straight-forward, unencumbered story telling, in no time at all, the new white 'male-hero' films were joined by a number of violent, sex-filled, white 'female-hero' films. *Super Chick* (1973), *They Call Her One Eye* and *Big Bad Mama* (both 1974), *Switchblade Sisters* (1975) and finally *Gloria* (1980) all used scenarios and themes more entertainingly presented in blaxploitation films.

Looking back it appears that the large group of low-budget, expeditiously produced white-action movies released in the mid-1970s, were purposely modelled after blaxploitation films, and shrewdly presented as an alternative to the politically-charged and still contro-versial black-cast pictures.

Yet another factor that accelerated blaxploitation's demise was Hollywood's side-by-side release of 'blockbuster' films like *Jaws* (1975) and *Star Wars* (1977), along with multi-cast disaster epics like *Earthquake* and *The Towering Inferno* (both 1974), all of which were enormously popular with African Americans. When a national survey revealed that a full 35% of tickets sold for *The Exorcist* and *The Godfather* were purchased by African Americans, blaxploitation's demise was cemented. If blacks would pay to see 'white-action' and/or 'event' films (and they did), why continue to make the problematic black ones?

THE BRIDE FINALLY DIED...HER TORTURE ENDED. FOR HIM, IT WAS THE BEGINNING OF A BRUTAL, SAVAGE TRAIL OF

POSSESSED HORROR!

HE BECAME **THE OBSESSED ONE** ...playing the GAME OF DEATH with the DEVIL!

starring MALC PANDAY • TRACY PARRISH • SALLY SAVALAS

directed by RAMDJAN ABDOELRAHMAN • an ELIZABETH PERSUAD Production

IN COLOR

1976, 'The Bicentennial Year', was blaxploitation's final year of note. Though many films still reached theatres that year, there were to be no more hits. *Hot Potato*, *Death Journey*, *Black Shampoo*, *Blast* (a re-release of 1972's *The Final Comedown*), *The Muthers*, *No Way Back*, *Black Samurai*, *Monkey Hustle* and *Black Fist* made very little money. The following year's latecomers (*Petey Wheatstraw: The Devil's Son-in-Law*, *Mr. Mean*, *The Guy from Harlem*, *Brothers*, *The Baron* and *Bare Knuckles*) did even worse.

By the time 1978 rolled around it was all over. In addition to the mounting number of pictures that never made it beyond the script stage (e.g. *Black the Ripper*, *Black Majesty*, *Billy Black*, and *The Werewolf from Watts*), and a few much-sought-after oddities for which there exist sundry rare promotional items such as soundtrack albums (e.g. *Hit 'em Hard*), those few that actually did get distributed (*Death Force*, *Fass Black*, *Youngblood* and *The Hitter* – a superior film that re-teamed *Super Fly*'s Ron O'Neal and Sheila Frazier) all played to empty houses. Like the disco phenomenon that was also entering its final stages, once blaxploitation films had run their course, the pictures were instantaneously devalued. What had once been considered an exciting new socially-responsive entertainment, was now totally dismissed.

above: Poster art for the elusive **The Obsessed One**, one of several blaxploitation films that disappeared after its, apparently brief, theatrical release.

above: Former Playboy bunny Jean Bell is anything but coquettish in this scene from 1974's Philippine-shot **TNT Jackson**. (J. Howard Collection).

Just as swiftly as it began it ended. An over-saturation of increasingly mediocre product combined with black audience indifference and the incorporation of blacks into less sensational mainstream film roles resulted in the unceremonious, almost total disappearance of low-budget, black cast, action-oriented motion pictures. As *Ebony* put it, "The black super stud as cinema hero is now officially a thing of the past."

POSTSCRIPT

Though 1980s films featured several genuine (bankable) African American cinema stars – including Eddie Murphy, Whoopi Goldberg and Richard Pryor – black film characters in the 1980s existed in a totally different world than that of their proud, defiant, anti-establishment, 1970s counterparts. No longer sexualised, objectified, politically-minded or out to get 'Whitey,' in order to be given the green light, films in this post-blaxploitation era, with the exception of Steven Spielberg's *The Color Purple* in 1985 and Spike Lee's outside-the-industry breakthrough *She's Gotta Have It* in 1986, were safe, slick, sanitised, multi-racial and wholly inoffensive.

There were black/white 'buddy pictures' like *Nighthawks* (1981), *White Nights* (1985), *Lethal Weapon* (1987) and *Lethal Weapon 2* (1989), straightforward comedies such as *The Toy* (1982), *D.C. Cab* (1983 – a not-too-subtle retread of 1976's *Car Wash*), *Brewster's Millions* (1985), *Jumpin' Jack Flash* (1986), and *Burglar* and *The Telephone* (both 1987), and box offices bonanzas that shrewdly incorporated both, including *Beverly Hills Cop* (1984) and *Beverly Hills Cop II* (1987). Even blaxploitation's jack-of-all-trades, Fred Williamson, couldn't keep the genre going in the 1980s. His attempt at expanding on the already proven formula kept him busy, but his pictures were neither financially successful nor popular with audiences. *One Down, Two to Go* (1982), *Vigilante*, *The Last Fight* and *The Big Score* (all 1983), *Foxtrap* (1986) – not to be confused with 1973's *Fox Style* – and *The Messenger* (also 1986) proved, once and for all, that the blaxploitation movie concept that was so big in the 1970s would not enjoy similar success in the 1980s.

What all these new-era films had in common was a determination to entertain (not provoke thought or speak directly to black needs, desires or expectations), appeal to (not exclude) all available markets, and, more than anything else, bring in the most amount of money for the motion picture industry's investment dollar.

More than thirty years have passed since "that bad mutha' (shut yo' mouth)" *Shaft* arrived on movie screens, and in the ensuing period the burgeoning home video and DVD markets have brought blaxploitation films out of the

above: One of blaxploitation's most violent and most popular films, 1972's **Trouble Man** (which spawned a top-selling soundtrack album by Marvin Gaye), starred Robert Hooks as private detective 'Mr. T.' (J. Howard Collection)

salt mines and into the hands of movie buffs around the world. Television documentaries like the Independent Film Channel's *BaadAsssss Cinema* continue to examine and highlight the genre, while in current-day Hollywood, a series of remakes and 'homages': *Action Jackson* and *I'm Gonna Git You Sucka* (1988); *Return of Super Fly* (1990); *Original Gangstas* (1996); *Jackie Brown* (1997); *Shaft* (2000); *Undercover Brother* (2002); *Baadasssss!* (2003); and *American Gangster* (2007) confirm blaxploitation's enduring appeal and ongoing significance.

If more evidence is needed, million-selling rap recording artist Foxy Brown took her name directly from Pam Grier's enormously successful 1974 film *Foxy Brown*, while the box-office smash *Austin Powers in Goldmember* (2002), unblushingly featured singer Beyoncé Knowles playing an Afroed, platform- and hot pants-wearing diva named Foxxy Cleopatra (appropriating not one, but *two* popular blaxploitation film character names!)

One of the reasons that blaxploitation movies remain of interest to film lovers is that the pictures cover all fronts. There are blaxploitation westerns, dramas, melodramas, bio-pics, comedies, horror films, science fiction epics, karate flicks, women's prison pictures, mysteries and, of course, action/adventure films. Whatever your taste or film preference, there is something in the blaxploitation canon that will appeal to you.

Equally important, yet less heralded than their mainstream counterparts, blaxploitation films did much more than simply entertain inner-city black audiences; they also captured and reflected (both black and white) America's predominant sensibilities, politics and fantasies and provided a visual cue that mitigated the rising tide of dissatisfaction with black representation in American motion pictures.

Through the innovative use of popular black entertainment icons, cutting edge musical soundtracks, topical, often controversial, subject matter and the presentation of a new group of totally contemporary, socially conscious black film heroes and heroines, blaxploitation films revised and updated the African-American cinematic image and laid the solid groundwork for the stellar reign of today's black superstars.

Long gone are the hand-illustrated posters that beckoned moviegoers with their garish colours and salacious headlines ("*Coffy...* she'll cream you!") Gone also are the rickety seen-better-days neighbourhood theatres (the 'Empire,' the 'Castle,' the 'Imperial') that came back to life one final time to thrill unsuspecting audiences. But here, still with us, and still very much alive and kicking, are the films – re-packaged, re-mastered and re-presented to a whole new generation of movie fans.

Chapter Two

Q & A: Ten Directors Discuss Their Films

Paul Bogart

Paul Bogart's long and esteemed career began in television. His directorial debut came in 1956, with an episode of the popular program *The Kaiser Aluminum Hour*, and from that point on he continued working in the medium, often on some of TV's most popular shows. His long list of directing credits includes episodes of *Get Smart*, *Way Out*, *All in the Family* (for which he won an Emmy award), *Alice*, *The Golden Girls*, *The Heidi Chronicles*, and over forty TV specials, movies of the week and television mini series.

Bogart's first feature film was 1970's contemporary-minded *Halls of Anger*, an ambitious story that dealt with the controversial issue of bussing white students into inner city black schools. *Halls of Anger* was a hit with black audiences, and Bogart quickly followed it up with 1971's *Skin Game*, the story of two con men – one black, one white – and then *Mr. Ricco*, a 1975 detective drama whose strong African-American subplot served as the film's centrepiece.

Bogart continued to work in television throughout the 1980s and '90s, only occasionally accepting film work. 1984's *Oh, God! You Devil* was a comedy vehicle for veteran actor/comedian George Burns. 1988's critically acclaimed *Torch Song Trilogy* marked a turning point for the director; despite the success of the film ensuring that he was in more demand than ever, he decided that the time was right for him to 'happily retire.'

Halls of Anger was your first blaxploitation film. How did you come to direct it?
I was invited to do so by producer Walter Mirisch.
Did the project come to you because you had enjoyed so much success in television?
I don't know why he picked me. I must say that I didn't think much of the script. The first time it was offered I turned it down. But then I figured, 'It's good money, I might as well do it.' I thought maybe I could work with it and make it better, but that didn't happen.
What was it about the script that didn't appeal to you?
I was very interested in the *idea* of the script – the whole controversial bussing issue that was going on at the time. But I felt that the point of the story was missing in the actual script. Walter Mirisch, on the other hand, was very excited about the project. He wanted to do the movie both because it had contemporary news value, and because he was interested in grooming leading man Calvin Lockhart as a screen replacement for Sidney Poitier.
I take it that you are not a fan of the film today.
Making that film was an excruciating experience for me. As you may know, there was enormous friction on the set, especially between me and Calvin Lockhart. I had the feeling that Mr. Lockhart just didn't want to be there. He didn't care about the film, he didn't like it; he was more concerned with the way he looked.
Would you say that Lockhart felt the project was beneath his capabilities?
Very much so. There were a lot of arched eyebrows on his part. A lot of attitude. He made my life absolutely

miserable. For instance on the very first day when we were having our first reading he came in over an hour late, sat down and demanded that someone bring him a hot cup of coffee. This immediately alienated him from all the other actors who were working on the film – and it only went downhill from there. He was late for almost every single day of shooting. I guess he was doing the film because he had a contract with Walter Mirisch. I really don't know.
Was your approach to making Halls of Anger very different from your approach to your work in television?
No. My interest has always been to present the truth of the event, the truth of the story, the truth of the characters.

above: 1970's **Halls of Anger** explored the effects of bussing suburban white students to inner city black schools. Here, high school teacher Quincy Davis (Calvin Lockhart) comes to the aid of honour student Doug (Jeff Bridges). (Soul Images)

What was your experience working on *Skin Game*?
I'd say that *Skin Game* is my favourite project from the period. It was done in a very warm atmosphere in which all of us were very much on the same page.
The story idea – that of a black man taking part in his own sale as a slave – must have been controversial.
It was. What I found interesting about the white character played by James Garner was that, even though he is highly likeable and not a racist, he is not above taking advantage of the black character played by Louis Gossett Jr. For instance, even though they are working together as scam artists, the white man doesn't mind taking a room at the hotel while his black friend has to sleep in the stable. They might be friends and equals but as the black character makes clear near the end of the film, there is a major difference. The black man can be bought and sold like a horse. The white man can't.

Mr. Ricco was released in 1975. How did it come about?
Well, that's a very minor piece of work.
I disagree. I think it's a very entertaining film.
Well, I enjoyed doing it because I really liked working with Dean Martin. That picture came about because Dean had a contract with the MGM Grand Hotel in Las Vegas. Part of his contract stipulated that they had to finance at least one picture for him to star in. It almost seems like it can't be true now, but I believe we did the film for $1,000,000. I treated the film as lavishly as I could under the circumstances, but I remember that I was sorry that I didn't have enough time to further develop the script. I just had to go ahead and do it as it was.
The film came and went without much notice.
It didn't leave a mark at all. To tell you the truth I had totally forgotten about *Mr. Ricco* until you mentioned it.

Did you put a great deal of time and effort into the casting of your films?

As far as the supporting players go, most definitely yes. But each of the films we are discussing came to me with stars already attached. *Halls of Anger* came with Calvin Lockhart; *Skin Game* came with James Garner; and *Mr. Ricco* came with Dean Martin.

Was your experience of making films for United Artists, Warner Bros., and MGM very different?

My experience depended on my relationship with the producer. A good producer played the role of buffer between the director and the studio. At the time I wasn't a very powerful director in Hollywood, so having a good producer was a great help to me.

Several directors I've talked to have spoken about racism behind the scenes in Hollywood. Did you experience any of this?

I think that by the time I did my films they were very sensitive about that issue and if there was any racism – and, yes I guess there must have been – they sat on it. The people in charge made sure that they didn't put themselves in a position where they could be exposed. For the most part Hollywood was reactionary anyway. At that time, and though few will admit it, Hollywood was very much a Republican town.

What did you think of other blaxploitation films, like *Shaft* and *Super Fly*?

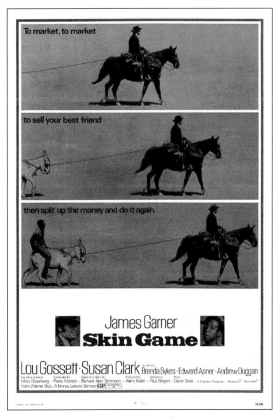

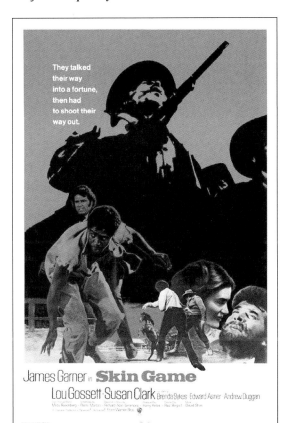

I never saw them. They seemed, for the most part, focused on violence and that did not interest me in the least.

Why do you believe the black action movie boom came to such an abrupt end?

Maybe because they weren't very good. I really can't tell you because I didn't go to see any of them.

Why do you believe blaxploitation films remain popular today?

I'm not really sure. I know that *Skin Game* has been treated very badly – it looks awful. It was a beautiful widescreen movie and it's been cut apart, panned and scanned and totally ruined. It's just so painful for me to watch now, that I never do. I wish someone would release it in its original widescreen splendour.

You have a ton of Emmy awards for your television work. Would you say you are more proud of your work on television or in films?

That's a very good question. I must say that I think I've done more significant, more meaningful, work in the television medium.

If I asked you how you would like to be remembered as far as your creative contribution to film goes, what would you say?

Well I think you can burn most of the stuff! I would say that I would like to be remembered as a good director. Someone who did the best they could with the often sub-standard material at hand.

Matt Cimber

Matt Cimber's career as a filmmaker began in 1968 when he cast his third wife, Hollywood sex symbol Jayne Mansfield, in a low budget exploitation movie that he had written, called *Single Room Furnished*. A filmmaker with a penchant for the unusual, he followed that picture with 1969's like-themed *Man and Wife* and then, in 1970, *Africanus Sexualis*, a titillating look at "the little-known love rights and mating habits of the Dark Continent."

By the mid-seventies, Cimber had made a name for himself as a producer/director who was not afraid to push the envelope. Though 1973's *The Black Six* was a good natured film featuring an all black cast consisting mostly of sports stars trying their hand at acting, the filmmaker's next two movies, *The Candy Tangerine Man* and *Lady Cocoa* (both released in 1975), raised the bar for blaxploitation in terms of the cinematic depiction of sex, violence, torture, obscene language and ostentatious nudity.

Three more infamous film entries – 1976's *The Witch Who Came from the Sea* (banned in England when it was released on video in the early 1980s), 1982's camp classic *Butterfly*, starring Pia Zadora, and 1984's *Yellow Hair and the Fortress of Gold* – have helped make Cimber – often cited as the last person to direct both Jayne Mansfield and Orson Welles – one of Hollywood's more eclectic filmmakers.

Matt Cimber's latest project, *Miriam*, a World War II drama based on a true story, was released in 2006.

***The Black Six* was your first black-cast film. How did it come about?**
I had seen several blaxploitation films at the time and realised that there was a lucrative, albeit limited, market for them. Since the films didn't call for very big budgets, it made sense for me to try a few.

What inspired you to cast football players?
The idea came to me both because I knew the market that I was making the films for and also because I got a heads-up from a guy named Moss, who represented them all. That's also the way I cast Gene Washington in the lead. His agent contacted me and told me he had this good-looking black actor that I should meet. Gene was great, one of the nicest people I met, so we sort of joined forces and did the film.

The picture carries a very strong positive message.

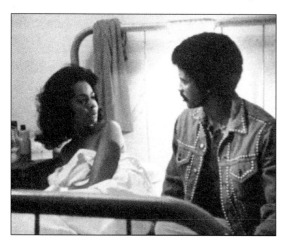

The film was heavily inspired by one of my favourite poems by Rudyard Kipling, called 'The Last of the Light Brigade.' I was attracted to the premise in the poem that there is a lesson and a message in every person's death and that, no matter what, you can't shirk the basic responsibility you have to your brothers.

I take it that the "Honky look out..." tag at the end was an homage to Melvin Van Peebles and *Sweet Sweetback's Baadasssss Song*.
You couldn't do enough homage to Melvin Van Peebles. I think he is a brilliant filmmaker. Yes that was my mini tribute to him.

***The Candy Tangerine Man* was at dramatic odds with *The Black Six*.**
Yes, and no. It is certainly the most potent of my three blaxploitation films, but again, I believe that as strong as all the over-the-top imagery in the film may be, the picture makes an equally strong statement about society. With *The Candy Tangerine Man* I wanted to show that this highly intelligent and capable person could be both a Sunset Strip pimp and a loving and caring husband and father of two. Everyone is putting him down for being a pimp, but what other opportunities did society offer him? He is doing the only thing that society had left for him to do.

Samuel L. Jackson says that *The Candy Tangerine Man* made a major impression on him.
Yes, and he's not the only one. Quentin Tarantino also loves the film. He says that whenever he and Sam get together that's all they talk about – for hours!

I must admit that I don't really get the title. What does it mean?

above: Returning Vietnam Vet Bubba (Gene Washington) and his girlfriend Ceal (Rosalind Miles) discover how much the world changed, in **The Black Six** (1973).

Well, it just came to me. I was thinking along the lines of a candy apple. The Baron is a candy man – he is bright, he is colourful. There is no special significance to it – I didn't want to call it *The Candy Apple Man*, so I came up with *The Candy Tangerine Man.* I think audiences got it at the time.

The film has everything – comedy, sex, action, gore – were you trying to outdo all the other blaxploitation films?

No, not really. You must remember that all my films are done a bit tongue-in-cheek and they can be very cynical. I wanted to get my message about society's injustices across and the sensational approach that I took seemed like the best way to do it.

***Lady Cocoa* came fast on the heels of *The Candy Tangerine Man*; how did the project come about?**

I was friendly with Sammy Davis Jr. and through him I knew that Lola Falana was looking for film work. At the time she was the biggest thing in Las Vegas – I think she was the highest paid black female performer who had ever played there. Sammy was always bugging me to write something for her to star in, so I did. I think she surprised us all – she did a really fantastic job.

The Nevada locations are a nice change.

Well, at the time, nobody had thought of it. I liked the fact that the backgrounds were really colourful and the terrain pretty raw. I also made a great deal with the King's Castle Lodge, which wasn't doing that well financially, so they were more than happy to have us. We did the film in about 17 days for $250,000. At one point I ran out of money and told the cast and crew that I needed a few more days of work out of them but couldn't pay them for it. I had a little money and offered to divide it up. Then someone suggested that, since we were in a casino, I should just go and shoot craps. Everyone agreed that if I lost they would perform for free. Don't you know I won a ton of money and was able to pay everyone more than their standard rate!

There is some confusion concerning the picture's title. Is it *Lady Cocoa* or *Pop Goes the Weasel*?

We filmed it as *Pop Goes the Weasel* and had the poster art ready before it was distributed. But when the distributor picked it up they thought *Lady Cocoa* had a broader appeal. Frankly, I didn't care which title they went with.

Did you ever experience any racism from the Hollywood community?

Not really. The only time I was ever worried about race relations was on the set of *The Black Six*. We had hired about 50 real Hells Angels and they had a reputation for being racist. Initially there was some tension but that soon passed when it became clear that the Angels were big fans of the football stars. That, and the fact that both factions were smoking a lot of pot, made the atmosphere very relaxed.

Why do you believe the black action movie boom came to a close?

Well, I can tell you that *I* stopped making the films because CORE (Congress Of Racial Equality) asked me to. In fact they camped out in my hall for a while. They were very congenial but they also put the pressure on. I thought it was a shame, because so many black people were finally getting a chance to work in the industry. Doors were finally opening up. But CORE didn't see it that way. As for the *studios* not making them anymore, I think that the idea of making films targeted for inner city black audiences became outdated. All types of black performers were starting to be featured in mainstream pictures and that rendered blaxploitation films unnecessary.

Why do you believe the films remain popular today?

Because they are an important part of film history. I don't believe it's just black films that are making a comeback. If you live long enough everything comes around again.

Which of your blaxploitation films is your favourite.

The Candy Tangerine Man is the best film that I have ever made. I'm not talking about production values, or star performances, but in terms of its feeling, its spirit and its effect on the viewer. I'm still, personally, very affected by the film.

How would you like to be remembered?

If I continue to meet people and they don't curse me out, I'll be very happy!

Larry Cohen

Though 1996's *Original Gangstas* marked director/writer/producer Larry Cohen's return to the blaxploitation genre (as well as the return of several of the genre's original star performers), Cohen's entrée into the film industry began in the 1960s as producer of the televisions series' *Never Too Young* and *Branded*. His first motion picture, 1972's *Bone*, was critically acclaimed but came and went without much notice. *Black Caesar* and *Hell Up in Harlem* (both released in 1973) changed all that, and when Cohen followed up with 1974's horror cult classic *It's Alive* (which he also wrote, produced and directed – and which was followed by two sequels) he had become a much-celebrated part of the film industry.

Larry Cohen's many other film successes include *God Told Me To* (1976), *The Private Files of J. Edgar Hoover* (1977), *Perfect Strangers* (1984) and *Phone Booth* (2002), for which he wrote the screenplay. Today, along with becoming well-established as a film historian/public speaker, Larry Cohen continues to write and produce films.

Bone is the first film in which you featured an African American in a leading role. What inspired you to write the story?
Well, that was the very first film that I directed. I can't really tell you what inspired me – I just sat down and wrote the script one day. I was looking for a film that I could direct without too much difficulty; you know, not too many locations, small cast, low budget. I thought it was an original idea that had something to say about racism in America.

It's an unusually sophisticated script.
It was way ahead of its time. It's an over the top, kind of wild story, and I must say that I am very pleased with the recent DVD release. It looks beautiful and the performers are all great. Yaphet Kotto always told me that he thought his performance is the best he has ever given in a film.

How did audiences respond to the picture?
Well, the response was odd because the distributor who bought the picture released it as a black exploitation action/adventure film, even though I told him it was a comedy. If you tell an audience that they are buying a ticket for an action film and they go in and get a comedy instead, they come away confused. Instead of thinking 'Oh, this is a great comedy,' they come out thinking 'That was the worst action picture I've ever seen.' And, unfortunately, that's what happened with *Bone*.

How did you come to cast Yaphet Kotto in the lead?
I had seen Yaphet in *The Liberation of L.B. Jones* and was greatly impressed with both his performance and the way he looked. He embodied the fantasy image that many people had of what a black man looks like. Since the film was about people's fantasies, I thought he was just perfect. In fact, I chose him over Paul Winfield, who also wanted the part.

Black Caesar remains one of blaxploitation's most exciting films. How did the project come about?

In the early '70s, Sammy Davis Jr. had aspirations of becoming a major movie star. He had been in films but was always cast as a sidekick to people like Frank Sinatra or Dean Martin. Sammy's manager contacted me and asked if I would write a treatment for Sammy. I suggested a gangster film. James Cagney and Edward G. Robinson were little guys who made great film villains and I thought that Sammy could continue in that tradition. Anyway, the money for the treatment, which I called *Black Caesar*, never came through. Finally I was told that Sammy was having tax problems, was short of money and wasn't going to be able to pay. Well, I wasn't about to sue Sammy Davis Jr. so I just kept the treatment. Not too long afterwards I had a meeting with Samuel Arkoff at American International Pictures and he told me he was looking for a black action vehicle to produce. I said, "Wait a minute, I have something in the car!" I went downstairs and got the *Black Caesar* treatment out of my trunk, and before I left the meeting that day I had a commitment from Arkoff to do the film.

How did you cast Fred Williamson in the title role?

I knew someone who knew Fred's manager and he arranged a luncheon between the two of us. Fred had just finished filming *The Legend of Nigger Charley*, which was controversial at the time. It had also done pretty good box office so Arkoff OK'd him and we went ahead and did it.

New York City locations add so much to the feel of the film. Did you prefer location shooting over studio shooting?

Absolutely. It's a much more enjoyable experience to go to a different location every day rather than sitting on a sound stage. To me, sound stage filming is almost like factory labour.

What was the audience response to *Black Caesar*?

It was an instant hit. When it opened it played to sold-out houses in three New York City theatres. The picture opened in February and it was a really cold winter but it didn't matter. Lines went around the block and the police had to put up barricades to contain the crowds. I must admit that I kept driving by the theatres just to see the crowds. I got a great kick out of it because *Bone* hadn't done much business and now I had this enormous hit.

James Brown's soundtrack adds a great deal to the picture.

I agree. James did a fantastic job but unfortunately the music he submitted wasn't timed out to fit the actual scenes in the film. I called up his manager and told him that James had not done what he had been contracted to do and his manager just said, "So, he gave you more than you paid for!" I said, "Unfortunately, that's not the way it works. We need the music to fit the scenes exactly – that's why we gave you a copy of the film." In the end, I made it work but AIP was furious. James had done the same thing with another one of their films, *Slaughter's Big Rip-Off*. Consequently, when it came time to do the sequel, James had to do his music on spec. When AIP refused it, he released it as a solo effort called *The Payback* and it became the biggest album of his career.

I know that the picture's ending was changed. How did that come about?

Well, at our first preview in Los Angeles audiences were very upset with the fact that the main character was killed at the end. The fact that white gangster films like *Public Enemy* and *Little Caesar* had the main character die at the end didn't matter to black audiences. They wanted *their* gangster to live. So after the screening I called up Arkoff and told him that we had a disastrous preview and he said, "I told you not to kill him!" The New York opening was just a few days away. He said, "Well there's nothing you can do now." And I said, "Yes there is. I can go to New York and cut off the last scene in the film by hand!" He said, "If you think you can do it – do it!" So I went to New York, arrived at the theatres where the picture was scheduled to open, introduced myself, went upstairs and cut off the ending – right there on the theatre's projection room floor! The film opened a few hours later, without the main character dying at the end, and it was exactly what audiences wanted to see.

Why did you choose to release the DVD version with the original ending – especially given that the edited version was such a success?

Well, for quality purposes we went back to the original negative. Today, the ending doesn't seem to disturb audiences as much as it did back then. Also, when the film was first transferred to VHS in the mid eighties, they used the original negative, which meant that the only people who had seen the edited version were those people who actually saw the film in movie theatres back in 1973.

How did you come up with the script for *Black Caesar*'s follow-up *Hell Up in Harlem*?

Well, I didn't want to do the same film twice, so we made the sequel more about Tommy Gibbs and his father. We gave Tommy's father a more prominent role – turned him into 'Big Poppa' and further developed his relationship with his son. Even so, a lot of *Hell Up in Harlem* was improvised. Fred Williamson was only available for filming on weekends. During the week he was doing another picture called *That Man Bolt*. Consequently, a great deal of the movie was shot using a double – which no one really seemed to notice, then or now.

How did *Hell Up in Harlem* fare?

It did pretty well. I must admit that I don't believe it is as good as *Black Caesar*. There are a lot of good scenes in it – but there are also a lot of action scenes that I don't believe are necessary. Ideally, I think the film should have been cut down but AIP wanted me to throw in everything but the kitchen sink, so I did.

How are you so familiar with the black experience presented in your films?

I'm not really sure I am. I went to City College in New York, which is located in Harlem, and I was there every day for four years. Maybe that has something to do with it.

Is your approach to directing actors loose, allowing them to improvise, or do you prefer a tightly structured working environment?

Improvising is a big part of my approach, especially when we go on location. I like to use whatever is there, make up a scene and give the actors the lines I have written right on the spot.

Why do you believe blaxploitation films are enjoying a renaissance?

Well, they are fast moving, they have a lot of action, many of the performers are exceptional – Ron O'Neal for instance, was a wonderful actor. *Shaft*, *Super Fly*, *Coffy*, those are all good films – they were good then and they are good now.

What do you say to critics who say the films are too violent and filled with negative stereotypes?

I'd say that action movies are generally *about* violence. Whether it's *Scarface* with Al Pacino or *The Godfather* series of films, violence is a major part of the story that the films are telling. They are, after all, movies about gangsters – outlaws. As for negative stereotypes, I don't believe blaxploitation films contain any more negative stereotypes than their white counterparts.

Which of your own blaxploitation films is your favourite?

I have a warm spot in my heart for *Black Caesar* because it was the first big hit that I had. It brought me into the big time and enabled me to keep working in Hollywood.

So many different types of films over such a long period of time; how would you like to be remembered?

If anyone remembers me at all, that would be great. I like the fact that my films constantly get reinvented; they come out in new versions and they still get played. I also enjoy going into video stores and seeing my movies on the shelves. I still get a lot of fan mail, people asking for an autograph, or just telling me how much they liked one of my films. That kind of appreciation, so many years after the fact, is extremely gratifying.

above: Rival gangs cause chaos as they settle their differences by shooting it out in **Black Caesar** (1973).

Robert A. Endelson

Robert A. Endelson's involvement with the film industry was fleeting but most definitely memorable. Following his directorial debut in 1972 with the little seen dating game show spoof *Filthiest Show in Town* – "It's about all those games you never played but wish you had," screamed the ads – Endelson combined forces with exploitation film promoter William Mishkin and helmed 1977's *Fight for Your Life*, a racially-charged black/white revenge picture that, today, three decades after it was first released, remains one of filmdom's most sensational, demented and base cinematic endeavours.

Robert A. Endelson retired from show business shortly after *Fight for Your Life*'s brief theatrical run. Though he remains proud of his work on *Fight for Your Life*, Endelson has, throughout the years, seldom spoken publicly about the film (he also did not participate in the picture's DVD release).

The following interview offers a rare opportunity to understand how Endelson became involved with *Fight for Your Life*, the behind-the-scenes challenges that he and the cast faced while making the film, and what he thinks of the picture today.

Wow! That's about all most people can say about *Fight for Your Life*. How did you come to produce and direct this remarkable film?
I pitched it to producer William Mishkin as a black *Desperate Hours*. He thought it was a great idea but he wanted a script whose prominent feature was escalating degradation followed by vengeance. Straw Weisman wrote the screenplay. At the time, Straw was working as a clerk, booking and tracking prints for theatres. *Fight* was his first big break. Straw was extraordinary with 'in your face' dialogue and that suited the project perfectly.

How was the picture received at the time of its release?
Before we released it we took it to a movie house in Newark, New Jersey, just to see how it would play in front of an audience. Sanderson was there and he slouched nervously in his seat wearing sunglasses and a hood. It was very quiet. You could feel the tension in the air. The screening went without incident but, as you can imagine, it was a very unnerving experience being a white guy in a theatre with 300 black people, most of them young and from the inner city, as they watched this movie.

Did the audience respond the way you thought they would?
Oh yes! I was very satisfied with the effect it had on them. They were emotionally engaged – it certainly wasn't a boring film. But even though the picture did exactly what I wanted it to do, I did consider having my name removed from the print. It was just such a hot potato and of course I knew that it was going to be very, very controversial.

What was the budget and shooting schedule for the film?
The budget was $75,000 and we shot it in ten days.

How did you manage to get so much with so little?
Economy of style in directing; no fancy camera work to detract from the documentary-like reality I sought to

achieve. For example, except for a few lines, like "tar baby" and "Deputy Dog," there was absolutely no improvisation. Every single scene was scripted and had been rehearsed. I also hired the best director of photography that I could find. Anybody can shoot; very few people know how to light. Additionally Ron Merk was a fantastic production designer. With just $100 to work with he made the Turner house look great.

The sound effects are particularly impressive.
They should be; I spent a lot of time doing them. I hated low budget films with their hollow sound and cheap, dirty sound effects. I recorded every footstep, door squeak and gun click myself. I used a portable cassette recorder and synched everything from screeching car wheels to the bell above the liquor store door – by hand. If I thought it would make the film seem more real, there was no effort that was too great. Along with the sound effects, good music was also very important to me. I wasn't exactly sure what I wanted so Jeff Slevin, the composer, would randomly play the piano. When I heard something I liked, I knew it, and we used it. Of course Jeff also wrote and performed the *Fight for Your Life* theme song, which plays over the opening credits.

Watching the film the viewer feels like he is in the room with the Turners.

And that's what I tried very hard to do. What makes the material itself so powerful is the juxtaposition of racism and context. Calling a person a racial slur is one thing. Using that slur when he can't talk back and in front of his family is another thing altogether. Initially the audience response is shocked silence. But then, pushed to their limit, they become very vocal and begin to angrily speak out – because the family cannot. Silent spectators are transformed into a furious mob, and when Grandma finally gets the gun and begins to talk back, the audience's pent-up rage just explodes.

How did you accomplish some of the picture's more violent visual effects?

Well, I shot the whole film in 35mm on a 3:1 ratio and edited it in 16mm. The bible beating was filmed at 8 frames per second with the actors performing their actions very slowly. Joey's murder was filmed in reverse with the rock being yanked *off* and *away* from his head. Of course, with our minimal budget, all the actors did their own stunts.

Did the controversial dialogue and film situations present any special challenges for the actors?

The black actors in the film consistently told me that the story of raw racism was important and worthy of their time and effort to tell. No one had any reservations about anything – and that was a green light for me. I think everyone's commitment to the project shows. You can't fake commitment like you can fake blood and guts.

It's true; the performers seem totally involved.

We took the cast and crew and put them in a hotel in upstate New York. Essentially we held them as hostages – just like the family in the film! This served the production very well. Everyone had just one thing on their minds at all times – the film.

William Sanderson gives a convincing performance.

Yes he does, and consequently, journalists always seem to focus on him. But I'd like to take a moment and talk about Robert Judd, who played Deacon Turner. First of all I called Robert 'One Take Judd'. I don't ever recall doing a second take with him. Look into his eyes. Not only is he one of the finest gentlemen you could ever meet, he was also an actor of the highest calibre. Without his presence, his quiet defiance and dignity, the film would never have worked on any level. It would simply have been a 'turn the tables' revenge picture without embodying any of the ideals of character – the reason the actors wanted to do the film in the first place.

Did any scenes not make it onto the screen?

As a matter of fact, yes. At one point I felt that I had to draw the line. In the script there was a scene in which Jesse Kane makes Floyd, the little boy, eat food from a dog bowl. Though I agreed that it would advance the good vs. evil element that I was trying to exploit, I thought that it was just taking things a bit too far. A few years ago I was pleasantly surprised to learn that Reggie Blythewood (Floyd) is now a successful writer and director. I'm glad I didn't have him eating food out of a dog bowl!

Several directors I've spoken to have talked about racism behind the scenes in Hollywood in the '70s. Did you experience any of this?

I don't know about racism behind the scenes – I was focused on the racism in front of the camera! *Fight for Your Life* was a virtual license to express racism and we were all completely into putting that license to good use!

Why was the picture's theatrical run so short?

I guess it was just too strong. Theatre owners didn't want mobs in their theatres at *any* price. To my knowledge the film never actually caused an out and out riot, but if I were a white projectionist looking down at an enraged black audience, I'm sure I would have thought so.

What was your opinion of some of the other blaxploitation films?

Actually, *Sweet Sweetback's Baadasssss Song* was my favourite blaxploitation film and Melvin Van Peebles, the writer and director, was my hero. He made that film against all odds and that was very inspiring to me.

Why do you believe the genre came and went so quickly?

I believe blaxploitation films were replaced by a very different kind of fantasy-escapist picture. For instance, when *Fight* was released the shift in public tastes was already underway. Our film came out around the same time as *Star Wars*, *Close Encounters of the Third Kind* and *The Cat from Outer Space*. A couple of years later there was *Alien*, and *Blade Runner*.

Why do you believe the pictures are becoming popular again?

I didn't know they were!

***Fight* is reaching a whole new audience via DVD. What do you think of the picture today?**

After all these years maybe the film is finally finding its audience. Regarding the DVD release, many people think that I did not offer any commentary because I am ashamed of the film. That's simply not true. I felt that it was the job of *other* people to talk about, examine and/or discuss the picture, not mine.

So, no regrets whatsoever?

Absolutely none. In fact I have a fantasy of remaking it. It would be called *Fight for Your Life – Resurrection: Turn the Other Cheek.* Can you imagine! "Grandma... sharpen your chainsaw!"

above: A cathartic moment: Grandma Turner (Lela Small) turns the tables on her racist captors in **Fight for Your Life** (1977).

Jamaa Fanaka

One of the film capital's very few successful African-American director/writer/producers, Jamaa Fanaka's Hollywood success story is a most unusual one. After directing *Welcome Home Brother Charles* and *Emma Mae* (both completed while he was a student at UCLA – and both theatrically released), Fanaka hit the big time with 1979's *Penitentiary*, a slice-of-life prison drama that topped critics' lists, won acclaim at the Cannes film festival and was followed by two sequels.

Today, the prolific filmmaker, whose 1992 *Street Wars* offered a rare look at drug and gang culture in America's inner cities, remains committed to black advancement in film. His 1990's lawsuit against the motion picture industry (in which he charged that African Americans continued to be systematically excluded) is indicative of his perseverance and longstanding passion to both advance and redefine the African American image in front of, and behind, the camera. Next up for Fanaka, a cinematic celebration of Hip Hop music and its far-reaching impact.

There were very few African-American directors working in the 1970s. How did you make your entrée into the film industry?

It just sort of happened. My family and I lived in Compton, California. After a brief stint in the Air Force I got out and didn't have a clue as to what I wanted to do with my life. I knew I wanted to make money but I just didn't know how. Then one day I saw a sign that was advertising an open-house outreach program at UCLA. I signed up and took it from there. At first, I was much more interested in writing – I still love to write. But part of the UCLA program was that you had to make a short film. I wrote, directed and starred in a short and then started thinking that maybe I should put my energies into directing, too.

Welcome Home Brother Charles **was your first big success.**

Yes, it was. That was the second film project we had to do as part of the program at UCLA. Usually students made a ten or twenty minute film, but I decided to go ahead and do a full-out feature length picture – and that turned out to be *Welcome Home Brother Charles*.

Tell me a little about the controversial subtext of the film.

I was very interested in the myth that has been thrust upon the black man – that of the black man's sexual superiority based upon the size of his penis. I don't believe that it serves black men well to have people thinking that his most valuable attribute is between his legs. With *Welcome Home Brother Charles* I wanted to show that the relentless focus on the size of the black man's penis has, throughout history, hurt everyone – both the people who focus on it as well as the black man himself, who, in response to all the sexual attention, often begins to neglect his many other fine attributes.

How did *Emma Mae* **come about?**

That was the second feature length film I made while I was at UCLA. The story was inspired by my cousin Daisy Lee. When I was about twelve years old my family moved from Jacksonville, Mississippi to Los Angeles. Daisy started coming and spending the

summer with us when she was about eight. Though she was young and not hip to the ways of the big city, she was very worldly and very tough. But as tough as Daisy Lee was, she also had a tremendous love for her family and friends, and that impressed me greatly. *Emma Mae* is her story.

How did *Penitentiary* come about?

It was my Masters thesis film – can you believe it! I had three theatrically released films out before I had even finished school. I don't think anyone else has ever accomplished that.

What was it about the story that interested you?

My parents used to tell me that no matter how formidable any given situation is, God has given each and every one of us the inner resources to deal with it. That got me to thinking about what would be the most challenging situation imaginable. Being locked up for something you didn't do has got to be at the top of the list. That was the story I was interested in telling.

It's safe to say, what with the two sequels that followed, that *Penitentiary* was your biggest success.

Yes, it was. The critics loved it. It got all kinds of awards, and I was invited to speak just about everywhere. I remember that at the time the movie was in theatres, the word was going around that the crime rate had dropped something like 50% in the Los Angeles area. I'm not sure if that's true, but the point is that the story in *Penitentiary* spoke to a lot of young, poor, black men. The primal reality of prison life was brought home to them in a very realistic way.

How were you able to write with such knowledge of the prison experience?

Well, though I've never spoken publicly about it before, when I was younger I served six months for being involved in a fight that broke out while I was playing dice. I did my time in Philadelphia, and while I was incarcerated I saw first hand all the personality types that you see in the film. What I was struck by

Jamaa Fanaka's critically acclaimed **Penitentiary** (1979) was one of only a few films written, produced and directed by an African American. Here 'Too Sweet' Gordone (Leon Isaac Kennedy) gets the upper hand over cellmate 'Half-Dead' Johnson (Badja Djola). (Soul Images)

most was the fact that no matter what your role was in society, you had to play by a whole different set of rules while behind bars. The dumbest person you meet on the street can be the most powerful and influential person behind bars.

Was boxing really such a large part of prison life?
Absolutely. Most of the guys who entered these boxing tournaments did so just to escape the drudgery of day-to-day living. They thought they were going to get to just kind of fool around for a while in the gym. Of course no one wanted to hear about the payment due at the end – each of the guys who participated in the program had to fight in a tournament. Two minutes in the ring seems like a lifetime when someone is swinging at your head!

Your films are very politically conscious. Was this something that was important to you?
Yes, it was. My father was a very politically minded man. He was very affected by the fact that blacks were not allowed to vote down in Jackson, Mississippi. To him that was an outrage. The truth was that he knew more about the political candidates of the day, and their various platforms, than the white people who had the right to vote. So at a very early age I was made aware of the politics and injustices around me. My father was a great inspiration to me. He was the kind of man that didn't have to say "Do what I say;" he could say, "Check out what I do and decide for yourself."

What did you think of some of the other successful blaxploitation films?
I thought, "Now, finally, Hollywood realises that we can do it." But more importantly I thought, "Now, finally, *we* realise what we can do." I likened the success of blaxploitation films to the success of Motown Records. Motown gave the world some good popular music, but, in my opinion, the bigger service they provided to blacks was that they taught us how to lead *behind the scenes*. We learned how to engineer; to produce; to manage; and to hone and effectively market our unique talents. We moved from being showmen to being masters of our own destiny.

Was racism a part of your experience while in Hollywood?
Yes, and I must say that I found it very strange. It was like a person telling themself a lie when the truth would actually help them. This was the reason I brought a lawsuit against the Director's Guild in the 1990s. It was a five-year affair and I eventually lost, but I held my own and I believe I brought attention to the great discrepancy in the hiring practices and opportunities made available to blacks. When blaxploitation films were no longer in vogue, Hollywood slammed and locked all its doors. The purpose of my lawsuit was to try to get those doors back open again.

above: Jerri Hayes and Ernest Williams II in the climactic fight scene from 1976's **Emma Mae** (re-titled **Black Sister's Revenge** on video).

What inspires you now?
Right now I'm finishing up a film on Hip Hop. I really champion the movement because, in many ways, Hip Hop artists are going through the same thing that I went through thirty years ago. I made my films *despite* Hollywood and they are making their music *despite* the recording industry. Perseverance is the key.

Gordon Parks refused to talk to me because he finds the term 'blaxploitation' derogatory. As an African-American filmmaker, what do you think of the term?
I think that at one time it may have had a negative connotation, but that has all been turned around. We [blacks] have reclaimed it. Certainly the young kids today don't find anything negative about the term. To them it references a major change in Hollywood – a time when blacks said 'what they can do, *we* can do too.'

Why do you believe the blaxploitation movie boom came to such an abrupt end?
Well, that's a really good question. I have a feeling that Hollywood just used the pictures to help them get back on their feet. Once they had moved away from bankruptcy – because most of the big studios were having real financial troubles in the '70s – they no longer had any interest in making the films.

Why do you believe the pictures are enjoying a renaissance?
The main reason is the autonomy we have gained through the Hip Hop revolution. Nobody thought that Hip Hop music was going to make it. They thought it was going to go the way of break dancing. When Hip Hop music not only endured, but prevailed, it created a renewed interest in black popular culture, past and present.

How would you like to be remembered?
As a man who helped pave the way for others. I wasn't the first; every person who effects change owes a debt to someone who came before them. I'd like to be remembered as a man who helped keep the ball rolling.

Jack Hill

Writer/director Jack Hill's name will forever be associated with both 'whitesploitation' and blaxploitation films that feature strong, ethnically diverse and sexually liberated women in leading roles. Having worked on several films in a co-director capacity between 1960 and 1963, his solo directorial debut came in 1964 with the camp classic horror movie *Spider Baby* (not released until 1968). Hill went on to make his mark with two women-in-prison films – 1971's *The Big Doll House* and 1972's *The Big Bird Cage* (which he also wrote) – and then followed with 1973's box office bonanza *Coffy* and 1974's 'sequel,' *Foxy Brown*.

After the release of his cult action/adventure female gang film *Switchblade Sisters* in 1975, Hill took a seven year break from directing but eventually returned to helm the 1982 fantasy/adventure film *Sorceress*. However, after the movie's budget was dramatically cut back mid-production, and the completed picture was then re-cut against his recommendations, Hill had his name removed from the film and decided that the time was right to take an extended sabbatical from the entertainment industry.

Today Jack Hill remains focused on his writing, both developing screenplays and working on a 'very ambitious novel.'

The Big Bird Cage featured a strong black subplot. How did you come to write and direct it?
I wouldn't say that it had a 'black subplot' by any understanding of the term that I have. Two of the characters just happen to be black. So what? But I must admit that Pam Grier, the main black character in the film, makes quite an impression and she has the best line. After a white gal calls her "nigger," Pam floors her and says: "That's *Miss* Nigger to you!" Pam came up with that line; I would never have thought of such a thing.

Which was the easier film to shoot? The Big Doll House – which you directed but didn't write – or The Big Bird Cage, on which you wore both hats?
The Big Bird Cage was much simpler to shoot, mostly because I didn't have to rewrite almost every scene and even invent new ones.

What were your ideas about the other blaxploitation films when you made Coffy?
Well, I had seen and admired *Super Fly*, but as a white man I didn't feel truly qualified to handle black characters and lifestyle on that level of reality. I also felt that black writers and directors should have the first crack at the opportunities that the success of the genre presented.

What changed your mind?
Larry Gordon – who was then head of production at American International Pictures – called me in and asked if I could create a 'black woman's revenge' picture. I said I thought I might be able to do it if I could work with Pam Grier. I had helped launch Pam's career a few years earlier and thought that she was the only actress that could generate the kind of screen persona I had in mind. To me, Pam has something magical; I can't put a name on it. Just 'It'! That special thing that only she has.

Coffy, even by today's standards, is still shocking. Did the violent situations, nudity and profanity present any special challenges?
By this time in the history of cinema, we were all used to it. I don't recall any profanity, though. I mean, nobody used 'fuck' as an expletive, did they? [Ed. Note: They do, many times]. The only challenge I recall was the fact that when we made the picture there were no experienced black stunt coordinators – and even more sticky for an action picture like *Coffy*, virtually no black stunt women. Which meant we had to train people on the job, presenting a serious safety concern that caused many a pair of crossed fingers on the set at times.

The film seems specifically created to shock and titillate.
You mean 'shock and awe'? What the hell – why not? But titillate! Perish the thought! Well, I can only say that I had to fight the studio to make the film something more than shocks and titillations. The 'awe' was my contribution.

How long was the shoot? What was the budget like?
Eighteen days, $500,000.

Foxy Brown came fast on the heels of Coffy. Did you have a freer hand given your success with Coffy?
Nobody had any idea that *Coffy* would be such a big hit, so nobody gave any thought to a sequel – least of all me. Did I have a freer hand after that? On the contrary! The studio idiots were afraid after such a big success I might have a big ego, so they tried to put me on an even tighter leash. But I fooled them.

Did you feel you were under pressure to do a bigger, more outlandish, follow up to Coffy?
Only because I hated the studio system so much at that time that I felt that only by really going over the top could I get my own sinister kind of revenge. Unfortunately, the result has haunted me ever since.

above: A rare shot of Claudia (Juanita Brown), Katherine Wall (Kathryn Loder) and Foxy Brown (Pam Grier) on the set of 1974's cult favourite **Foxy Brown**. (Soul Images)

It's certainly a more colourful production.

If you mean the title sequence and all the costume changes – which I didn't like at the time because I thought they took attention away from Pam's performance and beauty – I guess you're right. People think the budget for *Foxy Brown* was bigger than *Coffy*, but it actually ended up being less. $500,000 was all *AIP* was willing to pay for one of their so-called 'black pictures,' and because they had to pay me and Pam more the second time around, there was less money for the actual production. Even so, I brought the film in a day early and, because of that, became a hero at the studio.

It doesn't sound like *Foxy Brown* is a favourite film of yours.

Well, as you know originally I wrote the script as a sequel called *Burn, Coffy, Burn*. We were all pretty upset when, at the last minute, the studio decided to change it.

35

Oddly enough though, *Foxy Brown* has acquired a cult following and is even more popular today than *Coffy* – which in my opinion is the better film.

Switchblade Sisters followed Foxy Brown and is in many ways a 'whitesploitation' film.

Well, somewhat, yes. I really tried to do something special with *Switchblade Sisters*: a female version of the basic triangle of *Othello*; dealing with a woman provoking another woman's jealousy. When I first saw it in a theatre with an audience I felt that I had done everything wrong that I could possibly do wrong. Now it's considered a classic – 'post modern,' etc. Just goes to show you!

Many blaxploitation-era producers and directors have spoken about racism behind the scenes. Did you witness any of this?

Plenty. I was frankly appalled at some of the things I saw and heard. The studio had nothing but contempt for the audience they were making films for, but not just the black audience – everyone. They weren't shooting for an Academy Award, those guys – they had a popcorn machine in the screening room. But the studio guys weren't the only racists. Film critics were, too. I remember one reviewer referring to the character of Coffy as, "an unsympathetic black chick"; another as "a black tart."

But your experience making the pictures was a positive one?

Yes. It was one of the most enjoyable experiences of my life in film to collaborate with those wonderful young black players – so much enthusiasm, so full of marvellous ideas to enrich their characterisations and contribute elements to the film that alone I could never have dreamed of – and so happy just to be actually *working* at last. It was the age of 'black power' and 'black is beautiful' – and it *was* beautiful, and it *was* powerful. And still is!

Which of your blaxploitation films is your favourite?

Hey, I only made two! I think *Coffy* is actually a terrific movie. *Foxy Brown* – well, as I said, it continues to haunt me. Still, I would rather have made *Foxy Brown* than, say, *The Godfather: Part III*.

How would you like to be remembered?

Well, as far as my blaxploitation films go, one of my greatest satisfactions is that films like *Coffy*, *Foxy Brown* and a few others that were made by writers and directors who really cared about what they were doing, demonstrated that black characters and black lifestyles could appeal to a large white audience as well – what they called a 'cross-over audience.' And this ultimately helped open doors for black men and women in all categories of the film industry. So, if my work in any small way contributed to that transformation, I will be forever grateful for having been given the opportunity to make that contribution.

above: Pam Grier, blaxploitation's queen of sex and violence, prominently displays her "assets" in this moment of anguish from 1973's **Coffy**.

Jonathan Kaplan

Beginning his career as an apprentice for Roger Corman and his New World Pictures company, Jonathan Kaplan's first directorial efforts were 'sexploitation' pictures like 1972's *Night Call Nurses* – "They're always harder at night!" – and 1973's *The Student Teachers*. Kaplan then made a jump into the blaxploitation genre with 1973's *The Slams* and 1974's *Truck Turner*, which was followed by mainstream success with 1975's action-oriented *White Line Fever* (which he also wrote). 1988's *The Accused* (for which Jodie Foster won a Best Actress Oscar) solidified the filmmaker's position in the Hollywood hierarchy. The writer/director's many other film successes include *Love Field* and *Unlawful Entry* (both 1992) and *Brokedown Palace* (1999).

Today Jonathan Kaplan is one of television's most sought after craftsmen. His long list of TV credits include directing episodes of *ER*, *Crossing Jordan*, *The Man in Blue*, *The Court*, *Law & Order* and the two popular miniseries *In Cold Blood* and *Picture Windows*.

The Slams was your first black-cast film. How did you come to direct it?

I made a movie for Roger Corman called *The Student Teachers*. It was a low budget 'sexploitation' film – what we called a 'Soft Corman' picture! All I had to do was deliver the nudity, the thrills, the kinkiness and the comedy that had become Roger's trademark – and I did. *The Student Teachers* was very successful, and it had a black action subplot, so Roger recommended me to his brother Gene Corman. Gene went to check out *The Student Teachers* and walked out of the screening about two thirds of the way through. So I thought, "Oh well, I guess I didn't get that job!" But apparently Gene had seen enough to convince him that I could handle a larger, action oriented film. He went directly from the screening to go call my agent and hire me for *The Slams*.

The Student Teachers and The Slams were released the same year. Did your approach to the two pictures differ?

The Student Teachers was a Roger Corman formula film and *The Slams* wasn't. Gene wanted to stick to the script, so I really didn't get a chance to change too much, but *The Slams* had a longer, more complicated, shooting schedule and a bigger budget. The major challenge with *The Slams* was that it was very claustrophobic – it takes place in a prison. It was my job to make it as visually interesting as it could be.

Did working with a celebrated athlete like Jim Brown present any special challenges?

With Jim I was focused on making him the best he could be. I purposely made no mention of football, sports, or his past career as a star athlete. I looked at *The Slams* as being as close as I would ever get to something like a Warner Bros. gangster picture – like *White Heat* – and I directed him as if I were directing Cagney or Bogart or Pat O'Brien in one of their classic films.

What were your feelings about blaxploitation films when you became involved with The Slams?

To be honest with you, I didn't really see very many of them. I remember seeing *Super Fly* in New York when it first came out. I was amazed at how technically crude the picture was. I mean there were mikes in shots, shadows all over the place, all the sort of stuff that you assume won't be the case with a major studio movie. But I was also quite taken with Curtis Mayfield's soundtrack because I just thought it was so clear how much the movie owed to his fantastic score.

How did Truck Turner come about?

Producer Larry Gordon had seen *The Slams* and hired me to do something similar for his company American

above: A zebra-print dress, a grimace, and a gun: Madame Dorinda (Nichelle Nichols) can clearly take care of herself in **Truck Turner** (1974).

International Pictures. When I was first given the project the studio was thinking about using either Lee Marvin, Ernest Borgnine or Robert Mitchum in the lead role. But then I got a call from Larry telling me that I would be making the picture with Isaac Hayes. I said, "That's quite a switch from Robert Mitchum!"

Isaac Hayes seems like an odd choice for the lead in a film.

At the time Ike had made an incredible splash with the *Shaft* soundtrack album. Along with his fantastic score, everyone remembered his sensational performance of the song on the Academy Awards show, so AIP thought that they could exploit his popularity and make him an actor, too. What they really wanted was for him to do the film's music. *He* wanted to do some acting, so they threw the acting in to sweeten the deal.

What do you say to critics who say that blaxploitation films are filled with violence and negative black stereotypes?

Well, I tried to make the blaxploitation films that *I* worked on more about *class* and less about race. I tried to make the *world* be black in my films rather than it just being black vs. white. I thought that the pictures were more accurate if they were about good guys vs. bad guys, not black guys vs. white guys.

Another criticism of the films was that they were misogynist.

I agree. I found the treatment of women in blaxploitation films to be just horrible. For instance, in *Truck Turner*, I completely rewrote the relationship that Truck had with his girlfriend Annie (Annazette Chase). I made their relationship much more tender, much more gentle, and much more equal. Take the scene where Truck sets her up to get arrested – to protect her. That's a great scene! We, the audience, realise that he's doing the right thing, but *she* doesn't. And so you have a genuinely funny and emotional scene, where if it had just been "Bitch, shut the fuck up and do what I tell you," nobody would have cared.

It's a clever segment.

And it pays off. At the time, insisting on that kind of a change was a really big deal. I had to put up a fight to make it happen. But, you know, Ike was on my side too because he said, "I don't want to be slapping this girl around either." He was very aware that his audience was strongly female, and, you know, he's a very attractive guy, and all the love songs he had written and everything – it just didn't make sense for him to be playing some misogynist creep.

What about racism behind the scenes? Several prominent actors and directors have talked about how widespread it was.

I would say that the only time I experienced the provincialism of the movie directors was when I saw the way they dealt with Isaac Hayes's salary. They thought, because he was black, that they were going to get him for a lot cheaper than a white guy. Then they found out that, no, in fact, Ike was going to cost them *more* than a white guy – a lot more! They realised that Ike didn't need them; he was already making a lot of money just being Isaac Hayes. Being 'Black Moses' was very profitable for him. I'm not surprised by any racism in America.

above and right: Curtis Hook (Jim Brown) in 1973's **The Slams**, has got a plan: Stay out of trouble, blend into the crowd, and quietly execute a complicated prison escape!

opposite: **The Slams** returned Jim Brown's name to theatre marquees. A "black man's star" in the late 1960s, the film cemented Brown's position as a major draw in the '70s.

THE SLAMS

METRO-GOLDWYN-MAYER presents
JIM BROWN in 'THE SLAMS'
Written by RICHARD L. ADAMS · Directed by JONATHAN KAPLAN
Produced by GENE CORMAN

The scene where Nichelle Nichols is berating the local pimps is quite astonishing. It is, without a doubt, blaxploitation's most consistently vulgar and profane segment.

The thing about *Truck Turner* is that we all laughed our asses off while we made the film – especially that scene! We literally sat there and said, "How many 'mother fuckers' can we get in this scene?" We were just cracking up! It was like, "Who holds the record for the most 'mother fuckers?'" I didn't take the film too seriously. In many ways it was an affectionate parody, and the audience got it. When I saw the picture for the first time in a theatre, people were jumping up in the aisles and giving each other the high five. They were just having a great time laughing at all the shit that we laughed at when we shot it.

White Line Fever came on the heels of Truck Turner. Was your approach to making this 'whitesploitation' film vastly different than your approach to Truck Turner?

I looked at *Truck Turner* as sort of an action-comedy. *White Line Fever* is different. If you look at the film you can tell that it's heavily influenced by director Sergio Leone. It's really a western film – but with trucks instead of horses. I'm a huge fan of Sergio Leone.

Did White Line Fever come about because of your success with Truck Turner?

The real story of how I got to do *White Line Fever* is that when *Truck Turner* opened in Chicago and Detroit, it was announced in *Variety* that this movie, *Truck Turner* – directed by Jonathan Kaplan – had done huge business. That same weekend, Peter Guber, who was an executive at Columbia Pictures, had a treatment for *White Line Fever* pass across his desk. He looked at the treatment and saw that it was about trucks. He hadn't seen *Truck Turner* so he thought *Truck Turner* was about trucks too. So, he literally made the deal for *White Line Fever* on Monday morning – thinking he was getting Jonathan Kaplan's next 'trucking movie'! Only later did he find out that the main character was named Truck Turner and that *Truck Turner* had absolutely nothing to do with trucks or the trucking industry.

Do you believe that your association with blaxploitation films helped better position you for success in Hollywood?

Well, I never tried to position myself for anything in the movie industry. I just don't know how you would go about doing that. But I must say that I was very, very fortunate to make as many movies as I got to make before I made *White Line Fever*, which was my first major studio picture. I started off doing sexploitation, then blaxploitation, then action-adventure, and then female-driven drama. If you look at *The Accused* or *Brokedown Palace* and then you look at *Truck Turner* and *White Line Fever*, they are quite different. I've been very fortunate.

Why do you believe the blaxploitation cycle of films came to such an abrupt end?

You know, the first time that you see a pimp and he's flashy, and he's got a great car, and he's got all these hoes, that's cool. And then you can do it again, bigger, and then bigger still. But then at a certain point you just can't do it any bigger anymore. The car can't get any flashier – the women can't get any sexier – you've just sort of done it all. I also believe that the white movie executives misread the genre. They thought that the more violent they made the films, the more money they'd make. I remember going to see *Truck Turner* on Hollywood Boulevard for like a dollar on a Sunday night, and it was almost all families – moms, dads, grandmas, kids. But the white executives wouldn't be caught dead in a downtown movie theatre, so they really didn't know exactly who they were making the films for.

Why do you believe blaxploitation films remain so popular with audiences?

They're honest, they're authentic, they're entertaining, and the music is great. I also think that the pictures are relatively predictable and that makes them comforting. All of these elements, plus the fact that they have a twinkle in their eye – they don't take themselves too seriously – makes for some pretty good entertainment.

Arthur Marks

Talented movie business all-rounder Arthur Marks began his show business career in television. His long list of directorial credits includes the popular TV shows *Perry Mason*, *I Spy*, *Starsky & Hutch* and *The Dukes of Hazzard*. Marks's first feature film, *Togetherness*, was released in 1970. After forming General Film Corporation (a company that distributed several exploitation pictures), Marks made his own contributions to the genre with 1973's *Detroit 9000* (which he wrote, produced and directed), followed in rapid succession by: *Bucktown* and *Friday Foster* in 1975; and *Monkey Hustle* and *J.D.'s Revenge* in 1976 (the latter three of which he both produced and directed). Marks's other films include 1972's *Gabriella*, and *Bonnie's Kids* and *The Roommates* (both 1973).

Today Arthur Marks's experience as a director, producer, screenwriter and distribution company owner have made him a coveted guest speaker on college campuses.

Detroit 9000 was your first venture into blaxploitation. How did it come about?

Well, at the time I was heading a company called General Film Corporation. It was a distribution company but we also produced films. I saw a *Time* magazine cover story whose focus was the fact that Detroit, Michigan was the murder capital of the world. I thought, "there's a movie in there somewhere," so I wrote one!

Did you set out to write a blaxploitation film?

No, originally the film was designed to be a white picture with Alex Rocco, but the drive-in theatre market that we were creating the film for made it clear that they wanted a 'black' picture that could play in their inner-city movie houses as well, so we made sure that we fulfilled that particular need.

The rapid-fire editing in Detroit 9000 makes the film look totally contemporary.

I remember I was in a meeting with Sam Arkoff, who was the head of American International Pictures. Sam was very concerned about *Detroit*'s quick cuts and fast pace. At the time the movie companies thought that black audiences couldn't be barraged with images. They thought blacks preferred viewing films with steadily progressing narratives – scenes that they could view, digest and move forward from in a linear fashion. At one point they were going to re-edit the film. I told them they were crazy.

Does it surprise you that Detroit 9000 has such a large cult following?

Yes, it does. I thought the picture was always a good professional film but I never expected it to remain so popular – especially thirty years after the fact. About two years ago I got a call from Quentin Tarantino. He told me he was a big fan of the film and thought it should be re-released. We had a meeting and that lead to the current Miramax DVD.

You seem to make location – Detroit, Washington D.C., New Orleans, Chicago – a major part of your storytelling.

That is a very astute observation. Yes, I did that on purpose. I felt that genuine locations would not only enhance the story and add to the realism of the pictures, but would also increase the likelihood that the films would be played in the cities we were showing. Location filming also allowed me the opportunity to do

above: Fashion photographer Friday Foster (Pam Grier) and her smitten boyfriend Colt Hawkins (Yaphet Kotto) do their best to impress in 1975's **Friday Foster**, a film adaptation of the adventures of a comic book character. (J. Howard Collection)

things that I would not have been able to do in a union-based Hollywood situation.

Your films also share a readily identifiable format – they start out with a bang, either literally or figuratively – and then move forward from there.

The blaxploitation films I did were created to grab hold of an audience in the first ten to fifteen minutes and keep them hooked for the duration of the picture. I thought that approach was particularly useful for those types of action-oriented films.

***Bucktown* and *Friday Foster* were both released in 1975. Which was finished first?**

I think we did *Bucktown* first.

Was it difficult working with a star like Pam Grier, someone who had a very powerful pre-existing image?

At the time I cast Pam in *Bucktown* she was doing these shoot-'em-up films filled with big breasts and scanty clothes. I met with her, talked to her, and told her that if she would lend herself to me, I would feature her in a film that

she could be proud of. I told her, "You're going to play a waitress, a gal who works in a bar, who falls in love with a guy from Philadelphia and it's going to be a love story. You won't be shooting anyone or any of that stuff; your job is to provide a solid base as to why he wants to stay in this small town." I think she did an excellent job. Then I cast her again in *Friday Foster* and we got her everything she wanted; good clothes, expert makeup, perfect hairstyles – the whole glamorising treatment. She had a ball.

In *J.D.'s Revenge*, your use of black & white and colour photography is very interesting. Was this difficult to accomplish?

In those days we didn't have great computer or visual effects so we just shot a lot of the scenes in black & white or sepia right on the spot. There was a lot of improvising going on when we filmed *J.D.'s Revenge*.

Was the film inspired by *The Exorcist* or *The Reincarnation of Peter Proud* – both popular occult-themed films at the time?

above: Glynn Turman and Joan Pringle in the reincarnation themed **J.D.'s Revenge** (1976). (Soul Images)

No, not really. I liked the *J.D.* script and thought it would be a perfect vehicle for Glynn Turman. I had seen Glynn in *Cooley High* and thought, "Now there's a really fine actor."

Monkey Hustle is a 'feel-good' film – very different from J.D.'s Revenge. Did you make a conscious effort to depart from the action-adventure genre?

Oh yes! As a matter of fact I wanted to do *Oliver!* That's what *Monkey Hustle* is – *Oliver* in Chicago with a black cast! Yaphet Kotto is Fagin, and the boys are all his gang.

How did you come to cast Rudy Ray Moore?

I had never seen Rudy in any of his films but someone told me that I should really see *Dolemite* – that he was perfect for the part of the flashy, loud-talking character Goldie. I arranged a meeting to hear him read but he was just dreadful. So I threw away the script and told him to just be himself and then he was really terrific – exactly what the film needed.

What was your opinion of blaxploitation pictures at the time you made your films?

I must say that I often thought that blacks were presented very, very poorly. I won't mention any directors' names, but, more than once, I voiced my opinion and said, "You know, you are really off base in your presentation here. You really are making a 'Black Exploitation' film." I felt that the negative portrayal of blacks and black life in some of the pictures was giving directors like myself – someone who was trying to remain positive and not denigrate anyone – a bad name.

Did you ever experience any racism in Hollywood?

No, I never felt it anywhere. But don't forget that I was an independent and pretty much did what I wanted to do. Also, the fact that all my pictures were shot on location meant that I wasn't really too much involved with what was going on within the studio system back in Hollywood.

Why do you feel the genre came to such an abrupt end?

MONKEY HU$TLE

AN AMERICAN INTERNATIONAL PICTURE Starring

YAPHET KOTTO · RUDY RAY MOORE

Color by MOVIELAB

PG

I really can't answer that one; it's still not really clear to me. I'll tell you why the drive-in market dried up. The majors took a look at the money that the independent films were making in the black market and made their own half-assed 'black' pictures. Because the majors could spend a lot more on advertising, this pretty much pushed the independents out of the market. For instance Sam Arkoff told me that the main reason he sold AIP was because his bread and butter market – the drive-ins – were totally disappearing.

Why do you believe blaxploitation films remain popular today?

For one simple reason: they're worth seeing again.

above: Many blaxploitation films seemed to be quick rehashes of successful white films. Case in point 1976's **Monkey Hustle** – essentially a black-cast version of **The Sting**. Pictured are confidence man 'Daddy Fox' (Yaphet Kotto) and his young protégé 'Baby D.' (Kirk Calloway). (Soul Images)

Cirio H. Santiago

Cirio H. Santiago's eight blaxploitation pictures (five as director, three as producer, and all filmed in his native Philippines) are credited with injecting the genre with new life by taking familiar crime-centred narratives out of America's inner-cities and placing them in the scenic Filipino jungles.

Though Santiago had produced and directed several films in his native country before making his American directorial debut with 1973's 'sexploitation' epic *Fly Me*, it wasn't until that same year's *Savage!* that Santiago hit his stride and carved a niche for himself as a premier action/adventure director. The following year's box office smash *TNT Jackson* – a female-hero revenge epic that starred former *Playboy* playmate Jean Bell – solidified the director's new position as both an ambassador for the Philippines and a quick-working craftsman who could bring in crowd-pleasing pictures inexpensively. Along with his three other blaxploitation pictures, *Ebony, Ivory & Jade* and *The Muthers* (both 1976), and *Death Force* (1977), Santiago's films outside the blaxploitation genre include *Cover Girl Models* and *The Pacific Connection* (both 1975), plus *Vampire Hookers* (1978) and *Caged Fury* (1982).

Today Cirio H. Santiago has hung up in his directorial hat and remains one of the biggest producers of action/adventure pictures in the international film market.

You moved from producing films like *The Big Bird Cage* and *The Big Doll House* to directing. Was directing something you had always wanted to do?
After I graduated from college I started directing local films in the Philippines. Then I met Roger Corman while he was passing through Manila and he said, "some day when I get my own company together I want to work with you." First I started producing films for him and then I moved into directing.

I understand that your films were made expressly for the drive-in market.
Absolutely. At that time we were making films for less than $100,000. *The Big Doll House* was a bonanza for Roger, and once MGM picked it up and distributed it, that kind of got the ball rolling for everyone.

How did you come to produce and direct *Savage!*?
Savage! was my first blaxploitation film. Roger came to me and told me he wanted a "black soldier of fortune picture," so we did it. In fact, just last week I got my first copy of the film from the internet. I never owned a copy and hadn't seen it since it came out more than thirty years ago. Watching it was a very interesting experience for me.

***TNT Jackson* has a large cult following – not just the film, but the poster art as well. How did it come about?**
Well it's based on a famous book called 'Red Harvest'. Roger Corman got the rights, we re-wrote it, made the film and it became a huge hit. That film led the way for a large number of similar-themed pictures, most of them having to do with the after effects of the Vietnam War. I can tell you that I continue to make money on *TNT Jackson* from DVD and video sales.

***Ebony, Ivory & Jade* seems very much like a 'G'-rated film. Were you consciously trying to move away from the exploitation market?**

Yes, I was. I didn't do that one for Roger, I did that for a company called Dimension Pictures. A couple of years ago I got a call from Quentin Tarantino and he told me that *Ebony, Ivory & Jade* is one of his favourite films.

***The Muthers* is your other Dimension Pictures film.**
Yes, that one didn't do very well. *Ebony, Ivory & Jade* was the bigger success. Maybe that is the picture to re-make, since everyone is talking about the 2012 Olympics and the film centres around three female Olympic hopefuls.

***Death Force* starred husband and wife team Leon Isaac and Jayne Kennedy. How did that come about?**
I read the script and liked the whole concept of the film. The producer didn't have much money so we did it very cheaply – in just three weeks. At the time Leon and Jayne were a hot item. But the picture was never distributed properly. Consequently, even though they changed the title from *Death Force* to *Fighting Mad*, no one went to see it.

Your working relationship with Roger Corman has now spanned four decades.
Can you believe it? Just this week I counted up all the films that I did with him and there are 45! Roger has a catalogue of over 400 films. My work represents 10% of it! All together I've now been the producer, director or screenwriter on 61 feature films.

You are, undoubtedly, one of the busiest directors...
From Manila!

Well, from anywhere.
I'm very happy that I've been able to work so long.

The art of karate is a major element in many of your films.
You know, I had to convince Roger that it was worth showcasing. He wasn't so sure. But once Bruce Lee started to get a lot of press he understood that there was a big market for films that featured martial arts.

Your pictures seem more politically conscious than other films from the era.
Thank you for noticing. When I make a film I want to make a statement, I want to say something positive, especially for and about my people – Asians. The Philippine market was huge in the 1970s and I predict that, in the next five years, China will emerge as a major player too.

Did you ever experience any racism in Hollywood?
Well, not with Roger. But when I first started in Los Angeles, I had to Americanize my name. There really were no other Asian directors directing in the States at the time. Of course Hollywood preferred caucasian directors – that was what they were most comfortable with.

What did you think of some of the other blaxploitation films, like *Shaft* and *Super Fly*?
I thought that they were very entertaining and were doing exactly what they were supposed to do for their given market.

Why do you believe that the blaxploitation cycle of films came to such an abrupt end?
Because the black audience started to find fault with the images in the pictures. I think it's sad. I don't believe the films are anything to be ashamed of. They should be a source of pride – not embarrassment.

Why do you believe blaxploitation films remain popular today?
Well, it's a fact that every seven years there is a whole new audience for anything that is popular.

Which of your blaxploitation films is your favourite?
TNT Jackson. It's got great actors – Stan Shaw is a favourite of mine – it's got a great story, and it opened many, many doors for me.

Several of your films feature the same cast of players. Did you like working with the same people over and over again?
Yes. Because they knew what to expect from me and I knew what to expect from them. We looked forward to repeating an enjoyable experience.

In many ways your films are like a Filipino travelogue. Everything is beautiful, the land, the culture and the people.
I'm very proud of the way I presented Filipinos in my films. But I must say that I experienced many limitations at the time those films were made. Everyone kept telling me that if I made my pictures in the Philippines buyers would not be interested and audiences would not be able to connect with the characters or with the foreign locations. The idea was that blaxploitation films should take place in America's urban ghettos. I'm happy to say that I proved them wrong.

How would you like to be remembered?
I would like to be remembered as the guy who tried to put the Philippines on the map. As far as the film industry goes, I think I was quite successful. Big films like *Apocalypse Now* and *Platoon* were all filmed here. I believe my efforts on behalf of the Filipino film industry have been a good thing.

For the last thirty five years you've made at least one film a year. Why do you remain so incredibly active?
I don't talk about it often, but I support about eighty families who work for my film company in the Philippines. These are families that I inherited from my parents, who were also in the film industry. Making films allows me to express myself creatively and, at the same time, help my fellow countrymen. What more could you ask for?

Don Schain

During his forty-year show business career Don Schain has come full circle. Shortly after his directorial debut in 1967 with *The Love Object*, Schain hit the big time with 1971's box office smash *Ginger*, an exploitation film that he wrote and directed and in which his future wife Cheri Caffaro starred as a high-kicking, high-flying private detective. *Ginger*'s phenomenal success resulted in two 'sexsational' sequels, 1972's *The Abductors* and 1973's *Girls Are for Loving*. The director's most ambitious film, 1972's political mystery/thriller *A Place Called Today*, remains a relatively obscure work that very few have seen.

Today, Schain has traded in his director's hat for that of producer. His working relationship with cable TV's Disney Channel has meant that early-career R-rated films with titillating titles like 1977's *Too Hot to Handle* and 1979's *H.O.T.S.* are now, officially, a thing of the past. In their place are teen-oriented, suitable-for-all-family-members G-rated TV films with titles like *Mom's Got a Date with a Vampire*, *The World's Fastest Indian* and, most recently, *High School Musical*.

Ginger was a smash success. How did you come up with the story of a female private detective?
Well, we're going back a very long time. It just seemed to me that it was time to portray women in some of the roles that were traditionally reserved only for men.

Are you aware that many of the elements that made Ginger a success were appropriated in quite a few female-hero blaxploitation films?
I'm vaguely aware of it, but, you know, there are only so many storylines – so many different courses of action. When you take a strong female character and you make her a detective and you have her shooting guns, and you have her doing karate, and someone else comes along and creates a similar character, they might end up doing very similar things.

A Place Called Today is very different from Ginger. What made you want to write a black-themed political mystery-thriller?
My partner Ralph Desiderio and I always aspired to make *serious* movies. However, when you're a young filmmaker just starting out, and your first film is a serious movie that doesn't do much business, the chances of you getting to make a second film are greatly diminished. Our filmmaking strategy was to start out making films that were more commercial – like *Ginger* – and then reach a point where we could make more serious pictures.

A Place Called Today is most definitely serious.
That picture was my attempt to make a comment on the state of politics. Even though many critics have suggested that it was influenced by Watergate, it wasn't. Watergate hadn't even happened yet. *A Place Called Today* was filmed in 1971 and released in 1972. And it was written long before that.

How did you cast the film?
For me, one of the most satisfying things about the film is the casting. For instance, I had worked with Herbert Kerr

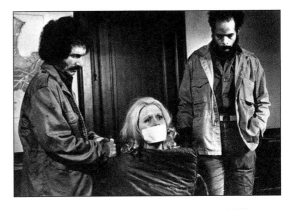

above: Rich society girl Cindy Cartwright (Cheri Caffaro) in 1972's **A Place Called Today**, a film that mixed politics, sex, race and contemporary events to produce a single sensational brew.

Jr. on *Ginger* and knew what he was capable of, so I gave him the lead without even auditioning anyone else. Woody Carter plays a black radical in the film. Woody had turned me down for the lead role in *Ginger* because he thought the character in that film was very stereotypical and a poor representation of African Americans. Even though he turned me down, I called him up and told him that I wanted him for *A Place Called Today*. He was very surprised that I remembered him or would even consider working with him again! He does an absolutely fantastic job in the picture.

How long was the shoot?
The shoot was about 38 days and the budget, at least by today's standards, was incredibly small.

Cheri Caffaro is one of the few likable characters in the film. Consequently, her on-screen demise is particularly disturbing. Was it your intention to shock the audience with her final scene?

above: When conventional interrogation tactics prove ineffective, Ginger (Cheri Caffaro) takes matters into her own hands – literally! Here, Caffaro is pictured with two unfortunate victims in a scene from 1973's **Girls Are for Loving**.

Cheri was playing a very rich woman and represented one of the many points of view in the film. Each character in the picture was meant to represent a different spectre in society. So the answer is no, I didn't write her character to shock. Her character was meant to represent the point of view of the rich entrenched society.

Many reviewers focused on Ms. Caffaro and her treatment in the film.

Again, I must say that my intention for Cheri's scenes, and for the film itself, was to hopefully get people to think about things. If certain events in the film are more shocking than others, they are there because I wanted to get people thinking.

Why do you believe *A Place Called Today* failed to reach a large audience?

I've never really understood why the film was not more successful. I know for a fact that blacks were particularly impressed with the picture. On several occasions, when I went to different film premieres, black audience members would come up to me and say, "You know, by just looking at the film, I could not tell whether it was written by a white man or a black man." I took those kinds of comments as a compliment – especially at that time. As for the critics, I must say that I believe they used the opportunity to take out their wrath on me for the phenomenal success of our *Ginger* films.

***Girls Are for Loving* is the third and final instalment in the *Ginger* series of films. How did it come about?**

It was just a natural progression from the other works that I had written and directed. The budget was a bit larger and because of that we got to film in a lot of different locations.

Your use of split screen photography and dissolves are staples of your films. Why are you attracted to them?

Well, split screens you hardly see anymore. At the time it just seemed to me that that was an interesting device to use to progress the action, and to give the audience a glimpse of simultaneous goings-on. As far as the dissolves go, that was just another creative tool which I found visually satisfying

What was your opinion of the blaxploitation films that were in theatres at the time?

I saw some of them but not all of them. I remember thinking that the *Shaft* series of films was excellent.

What do you say to critics who contend that exploitation and blaxploitation films are filled with too much violence and sex?

When you're talking about pictures like *Ginger*, or *Girls Are for Loving*, you're talking about pictures that were meant to *entertain*. They were meant to give an audience what an *audience* wanted. They were never expected to be something that the critics would enjoy. I think that critics were more bothered by the fact that these types of films were phenomenally successful, than by their actual content. If they had just been these little unknown pictures we wouldn't be talking about them today, and they wouldn't have talked about them back then.

Did you ever experience or witness any racism or discrimination in Hollywood?

No, not at all. I was, frankly, not aware of any of that.

Why do you believe the blaxploitation genre came to such an abrupt end?

It came to an end for a number of reasons. Among them was the advent of cable television. Additionally, videocassettes and the whole home-movie business removed the films from the possibility of being theatrically released. A bigger problem, that is not often discussed, is the change in the way films were promoted. In the early 1980s, the big movie studios began buying huge blocks of television promotion time. Small exploitation and blaxploitation films just could not compete with that kind of industry muscle. Movie theatres preferred to book films that were supported by million dollar ad campaigns and lost all interest in small films that relied, for the most part, on word-of-mouth.

Why do you believe the pictures remain popular today?

Well that's a good question and I wish I had a good answer for you. I know that the films had an extremely large following and in some respects they became cult films. For instance, I remember going on a publicity tour for *Girls Are for Loving*. We were somewhere in Ohio – I don't remember where – but a couple came up to me with their newborn baby girl and they told me that they had named her Ginger, because they were dating at the time and loved the character Ginger in all three of the films. So, for whatever reason, my films had an impact on people that went way beyond what was originally intended.

Which of your blaxploitation-era films is your favourite?

I would have to say that *A Place Called Today* is my personal favourite because I think that even though that film was not so successful, I really believe that it had some very, very, important things to say.

He's more than a man
He's a death machine!

SEE WHAT HE DOES TO STICK IT TO THE FUZZ

MEN CALL HIM SAVAGE...
WOMEN CALL HIM ALL THE TIME

SAVAGE!

above and top right:
Poster art and stills for **Savage!** (1973), just one of several blaxploitation films – including **Death Force** (1977), **TNT Jackson** (1974), and **The Muthers** (1976) – all directed by Cirio H. Santiago, that were expeditiously and, more importantly, inexpensively filmed in the Philippines.

right:
Not afraid to roll around in the mud – literally – Pam Grier made quite an impression in Jack Hill's **The Big Bird Cage** (1972), a film that had a great deal in common with **Savage!**; namely violence, female nudity and Philippine locations.

"...dem a loot, dem a shoot, dem a wail in shanty town "

This page and opposite:
Guns (along with "jive talk," hip fashions and catch phrases) were staples
of both blaxploitation advertising campaigns and the films themselves,
as typified in these promotional images for **Mean Johnny Barrows** (1975),
The Harder They Come (1973), **Cotton Comes to Harlem** (1970),
Trouble Man (1972), and **Hit!** (1973).

ONE CAT...
WHO PLAYS LIKE AN ARMY!

TROUBLE MAN

HIS FRIENDS CALL HIM MR. T...HIS ENEMIES CALL FOR MERCY!

20TH CENTURY-FOX Presents TROUBLE MAN Starring ROBERT HOOKS
Co-Starring PAUL WINFIELD RALPH WAITE BILL SMITHERS PAULA KELLY JULIUS HARRIS
Produced by JOEL D. FREEMAN Executive Producer JOHN D. F. BLACK Directed by IVAN DIXON
Written by JOHN D. F. BLACK Music by MARVIN GAYE
COLOR BY DE LUXE

Original MARVIN GAYE SCORE
Available On MOTOWN RECORDS

To pull off a job no one would ever dare,
you need a team no one would ever believe.

Paramount Pictures Presents
BILLY DEE WILLIAMS in "Hit!"
RICHARD PRYOR PAUL HAMPTON GWEN WELLES
Written by ALAN R. TRUSTMAN and DAVID M. WOLF Produced by HARRY KORSHAK Directed by SIDNEY J. FURIE
Executive Producer GRAY FREDERICKSON Music LALO SCHIFRIN PANAVISION TECHNICOLOR A PARAMOUNT PICTURE
R RESTRICTED

20th Century-Fox
presents   **TROUBLE MAN**   Color by De Luxe®   72/346

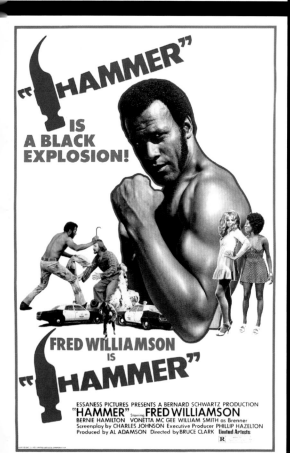

this page:
The Candy Tangerine Man (1975; action/adventure), **Big Time** (1977; comedy),
Hammer (1972; boxing) and **Three the Hard Way** (1974; a smorgasbord of the genre's
three biggest male stars) appealed to film goers on a variety of different levels.

opposite:
Without question, Pam Grier, featured here in artwork for **Sheba Baby** (1975), was
blaxploitation's most popular female performer; both a genuine African-American film star
and a feminist icon.

HOTTER'N "COFFY" MEANER'N "FOXY BROWN"

PAM GRIER is *Sheba, Baby*

QUEEN OF THE PRIVATE EYES

Starring AUSTIN STOKER · Special Guest Star D'URVILLE MARTIN as 'Pilot'

Music Composed by MONK HIGGINS & ALEX BROWN · Vocals by BARBARA MASON · Screenplay by WILLIAM GIRDLER
Story by WILLIAM GIRDLER & DAVID SHELDON · Produced by DAVID SHELDON · Directed by WILLIAM GIRDLER
A WILLIAM GIRDLER/DAVID SHELDON PRODUCTION · Color by MOVIELAB · AN AMERICAN INTERNATIONAL PICTURE

PG PARENTAL GUIDANCE SUGGESTED
SOME MATERIAL MAY NOT BE SUITABLE FOR PRE-TEENAGERS

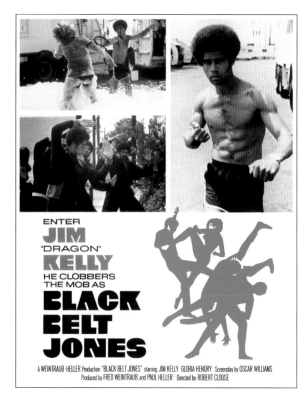

this page and opposite:
No room for misunderstanding: The word "black" appears in the title of more than forty blaxploitation features. Shown on these two pages: promotional artwork for **Black Samson** (1974), **Black Belt Jones** (1974), **Black Fist** (1977), **Black Shampoo** (1976) and **Black Lolita** (1974).

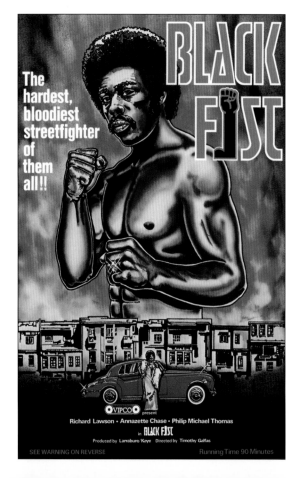

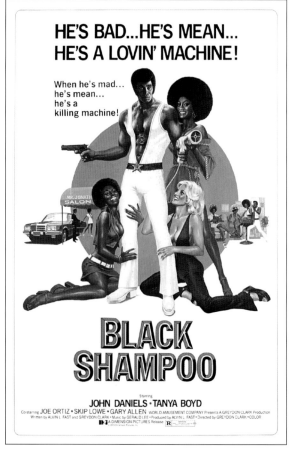

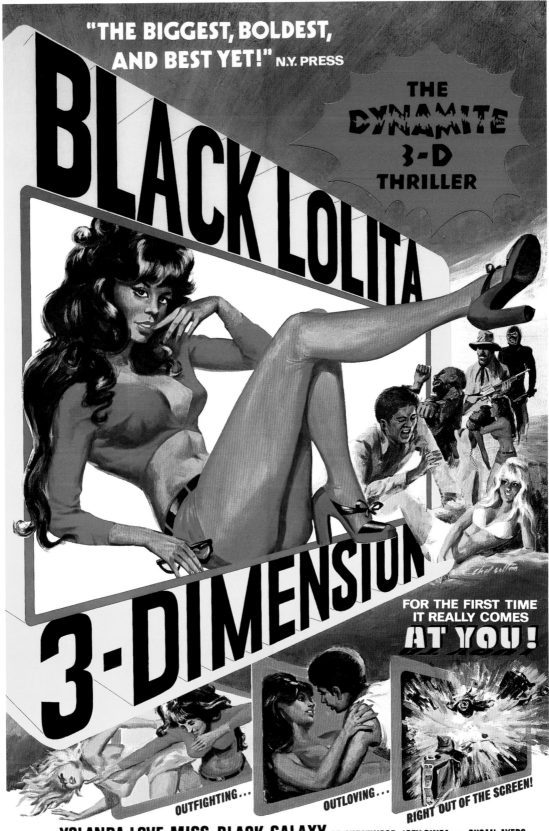

Proizvodnja **Warner Bros.**

Distribucija VESNA FILM

Cleopatra Jones

Tamara Dobson   **Bernie Casey**   **Shelley Winters**

Režija **Jack Starret**

TECHNICOLOR

PANAVISION

Model-turned actress Tamara Dobson is often considered to have been in competition with Pam Grier for the dubious title "Queen of the Bs," but there really was no rivalry, because Dobson was the suitable-for-all-ages version of Grier's over-the-top adult audience counterpart.

bottom left:
Dobson is glazed, glistening and objectified in the James Bond-like sequel to **Cleopatra Jones** (1973), **Cleopatra Jones and the Casino of Gold** (1975). Defined by its baroque sense of style, this action/adventure film often looks more like a science fiction fantasy.

opposite:
Three of Pam Grier's biggest hits:

Black Mama, White Mama (1973, a re-worked version of 1958's **The Defiant Ones** which starred Sidney Poitier and Tony Curtis);

Foxy Brown (1974, a sequel to **Coffy** originally slated to be entitled **Burn, Coffy, Burn**);

and **Coffy** (1973), blaxploitation's pre-eminent "female hero" picture and the film that made Pam Grier a star.

6 ft. 2 in. of dynamite explodes into action.

TAMARA DOBSON · STELLA STEVENS IN CLEOPATRA JONES AND THE CASINO OF GOLD IN A RUN RUN SHAW / WILLIAM TENNANT PRODUCTION

Written and Produced by WILLIAM TENNANT   Based on characters created by MAX JULIEN   Directed by CHUCK BAIL   PANAVISION® TECHNICOLOR®   **R** RESTRICTED Under 17 requires accompanying Parent or Adult Guardian

from Warner Bros 🅦 A Warner Communications Company

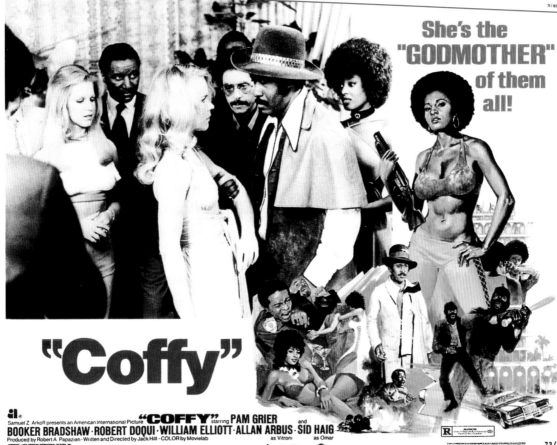

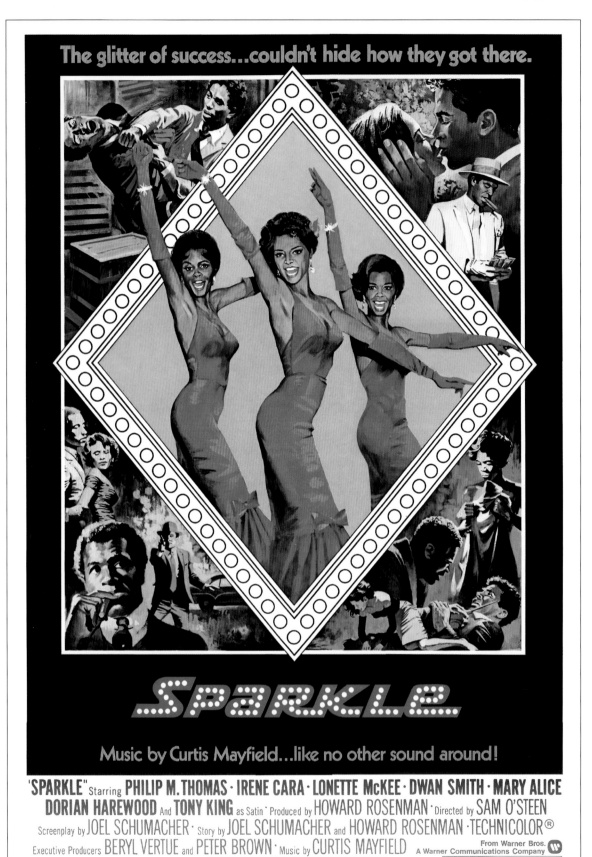

this page and opposite: Music-centred films like **Sparkle** (1976), **The Wiz** (1978) and **Wattstax** (1973) were a safe way to present already-established African-American recording artists, but singer/musicians in straight dramatic narratives (such as Isaac Hayes in 1974's **Truck Turner**) often stretched the parameters of believability.

bottom left: Former NFL fullback Jim Brown, seen here in a still from **Black Gunn** (1972), turned from sports to film and enjoyed immense popularity – especially with African-American audiences. Also shown on this page is artwork for three of his starring vehicles: **Black Gunn** (1972), **Slaughter** (1972 – which was followed by the sequel **Slaughter's Big Rip-Off** in 1973), and **I Escaped From Devil's Island** (1973).

opposite: **Brother on the Run** (1973), which starred Terry Carter, is one of only a handful of blaxploitation films that, to date, have not been released on home video.

BROTHER ON THE RUN!

WHEN HE STOPS RUNNING . . . WATCH OUT!

Starring TERRY CARTER·GWENN MITCHELL·KYLE JOHNSON
Also starring JAMES SIKKING · DIANA EDEN · A FRED WILLIAMS Production · Written and
Directed by HERBERT STROCK · Music Composed and Conducted by JOHNNY PATE · ADAM
WADE sings "BROTHER ON THE RUN" · Eastman Color · A Southern Star Release

73/216

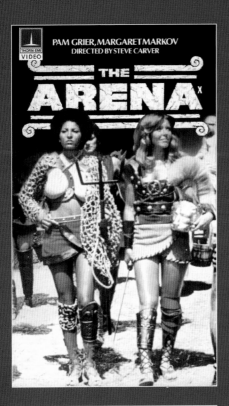

PAM GRIER, MARGARET MARKOV
DIRECTED BY STEVE CARVER

THE
ARENA x

DRUM

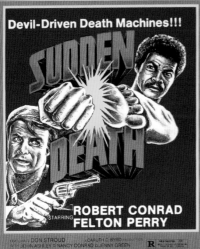

Devil-Driven Death Machines!!!

SUDDEN DEATH

starring
ROBERT CONRAD FELTON PERRY

BILL COSBY · RAQUEL WELCH · HARVEY KEITEL

Mother, Jugs & Speed

(A Black and Blue Comedy)

The F + B Ambulance Co. is looking for a few good men... but they will take any body they can get.

A PETER YATES | TOM MANKIEWICZ PRODUCTION
starring
ALLEN GARFIELD · DICK BUTKUS · L. Q. JONES · BRUCE DAVISON and LARRY HAGMAN
executive producer JOSEPH R. BARBERA
produced by PETER YATES and TOM MANKIEWICZ
directed by PETER YATES · TOM MANKIEWICZ
screenplay by STEPHEN MANES and TOM MANKIEWICZ
COLOR BY DELUXE
SOUND TRACK AVAILABLE ON A&M RECORDS AND TAPES

PG PARENTAL GUIDANCE SUGGESTED

"There's a sexual revolution going on...and all the leaders are in my family."

METRO-GOLDWYN-MAYER presents
A GEORGE SCHLATTER FILM
REDD FOXX · PEARL BAILEY
"NORMAN... IS THAT YOU?"

DENNIS DUGAN · MICHAEL WARREN
TAMARA DOBSON · VERNEE WATSON
also starring JAYNE MEADOWS

Black Godfather's Mad... and that's Real Bad!

Black Caesar Gibbs has the Mafia on the run, the Man on the lam and he's taking over the town.

Hell Up in Harlem

FRED WILLIAMSON "HELL UP IN HARLEM"

opposite: **Sweet Jesus Preacher Man** (1973; released in the sensitive Southern states as **Sweet James Preacher Man**) was omitted from its film company Metro Goldwyn Mayer's "all inclusive" coffee-table book *The MGM Story*.
this page: From "Devil-driven death machines" (**Sudden Death**, 1977) to "A black and blue comedy," (**Mother, Jugs & Speed**, 1976), blaxploitation films covered it all.

Whenever the cane turns up, someone turns up dead.

BLACK EYE
knows why

"BLACK EYE" Starring FRED WILLIAMSON Co-Starring ROSEMARY FORSYTH · TERESA GRAVES · FLOY DEAN
Music—Mort Garson · Screenplay by Mark Haggard and Jim Martin Directed by Jack Arnold
A Pat Rooney Production · TECHNICOLOR® A Warner Communications Company [PG]

★ Lone Star Pictures International Presents....

MR MEAN

If the price is right, the job gets done!

Featuring
THE OHIO PLAYERS
Hit Single:
"GOOD LUCK CHARM"

STARRING FRED WILLIAMSON

LOU CASTEL · RAIMUND HARMSTROF · CRIPPY YOCARD
Produced, Directed and Written by FRED WILLIAMSON
Associate Producer LEE THORNBURG [R]

HAIL CÆSAR
Godfather of Harlem!
...The Cat with the .45 caliber Claws!

BLACK CÆSAR

FRED WILLIAMSON starring in "BLACK CAESAR"   Music composed and performed by JAMES BROWN
Sound Track Album available on Polydor Records.

WHITE
MAN'S
TOWN...
BLACK
MAN'S
LAW!

PART DEVIL...PART LEGEND...ALL MAN!
FRED WILLIAMSON as
BOSS NIGGER

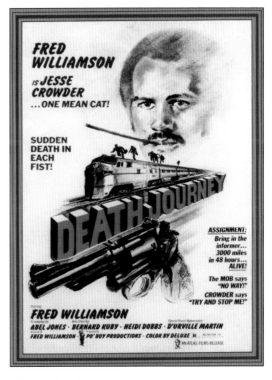

FRED
WILLIAMSON
IS JESSE
CROWDER
...ONE MEAN CAT!

SUDDEN
DEATH IN
EACH
FIST!

DEATH JOURNEY

ASSIGNMENT:
Bring in the
informer...
3000 miles
in 48 hours...
ALIVE!
The MOB says
"NO WAY!"
CROWDER says
"TRY AND STOP ME!"

FRED WILLIAMSON

this page and opposite:
Fred Williamson was one of the few African-Americans to write, produce and
star in his own films. Shown on these two pages, artwork from: **Black Eye**
(1973), **Mr. Mean** (1977), **Black Caesar** (1973), **Boss Nigger** (1974),
Death Journey (1975) and **That Man Bolt** (1973).

THAT MAN
BOLT

The highest
flyin', slickest,
meanest
dude you'll
ever face is
Jefferson Bolt
...on the case.

See
these famous
MARTIAL ARTS
experts in action:

MIKE STONE
World Professional Light Heavyweight
Karate Champion

KEN KAZAMA
Japan Kick Boxing Champion

EMIL FARKAS
European Black Belt Karate Champion

DAVID CHOW
Former California State Judo Champion

Universal Presents A BERNARD SCHWARTZ Production • FRED WILLIAMSON in
"THAT MAN BOLT" • Screenplay by QUENTIN WERTY and CHARLES JOHNSON
Story by CHARLES JOHNSON • Directed by HENRY LEVIN and DAVID LOWELL RICH
Produced by BERNARD SCHWARTZ • A UNIVERSAL PICTURE • TECHNICOLOR®

above: **The Soul of Nigger Charley** (1973; a sequel to 1972's **The Legend of Nigger Charley**), and **Detroit 9000** (1973; the title is police code for "officer needs assistance").
below: Scenes from **The Mack** (also from 1973, one of the genre's most productive years).
opposite: **Trick Baby** (1972) was based on a best selling novel by former Harlem pimp Iceberg Slim.

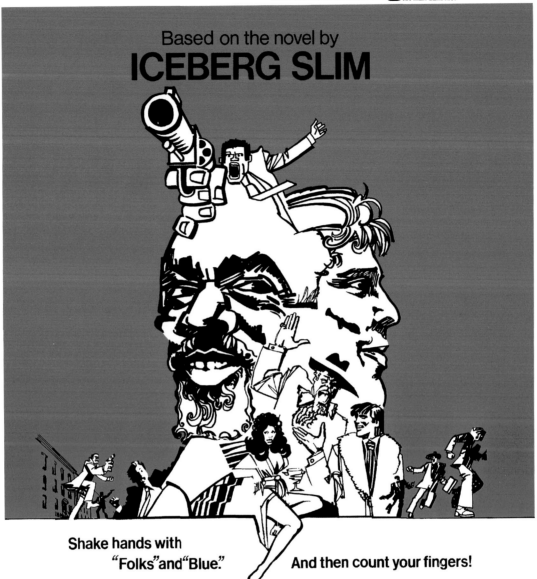

Based on the novel by
ICEBERG SLIM

Shake hands with
"Folks" and "Blue."   And then count your fingers!

TRICK BABY

A MARSHAL BACKLAR / JAMES LEVITT PRODUCTION
Starring KIEL MARTIN • MEL STEWART
Screenplay by A. NEUBERG, T. RAEWYN and LARRY YUST • Directed by LARRY YUST
Produced by MARSHAL BACKLAR • Executive Producer JAMES LEVITT
A UNIVERSAL RELEASE • TECHNICOLOR   R RESTRICTED Under 17 requires accompanying Parent or Adult Guardian

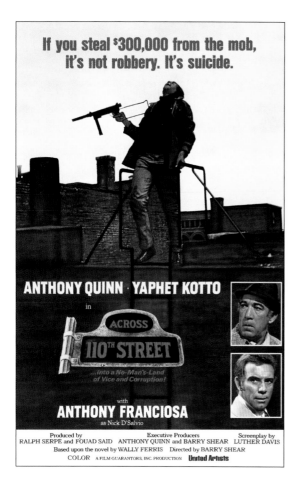

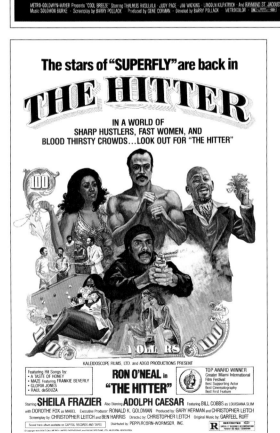

this page: Tools of the trade: 1973's **Mean Mother** poster art cleverly combines photography and illustration, while 1972's **Cool Breeze** references an earlier hit film, **Shaft**, and **The Hitter** (1978, which also references an earlier film – **Super Fly**) re-teams two of the genre's stars, Ron O'Neal and Sheila Frazier. The top image is from 1978's **Fass Black**.

opposite: From New York City's Harlem (**Across 110th Street**, 1972) to America's Midwest (**The Legend of Nigger Charley**, 1972). From the Orient (**Hot Potato**, 1975) to the streets of Los Angeles (**Willie Dynamite**, 1974), blaxploitation films often made location a major part of the narrative.

Never a dude like this one!
He's got a plan to stick it to The Man!

THE SIG SHORE PRODUCTION

Super Fly

STARRING
RON O'NEAL
AS PRIEST

See and hear CURTIS MAYFIELD play his Super Fly score!

Original soundtrack available on Curtom Records

The SIG SHORE Production "SUPER FLY" Starring RON O'NEAL · CARL LEE · JULIUS W. HARRIS · SHEILA FRAZIER CHARLES McGREGOR · Music Composed and Arranged by CURTIS MAYFIELD · Screenplay by PHILLIP FENTY · Produced by SIG SHORE · Directed by GORDON PARKS, JR. · from Warner Bros., a Warner Communications company

R RESTRICTED Under 17 requires accompanying Parent or Adult Guardian

72/319

Same dude with a different plan ...
in another country with a different man.

The
All NEW
SIG SHORE
Production

SUPER FLY T.N.T.

ORIGINAL SOUNDTRACK ON BUDDAH RECORDS

Paramount Pictures Presents The SIG SHORE Production
Starring **RON O'NEAL** in **"SUPER FLY T.N.T."** Co-starring **ROSCOE LEE BROWNE**
SHEILA FRAZIER · ROBERT GUILLAUME · JACQUES SERNAS · WILLIAM BERGER · Produced by **SIG SHORE**
Directed by **RON O'NEAL** · Original Story by RON O'NEAL and SIG SHORE · Screenplay by **ALEX HALEY** · Music composed and performed by OSIBISA
R RESTRICTED · Prints by MOVIE LAB · TECHNICOLOR · A Paramount Release
73/233

HIT MAN

He aims
to please.

MGM presents "HIT MAN"
Starring BERNIE CASEY · Co-starring PAMELA GRIER
Screenplay by GEORGE ARMITAGE
Based Upon the Novel "Jack's Return Home" by TED LEWIS
Produced by GENE CORMAN
Directed by GEORGE ARMITAGE · METROCOLOR
R RESTRICTED   MGM

opposite:
Super Fly (1972) was one of several
blaxploitation films that was deemed
"objectionable" and met with
nationwide picketing and protests
upon release.

this page:
Super Fly T.N.T. (1973; a surprise
flop sequel to **Super Fly**) and **Hit Man**
(1972), both featured dissatisfied,
combative, over-the-top anti-heroes.

top right, and right:
Three images from **Super Fly** (1972)
say it all: fighting, lovemaking and life-
threatening intimidation!

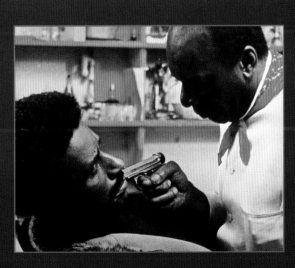

THE Brother Man in the Motherland.
Shaft is stickin' it ....all the way.

SHAFT in Africa

starring
RICHARD ROUNDTREE as **JOHN SHAFT**

The mob wanted
Harlem back.
They got Shaft...
up to here.

SHAFT

SHAFT's his name. SHAFT's his game.

METRO-GOLDWYN-MAYER Presents "SHAFT" Starring RICHARD ROUNDTREE Co-Starring MOSES GUNN
Screenplay by ERNEST TIDYMAN and JOHN D.F. BLACK Based upon the novel by ERNEST TIDYMAN
Music by ISAAC HAYES Produced by JOEL FREEMAN Directed by GORDON PARKS METROCOLOR

MGM Presents
A STIRLING SILLIPHANT-ROGER LEWIS Production
"SHAFT IN AFRICA"
Starring RICHARD ROUNDTREE · VONETTA McGEE
Written by STIRLING SILLIPHANT · Produced by ROGER LEWIS
Directed by JOHN GUILLERMIN
Metrocolor · Panavision®

R RESTRICTED

SWEET SWEETBACK

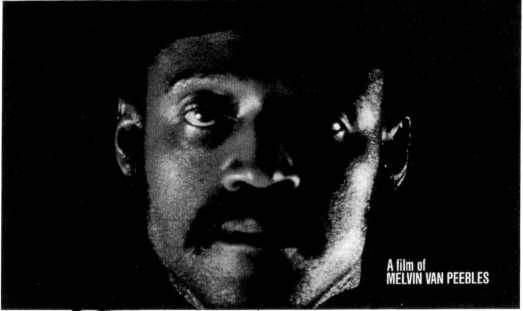

A film of
MELVIN VAN PEEBLES

YOU BLED MY MOMMA — YOU BLED MY POPPA — BUT YOU WONT BLEED ME

ORIGINAL SOUNDTRACK ALBUM AVAILABLE ON STAX RECORDS   ORIGINAL PAPERBACK SOON AVAILABLE AS A LANCER PUBLICATION

MELVIN VAN PEEBLES and JERRY GROSS present "SWEET SWEETBACK'S BAADASSSSS SONG"
a CINEMATION INDUSTRIES Release · COLOR

RATED **X** BY AN ALL-WHITE JURY

left and above: **Shaft** (1971, starring Richard Roundtree) and **Sweet Sweetback's Baadasssss Song** (1971, starring Melvin Van Peebles) ushered in a new, tough, street-smart African American cinema hero. **Shaft** is the only film in the genre to be followed by two sequels: **Shaft's Big Score!** (1972) and (pictured) **Shaft in Africa** (1973)

Abby doesn't need a man anymore...

The Devil is her Lover Now!

FRSCO PRESENTS...

NOT SINCE "FRANKENSTEIN" STALKED THE EARTH
HAS the WORLD KNOWN SO TERRIFYING A DAY ... OR NIGHT

BLACK FRANKENSTEIN
BLACKENSTEIN

A FRSCO PRODUCTIONS LIMITED FILM

STARRING JOHN HART, IVORY STONE. FEATURING ANDREA KING, LIZ RENAY, ROOSEVELT JACKSON, JOE DE SUE, NICK BOLIN, CARDELLA DI MILO, ANDY C. AND INTRODUCING JAMES COUSAR.
ALSO INTRODUCING MARVA FARMER

WRITTEN AND PRODUCED BY FRANK R. SALETRI   EXECUTIVE PRODUCER TED TETRICK   DIRECTED BY WILLIAM A. LEVEY

COLOR BY DE LUXE

Her HUSBAND	Her BROTHER	Her FRIEND	The EXORCIST

Abby ®
...the story of a woman possessed!

starring
WILLIAM MARSHALL · TERRY CARTER · AUSTIN STOKER
· **CAROL SPEED** as "**ABBY**" co-starring **JUANITA MOORE**

Screenplay by G. Cornell Layne · Story by WILLIAM GIRDLER & G. Cornell Layne

Produced by WILLIAM GIRDLER, MIKE HENRY & GORDON C. LAYNE · Directed by WILLIAM GIRDLER · COLOR BY MOVIELAB

Music Composed and Conducted by ROBERT O. RAGLAND · A WILLIAM GIRDLER PRODUCTION · Released by Roadshow

M.A.P.S. LITHO PTY. LTD.

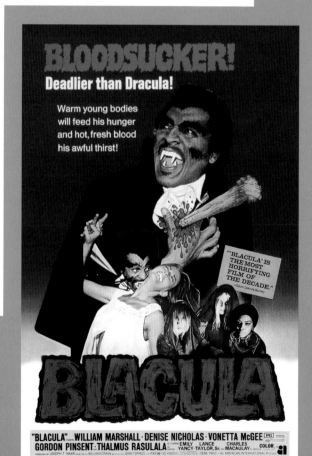

BLOODSUCKER!
Deadlier than Dracula!

Warm young bodies
will feed his hunger
and hot, fresh blood
his awful thirst!

"BLACULA' IS
THE MOST
HORRIFYING
FILM OF
THE DECADE."

BLACULA

"BLACULA" **WILLIAM MARSHALL · DENISE NICHOLAS · VONETTA McGEE**
GORDON PINSENT · THALMUS RASULALA   EMILY · LANCE · CHARLES
YANCY · TAYLOR, Sr. · MACAULAY   **COLOR**

bottom right this page, and opposite top: **Blacula** (1972) opened the floodgates for a string of black-cast horror films that included **Abby** (*above*, 1974; a not-too-subtle appropriation of **The Exorcist**) and **Blackenstein** (*top right*, 1973; a not-too-subtle appropriation of the classic Mary Shelley novel 'Frankenstein').

opposite bottom: Both the poster art and the two stills shown here from 1973's quickie follow-up to **Blacula**, entitled **Scream Blacula Scream**, gave audiences the impression that the sequel might be an improvement on the original. However, despite its bigger budget the result was something of a disappointment.

THE BLACK PRINCE OF SHADOWS STALKS THE EARTH AGAIN!

SCREAM BLACULA SCREAM

AMERICAN INTERNATIONAL PICTURE PG

WILLIAM MARSHALL · DON MITCHELL · PAM GRIER
MICHAEL CONRAD · BERNIE HAMILTON ..... RICHARD LAWSON color
...... SAMUEL Z. ARKOFF ..... JOAN TORRES & RAYMOND KOENIG AND MAURICE JULES
...... JOAN TORRES & RAYMOND KOENIG ..... JOSEPH T. NAAR ..... BOB KELLJAN

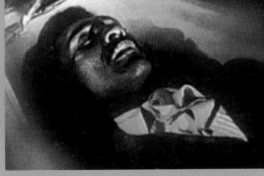

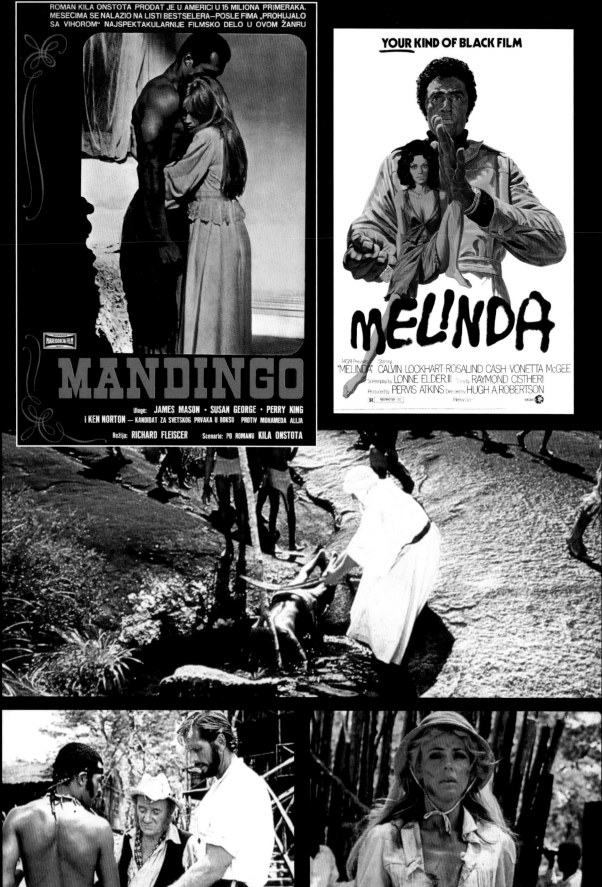

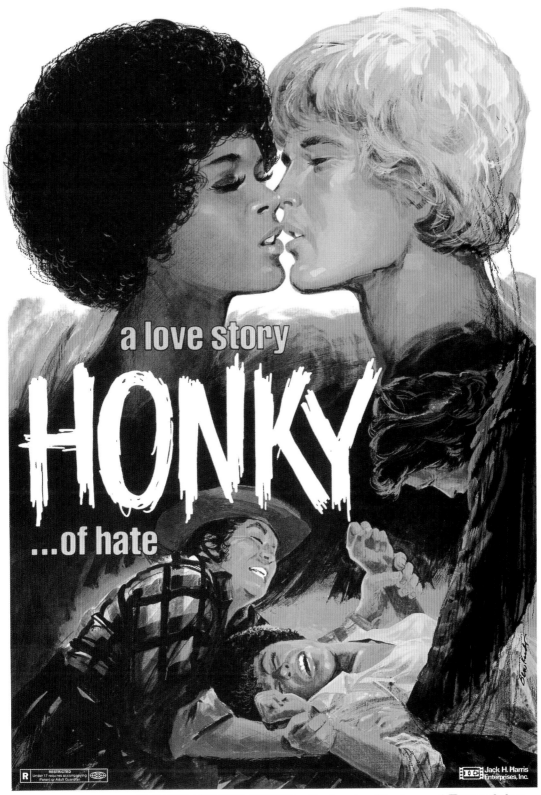

a love story

HONKY

...of hate

JACK H. HARRIS PRESENTS A GETTY-FROMKESS / STONEHENGE PRODUCTION
INTRODUCING BRENDA SYKES AND JOHN NEILSON • WRITTEN BY WILL CHANEY. BASED
ON THE NOVEL SHELIA BY GUNARD SOLBERG • EXECUTIVE PRODUCER J. RONALD GETTY
PRODUCED BY WILL CHANEY AND RON ROTH • DIRECTED BY WILLIAM A. GRAHAM

Color by De Luxe / Panavision
Music by Quincy Jones

Jack H. Harris
Enterprises, Inc.

R RESTRICTED
Under 17 requires accompanying
Parent or Adult Guardian

above: **Honky** (1971), a sensationally titled tale of interracial romance, proved to be genuinely engaging.

opposite: **Mandingo** (1975), a big-budget plantation melodrama adapted from a best-selling novel, and (*stills, opposite bottom*) **Slavers** (1977), both dealt with the brutal
and bloody slave trade, while **Melinda** (1972) was a fully-realised murder mystery that didn't quite hit its mark.

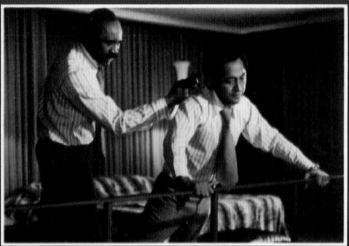
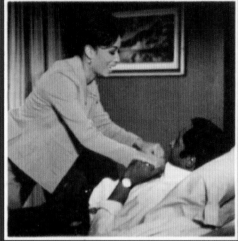

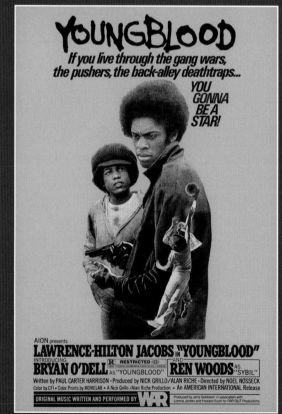

They transplanted a **WHITE BIGOT'S HEAD** onto a **SOUL BROTHER'S BODY!**

The doctor blew it—the most fantastic medical experiment of the age. And now, with the fights, the Fuzz, the chicks and the choppers ...Man, they're really in deeeeep trouble!

SAMUEL Z. ARKOFF Presents

Ray Milland and **"Rosey" Grier** as...

THE THING WITH TWO HEADS

CO-STARRING
DON MARSHALL · ROGER PERRY · KATHY BAUMANN and **CHELSEA BROWN** as "Lila"

A Saber Production   An American International Release

COLOR by DE LUXE

PRODUCED BY **WES BISHOP** · EXECUTIVE PRODUCER **JOHN LAWRENCE** · DIRECTED BY **LEE FROST** · SCREENPLAY BY **LEE FROST & WES BISHOP** and **JAMES GORDON WHITE** · STORY BY **LEE FROST & WES BISHOP**

PG PARENTAL GUIDANCE
May not be suitable for pre-teenagers

above: **The Thing with Two Heads** (1972), a drive-in/blaxploitation/exploitation horror/comedy starred Ray Milland and Rosey Grier.

opposite: **The Spook Who Sat by the Door** (*top four images*) (1973; based on a best selling book; pointedly political), **Maurie** (1973; pointedly sentimental) and **Youngblood** (1978; pointedly youth-centered) spoke to audiences in a language that was "pointedly familiar".

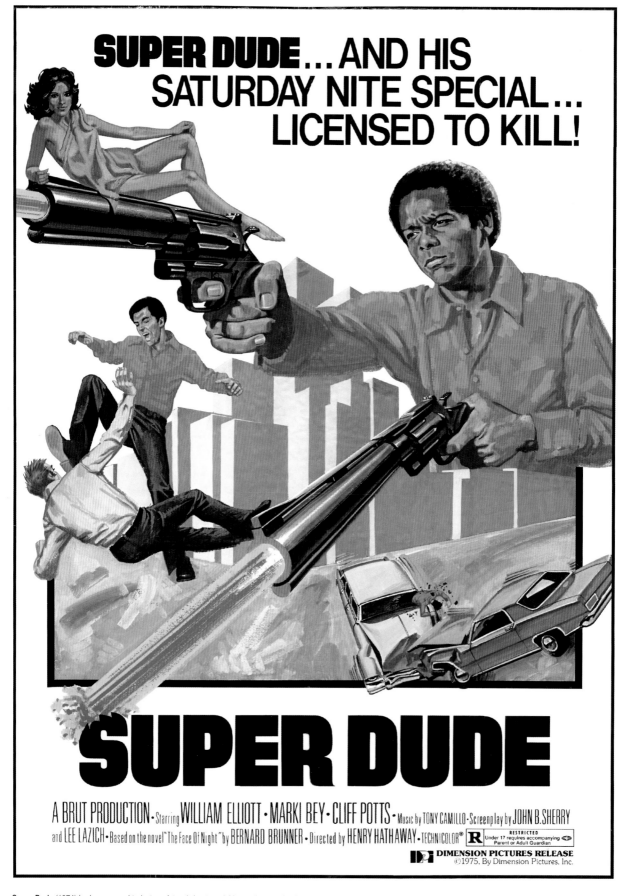

SUPER DUDE... AND HIS
SATURDAY NITE SPECIAL...
LICENSED TO KILL!

SUPER DUDE

A BRUT PRODUCTION · Starring WILLIAM ELLIOTT · MARKI BEY · CLIFF POTTS · Music by TONY CAMILLO · Screenplay by JOHN B. SHERRY
and LEE LAZICH · Based on the novel "The Face Of Night" by BERNARD BRUNNER · Directed by HENRY HATHAWAY · TECHNICOLOR® [R] RESTRICTED Under 17 requires accompanying Parent or Adult Guardian

DIMENSION PICTURES RELEASE
©1975, By Dimension Pictures, Inc.

Super Dude (1974) had an unusual trajectory. Artwork (posters, lobby cards, pressbooks, etc.) was issued by Warner Bros. under the title **Hangup**, but wide distribution only came the following year when Dimension Pictures released it as **Super Dude**. The film is so derivative and clichéd that the poster art shown here almost makes it look like a spoof of the genre.

Chapter Three

Blaxploitation Filmography

Distributors and MPAA Ratings

For each of the A-to-Z entries, the original US theatrical distributor is shown along with the MPAA rating given to the film and the certificate number in parentheses. NR indicates that the MPAA database records no rating for the film in question. NR followed by an MPAA rating in parentheses – e.g. NR (PG) – indicates that, although there is no record of an official MPAA certificate for the film in question, it was released theatrically with the indicated rating shown on advertising materials. In the interests of clarity, it is worth quickly summarising the history of MPAA ratings:

Original ratings
The original movie ratings (in use from 1968 to 1970) consisted of:
Rated G: General Audiences. All ages admitted.
Rated M: Suggested for Mature Audiences. Parental discretion advised.
Rated R: Restricted. Persons under 16 are not admitted unless accompanied by parent or adult guardian.
Rated X: Persons under 17 not admitted.

M rating replaced by GP
When it became clear that many patrons were confused as to whether M-rated films contained more mature content than those rated R, in 1970, M was replaced by the new GP rating:
Rated GP: All Ages Admitted/Parental Guidance Suggested.
GP could be interpreted as meaning 'General Patronage'. Alternatively, the G in GP designated that the film was not age restricted (in common with the G rating), while the P informed audiences that parents should use their discretion in deciding whether their children should be admitted to the screening.

Age restrictions change with regard to the R and X ratings
During 1970 the age restriction applicable to the R rating was increased from 16 to 17, although the age at which a patron would be admitted to a film with the X rating varied between 17 and 21 according to the wishes of the local jurisdiction. The minimum age for admission to films considered too strong for the R rating was eventually standardised by the introduction of the NC-17 rating.

The GP rating is replaced
During 1971 the MPAA appended specific warning labels to some GP-rated movies. The precise wording varied, but typically the labels were along the lines of, "Contains material not generally suitable for pre-teenagers." It can therefore be considered an early form of the PG-13 rating. The added message was referenced by an asterisk next to the GP symbol, so this short-lived rating is often referred to as GP*. When, in early 1972, the percentage of GP* films started to outnumber GP films without the appended special advisory, both GP and GP* were redesignated, and the new PG ('Parental Guidance') rating was introduced.

A.K.A. CASSIUS CLAY

1970, USA
Alternative Titles: *Muhammad Ali a.k.a. Cassius Clay*; *Muhammad Ali alias Cassius Clay*
GP (22752), Documentary, 79m.
United Artists.
Director (D): Jim Jacobs; Producer (P): William Cayton; Script (S): Bernard Evslin.
Cast: Muhammad Ali, Richard Kiley, Cus D'Amato.

"See the punches that won the championship and the ideals that lost it!"

A look at prize fighter Muhammad Ali's triumphs and setbacks.

This short (only 79 minutes) black & white documentary film played in theaters a full seven years before Muhammad Ali reprised his role (as himself) in 1977's *The Greatest*. Basically a collection of archival footage inter spliced with interviews, this celebration of all things Ali (including his 1960 Olympic win and his 1964 upset of boxer Sonny Liston) also includes a matter-of-fact examination of his conversion to the Nation of Islam, his mid-career name change, and his refusal to serve in the military. The vintage archival footage of a host of fascinating characters, from Ali and Joe Louis to Malcolm X and John Lennon, makes this forgotten film worth a look.

AARON LOVES ANGELA

1975, USA
R (24423), Drama, 99m. Columbia Pictures.
D: Gordon Parks Jr.; P: Robert J. Anderson; S: Gerald Sanford.
Cast: Moses Gunn, Kevin Hooks, Irene Cara, Ernestine Jackson, José Feliciano, Walt Frazier.

Against the odds, two teenagers – one African American and one Puerto Rican – fall in love and learn about life in New York City's Spanish Harlem.

Excellent on every level, *Aaron Loves Angela* is perhaps the most fully realised youth-centred blaxploitation movie. As Aaron James, a young African-American teenager in search of himself, Kevin Hooks is both endearing and believable. His Puerto Rican girlfriend Angela (Irene Cara) is even more credible. In possession of a rarely-noted command of both voice and manner, the actress/singer (best known for her movie theme songs 'Fame' and 'What a Feeling (Theme from Flashdance)') is an admirably natural and intuitive screen presence.

Moses (*Shaft*) Gunn provides support in the role of Ike James, Aaron's ex-pro football player-turned-alcoholic father, Ernestine Jackson is Cleo, a prostitute neighbour who teaches Aaron the dos and don'ts of sex, and there are cameo roles for José Feliciano (who also performs the soundtrack) and basketball star Walt Frazier.

Be it the liberal use of slow motion sequences, the extensive segments filmed in long-shot which feature overdubbed dialogue, the superior soundtrack, or the plot device of having a stash of stolen drug money look like the only means out of the ghetto, *Aaron Loves Angela* seems to have borrowed from African-American director Gordon Parks Jr.'s earlier *Super Fly*. Vintage New York locations (Coney Island, Spanish Harlem and the Brooklyn Bridge) all contribute to the film's authentically gritty and desperate atmosphere. Gordon Parks Jr.'s other films include *Thomasine & Bushrod* and *Three the Hard Way*.

"...a refreshing look at love across ethnic lines..."
(Nelson George, Blackface: Reflections on African Americans and the Movies, 1995)

ABAR

1975, USA
Alternative Titles: *In Your Face*; *Abar: The First Black Superman*
PG (24443), Science Fiction, 85m.
Mirror Releasing.
D: Frank Packard; P: J.P. Joshua; S: James Smalley.
Cast: J. Walter Smith, Tobar Mayo, Art Jackson, Roxie Young, Lonnie James.

"The first black science fiction film!"

When a black doctor and his family are harassed by white neighbours in their new community, a black activist is hired to protect them.

Rarely-seen super-low-budget and preachy film that is nonetheless irresistible. The plot revolves around Dr. Kenneth Kinkade (J. Walter Smith), an urbane, righteous-minded physician who is doing "historical research" in his basement! Helping out are Roxie Young as Beth, Dr. Kinkade's immaculately coiffed and incessantly sceptical wife, and Tobar (*Big Time*) Mayo as John Abar, a hired bodyguard (from a local black activist group) who volunteers to try Dr. Kinkade's new potion.

Abar's fantastic, overwrought atmosphere is best illustrated by a brief exchange between the well-meaning Dr. Kinkade and his more practical-minded wife:

> Dr. Kinkade: *Beth, the greatest scientific achievement ever known to mankind is about to become a frightening nightmare.*
> Beth: *Ken, what are you trying to say?*
> Dr. Kinkade: *I've created a super-human!*

In addition to Abar's interesting documentation of Los Angeles's black upper middle class, this juvenile, poorly acted, atrociously directed and just plain silly film's most appealing feature is the out of this world '70s kitsch house in which the Kinkades live.

"Completely inept, dismally acted, but so crazy, I couldn't help but love it!"
(Steve Puchalski, Baad Mutha@*!#ers)

ABBY

1974, USA
Alternative Title: *Possess My Soul*
R (24030), Horror, 89m.
American International Pictures.
D: William Girdler; P: William Girdler, Mike Henry, Gordon C. Layne; S: Gordon C. Layne, William Girdler.
Cast: Carol Speed, William Marshall, Terry Carter, Austin Stoker, Juanita Moore, Nancy Lee Owens, Bob Holt [voice].

"Abby doesn't need a man anymore... the devil is her lover now!"

When a minister's wife becomes possessed by Eshu, the Nigerian god of sexuality, an exorcist is called in to drive the evil spirit away.

Derivative, stilted and flat, *Abby* remains a must-see film if only for its shameless appropriation of *The Exorcist* (In the 8 January, 1974 edition of *Variety*, it was confirmed that, after playing to sell-out audiences for a full ten weeks – in the process grossing $2,106,072 – *Abby* was suddenly and inexplicably removed from theatres). In the titular role of Abby Williams, Carol Speed is embarrassingly miscast. Squat, eager to 'put on,' and difficult to sympathise with, her church-going good girl also happens to be a terrible singer (her breathtakingly bad church solo will leave your mouth agape). As Bishop Garnet Williams, a man who also teaches anthropology at a local college, William (*Blacula*) Marshall is, as always, assured.

In fact the actor's committed performance seems a bit out of place amidst this film's cartoonish surroundings. Joining him are Terry (*Brother on the Run*) Carter as Emmett Williams, Abby's put-upon husband, and Juanita (*The Mack*) Moore as Mama Potter, Abby's emotional mother.

Complete with green vomit, dirty sexual talk, levitation, several violent murders and of course the sudden visual transformation of a young, 'innocent' female into a monstrous, marauding demon, *Abby* (which was almost released as *The Blaxorcist*), is a not-to-be-missed camp classic. There is a notable exchange between the bed-bound, newly clairvoyant and 'possessed' Abby and Mrs. Sadie Wiggins (Nancy Lee Owens), the organist at Abby's church, which is typical of the picture's over-the-top tone:

Sadie (entering Abby's bedroom): *I rang the bell, I guess you didn't hear it. Your mother thought that you might like some company. Mrs. Williams? Don't you know me? I'm your friend Mrs. Wiggins.*
Abby (suddenly snarling): *No you're not!*
Sadie: *Pardon?*
Abby: *Wiggins isn't your name you damned liar! And why do you bother calling yourself 'Mrs.'?*
Sadie: *Please – you stop this. My husband is dead.*
Abby (laughing evilly): *Oh you're funny Sadie. Horace Williams never married you. Screwed you once and left you to rot like a rotten apple!*

Abby's she-devil voice was provided by the well-known and extremely versatile Bob Holt (he voiced animated flms such as 1974's *The Nine Lives of Fritz the Cat* and the 13-episode 1982 series *The Incredible Hulk*, and also provided vocal effects for *Gremlins* in 1984). *Abby*'s exciting theatrical trailer remains the only promo spot in the entire blaxploitation canon to use a *female* voiceover. "This is Abby," says a calm voice over a rapidly edited collection of violent and increasingly out-of-control images, "a woman loved – and in love. Until that night – when something evil came looking for a soul to possess. Abby... rated R." William Girdler's other films include *The Zebra Killer* and *Sheba Baby*.

"More silly than shocking even if it seems to take itself seriously..."
(A.H. Weiler, New York Times)

ACROSS 110TH STREET

1972, USA
R (23484), Action/Adventure, 102m.
United Artists.
D: Barry Shear; P: Ralph Serpe, Fouad Said; S: Luther Davis from the novel by Wally Ferris.
Cast: Yaphet Kotto, Anthony Quinn, Anthony Franciosa, Richard Ward.

"If you steal $300,000 from the mob. It's not robbery. It's suicide."

When three black men rob a Harlem numbers racket, they find themselves pursued by both the NYC mob and the NYC police.

A smash hit at the box office, this over-praised 'examination' of racism and corruption in the New York City police department (played against a backdrop of two feuding mob factions, one in Harlem, one in Little Italy) is a stretched and very tired, super-violent and relentlessly downbeat attempt to create a blaxploitation film that not only entertains but also sheds light on the socio-political issues of the day.

Former matinee idol Anthony Quinn (who also co-executive-produced the film) is woefully miscast in the lead as 55-year-old Captain Frank Mattelli. Totally unbelievable as a mean, way-past-his-prime (and now corrupt) police department supervisor, Quinn's outing is the sort of late-career performance meant to solidify the performer's place in Hollywood's pantheon of great actors. Sadly it does not succeed. Far more believable, contemporary looking and natural is the new upstart in the police station, Detective Lieutenant William

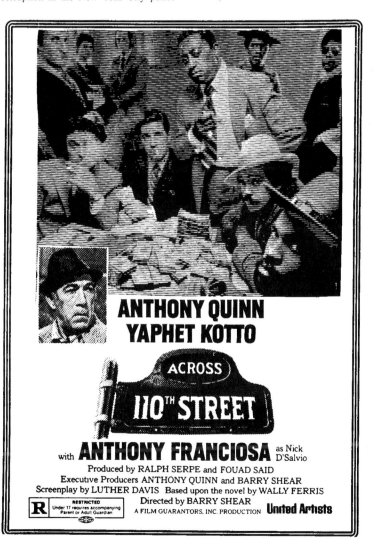

Pope (Yaphet Kotto). Overshadowing his paint-by-numbers 'inspirational' character, Kotto's appearance, mannerisms and speech patterns add an air of authenticity to an otherwise lacklustre project. Also better than the material at hand is Anthony Franciosa as Nick D'Salvio, a small-time, desperate-for-power, Italian mobster.

Admittedly action and violence packed (there is police brutality, a shootout, a slum apartment robbery, a castration and a death due to a 'fall' from a rooftop) *Across 110th Street*'s Top 40 theme song, performed by Bobby Womack & Peace, is more memorable than the film itself. Incidentally, director Quentin Tarantino used the picture's theme song in his 1997 blaxploitation homage *Jackie Brown*.

"... a desperate rip-off of the latest news reports about the death of our cities." (Roger Greenspun, New York Times)

ADIOS AMIGO

1975, USA
Alternative Title: *No Sweat*
PG (24375), Comedy/Western, 87m.
Atlas Films.
D: Fred Williamson; P: Fred Williamson; S: Fred Williamson.
Cast: Fred Williamson, Richard Pryor, Thalmus Rasulala, James Brown.

"Boozin'! Brawlin'! Blastin'! Two sharp dudes taking turns with chicks and tricks!"

An African-American man living on the prairie is befriended by a scheming drifter.

Unbearably unfunny, this atrocity took just nine days to shoot – and it most definitely shows. Obviously inspired by the previous year's *Blazing Saddles*, with his (twelve page) script in hand, writer/director/producer Fred Williamson hoped that a few of his talented actor-friends would do the work he didn't do himself. They don't.

Playing Big Ben, a black cowboy unfairly uprooted from his land, Williamson seems more interested in his directing and 'screenplay' than in his performance which, such as it is, has a just-passing-through air about it that does not flatter him or the production. As his obviously named sidekick Sam Spade, Richard Pryor is no better.

Distracted, uncomfortable, and at a loss for what to do with his sketchily written role, Pryor would later confess that he was embarrassed by his participation in the project.

What one comes away from *Adios Amigo* remembering (if you remember anything at all) are not the two principal players, but a brief though dazzling cameo by Thalmus (*Cool Breeze*) Rasulala, embodying the role of a toothless illiterate named Noah Abraham Lincoln Brown; his characterisation is the only believable one in the entire film.

Slapdash, episodic and featuring juvenile on-screen illustrations and a shrill, obnoxious theme song (relentlessly reprised throughout) *Adios Amigo* is a picture that will only appeal to the Fred Williamson completist. Williamson also directed *Death Journey*, *Mean Johnny Barrows*, *No Way Back* and *Mr. Mean*.

"...little more than a series of skits better suited for television." (Donald Bogle, Blacks in American Films and Television, 1988)

AIN'T THAT JUST LIKE A HONKEY!

1976, USA
NR (R), Comedy, 85m.
Gulf-United Productions
D: Charles Harder; P: Jerry Kohake.
Cast: Wildman Steve and others.

"See Wildman Steve put honkey where he belongs! Wildman tells it like it is! It's What's Happening Baby!"

Lost, and not seen since its original 1976 theatrical release, this was a vehicle for Laff Records recording artist Wildman (*The Six Thousand Dollar Nigger*) Steve.

"While most of the humor is black-oriented, it is in good taste and a crossover to the white market is possible." (Boxoffice)

ALABAMA'S GHOST

1973, USA
PG (669), Comedy, 92m. Ellman Enterprises.
D: Fredric Hobbs; P: Fredric Hobbs; S: Fredric Hobbs.
Cast: Christopher Brooks, Peggy Browne, E. Kerrigan Prescott, Steven Kent Browne.

"A Satanic journey into the depths of black magic!"

After finding a dead magician's personal belongings, a black handyman unwittingly enters into a pact with a ghost.

Protracted, talky and 'psychedelic,' *Alabama's Ghost* is an early 1970s film in the spirit of the late '60s counter-culture.

As 'Alabama: King of the Cosmos,' Christopher (*The Mack*) Brooks is game for the shenanigans even though Hobbs's frequent extreme close-ups do not flatter him or anyone else in the film. E. Kerrigan Prescott is good enough (but not quite great) as the resurrected 1920s stage magician 'Carter the Great,' and Peggy Browne as Zoerae, an ever-present vampire/seductress makes what can best be called a capable display of her fangs.

Nazis, jazz, cannibalism, motorcycle races, voodoo, hippies, transvestism, marijuana parties, go-go dancers, an automobile that looks like a parade float, scenes (many of them) at an outdoor music festival and, yes, a stampeding elephant, combine to make a colourful but distractingly student film-like experience.

AMAZING GRACE

1974, USA
G (23890), Comedy, 98m. United Artists.
D: Stan Lathan; P: Matt Robinson; S: Matt Robinson.
Cast: "Moms" Mabley, Rosalind Cash, Slappy White, Moses Gunn, Butterfly McQueen, Stepin Fetchit.

"Who's comin' to put an end to dirty tricks, crooked politicians and lyin' mayors! Who? America's most glamorous, sexiest female superstar! 'Moms' Mabley... it's about time!"

A corrupt Bostonian mayoral candidate is exposed, then transformed, by a feisty elderly neighbour.

Created to showcase bawdy (but here much watered down) comedian "Moms" Mabley, *Amazing Grace* is an affecting showcase for both her as Grace Teasdale Grimes, a very nosey pie-baking suburbanite, and Slappy White as Fortwith Wilson, her past-his-prime tap dancer/friend. Also in the cast and deserving of a mention are two other veteran African-American performers; helium-voiced Butterfly (*Gone with the Wind*) McQueen as Clarine, Grace's gossipy best friend, and Stepin Fetchit in a don't-blink-or-you'll-miss-him cameo as Cousin Lincoln, Grace's well wishing cousin. Rosalind Cash as Creola Waters, an African-American woman who is supposedly passing for white, and Moses Gunn as Welton J. Waters, a misguided politician, round things out. A typical Mabley exchange:

Mabley (to a young stranger): *Would you like some chicken son?*
Stranger: *No thank you sister, I just ate.*
Mabley: *Well in the first place I ain't your sister, you know that. In the second place if you already ate you ain't ate enough. And in the third place, you ain't tasted nothin' son till you tasted some of this!*

Scenic locations and good use of the mostly African-American students at Boston's Morgan State College (who get to hear Mabley's rousing endorsement of a political candidate) enliven the proceedings. The movie's final segment, which features Mabley alone in her house talking to herself (and then directly to the camera), is unexpectedly moving in that it

seems like the free association ramblings of an old woman who doesn't know that she is being watched. Not always funny, but most definitely worth a look. African-American director Stan Lathan also directed *Save the Children*. Writer/producer Matt Robinson is also African American.

"She's a legend long past her prime, but a legend captured on celluloid nonetheless." (Donald Bogle, Blacks in American Films and Television, 1988)

THE ANGEL LEVINE

1970, USA
GP (22494), Comedy/Drama, 105m.
United Artists.
D: Jan Kadar; P: Chiz Schultz; S: Bill Gunn and Ronald Ribman based on a story by Bernard Malamud.
Cast: Harry Belafonte, Zero Mostel, Ida Kaminska, Milo O'Shea, Gloria Foster, Barbara Ann Teer.

A hip African-American angel returns to earth to help a Jewish tailor re-examine his life.

Seldom seen 'vanity' film (a "Belafonte Enterprises Production") that contains energetic performances, wonderfully detailed sets, inventive photography and clever editing but still, somehow, never really comes together.

In the role of befuddled former store owner Morris Mishkin, Zero Mostel turns in an animated, (and expressly ethnic) performance that is at times funny, poignant, and recognisable from real life. Harry Belafonte is also very good as Alexander Levine (a Jewish angel reincarnated in the form of a rough-edged African-American male). He neatly sums up his predicament: "Every white mother up there is going through them pearly gates, but me, they put on probation!"

Pluses in the film include an interesting use of black & white and colour photography, and a few sassy supporting characters, including Mishkin's invalid wife Fanny (Ida Kaminska), Levine's earthbound girlfriend Sally (Gloria Foster), and, in a distinct and memorable cameo as a proud, combative, and very sceptical 'Welfare Clerk,' Barbara Ann Teer. Not quite what it set out to be, but still worth a look.

"...nervously at odds with itself, timid in its impulses, and mistaken in its choices." (Roger Greenspun, New York Times)

THE ARENA

1973, USA/Italy
Alternative Title: *Naked Warriors*
R (23846), Action/Adventure, 82m.
New World Pictures.
D: Steve Carver; P: Mark Damon; S: John Corrington, Joyce Corrington.
Cast: Pam Grier, Margaret Markov, Lucretia Love, Paul Muller, Marie Louise, Sid Lawrence [Silvio Laurenzi], Peter Cester [Pietro Ceccarelli].

"Black slave, white slave... see wild women fight to the death!"

In ancient Rome audiences have grown tired of gladiators fighting to the death. Something new is needed... women!

An entertaining, over-the-top blaxploitation visit to ancient Rome. The four female leads, all beautiful (and all comfortable

"You'd better pray she's working for you!"

specialist director and cinematographer Joe D'Amato / Aristide Massaccesi).

"'The Arena' is primitive entertainment but it does have a certain raw appeal..." (Richard Coskelly, L.A. Herald Examiner)

BABY NEEDS A NEW PAIR OF SHOES

1974, USA
Alternative Titles: *Jive Turkey*; *Nigger Rich*
R (1149), Action/Adventure, 86m.
Alert Film Releasing, Inc.
D: Bill Brame; P: Howard, Edith Ransom; S: Fredricka DeCosta, from a story by Howard and Elizabeth Ransom.
Cast: Paul Harris, Frances Williams, Frank De Kova, Don Edmondson.

"Gambling with lives in the numbers game... a game of wine, women and fast cars."

In 1956 Ohio, the head of a lucrative numbers game is pursued by both the mob and the local police.

Not bad, low-budget re-enactment of a 'true story.' All the key-elements of blaxploitation are here: shootouts, car chases, sex scenes, bar-room (this time pool-room) brawls and a few bloody murders. What sets this film apart, aside from the fact that it is distractingly set in the past (there are at least four references to it being 1956) is the clever casting of Don Edmondson in the role of Serene, a transvestite murderer-for-hire who is as glamorous as he is deadly! Paul (*Truck Turner*) Harris holds his own as Pasha, a beleaguered African-American numbers king, along with Frank (*The Slams*) De Kova as Big Tony, a Russian Roulette-playing Italian mob boss.

Seen by very few, this independently produced film whose title is an appropriation of a popular gambling phrase, is a fairly clever, violent, vulgar and shoddy little picture with a twist. Bill Brame also directed *Miss Melody Jones*.

BAD, BLACK AND BEAUTIFUL

1976, USA
R (1600), Action/Adventure, 83m.
Contemporary Films.
D: Bobby Davis; P: Bobby Davis; S: Bobby Davis.
Cast: Gwynn Barbee, Sammy Sams, Levi Balfour, Luke Ward, Terry Seazares.

When an innocent man is accused of murder, a lawyer and a private detective join forces to crack the case.

Hampered by poor sound and lighting, and actors who occasionally look off-screen for cues mid-sentence, *Bad, Black and Beautiful* (an admittedly great title) is so technically inept and ugly to look at that it's not even enjoyable on a camp level.

There's a dead-voiced 'foxy female attorney' / race car driver / pilot / nightclub performer named Eva Taylor (Gwynn Barbee); a carved-from-wood PI named Rich Jacobs (Levi Balfour); a philandering 'newspaperman' named Mike Copeland (Sammy Sams); and a falsely accused former Vietnam Vet named Johnnie Boyles (Terry Seazares). For what it's worth, there's a topless dance in a bar, a bathtub drowning, and a courtroom shootout. Texas never looked so dull and dreary. Director/writer Bobby Davis is African American.

"Bad, Black and Beautiful has now become the ultimate stick by which all other bad films must be measured." (David Walker, BadAzz MoFo issue #6)

BAMBOO GODS & IRON MEN

1974, Philippines/USA
Alternative Title: *Black Kung Fu*
R (23831), Action/Adventure, 96m.
American International Pictures.
D: Cesar Gallardo; P: Cirio H. Santiago; S: Ken Metcalfe, Joseph Zucchero.
Cast: James Iglehart [Inglehart], Shirley Washington, Chiquito, Eddie Garcia.

being photographed in the nude) satisfy both the narrative and the male gaze.

The bevy of women captured and forced to perform for the Romans include: Mamawi (Pam Grier), an African ceremonial dancer; Bodicia (Margaret Markov – who co-starred with Grier in the previous year's *Black Mama, White Mama*), a druid princess; Livia (Marie Louise), a Roman sympathiser; and Deidre (Lucretia Love), an easily-intimidated woman who likes to sneak a drink whenever she can. Fighting their corners in equally colourful supporting roles are Silvio Laurenzi as Priscium, a diminutive, over-made-up, and ostentatiously effeminate slave organizer, and Pietro Ceccarelli as Septimus, a gargoyle-faced warrior with a heart of gold.

A nude shower scene, an erotic dance (performed by Pam Grier), two public rapes, a deadly slave revolt, two love scenes, and a trip into the secret underground catacombs of Brundisium are all part of the costume-clad, set-heavy and often very funny proceedings. Steve Carver also directed *Drum*.

Note: There are two distinct versions of this American/Italian co-production. The American release is reviewed here. The Italian version (*La rivolta delle gladiatrici*) is credited to 'Michael Wotruba' (actually notorious horror/porn

"From Harlem to Hong Kong they fear the name, the fame and the fury of Black Cal Jefferson, the Champ!"

While vacationing in China an African-American boxer unknowingly becomes a pawn in the search for an ancient secret formula.

Awkwardly titled, super-low-budget and filled with more action than dialogue, *Bamboo Gods & Iron Men* is, nevertheless, an entertaining distraction.

In the lead role of vacationing prizefighting boxer Calvin Jefferson, football star-turned-actor James (*Savage!*) Inglehart is surprisingly good. Brawny (he often appears shirtless), laid back and comfortable in front of the camera, his is, by far, the most believable performance in the film. Other characters include his devoted young wife 'Mrs. Jack Jefferson' (Shirley Washington), and Charley (Chiquito), a timid Filipino wanderer who also happens to be a karate expert.

Incorporating both comedy and action (there is a Laurel & Hardy-like moment when a fat detective and a skinny detective get stuck in a doorway), *Bamboo Gods & Iron Men* (filmed in the Philippines but set in China) is a briskly-paced blaxploitation entry that does not attempt to do more than its modest budget allows.

BARE KNUCKLES

1977, USA
R (24984), Action/Adventure, 94m.
Intercontinental Releasing Corporation.
D: Don Edmonds; P: Don Edmonds;
S: Don Edmonds.
Cast: Robert Viharo, John Daniels, Gloria Hendry, Sherry Jackson, Michael Heit.

"Zack and Black manhunters... back to back!"

When a homicidal maniac targets women in Los Angeles, a bounty hunter sets out to capture him – and claim the $15,000 reward.

Violent and gory, *Bare Knuckles* is the kind of relentlessly base and uninventive film that even blaxploitation fans found difficult to enjoy.

Robert Viharo is more than competent in the role of bounty hunter Zachary Kane. Charismatic, determined and believable as an expert street fighter, his character (and performance) seem more than a little influenced by actor Charles Bronson and his string of super-successful *Death Wish* pictures. The film is given a bit of urban authenticity by John (*Black Shampoo*) Daniels, who plays Black, Kane's African-American nightclub owner friend. Others in the cast include: Michael Heit as Richard Devlin, a psychotic mama's boy; Gloria (*Black Belt Jones*) Hendry as Barbara Darrow, a nightclub singer on the run; and Sherry Jackson as Jennifer Randall, Zach's well-meaning girlfriend.

There is a love-story subplot that, if cast differently, might have worked. (Jackson is no great actress and the clichéd dialogue that she is forced to read makes a bad situation even worse):

Jennifer (to Zachary): *You're gonna hurt me, you know.*
Zachary: *I wouldn't do that.*
Jennifer: *Not the me on the outside, the me on the inside – the one that nobody sees.*

Worth a look, if only to see Viharo – one of those performers who, given a few more opportunities, might have become a star.

Note: The nightclub where John Daniels's character Black works is Maverick's Flat, the popular L.A. nightclub owned by Daniels himself – and also seen in *Coffy*.

THE BARON

1977, USA
Alternative Title: *Black Cue*
NR (R), Action/Adventure, 89m.
Tripps Production Corp.
D: Phillip Fenty; P: Chiz Schultz; S: Nelson Lyon with Linda and Phillip Fenty.
Cast: Calvin Lockhart, Joan Blondell, Charles McGregor, Raymond St. Jacques, Marlene Clark, Beverly Johnson.

"A film about a hustling cat determined to finish his first film... by any means necessary."

An African-American independent filmmaker unknowingly borrows money from a friend who is tied to the mob.

Model-turned-actress Marlene Clark starred in several blaxploitation horror films, including **Night of the Cobra Woman** (1972), **Ganja & Hess** (1973), and, shown here, **The Beast Must Die** (1974). (J. Howard Collection)

There is a good idea for a movie here (this is the first and only blaxploitation film about *making* a film) but the script is poor, scenes are overlong and the photography is lacklustre.

In the lead as Jason, a man-about-town who is looking for an entrée into California's lucrative film industry, Calvin Lockhart is pleasant to look at (and listen to) but ultimately unremarkable. His girlfriend Caroline, played by Marlene (*Ganja & Hess*) Clark fares slightly better. Emotionally committed to her sketchily written role, and eager to please, hers is a performance and visual display of beauty that is both rare and memorable. Star turns are also provided by: Charles (*Aaron Loves Angela*) McGregor as Cokeman, Jason's beleaguered and befuddled, yet well-meaning, dope-pushing friend; veteran Hollywood movie actress Joan Blondell as Mama Lou, an aged, bloated, sequin-and-feather-clad lounge proprietress; Raymond St. Jacques as Peter Mosten, a wealthy yet highly sceptical black investor; and, in a cameo role, Beverly Johnson (the first African-American model to appear on the cover of *Vogue*) as 'The Receptionist.'

Sadly the vintage New York City locations – including Central Park, Harlem and Greenwich Village – don't make up for the lack of incident and unbearably sluggish pace. African-American director Phillip Fenty also wrote *Super Fly*.

THE BEAST MUST DIE

1974, UK
Alternative Title: *Black Werewolf*
PG (23810), Horror, 93m.
Cinerama Releasing.
D: Paul Annett; P: Max J. Rosenberg, Milton Subotsky; S: Michael Winder from an original story by James Blish.
Cast: Calvin Lockhart, Charles Gray, Peter Cushing, Anton Diffring, Marlene Clark.

"See it... Solve it... But don't tell!"

A millionaire sportsman invites six friends to his isolated country estate. His objective... discover which one is a werewolf!

"This is a detective story. The question is not 'who is the murderer?' but 'who is the werewolf?' After all the clues have been shown you (the viewer) will get a chance to give your answer. Watch for the 'Werewolf Break'!"

All the elements are in place; six diverse guests summoned to a deserted mansion and a rich history of similar motion pictures that have preceded it. But the film has a major challenge: the marauding 'werewolf' is not really a werewolf at all – it's a rather friendly looking, obviously domesticated and over-fed, medium sized dog!

Calvin Lockhart plays Tom Newcliffe, a wealthy sportsman with too much time on his hands. Handsome, authoritative, urbane (if a bit pretentious), the star is game for the shenanigans at hand. Joining the hunt are several horror film veterans including: Marlene (*Night of the Cobra Woman*) Clark as Newcliffe's estranged wife Caroline; Peter (*Tales from the Crypt*) Cushing as Dr. Christopher Lundgren; and Anton (*Circus of Horrors*) Diffring, Newcliffe's old friend, a landscape architect named Pavel.

Worth a look for an impressive helicopter explosion (that seems borrowed from the previous year's *Shaft's Big Score!*) as well as the 30-second "werewolf break," an on-screen pause that allows the audience to guess who's the werewolf!

THE BIG BIRD CAGE

1972, USA
R (580), Action/Adventure, 93m.
New World Pictures.
Alternative Title: *Women's Penitentiary II*
D: Jack Hill; P: Jane Schaffer; S: Jack Hill.
Cast: Pam Grier, Anitra Ford, Sid Haig, Vic Diaz, Carol Speed, Karen McKevic.

"Women so hot with desire they melt the chains that enslave them!"

Two idealistic thieves, aided by a Filipino revolutionary cult, plot to break into a women's prison and liberate the inmates.

This unfunny 'spoof' (a follow up to the super-successful and much more entertaining *The Big Doll House*) is a tasteless and inexcusably derivative hodgepodge of over-familiar scenes and situations.

All the clichés are here – lesbianism, nudity, oversexed female inmates and cat fights – but unfortunately every line, action and situation has an I've-seen-this-all-before feel to it.

The bevy of 'incarcerated' females includes: Pam Grier as Blossom, a revolutionary freedom fighter; Anitra Ford as Terry, an unjustly imprisoned aristocrat; Karen McKevic as Karen, a six-foot-five blonde-haired blue-eyed walking (and running – slathered in chicken fat!) skeleton; and Carol (*Abby*) Speed as Mickie, a squat, always grimacing jailhouse 'supervisor.'

Add a not-too-fun gang rape (for the record the female inmates also 'gang rape' a male prison guard), an extended segment in which a male character named Django (Sid Haig) pretends to be gay and flirts with two ostentatiously effeminate gay guards, and an eye-crossingly dull 'mud fight,' and the result is a generally unpleasant film whose best moments are supplied by Grier, who is in imperious form here. Jack Hill's other films include *The Big Doll House*, *Coffy*, and *Foxy Brown*. See *Q & A: Ten Directors Discuss Their Films*.

"A perfect showcase for nudity, sex, violence, raw language and comic relief..."
(Addison Verill, *Variety*)

THE BIG DOLL HOUSE

1971, USA
R (352), Action/Adventure, 95m.
New World Pictures.
D: Jack Hill; P: Jane Schaffer; S: Don Spencer.
Cast: Pam Grier, Judy Brown, Roberta Collins, Kathryn Loder, Pat Woodell, Brooke Mills, Gina Stuart, Sid Haig, Christiane Schmidtmer.

"Their bodies were caged, but not their desires. They would do anything for a man – or to him."

Female prisoners in a Philippine jail are being subjected to sadistic torture. Five of the women – along with the help of two men – plot an escape.

Fast-moving, funny, totally engaging, if you see only one 1970s 'Women In Prison' blaxploitation film, see *The Big Doll House*.

The female leads are: Grear (Pam Grier), an opportunistic 'lesbian' prostitute ("I'm not this way because I want to be... it's this place!"); Collier (Judy Brown), a woman imprisoned because she murdered her cheating husband; Alcott (Roberta Collins), a Cheryl Ladd look-alike who also happens to be a nymphomaniac (she 'rapes' a delivery man at knifepoint snarling "get it up – or I'll cut it off!"); Bodine, played by Pat (*The Twilight People*) Woodell, a tough military leader's faithful girlfriend;

Harrad (Brooke Mills), a heroin-addicted inmate incarcerated because she murdered her newborn baby; and Ferina (Gina Stuart), a cat-loving and cat-like (she gouges someone's eyes out) inmate whose beloved pet helps her female comrades in an escape. Also strong in the cast are: delivery man Harry, played by Sid (*Coffy*) Haig; prison Matron Miss Dietrich (Christiane Schmidtmer); and Kathryn (*Foxy Brown*) Loder in the role of head guard Lucian.

The many over-the-top scenes in this film include a head-in-a-toilet catfight, a cockroach race, two nude shower scenes and, most memorable of all, a knock-down-drag-out female wrestling match – in a mud pit! (This particular scene was such an audience-pleaser that it was shamelessly repeated in the following year's *The Big Bird Cage*.) Add to this a subplot involving sadomasochism, a high number of lascivious one-liners ("shit – it's like a vice!"), and not one, but two, dramatic finales, and you've got a film that does everything it's supposed to – and then some.

Notes: The video and DVD of *The Big Doll House* contain a downbeat ending (a voiceover added after the film played on television) that audiences did not see at the time of the picture's theatrical release. For the uninitiated, cast-member Gina Stuart (Ferina) is a transgendered male. Pam Grier performs the film's theme song 'Long Time Woman.' See *Q & A: Ten Directors Discuss Their Films*.

BIG TIME

1977, USA
PG (24978), Comedy, 96m.
Joyce Distributing Co.
D: Andrew Georgias; P: Christopher Joy, Leon Isaac Kennedy, Andrew Georgias, Louis Gross; S: Anton Diether.
Cast: Christopher Joy, Roger E. Mosley, Tobar Mayo, Jayne Kennedy, Art Evans.

A small-time con artist gets between the FBI and a suitcase full of mob money.

Big Time is a well-done *Car Wash*-like comedy 'presented' by William 'Smokey' Robinson (who also sings several songs on the soundtrack).

Christopher Joy plays Eddie Jones, a low-level crook looking for a scam that will place him in the 'big time.' A cross between Richard Pryor and Chris Rock (he closely resembles Rock), his confidence, on-the-money comic timing, and ease of delivery make him stand out in what is meant to be an ensemble piece.

Also in the cast are: Tobar (*Abar*) Mayo as Harold Johnson, Eddie's bald-headed, well-meaning but goofy sidekick; Art Evans as Buzz Murdock, a Private Investigator who sounds and acts like Humphrey Bogart (just in case you don't get it there is a poster of Bogart in his office); and 'Special Guest Star' Roger E. (*Sweet Jesus Preacher Man*) Mosley as J.J., a loan shark with a heart of gold.

The only distractingly poor performance in the film comes from beauty queen Jayne Kennedy (she was crowned Miss Ohio in 1970) as Shana Baynes, a Private Investigator who succumbs to Eddie's relentless romantic pursuit. Flat, self-conscious and unconnected to the proceedings at hand, she is lovely to gaze upon (particularly in a wedding gown – in which she looks like a perfectly proportioned store-window mannequin) but a difficult-to-endure screen presence.

The mud fight between Grear (Pam Grier) and Alcott (Roberta Collins) in **The Big Doll House** (1971) was so popular with audiences that it was reprised in the picture's sequel, 1972's **The Big Bird Cage**. (Soul Images)

above: Miss Ohio 1970, Jayne Kennedy plays Private Investigator Shana Baynes in **Big Time** (1977).

Filled with a large number of one-liners ("Hey don't get a rash we'll be back in a flash," and "I make love cafeteria style – help yourself!"), *Big Time's* shenanigans include shootouts, car chases, and a pivotal high-stakes suitcase switch. Worth a look.

THE BINGO LONG TRAVELING ALL-STARS & MOTOR KINGS

1976, USA
PG (24566), Comedy, 111m.
Universal Pictures.
D: John Badham; P: Rob Cohen; S: Hal Barwood.
Cast: Billy Dee Williams, James Earl Jones, Richard Pryor, Ted Ross, Sam Laws.

"To laugh you listened to radio, to cry you went to the movies, for excitement you went to the ball game. But if you wanted all three, you went to Bingo Long."

In hopes of competing with the Negro National League, an African-American baseball star puts together his own highly theatrical team.

Beautifully photographed period film (based in 1939) with a large budget for authentic costumes, automobiles and sets, this well-intentioned piece of entertainment is everything it wants to be. No cursing, no sex scenes, no drugs, this decidedly PG-rated tale of male bonding in the sports arena is a film that, necessarily, overlooks the litany of deeply disturbing issues and concessions made by African-American ball players at the time.

Billy Dee Williams is superb as the overly-confident, showy but undeniably persuasive baseball team leader Bingo Long. James Earl Jones, as Long's more practical minded best friend Leon Carter,

also supplies a noteworthy performance. Along for the ride (in a role that seems too small to accommodate his immense talent) is Richard Pryor as Chief Takahoma, an always-looking-at-girls teammate who will do anything (including posing as a Mexican and/or American Indian) to break into the white baseball league. Fun film touches include a faux newsreel, split screen photography, vintage radio show broadcasts, and a steady stream of 'gin-house' music. Look for versatile actor Sam (*Cool Breeze*) Laws in a one-line supporting role.

"A genial, slapdash, high-spirited, and occasionally moving comedy."
(Vincent Canby, New York Times)

THE BLACK ALLEYCATS

1973, USA
NR (X), Action/Adult, 83m.
Entertainment Pyramid.
D: Henning Schellerup; P: John Munchkin; S: Joseph Drury.
Cast: Sandy Dempsey, Marsha Jordan, Uschi Digard, Norman Fields.

"So cuddly by day... so deadly by night! These pussies mean business!"

When four finishing-school students are raped by a gang of hoodlums, the girls band together and exact their vengeance.

Softcore porn movie with lots of bare breasts and simulated sexual activity. The plot involves four young women (two black and two white) who wear schoolgirl uniforms during the day and then don black satin jackets emblazoned with a pink cat at night. When the sun sets this "ebony and ivory female vigilante group" rob, act out sexually and cause all-around general havoc.

Borrowing much from the 'Women In Prison' film genre – a lesbian headmistress (the voluptuous proprietor of Miss Emerson's School for Girls); sexually deprived, yet sexually obsessed young women; female camaraderie which leads to female rebellion – today, *The Black Alleycats*, even with its lingering nudity, would probably be rated R. *The Black Alleycats* is one of several 1970s 'adult' films whose advertising campaigns, poster art, and crime-centred story lines were pointedly fashioned to appeal to the blaxploitation film fan. Henning Schellerup also directed *Sweet Jesus Preacher Man*.

BLACK ANGELS

1970, USA
Alternative Titles: *Black Bikers from Hell*; *Angels Revenge*; *Outlaw Bikers: The Gang Wars*
R (22591), Action/Adventure, 85m.
Merrick International.
D: Laurence Merrick; P: Leo Rivers, Laurence Merrick; S: Laurence Merrick.
Cast: Robert Johnson, Des Roberts, King John III, Linda Jackson, James Whitwirth, Clancy Syrko.

"God forgives... the Black Angels don't!"

When an African-American biker gang is tricked into believing that a white biker gang is planning a war, all hell breaks loose.

A peek at the clothing, lifestyles and dubious aspirations of two travelling biker gangs; one white ('Serpents Angels'), one black ('Choppers'). The characters, none of them interesting, include: Knifer (Robert Johnson), the black biker gang leader; Chainer (Des Roberts), the white biker gang leader; and Lt. Harper (Clancy Syrko), a scheming police detective. Linda Jackson plays Jackie, a free-spirited biker groupie.

Filled with freeze-frame photography, flashbacks, and an overtly dull ten-minute motorcycle chase, the most memorable moment in the film comes when one biker responds to another biker who has climbed into a tree and urinated on him:

Biker: *I'm gonna kill you, you filthy, no good, egg-sucking, finger-licking, fat-picking, skuzzy-faced, rat!*

Note: The Choppers are played by actual L.A. gang members.

BLACK BELT JONES

1974, USA
R (23807), Action/Adventure, 85m.
Warner Bros.
D: Robert Clouse; P: Fred Weintraub, Paul Heller; S: Oscar Williams.
Cast: Jim Kelly, Gloria Hendry, Scatman Crothers, Malik Carter, Marla Gibbs.

"Enter Jim 'Dragon' Kelly... Black Belt Jones."

When the mob puts pressure on an African-American karate school to close down, an African-American federal agent is asked to intervene.

A comic-book, TV-movie-like, karate action film worth seeing just for the many elaborately staged, high-kicking fight sequences.

In the lead as Black Belt Jones, middleweight martial arts champion Jim Kelly, with his outsize afro, pork chop sideburns and platform shoes, is as colourful and one-dimensional as any super hero could ever be. (Kelly's rather flat line delivery and intonation work in his favour, making him even more cartoonish and otherworldly.) Jones's girlfriend, Sydney Byrd, is played by Gloria Hendry; the *Playboy* bunny-turned-actress is the perfect powerhouse sidekick – as sexy as she is deadly. "What trouble could I possibly cause – I'm just a woman?" she asks an acquaintance before proceeding to pummel a trio of intimidating thugs. Also in the cast are Scatman Crothers as Pop Byrd, a karate school owner whose modest business is in the way of a proposed Watts redevelopment project, and Malik Carter (the only actor in the film who appears genuinely comfortable in front of the camera) as Pinky, the local pimp who wants to 'educate' his many adversaries.

Marla Gibbs (best known as Florence the maid from hit TV show *The Jeffersons*) plays Mrs. Williams, a recently-widowed benefit organiser.

A lights-on, lights-off, fight sequence, an on-train showdown (in which ten assailants are kicked through the locomotive's windows), and a raucous (and very messy) finale that takes place inside and outside of a downtown car wash, are all colourful, high spirited and thoroughly entertaining distractions. Robert Clouse also directed *Enter the Dragon* and *Golden Needles*.

"...it's popcorn, comic-strip entertainment that moves swiftly and has a good kick now and then."
(Donald Bogle, Blacks in American Films and Television, 1988)

BLACK CAESAR

1973, USA
Alternative Title: *The Godfather of Harlem*
R (23539), Action/Adventure, 94m.
American International Pictures.
D: Larry Cohen; P: Larry Cohen; S: Larry Cohen.
Cast: Fred Williamson, Art Lund, Julius W. Harris, Gloria Hendry, D'Urville Martin, Val Avery.

"Hail Caesar Godfather of Harlem! The cat with the .45 caliber claws!"

From shoe-shine boy to top mafia kingpin, the story of a Harlem youth's rise and fall in New York City's crime world.

The tragic tale of a broken home and misguided dreams, *Black Caesar* holds its own against *Super Fly* as one of blaxploitation's most carefully constructed and consistently engaging entries.

As Tommy Gibbs, a mistreated Harlem youngster bent on getting even and rising to the top of the Harlem underworld, Fred Williamson is everything he was hired to be. Tall, dark, handsome, charismatic and, most of all, believable, he is perfectly cast and seems to be exactly the type of overly-confident, egocentric man who would be able to succeed in the cutthroat underground world of organised crime. Gibbs's nemesis is racist cop John McKinney (Art Lund), who viciously attacks the young Gibbs and leaves him with a limp. On hand, and adding a great deal of energy and excitement to the fast-moving narrative, are: Gloria Hendry as Helen, Tommy's turncoat ex- girlfriend; Julius W. Harris as Mr. Gibbs, Tommy's remorseful 'just-visiting' father; and D'Urville Martin as Reverend Rufus, a good-natured but shamelessly corrupt evangelist. There is also a great performance by Val Avery as Sal Cardoza, a life-worn, but still very powerful mafia don.

The bloody shootouts, car chases and under-the-table deals are deftly photographed, and the picture contains one of the genre's most discussed segments – a scene in which Gibbs brutalises corrupt cop McKinney by making him rub shoe shine polish on his face and sing 'Mammy!'

Originally intended to be a star vehicle for Sammy Davis Jr., *Black Caesar* (fastidiously shot in just 18 days for only $300,000) raked in over $2,000,000 and spawned a quickly released sequel, *Hell Up in Harlem*. The outstanding soundtrack is by James Brown. (See *Q & A: Ten Directors Discuss Their Films*.

"With his powerful frame, good looks and cultured demeanour... [Williamson] gives the focal part conviction... not only in the menacing gangster fisticuffs and gunplay... but also in the more intimate one-on-one encounters."
(Parish/Hill, Black Action Films, 1989)

BLACK CHARIOT

1971, USA
NR, Action/Adventure, 90m. Goodwin.
D: Robert L. Goodwin; P: Robert L. Goodwin; S: Robert L. Goodwin.
Cast: Bernie Casey, Richard Elkins, Barbara Jones, Pauline Myers.

When a member of a black empowerment organisation frames one of his fellow members, a moral crisis evolves.

Receiving only a very brief theatrical release, this super-low-budget film is one of only a handful of blaxploitation pictures that appears to have been lost, never to be seen again. Completed on a budget of just $44,000, *Black Chariot* is notable for featuring a performance by Bernie (...*tick...tick...tick*...) Casey.

"Displays tremendous feeling but no sense of pace or style or, in some cases, characterization."
(Kevin Thomas, Los Angeles Times)

THE BLACK CONNECTION

1974, USA
Alternative Titles: *Run Nigger ...Run*; *The Black Connection: Run Nigger ...Run*
R (23827), Action/Adventure, 87m.
Box-Office International.
D: Michael J. Finn; P: Harry Novak; S: Michael J. Finn.
Cast: Bobby Stevens, Sonny Charles, Tommy Moe Raft, Martha Washington, Sweet Louie, Steve Edwards, Sergio Escobar.

"What's wrong with the black man winning for a change?"

A 'confidence man' gets caught between two warring crime syndicates.

Super-low-budget, with atrocious acting, poor sound, and lit like an operating room, *The Black Connection* should still, somehow, manage to keep your attention until the picture's 'shocking' conclusion; it doesn't.

Bobby Stevens is unimposing, not particularly photogenic, and just plain ordinary in the lead as drug pusher/pimp Miles Carter. Faring a bit better (but no more attractive to look at) is the overweight, constantly sweating Italian mobster, Don Juliano (Tommy Mo Raft). Other self-explanatory characters include The Bruiser (Sonny Charles), The Hit Man (Steve Edwards), and The Cuban (Sergio Escobar), but without question this film's star is black prostitute Magda (played by Martha Washington). Loudmouthed, ballsy and crass, her brief appearance (sitting up topless in bed with a white 'John' by her side) is this shoddy production's indisputable highlight.

John (to Magda): *Baby, you're the best buy in town.*
Magda: *I'm glad you feel that way because... All Sales Are Final!*

Later, after Magda's pimp comes to collect his percentage of her money:

Magda (to John): *That Larry just doesn't know how to treat a lady*

like a lady... [snarling] ...and I am a motherfuckin' lady!

Vintage Las Vegas (and Albuquerque, New Mexico) locations, a deadly poolside karate fight, and a novel (and disgusting) way of delivering packets of heroin, are just a few of this picture's badtaste amusements.

Populated with a bevy of siliconeenhanced, old-school showgirls (with names like Sherry Wine and Suzanne Vegas), *The Black Connection* is also a showcase for the not-very-good (if the soundtrack to this movie is any indication) band, The Checkmates Ltd.

"A vile, boring film that has, at its heart and soul, not one single redeeming value..."
(David Walker, BadAzz MoFo magazine issue #6)

THE BLACK DRAGON

1974, Hong Kong
Alternative Titles: *Super Dragon*; *Tough Guy*; *Chueh tou lao hou chuang*
R (1236), Action/Martial Arts, 93m.
Howard Mahler Films.
D: Tommy Loo Chung [Tony Liu Jun Guk]; P: Joseph E. Estrada, Yeo Ban Yee; S: Tommy Loo Chung.
Cast: Jason Pai Piao, Ron Van Clief, Nancy Veronica, George Estregan [Jorge Estraga], Angie Rau.

A naive Chinese farmhand travels to the Philippines and discovers the truth about his estranged wealthy brother.

From the opening credits (which show ancient Chinese illustrations accompanied by a perky banjo and harmonica arrangement) to the climactic brother-against-brother fight, *Black Dragon* is a thoroughly engaging, meticulously choreographed and wholly likeable picture.

In the lead as Thai Lu, an illiterate yet big-hearted country bumpkin who also happens to be a martial arts expert, Jason Pai Piao is pleasant-faced, amiable and exceedingly agile. The film also features African-American karate champion Ron Van Clief (in an overly promoted cameo as a gang leading freedom fighter named "The Black Dragon." Support is provided by (an un-credited) Angie Rau as Chu, Thai Lu's corrupt, heroin-dealing brother, and Nancy Veronica as Thai Lu's sympathetic girlfriend.

Wonderfully entertaining fight sequences, likable characters and clichéd phrases – "Just like my mother used to make!" and "with you as a friend, who needs enemies?" – along with the English dubbing by a bevy of awkward Chinese voices, add an unintended levity to what would otherwise be a straightforward martial arts film. Good story, good performances and an eagerness on the part of the filmmakers to please the audience make this hard-to-find film worth a look.

BLACK DRAGON FEVER

1979, Hong Kong
Alternative Title: *Kung Fu Fever*
NR, Action/Adventure, 75m.
Yangtze Film Company.
D: Kao Ke; P: David Poon; S: Ngai Hong.
Cast: Ron Van Clief, Dragon Lee, Amy Chum, Sze Chung-Tin.

"Non-stop, bone-breaking, gut-wrenching action!"

Three rival gangs embark on a search for Bruce Lee's handwritten 'Finger Fighting' manual.

The opportunistic plot of this film is fashioned around the sudden and unexpected death of martial arts legend and film star Bruce Lee. Dim-witted and painfully straightforward, but containing the requisite number of deftly executed karate fight scenes (in the woods; on a highway; on a balcony; on the beach; in a parking lot) as well as a bevy of young, attractive and extremely agile players, *Black Dragon Fever* (which has nothing to do with the first *Black Dragon*) is a favourite of schlock karate film lovers.

THE NEW AMERICAN SUPERSTAR

RON VAN CLIEF
7th degree
BLACK BELT

4 times
WORLD
CHAMPION

starring JASON PAI POW   JORGE ESTRAGA and
introducing RON VAN CLIEF as

SERAFIM KARALEXIS presents
THE BLACK DRAGON

IN COLOR [R]

starring JASON PAI POW • RON VAN CLIEF • JORGE ESTRAGA • NANCY VERONICA
MENG FU • THOMSON KAO KANG • CHANG LAU CHU • Screenplay by TOMMY LOO CHUNG
Directed by TOMMY LOO CHUNG • Action Directors JASON PAI POW, MENG FU, CHEN LAW
A co-production by SERAFIM KARALEXIS & YEO BAN YEE

A MADISON WORLD FILM   A HOWARD MAHLER Release

Ron Van Clief is believable, but oddly un-engaging, as a hired killer and karate expert. Not much of an actor, in fact not an actor at all, the 'performer' does make up for his dead-voiced line deliveries by screeching, groaning and roaring during his many fight scenes. Ron's nemesis is Ricky Chan (Dragon Lee – no relation to Bruce), a hip-dressing, always smirking karate master. Rounding out the cast is Amy Chum as Ms. Lu, a leather-clad motorcycle mama (and the only person in the entire film who comes across as a human being and not an automaton).

Both a celebration and an exploitation of Bruce Lee and his legend (he is mentioned at least thirty times and his photographic images are displayed throughout – in fact the film even features a clip of the real Lee talking on the telephone), *Black Dragon Fever* is a curiosity piece, an atrociously dubbed and poorly acted film that, like so many others in the genre, is much more fun than it has any real right to be.

THE BLACK DRAGON REVENGES THE DEATH OF BRUCE LEE

1975, Hong Kong
Alternative Titles: *The Black Dragon's Revenge*; *Long zheng hu dou jing wu hun*
R (1374), Action/Martial Arts, 90m.
Madison World Films.
D: Tommy Loo Chung [Tony Liu Jun Guk];
P: Serafim Karalexis; S: Norbert Albertson.
Cast: Ron Van Clief, Charles 'La Pantera' Bonet, Jason Pai Pow [Jason Pai Piao], Linda Ho.

"Starring Ron Van Clief... The 4 Times World Champion!"

A wealthy Chinese merchant hires an African American karate champion to discover the truth behind the death of martial arts superstar Bruce Lee.

A film fashioned around (and capitalising on) the sudden death of martial arts superstar Bruce Lee, *The Black Dragon Revenges the Death of Bruce Lee* is the second of three 'Black Dragon' entries designed to showcase the high-kicking talents of Ron Van Clief.

Filmed on location in Hong Kong, this quickie sequel to the previous year's *Black Dragon* stars Van Clief as a karate expert who is paid $100,000 to discover the actual circumstances behind Bruce Lee's death. Interested parties include: Jason Pai Piao as the Black Dragon's fighting companion; Charles 'La Pantera' Bonet as Charlie, an antique shop owner who is also a karate expert; and Linda Ho as Lulu, a gangster's moll who uses poisonous snakes as a weapon.

BLACK EYE

1973, USA
PG (23753), Action/Adventure, 97m.
Warner Bros.
D: Jack Arnold; P: Pat Rooney; S: Mark Haggard and Jim Martin, based on a novel by Jeff Jacks.
Cast: Fred Williamson, Teresa Graves, Rosemary Forsyth, Floy Dean, Nancy Fisher, Bret Morrison.

"The name of the game is the cane of pain."

A former police officer-turned private detective tries to solve a case involving a missing girl.

The clever use of a black & white silent-movie era opening segment contrasts nicely with the vivid 1970s fashions, cars and interiors that follow in this amiable TV movie-like film that is centred around a mysterious walking stick.

Fred Williamson as private eye Shep Stone is competent yet slightly less effective than he is in his harder-edged films. A little too self-aware, a little to eager to mug for the camera, he is nonetheless a fantasy match for gorgeous Teresa (*Get Christie Love!*) Graves as Cynthia, a bisexual woman who is enjoying an open romantic relationship with Stone. Graves,

Best known for the sassy-talking, irresistible police detective she played in TV's **Get Christie Love!**, beautiful Teresa Graves also appeared in three blaxploitation films; **Black Eye** *(above)* and **That Man Bolt** (both 1973), and **Old Dracula** (1974).

whose on-screen charisma and breath-taking likeability have rarely been seriously considered (perhaps because she only made two more feature films (*That Man Bolt* and *Old Dracula*) before turning to religion, is a pleasure to behold and listen to. Also featured in the cast are Nancy Fisher as a prostitute named Vera, turning in a performance that is so visceral it almost throws the film off, and Bret Morrison as a pornographic filmmaker.

Black Eye, with its over-lit cardboard sets (many of which become completely obliterated), Venice California locations, and catchy theme song (the singer of the fantastic tune 'I Know Where I'm Going, Because I Know Where I've Been' does not receive an on-screen credit) is one of very few films that examines the ties that bound organised crime and the pornography industry during the 1970s. Jack Arnold also directed *Boss Nigger*.

"...almost savage commentary juxtaposing the traditional private eye to a modern California background of Jesus freaks, pornographic film makers, the narcotics trade and transitional sexual lifestyles..." (Lawrence Van Gelder, New York Times)

BLACK FIRE

1979, Mexico
Alternative Title: *Fuego Negro*
NR, Action/Adventure, 98m. Scope Films.
D: Raúl Fernández; P: Xavier Rezzo;
S: Raúl Fernández.
Cast: Cesar Imbert, Susana Kamini,
Aurora Clavel, Yvonne De Carlo.

Slaves on a Southern plantation revolt when they are not set free following the Civil War.

Yet another 'slaves-in-the-old-South' melodrama influenced by *Mandingo*, this Mexican-shot tale of interracial romance and vigilantism is better than expected.

In the lead as Manuel, an African-American slave in love with the plantation owner's beautiful white daughter, Cesar Imbert is an attractive mannequin, on hand to look good picking cotton and making passionate love to the object of his desire. Susana Kamini as Gabriella, the daughter of a wealthy plantation owner, is also attractive, both with her clothes on and off. Supporting roles are filled by Latin actress Aurora Clavel (in blackface!) as Nanny, a bumbling but well-meaning servant, and Yvonne De Carlo (post *The Munsters* TV series), as the evil plantation owner's sometimes-empathetic wife.

Rape, violence, miscegenation, whippings, and general unrest permeate the film. What elevates this patently derivative tale is an intriguing script that takes more than a few unexpected turns.

Stunning Oaxaca locations, period clothing and unusual casting (Mexicans playing African Americans) help make this a peculiarly satisfying novelty film.

BLACK FIST

1977, USA
Alternative Titles: *Homeboy*; *Bogard*; *The Black Street Fighter*
R (1242), Action/Adventure, 94m.
Worldwide Films.
D: Timothy Galfas, Richard Kaye;
P: William Larrabure and Richard Kaye;
S: Tim Kelly, Andrew Maisner, Richard Kaye.
Cast: Richard Lawson, Philip Michael Thomas, Dabney Coleman, Annazette Chase, Robert Burr.

"He's all white hot fury... he's all stone cold nerve... he's all big black fists... he's 60,000 volts of black power!"

A promoter with mob connections brings an out of work young man up through the ranks in the illegal street-fighting racket.

Sensational but realistic, *Black Fist* takes a look at the highly lucrative back-alley world of illegal bare-fist fighting.

Richard Lawson is simply superb as Leroy Fisk, a down-on-his-luck day worker turned street fighter. Natural, comfortable in front of the camera and streetwise, he is the highly deserving centrepiece around which the rest of the film is built. Philip Michael Thomas is stunning in two smal roles – at first a clever bearded and grungy black wino (and mob informant), and then a Puerto Rican hustler/hit man. This is due to the fact that this is basically two films edited together: In 1975, Timothy Galfas directed *Bogard*, an X-rated action movie that had a limited theatrical run, then in 1977, a re-edited version of the film, with new footage shot by Richard Kaye, was released as *Black Fist*; it is this version of the film that survives today. Striking performances are also put in by Dabney Coleman in the role of Heineken, a cocky, corrupt white police officer, and Robert Burr as Mr. Logan, a greasy-faced, verbally and physically abusive mob boss.

The underlying theme of the film – the idea that blacks are never really in control of their own destiny as long as there are corrupt white people around – is forcefully presented:

Fighter (to extortionist): *One of these days you're going to pay the piper.*

Extortionist: *No man, you don't understand. Some of us never pay the piper because some of us **are** the piper.*

Filled with realistic-looking violence (a relentless and bloody beating in a men's bathroom; a brawl in which a character's head is smashed into the steel frame on the back of a truck; a poolside shooting; a character placed on a meat hook and dumped in a freezer), *Black Fist* is self-indulgent, shameless and thoroughly engaging. Most definitely worth a view.

THE BLACK GESTAPO

1975, USA
Alternative Titles: *Ghetto Warriors*; *The Black Enforcers*
R (1269), Action/Adventure, 94m.
Bryanston Pictures.
D: Lee Frost; P: Wes Bishop; S: Lee Frost, Wes Bishop.
Cast: Rod Perry, Charles P. Robinson, Phil Hoover, Angela Brent, Dona Desmond.

"The new master race!"

Members of a neighbourhood organisation called The People's Army drive the mob out of their community only to, themselves, adopt the mob's self-serving tactics.

Narrator: *"Work them hard, to the very end of their endurance. I want my army to be ready for anything and everything that comes their way. No one will stop us. Whether they live or die is not the question. Whether they live or succeed is the only answer."*

Upon its release this oddly compelling film sparked a small measure of controversy because the opening credits use vintage footage of Hitler, marching Nazi soldiers, and cheering German crowds. One of the very few blaxploitation films that dare to present African-American characters that are as corrupt as 'whitey,' *The Black Gestapo* (like *Bucktown*), also offers an intimate look at the organised, extremely profitable underground world of sex and drugs.

In the lead role of righteous, yet still somewhat militant-minded community leader General Ahmed, Rod (*Black Godfather*) Perry is everything that he needs to be. Appropriately guarded, determined yet sceptical, Perry's commitment to character is both plausible and recognisable from real life. As his

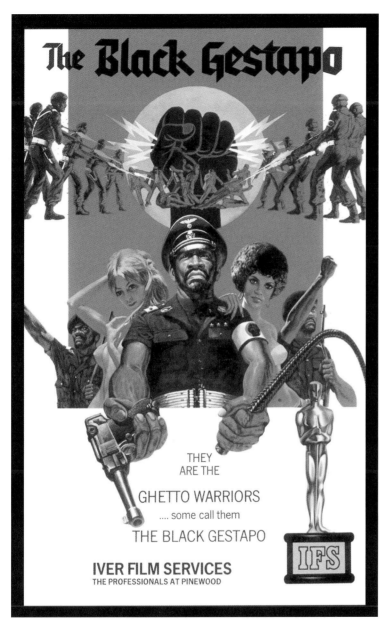

THEY
ARE THE

GHETTO WARRIORS
.... some call them
THE BLACK GESTAPO

IVER FILM SERVICES
THE PROFESSIONALS AT PINEWOOD

BLACK GIRL

1972, USA
PG (23471), Drama, 97m.
Cinerama Releasing.
D: Ossie Davis; P: Lee Savin; S: J.E.
Franklin.
Cast: Peggy Pettit, Brock Peters, Louise
Stubbs, Claudia McNeil, Leslie Uggams,
Damu King.

*"She's got to cut it... or cut out. She's a
Black Girl ...your girl."*

**The ongoing discoveries and challenges
of three generations of African-
American women.**

Not as fully realised as you would like it
to be, *Black Girl* is still a rare film that
offers a seldom-seen look at the dreams,
fantasies, aspirations and special
challenges that many African-American
women face.

Young Peggy Pettit (in her screen
debut) is refreshingly natural in the lead
as Billie Jean, a young girl with dreams

nemesis, the separatist (and violence-
condoning) Colonel Kojah, Charles P.
Robinson effectively embodies contemporary black impatience and frustration.
Also true to her role is Dona Desmond as
a drug-addicted prostitute whose vividly
enacted display of emotion (and unself-
conscious nudity) offers a chillingly
realistic portrait of a woman who is living
on the very edge of society

Revelling in both atrocity and controversy, *The Black Gestapo*'s berserk mix of
pathos, farce and social commentary
includes: a gang rape; a castration after
which the victim's severed penis is
flushed down the toilet; and a lingering

visit to a black anti-establishment
'Training Camp' where neo-black fascists
chant "vengeance" using body language
that makes a clear alignment with the
militaristic images of Nazi Germany.

Not for those seeking light-hearted
entertainment, but worthy of examination –
if only for its sheer audacity, *The Black
Gestapo* is, today, a cult movie favourite
that was one of the very first blaxploitation
films to show up on DVD. Lee Frost also
directed *The Thing with Two Heads*.

*"...surely one of the more crass, prepos-
terous, and disturbing films of its vintage."*
(Parish/Hill, Black Action Films, 1989)

(she wants to be a dancer) that seem unrealistic to both her practical-minded mother and troublemaking sisters. Louise Stubbs is nothing short of incredible as her life-embittered mother Roseanne. Angry, doubtful and frustrated, hers is an onscreen performance that has the chilling air of truth about it. Also present in this overpopulated and extremely talky ensemble piece are: Leslie (*Poor Pretty Eddie*) Uggams as Netta, Roseanne's 'adopted' daughter; Claudia (*A Raisin in the Sun*) McNeil (in what feels like a repeat performance) as Mu' Dear, a rotund Mammy-like grandmother; and Damu (*Shaft*) King, as a church reverend who delivers a totally realistic and utterly engaging sermon.

Black Girl's virtues lie in its realistic handling of personal family matters like sibling rivalry, parental favouritism, and the often-considerable discrepancy between what people *say* they do and what they *actually* do. Also examined is the trap that many poor black girls fall into (believing their only worth to a man, and to themselves, lies in their ability to procreate). African-American director Ossie Davis's other films include *Cotton Comes to Harlem*, *Gordon's War* and *Countdown at Kusini*. Screenwriter J.E. Franklin is also African American.

"...still as much a play as a movie... a fierce, clear and eloquent testament about growing up black in America."
(Jay Cocks, Time)

THE BLACK GODFATHER

1974, USA
Alternative Title: *Street War*
R (1140), Action/Adventure, 94m.
Cinemation Industries.
D: John Evans; P: John Evans; S: John Evans.
Cast: Rod Perry, Jimmy Witherspoon, Diane Sommerfield, Damu King, Don Chastain.

"There's a new Godfather in town and everybody wants his body, the FBI, some very foxy chicks... and the Mafia!"

With the intention of wiping out drugs in their community, a team of community-minded African Americans take control of their neighbourhood.

Longwinded and talky, *The Black Godfather* (filmed under the working title *The Blackfather*) is a literally dark, poorly presented tale of black mafia infighting for a 'just cause.'

Rod Perry is good enough in the role of J.J. Johnson, a petty criminal who organises a team to help rid his ghetto neighbourhood of drugs, but he proves unable to transcend the limitations of his poorly written role. Older ghetto boss Big Nate Williamson (Jimmy Witherspoon) also teeters on the edge of believability but is, unfortunately, undermined by ridiculous dialogue and highly unlikely situations. Other cast members include:

Damu King as Diablo, a community recruiter for justice; Don Chastain as Tony, a corrupt white Mafia adversary; and Diane (*Blackjack*) Sommerfield as Yvonne, Big Nate's handy-with-a-meat-cleaver daughter.

The best line in the movie is a rare humorous one. A father who is confused by his foolish son's antics asks, "Boy, is you on that dope again?!"

Stilted performances, flat photography, message-heavy ("Down with the man – Power to the People,") and just an all around mess, *The Black Godfather* is a film whose trailer (in common with so many other blaxploitation movie trailers) is infinitely more exciting than the film it was created to promote. African-American director/producer/writer John Evans's other films include *Speeding Up Time* and *Blackjack*.

"Slovenly, poorly directed... a good example of the type of black action film that killed off the black movie market."
(Donald Bogle, Blacks in American Films and Television, 1988)

BLACK GUNN

1972, USA
R (23451), Action/Adventure, 97m.
Columbia Pictures.
D: Robert Hartford-Davis; P: John Heyman, Norman Priggen; S: Franklin Coen
Cast: Jim Brown, Brenda Sykes, Bernie Casey, Martin Landau, Bruce Glover, Rick Ferrell, Jeanne [Jean] Bell, Chuck Daniel, Timothy Brown.

"For every drop of black blood spilled... a white man pays!"

A Los Angeles nightclub owner seeks revenge after his brother is brutally murdered and left on his doorstep.

Another Jim Brown vehicle that presents the former football star as the regal and powerful embodiment of black pride and righteousness, *Black Gunn* covers all the necessary bases and covers them well.

As Gunn, the take-nothing-from-nobody owner of a popular nightspot called Gunn's Club, Brown seems to have it all; good looks, a beautiful girlfriend, money, respect and a bevy of genuinely caring friends and supporters. Unfortunately for him, both the mob and the local police are looking for a way to

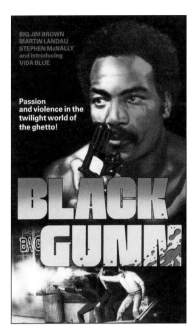

make Gunn eat humble pie. Displaying an emotional commitment to character not seen in any of his other films (he is genuinely moving in a family death scene) Brown is at turns funny, seductive, touching and worn. Standing in Brown's shadow, both literally and figuratively, are Brenda (*Honky*) Sykes as Judith, his beautiful and eminently committed girlfriend, and Bruce Glover as Ray Kriley, an eerie-voiced 'degenerate' mobster.

Quite incredibly *Black Gunn* also features four other blaxploitation *headliners* in minuscule early-career film roles. There's Jean (*TNT Jackson*) Bell, Bernie (*Hit Man*) Casey, Chuck (*Fox Style*) Daniel, and Timothy (*Dynamite Brothers*) Brown. Add to this a small yet memorable performance by character actor Rick Ferrell as Jimpy, a drug dealer turned informant, and you've got a superb collection of supporting players that fill every nook and cranny of the plot.

High-speed car chases, shootouts, politically incorrect language, ("freak, nigger, coon, monkey, spade, spook, boy") bloody beatings, and an elaborately staged multi-cast shoot-out finale are all part of the mix. A wholly underrated genre entry. Robert Hartford-Davis also directed *The Take*.

"Jim Brown's search and destroy tactics often destroy his shirt to expose him as a fine figure of a man."
(A.H. Weiler, New York Times)

BLACK HEAT

1976, USA
Alternative Titles: *Intrigue*; *Girl's Hotel*; *The Murder Gang*; *Syndicate Vice*; *US Vice*
R (1479), Action/Adventure, 94m. Independent-International Pictures Corp.
D: Al Adamson; P: Al Adamson; S: John D'Amato, Sheldon Lee, Budd Donnelly.
Cast: Timothy Brown, Tanya Boyd, Russ Tamblyn, Geoffrey Land.

"The word was out: Smash him! Stomp him! Stop him at all costs!"

Police sergeant 'Kicks' Carter and his television journalist girlfriend crack the case of a major underground exchange of drugs for firearms.

Padded with overlong shots of a car chase, a shopping spree, a shootout and countless scenes of characters driving around Los Angles, Las Vegas and the California desert, *Black Heat* is one of those low budget entries that seems purposely stretched to meet the usual 90 minute theatre-owner time requirement.

In the lead role of Kicks Carter, a Las Vegas cop out to get the bad guys, baseball player-turned actor Timothy (*Dynamite Brothers*) Brown is better than one would expect. Playful and comfortable in front of the camera, Brown is both lively and natural. Kicks's girlfriend Stephanie is played by the wooden Tanya (*Black Shampoo*) Boyd, who always seems to

appear in films that require her to disrobe, and also worthy of mention are Russ Tamblyn as Ziggy, an oversexed mobster, and Geoffrey (*Nurse Sherri*) Land as Tony, Kicks's doomed sidekick.

Scenes including a brutal gang rape, a man whose legs are run over by a car, a lesbian seduction, and a villain who is gored to death, all seem forced, unnatural and specifically designed to shock. They don't. Director Adamson's other films include *Mean Mother*, *Dynamite Brothers*, *Black Samurai*, *Nurse Sherri* and *Death Dimension*.

BLACK HOOKER

1974, USA
Alternative Titles: *Black Mama*; *Street Sisters*
R (1028), Drama, 90m. Movie Company.
D: Arthur Roberson; P: Joseph Holsen; S: Arthur Roberson, from his stage production.
Cast: Sandra Alexandra, Jeff Burton, Teddy Quinn, Durey Mason.

"What would you do if your mother was a hooker?"

The daughter of an African-American preacher has an illegitimate son who appears to be white. Against overwhelming odds, the boy sets out to build a relationship with his abusive prostitute mother.

An uninteresting, stage-bound and thoroughly unrealistic adaptation of a theatrical production, *Black Hooker* is one of those select few films that misses its mark at every turn. There is a blonde, blue eyed, totally Anglo-featured 'bi-racial' child; an overweight, backwoods, mammy type grandmother who can barely speak proper English; a Baptist minister who looks, acts and orates like a used car salesman; and of course, the title character, a young woman who has abandoned her child, teases her mother and father and, for a full 90 minutes, displays no redeeming qualities whatsoever.

Matching the poor timing, misdirected energy (the improbably named Sandra Alexandra does the best she can with a thankless role) and insultingly bad script, are the over-lit cardboard theatrical sets (one features a 'window' with a painting of the outdoors!) and a succession of disjointed, obviously photographed-after-the-fact close-ups. An appallingly rotten conglomeration of noise and moving images.

"You'll just want it to be over..."
(David Walker, BadAzz MoFo magazine issue #5)

BLACK LOLITA

1974, USA
Alternative Title: *Wildcat Women*
R (1239), Action/Adult, 80m.
Parliament Films Ltd.
D: Stephen Gibson; P: Stephen Gibson; S: Mike Brown, Stephen Gibson.
Cast: Yolanda Love, Susan Ayers, Joey Ginza.

"They obey no rules, only desires!"

A young woman and her two girlfriends combine forces to take action against neighbourhood thugs.

Originally released in 3-D, *Black Lolita* must have been a lot of fun to see in theatres. Unfortunately most of the effects do not carry over very well to the small screen (the DVD has been issued in 3-D – and comes with two pairs of glasses). Not to worry, with or without the glasses, this notably exploitative and shamelessly trashy film is filled with a little bit of everything – and all of it is entertaining.

As Lolita, Yolanda Love is resplendently energetic; a sheer delight to both gaze upon and listen to. Riding around town in her blue Corvette, singing at her piano in a nightclub, or screaming, rather than emoting, her lines, Love's youthful enthusiasm, broad smile and southern drawl are utterly disarming. A good example of how the actress makes the material at hand her own comes during a segment in which she has to distract an overweight mob henchman by delivering a pizza to him! When he refuses, telling her that he is "on the job," she responds with genuinely funny exasperation, "Come on fat boy, eat it before it gets cold!"

The film is often notably awkward in its presentation, as a great many shots (cars, people, fists) are photographed in order to best accommodate the 3-D process, but *Black Lolita*, with its psychedelic colours, funky clothing and game-for-anything, top-heavy, female players is a definite hoot.

The best line in the movie comes from the mouth of our lovely heroine. After foiling her boyfriend (who had intended to murder her) she literally kicks him out of her car and says to herself, "Wait till I tell 'Dear Abby' about this one!"

"'Charlie's Angels' meets 'Shaft' in a wild 3-D flashback!"
(Hollywood Press)

BLACK MAMA, WHITE MAMA

1973, Philippines/USA
R (23494), Action/Adventure, 86m.
American International Pictures.
D: Eddie Romero; P: John Ashley, Eddie Romero; S: H.R. Christian, from an original story by Joseph Viola and Jonathan Demme.
Cast: Pam Grier, Margaret Markov, Sid Haig, Lynn Borden, Eddie Garcia, Vic Diaz.

"Chicks in chains - where they come from this is fun!"

Two female convicts, one black, one white, escape from a Filipino prison and develop a mutual respect for one another.

This hip-titled, lively and well-done women's prison yarn contains all the expected elements, but somehow never really hits its mark.

above: Margaret Markov and Pam Grier in the Women In Prison drama **Black Mama, White Mama** (1973).

In the equal-screen-time leads as two 'desperate and dangerous' prison escapees, Pam Grier (playing prostitute Lee Daniels) and Margaret Markov (as Karen Brent, a revolutionary) both do exactly what they need to do, no more and no less. Lovely to look at, coquettish and clever (at one point they mug a pair of nuns and don their habits!) the filmmakers do little to distance themselves from the tired trick (borrowed from the 1958 Tony Curtis/Sidney Poitier film *The Defiant Ones*) of having key characters shackled together for almost the entire length of the picture. Supporting characters include: Sid Haig as Ruben, a 'greasy cowboy' for hire; Eddie Garcia as Captain Alfredo Cruz, a military man with a conscience; and Vic Diaz as Vic Cheng, a fat-bellied island pimp/drug lord.

A nude shower scene (during which a lesbian guard masturbates while peeping through a hole in the shower room wall), a loud, raucous and very messy cafeteria riot, and a lively wrestling/slapping match that takes place between Lee and Karen as they roll over and over on a hillside, are just minor distractions. Harry Betts's superior ambient music soundtrack (available on CD) is much more sophisticated than the film that it was created for. A hit with audiences, Pam Grier and Margaret Markov were paired again in the following year's *The Arena*. Eddie Romero's other films include *The Twilight People*, *Savage Sisters*, and *Sudden Death*.

"Performances run from bad to mediocre." (Variety)

THE BLACK MOSES OF SOUL

1973, USA
G (23759), Concert, 80m.
Aquarius Releasing.
D: Chuck Johnson; P: Chuck Johnson.

"The superbad music event of a lifetime!"

Singer/musician Isaac Hayes captured in concert at the height of his popularity.

"Superbad" is right! *The Black Moses of Soul* is un-inventively photographed, long on instrumentals and short on vocals, and padded with over-long meandering stories that precede the concert segments.

More disappointing for blaxploitation movie fans than the lack of exciting visuals, creativity and inspiration is the fact that the film does not even include Hayes's signature hit, 'Shaft'. In its place are well-known covers like 'The Look of Love,' 'Light My Fire' and 'I Just Don't Know What to Do with Myself;' songs that were, unfortunately, much better the first time around.

A concert film that is a failure because it does not expand upon or show its star performer to his best advantage, *The Black Moses of Soul* diminishes Isaac Hayes and his many talents, making him appear to be less – much less – than the substantial legend that precedes his arrival on stage.

THE BLACK RIDER

1976, USA
Alternative Title: *Joshua*
R (24765), Western, 84m.
Lone Star Pictures.
D: Larry Spangler; P: Larry Spangler; S: Fred Williamson.
Cast: Fred Williamson, Calvin Bartlett, Brenda Venus, Isela Vega.

A war veteran combs the Midwest in search of the five men who murdered his mother.

As Joshua, a recently-released Union Army officer bent on avenging his mother's murder, Fred Williamson offers nothing more than his trademark laid-back screen persona, which – though effective in some of his other pictures – does not work, and is not enough, here. Gamely attempting to enliven his own plodding, feeble-minded script, director Larry Spangler tries to divert our attention away from the actor by constantly focusing on the expansive and very beautiful Arizona desert. The result is a 'Western' (filmed in the Todd-AO widescreen process) that feels more like a celluloid version of *National Geographic* magazine.

Blissfully unaware of its own inherent dullness, this self-centred, bottom-of-the-barrel spaghetti western is the kind of picture you'd walk out on. Not just bad, but embarrassing. Larry Spangler also directed *The Soul of Nigger Charley*.

"Moves at a turtle's pace... even at just 84 minutes, it seems too long." (David Walker, BadAzz MoFo magazine issue #4)

BLACK RODEO

1972, USA
G (23354), Documentary, 87m.
Cinerama Releasing.
D: Jeff Kanew; P: Jeff Kanew, Don Saffrin.
Cast: Muhammad Ali, Woody Strode, Bud Bramwell, Cleo Hemm.

"Nobody ever told you there were black cowboys."

Filmed in Harlem, New York City and featuring cowboys, cattle rustlers, and the African American community as its stars, this relatively fun-spirited "black

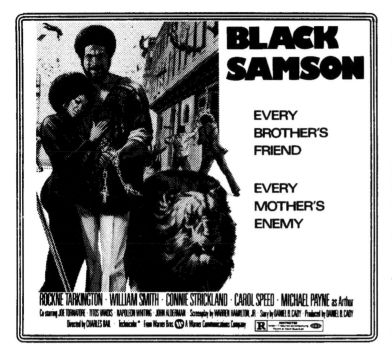

"In the guise of presenting a story of courage against all odds, it is, in truth, an ugly and brutal film, revelling in cruelty and the bloody abuse of women."
(Lawrence Van Gelder, New York Times)

BLACK SAMURAI

1976, USA
Alternative Title: *Black Terminator*
R (24801), Action/Adventure, 84m.
BJLJ International.
D: Al Adamson; P: Barbara Holden; S: B. Readick, based on a novel by Marc Olden.
Cast: Jim Kelly, Roberto Contreras, Marilyn Joi, Essie Lin Chia, Felix Silla, Bill Roy.

"Jim Kelly as the Black Samurai... agent for DRAGON."

When a Chinese minister's daughter is kidnapped, her former lover, an African-American martial arts expert, comes to the rescue.

Even though the fight sequences are cleverly choreographed (by Kelly), at just 84 minutes *Black Samurai* seems way too long. The problem is the one-note, paint-by-numbers script.

Karate expert Kelly's acting has always been a problem for critics. In an interview with the Independent Film Channel, conducted in the year 2000, Fred Williamson admitted, "the guy just couldn't act to save his life!", and as investigator Robert Sand (agent for DRAGON), Kelly is no more or less accomplished than he is in any of his other films. Making the most of Kelly's own view of himself, director Al Adamson delivers the picture's most memorable moment, a silent visual homage in which a shirtless Kelly practices his karate moves in front of a mirror.

This strikingly unreal film also features: Essie Lin Chia as Toki Konuma, Sand's lovely Asian girlfriend; Bill Roy as Janicot, a Fu Manchu-like crime lord; Felix Silla as Rheinhardt, a clever and very deadly midget henchman; and Marilyn (*The Candy Tangerine Man*) Joi as Synne, a beautiful, if overly affected, whip-wielding sadist.

A machine-gun-equipped blue Ferrari, a strap-on jet-propelling backpack, and several attractive locations (Sand's funky mod style house is a winner) do not make up for what feels like a one-more-visit-to-the-well cinema concoction that is tired, stretched and over-familiar.

Woodstock" attempts to shed light on the important role that African Americans played in America's old West.

Commentary by Muhammad (*The Greatest*) Ali and Cleveland Rams football player-turned-actor Woody Strode, as well as 'man on the street' interviews, accompany scenes depicting steer wrestling, roping and bareback bronco riding. A film that came and went without much notice, *Black Rodeo*, whose movie soundtrack boasted tunes by Aretha Franklin, B.B. King, Ray Charles and Little Richard, among others, is one of only a handful of 'lost' blaxploitation entries that, at the time of writing, have not surfaced on tape or DVD.

BLACK SAMSON

1974, USA
R (23877), Action/Adventure, 88m.
Warner Bros.
D: Charles [Chuck] Bail; P: Daniel B. Cady; S: Warren Hamilton Jr., from a story by Daniel B. Cady.
Cast: Rockne Tarkington, William Smith, Connie Strickland, Carol Speed.

"Every brother's friend. Every mother's enemy."

An influential nightclub owner goes into action when the mob tries to set up a drug ring in his neighbourhood.

The tale of one 'righteous' man's battle against the infiltration of mobs into his neighbourhood, *Black Samson* (shot under the title *Black Samson, White Delilah*) is a well-intentioned look at the complicated and very profitable business of selling drugs to disenfranchised inner-city blacks.

Dressed in Dashikis, and always carrying a six-foot staff, Rockne Tarkington is both regal and believable as nightclub owner/neighbourhood watchdog Samson. His nightspot, 'Samson's,' on the other hand, is something else altogether. Along with a bevy of topless go-go dancers and a resident past-his-prime organ player, the club features, as one of its main attractions, a pedestal-bound, real life lion!

On hand as Samson's adversary Johnny Nappa – an Italian mobster who has a penchant for beating up women, attacking subordinates, and using the word 'nigger' – is William (*Blackjack*) Smith; as always Smith turns in a frighteningly real performance. The film also features Carol (*Abby*) Speed – irritatingly overwrought in most of her scenes – as Leslie, Samson's ever-faithful companion, and Connie Strickland as Tina, Johnny Nappa's conflicted sometime-prostitute girlfriend.

A run of the mill film made better by a few good performances (and Rockne Tarkington's kendo skills), *Black Samson* concludes with a triumphant showdown between an entire inner-city community and the mob. Chuck Bail also directed *Cleopatra Jones and the Casino of Gold*.

Note: *Black Samurai* was originally fashioned as a vehicle for Kelly's only other real competitor in the film industry, African-American karate champion Ron (*Black Dragon*) Van Clief.

BLACK SHAMPOO

1976, USA
R (1356), Action/Adventure, 85m.
Dimension Pictures.
D: Greydon Clark; P: Alvin L. Fast;
S: Alvin L. Fast, Greydon Clark.
Cast: John Daniels, Tanya Boyd, Joe Ortiz, Skip E. Lowe, Gary Allen.

"He's bad... he's mean... he's a lovin' machine! When he's mad... he's mean... he's a killing machine!"

When a beauty salon owner's girlfriend is kidnapped by the mob, 'Mr. Jonathan' springs into action.

Now *this* is a blaxploitation film! Super-low-budget, poorly written, terribly acted and filled with ostentatious sex, violence and nudity, *Black Shampoo* is a gleefully crude picture, that though it is distractingly sexist and homophobic, remains irresistibly entertaining.

John Daniels stars as Jonathan Knight, Hollywood's most popular (heterosexual) hairstylist; a man who takes care of his female customers by doing much more than just their hair. He is also a macho fantasy figure who, along with bedding women, beating up adversaries and falling in love with his receptionist, has a genuine affection for his two ostentatiously gay employees. Jonathan's well-meaning receptionist/girlfriend Brenda is played by Tanya (*Black Heat*) Boyd. Obviously comfortable being naked in front of the camera and participating in her many softcore sex scenes, Boyd's extremely flat, monotone line readings keep the entire production (even with its sometimes creative photography and special effects) lewd, low-grade and laughable. On board at Mr. Jonathan's are Artie (Skip E. Lowe), a mincing, overly effeminate gnome-like hairstylist (Lowe played a similar cameo in *Bare Knuckles*), and Richard (Gary Allen), a flittery, soft-voiced, black shampoo boy. Joe Ortiz plays Mr. Wilson, a mob boss who wants Brenda to quit her job and return to his side.

The dialogue, written for hoots and hollers, is fast and quotable: On unbuttoning Mr. Jonathan's pants an

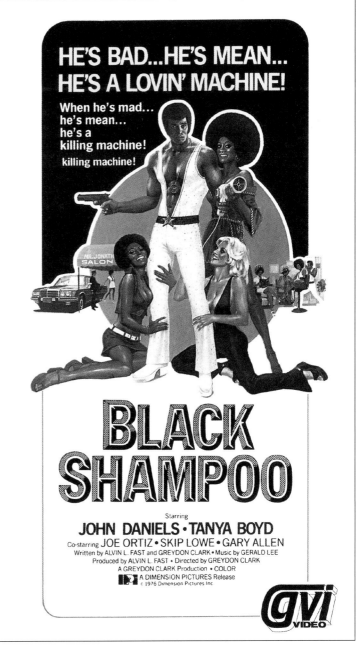

attractive blonde 'customer' shrieks with delight, "Oh my god! Mr. Jonathan it is bigger and better!" When a bosomy receptionist hugs the gay Artie at a party, Artie turns to the camera and says "Oh God! She'll never *drown* – believe me!"

A 'western style' barbecue, a poolside ménage a trois, and a film hero who drives around North Hollywood in a Rolls Royce while sporting a huge afro, pork chop sideburns and a white polyester jumpsuit with matching 'marshmallow' platform shoes, are all part of the fun.

Outrageous, shamelessly derivative and unexpectedly grisly – equal parts *The Godfather*, *Shampoo* and *The Texas Chain Saw Massacre* – the only popular 1970s film that *Black Shampoo* doesn't seem to borrow from is *Jaws*! Cinema trash at its best.

"There is so much gratuitous sex and violence in 'Black Shampoo' there really isn't room for anything else, least of all story."
(Variety)

THE BLACK SIX

1973, USA
R (895), Action/Adventure, 85m.
Cinemation Industries.
D: Matt Cimber; P: Matt Cimber;
S: George Theakos.
Cast: Gene Washington, Carl Eller, Lem
Barney, Mercury Morris, 'Mean' Joe
Greene, Willie Lanier, Rosalind Miles,
Lydia Dean.

"Six times tougher than 'Shaft'! Six times rougher than 'Super Fly'! See the six biggest, baddest and best waste 150 motorcycle dudes!"

A black biker returns home to avenge his younger brother's murder.

The Black Six is an action-adventure vehicle put together to showcase the football icons of the day. On hand are 'Mean' Joe Greene (Pittsburgh Steelers), Willie Lanier (Kansas City Chiefs), Lem Barney (Detroit Lions), Carl Eller (Minnesota Vikings), and Mercury Morris (Miami Dolphins). What could have been a thoroughly charmless exercise in ego gratification (given the super-low-budget and a cast of non-actors) is, instead, a mostly endurable guilty pleasure.

In the lead as Bubba, a member of a wandering black biker gang who has returned to his backwoods hometown intent on finding out the true circumstances surrounding his brother's death, actor Gene Washington gives it his all and is both charismatic and believable. His black biker friends (the black six) are equally entertaining; sometimes unintentionally funny, but totally up for the often-outlandish proceedings at hand. Along with our ever-frolicking heroes the film's characters include Bubba's drug-addicted prostitute girlfriend Ceal (Rosalind Miles), who gives an emotionally charged performance that seems a bit out of place in this good-natured confection), and Sissy (Lydia Dean), Bubba's sassy, militant-minded younger sister.

above: The climactic motorcycle gang war is the highlight of **The Black Six** (1973).

Ostensibly a revenge epic, *The Black Six* takes a look at everything from interracial dating to the plight of returning Vietnam Veterans. The film's philosophy is best summed up by an exchange that Bubba has with an elderly white woman who has hired the Black Six to perform chores on her farm:

Mrs. Perkins: *What about the future? Aren't you thinking about tomorrow?*
Bubba: *There is no tomorrow. Just right now.*

Atrocious line readings, poor production values, sloppy editing and an AWOL main character ('Mean' Joe Greene inexplicably disappears mid-film) don't get in the way of this alternately violent (one character is beaten to death with chains; another is torched), and funny (the gang completely demolishes a roadside shack called 'Flora's Truck and Beer Stop') tale whose closing on-screen coda, "Honky... look out. Hassle a brother and 'The Black Six' will return!" is not so much a threat, but an invitation to another fun-filled bout of entertainment. Matt Cimber also directed *The Candy Tangerine Man* and *Lady Cocoa*. See *Q & A: Ten Directors Discuss Their Films.*

"Gene Washington and his fellow athletes have considerable charm, which comes through despite the arthritic development."
(Nora Sayre, New York Times)

BLACK SNAKE

1973, USA
Alternative Titles: *Sweet Suzy*; *Slaves*; *Blacksnake: The Whip*
R (771), Action/Adventure, 82m.
Signal 166, Inc.
D: Russ Meyer; P: Russ Meyer; S: Russ Meyer, Len Neubauer.
Cast: Anouska Hempel, David Warbeck, Bernard Boston, David Prowse, Thomas Baptiste.

"To some a tropical paradise. To others, a green hell of never ending servitude."

On St. Cristobel Island in the British West Indies, there resides a profitable illegal slave ring that is run by a sadistic female plantation owner.

Wow! This was Russ Meyer's (*Faster, Pussycat! Kill! Kill!*; *Beyond the Valley of the Dolls*) only blaxploitation film. An

expansively photographed period piece (based in 1835), *Black Snake* is lovely to look at but, unfortunately, never much fun.

Doll-like actress Anouska Hempel (who resembles Brigitte Bardot) plays Lady Susan Walker with a tongue-in-cheek pathos that is similar to that of Faye Dunaway in the infamous *Mommie Dearest*. The actress snarls, shrieks ("black and white together? Never!"), swears and is obviously very comfortable being photographed in the nude. Others in the film include: David Warbeck as Charles Walker, a handsome young Brit who has travelled to St. Cristobel in search of his long-missing brother; Thomas Baptiste as Isiah, a haughty black homosexual slave organizer; and Bernard Boston as Capt. Raymond Daladier, a bigoted and ineffectual competitor for Lady Susan's affections.

It's all here; crucifixions, spread-eagle bloody whippings, castrations, executions, rapes, hangings, a severed leg, and even a shark attack! Even so, an unseemly air (particularly the use of obviously untrained local islanders as actors in scenes of degradation) is a bit discomforting.

Black Snake (a reference to the slave master's whip) is an unintentionally disturbing and distractingly uneven attempt to combine comedy, horror, sensationalism and melodrama. A queasy mix that, though spirited, just doesn't come off.

"There is a good reason that director Russ Meyer waited so long to release this film on video – it's one huge mess."
(Mike Accomando, Baad Mutha@*!#ers)

BLACK STARLET

1974, USA
Alternative Title: *Black Gauntlet*
R (1223), Drama, 85m. Omni Pictures.
D: Chris Munger; P: Daniel B. Cady;
S: Howard Ostroff.
Cast: Juanita Brown, Rockne Tarkington,
Eric Mason, Diane Holden, Al Lewis.

"They set a high price for stardom...was it worth it?"

A young woman travels from Gary, Indiana to Hollywood, in search of fame and fortune.

A young woman travels from Gary, Indiana to Hollywood, in search of fame and fortune. The often-told tale of the film capital's seedy underbelly, *Black Starlet* is a highly predictable low-budget melodrama, told in flashback, and filled with worn dialogue ("I think you're going to find it very lonely at the top") that, ultimately, does not deliver the goods.

Juanita (*Foxy Brown*) Brown is Carla/Clara, an "extremely talented actress" looking-for-someone's coat-tails-to-ride-on. Brisco (Eric Mason) is Carla's resigned agent, and Rockne (*Black Samson*) Tarkington is Ben, Carla's well-meaning business manager. A delightful turn in casting comes in the form of Al Lewis (Grandpa Munster on TV's *The Munsters*) as Sam Sharp, a highly ethnic Jewish dry-cleaning store-owner. Both comical and compassionate, Lewis's character understands Carla's frustrations and, when she gets angry and calls him a "honky ass," does not fire her but, instead, turns to one of her co-workers and asks, "what's wrong with her?"

Along with the usual assortment of perverts, con-men and pretentious Hollywood wannabes, there are two bar scenes that feature topless dancers, a degrading multiple-partner 'consensual' sex scene, a Hollywood wrap party (for a porno film), and a mad shopping spree in which Carla purchases clothes, a car and a house!

Not very good, but still strangely compelling, this stale, sordid, rags-to-Hollywood-riches tale is at least vastly superior to blaxploitation's other like themed, but patently unbearable *Miss Melody Jones*.

BLACK TRASH

1976, South Africa/UK/USA
Alternative Titles: *Soul Patrol*; *Death of a Snowman*
NR (R), Action/Adventure, 87m.
Madison World Films.
D: Chris Rowley; P: Martin Wragge;
S: Bima Stagg.
Cast: Ken Gampu, Nigel Davenport, Peter Dyneley, Bima Stagg, Joe Lopes.

"From the USA to South Africa."

When a string of known drug dealers are murdered in London, a newspaper reporter and policeman join forces to discover who is behind the killings.

Black Trash's main calling card is its rare look at England's (and South Africa's) 1970s black youth culture.

Ken Gampu plays Steve Chaka, a black 'crusading crime reporter' on the hunt for an organised gang of killers responsible for a series of inner-city murders. Not one of filmdom's most attractive players, Gampu is neverthe-less convincing in the role of a concerned citizen trying to solve a case. His friend and helpmate is Ben (Nigel Davenport), a police detective with the will, means and know-how needed to uncover the truth. Supporting roles include a by-the-books white cop played by Peter Dyneley, and a looking-for-love-in-all-the-wrong-places mob assassin, Chops (Joe Lopes).

An exciting opening scene – in which two flamboyant characters the viewer assumes are to be the stars of the film are violently murdered – is followed by an equally violent, messy and disjointed story whose disparate elements include a troubled father-son relationship, a 'War on Crime' vigilante group, and a cursory examination of the British underworld's connection with American mobster 'Crazy' Joe Gallo (who is the subject of his own blaxploitation entry, *Crazy Joe*).

Black Trash's vintage tour of Britain's airports, trendy nightclubs, hip houses and modern-furnished apart-ments, coupled with the spectacle of watching a cast of what looks like young African Americans speak with strong British accents, make this under-whelming feature a somewhat enjoyable novelty.

BLACKENSTEIN

1973, USA
Alternative Title: *Black Frankenstein*
R (1094), Horror, 83m.
Prestige Pictures Releasing Corp.
D: William A. Levey; P: Frank R. Saletri; S: Frank R. Saletri.
Cast: John Hart, Ivory Stone, Joe De Sue, Roosevelt Jackson.

"No bullet can kill him... no chains can hold him... it walks the night... the king of monsters!"

A Nobel Prize-winning doctor attaches arms and legs to an African American whose body was destroyed in the Vietnam War.

This black version of the horror classic *Frankenstein* is not only inexcusably dull but also – surprisingly, given its rather fun title – humourless.

As Dr. Stein, a reclusive medical genius who is conducting experiments in his basement laboratory, actor John Hart is less than engaging, but at least he's better than everyone else in the cast. His star-struck young assistant, Dr. Winifred Walker – a recent PhD graduate looking for an interesting project to fill her time – is played by Ivory Stone who, though attractive, is neither likeable nor convincing. In the role of damaged returning Vietnam Veteran Eddie Turner (it just so happens that he has been shipped home missing both his arms and both his legs, making him a perfect candidate for Dr. Stein's 'replacement limbs' experiment) Joe De Sue is large (we are told 15 feet), amiable and at times intimidating. Stirring things up is a competitor for Winifred's affections, houseman Malcolm (Roosevelt Jackson).

Tiresome, dim-witted, unsure of what it wants to be (there is a scene in a nightclub where we witness a comedian and a blues singer perform their entire routines), *Blackenstein* fails miserably even as kitsch. A missed opportunity.

Note: In his book *Blaxploitation Films*, author Mikel J. Koven points out a nagging problem with the film's title. In the original book *Frankenstein*, by Mary Shelley, the mad doctor who creates the monster names the beast Frankenstein after himself (using his surname). But the mad doctor in *Blackenstein* is neither black nor named Blackenstein.

"There is a certain degree of crap tolerance that one needs when exploring blaxploitation films, but this one challenges even that level."
(Mikel J. Koven, Blaxploitation Films, 2001)

BLACKJACK

1978, USA
R (25342), Comedy/Adventure, 104m.
Blackjack Film Company.
D: John Evans; P: John Evans; S: John Evans.
Cast: Bill [William] Smith, Damu King, Tony Burton, Diane Sommerfield, Ted Harris.

"They came with a mission and nothing could stop them!"

A team of recently-released convicts stage a series of intricately choreographed Las Vegas casino robberies.

Talky, over-long and unfocused, *Blackjack* is a tired, patently derivative bank caper from writer/producer/director John (*Speeding Up Time*) Evans.

William (*Black Samson*) Smith is utterly convincing in the lead role of Andy Mayfield, a corrupt Italian American casino supervisor with ties to the mob. Filled with a palatable frustration and determined to do things 'the right way,' the large mean-looking actor proves to be a skilled, emotionally involved performer. Tony Burton plays Charles, the head of a group of Las Vegas would-be robbers. Diane (*Black Godfather*) Sommerfield plays Charles's romantic interest, Nancy, the lovely nightclub singer wife of his former prison mate. Featured in a notable supporting role is Ted Harris (who made a striking impression as an ostentatiously gay interior decorator in *Blacula*) as Akbar, a clever yet slightly kooky robbery team member.

More interesting than the murders by shotgun, scalding and beatings, and the film's acidic dialogue ("Since you stopped sleeping with the rats and cockroaches in the ghetto you've forgotten who you are, nigger!") are the vintage Las Vegas, Nevada locations.

Note: Director Evans's *Blackjack* (1978) is sometimes confused with another *Black Jack* (1972), a film (originally titled *Wild in the Sky*), written and directed by William T. Naud.

BLACULA

1972, USA
PG (23355), Horror, 93m.
American International Pictures.
D: William Crain; P: Joseph T. Naar; S: Raymond Koenig, Joan Torres.
Cast: William Marshall, Denise Nicholas, Vonetta McGee, Thalmus Rasulala, Ketty Lester, Elisha Cook Jr.

"Rising from the echoing corridors of hell an awesome being of the supernatural - with satanic power of sheer dread. Chained forever to a slavery more vile than any before endured!"

In 1780, an African Prince on a trip abroad is bitten by Count Dracula and placed in a coffin. 200 years later the coffin is opened in Los Angeles and havoc ensues.

'Blacula' (his actual character name is Mamuwalde) is played by William Marshall, who is, as always, refined, grand and erudite. Taking his part very seriously (except when he orders a 'Bloody Mary' at a bar!), and looking genuinely scary in his transformation makeup, Marshall is perfect as the all-knowing vampire. As his lost love Luva (reincarnated in modern-day Los Angeles as a young woman named Tina), Vonetta McGee is wide-eyed, game and magnificent to behold.

Exhibiting a heightened level of emotion and commitment to her sketchily written role is Denise (*Let's Do It Again*) Nicholas, who plays Michelle, Luva's confused sister. Nicholas's visual display of emotion is so visceral that it throws several light-hearted scenes off. Also appearing in the cast are: Thalmus (*Cool Breeze*) Rasulala as Dr. Gordon Thomas, an inquiring detective; Ketty Lester as Juanita Jones, a cab driver-turned vampire-turned rising corpse; and, in a fun cameo, horror film veteran Elisha (*House on Haunted Hill*) Cook Jr. as Sam, the local hospital morgue keeper.

Man-to-bat transformations, deaths by exposure to sunlight, and several stake-through-the-heart ritualistic sacrifices are all part of the madness at hand. Along with dialogue that is specifically written for hoots and hollers (at one point an incidental character turns to the camera and declares [referring to Blacula] "That is the rudest nigger I have ever seen!"), this box-office bonanza includes not one, but two, halt-the-narrative musical

performances by the then-popular group The Hues Corporation (best known for their No.1 hit 'Rock the Boat').

Note: The animated Sandy Dvore opening credit sequence and the Gene Page soundtrack album are worth the rental price alone. African-American director William Crain also directed *Dr. Black, Mr. Hyde.*

"...heroes vs vampires with soul music and a couple of good gags."
(Leonard Maltin, Movie & Video Guide, 1999)

BLAZING SADDLES

1974, USA
R (23752), Comedy, 93m. Warner Bros.
D: Mel Brooks; P: Michael Hertzberg; S: Mel Brooks.
Cast: Cleavon Little, Gene Wilder, Madeline Kahn, Harvey Korman, Slim Pickens.

"Blazing Saddles... or never give a saga an even break!"

An African-American sheriff, residing over a backwoods white town, succeeds against all odds.

This vastly overrated, only occasionally amusing bad-taste spoof of Westerns and American movie clichés, prides itself on sparing no one from its critical barbs. Jews, blacks, whites, Germans, Chinese, gays, politicians, the rich, the poor and American society at large are all poked fun at. Too bad it's not really all that funny.

In the lead as Bart, a railroad man turned Sheriff, Cleavon Little gives a sly and understated performance that seems a bit removed from the general slapstick atmosphere at hand (it is, in fact, difficult to enjoy Little's performance when one knows that he was a replacement for Richard Pryor). Gene Wilder as Jim 'The Waco Kid' – a man who briefly enjoyed notoriety as the West's fastest gun shooter – contributes a reserved performance that serves the narrative well.

Eclipsing the two leads are Harvey Korman – who at the time was a regular on TV's *Carol Burnett Show* as Hedley Lamarr, an opportunist and perpetually horny (he molests a statue) Mayoral assistant – and Slim (*Poor Pretty Eddie*) Pickens as Taggart, the bumbling but good-natured spokesperson for the 'plain folk' inhabited town of Rock Ridge. Another noteworthy performance comes from Madeline Kahn as Lili Von Shtupp, a German chanteuse (modelled on Marlene Dietrich) who does a nightclub performance of a song called 'I'm So Tired' (Kahn received a best supporting actress Oscar nomination the following year).

Along with a large number of sight gags and a bit of fast-action photography, there is a chain gang performance of 'I Get a Kick Out of You', a visit to Grauman's Chinese Theater on Sunset Boulevard in Hollywood, and an admittedly exciting finale involving a marauding gang of Rock Ridge residents who literally crash onto a movie set where a bevy of (ostentatiously gay) male dancers are in the midst of performing a complicated top-hat-and-tails song and dance production number – "Throw out your hands/Stick out your tush/Hands on your hips...!"

Not quite the 'hilariously funny' film that many critics continue to proclaim it to be – some have even called it one of the top ten funniest American movies ever made – *Blazing Saddles* is, instead, a sometimes fun, extremely visual collection of comedy vignettes.

"Essentially a series of TV skits and routines, 'Blazing Saddles' is embarrassingly uneven."
(Donald Bogle, Blacks in American Films and Television, 1988)

BLIND RAGE

1978, Philippines
R (25189), Action/Adventure, 81m.
Trans World Films.
D: Efren C. Pinon; P: Leonardo Velasco Uy, Leoncio Imperial; S: Jerry O. Tirazona, Leo Fong.
Cast: Fred Williamson, D'Urville Martin, Leo Fong, Tony Ferrer, Dick Adair, Darnell Garcia, Charlie Davao.

"Revenge made them hate the man... but money was the excuse to blast him."

top: William Marshall puts the bite on a nightgown-clad young victim in **Blacula** (1972).
above: Veteran horror film actor Elisha Cook Jr. is the recipient of a rather intense "soul kiss" in **Blacula**.

A gang of blind men steal $15,000,000 from a bank vault in Manila.

A virtual travel guide of 1970s Mexico, Las Vegas, Hong Kong, Tokyo and Manila, *Blind Rage* is a thoroughly entertaining film filled with good music, well-done karate fights and an intriguing, briskly-paced script.

An ensemble piece, the film's cast includes Willie Black (D'Urville Martin); Lin Wang (Leo Fong); and Ben Guevara (Tony Ferrer), three film characters who double-crossed the mob and had to pay for it with their eyesight. The unusual robbery team also includes Amazing Anderson (Dick Adair), a born-blind travelling magician, and Hector Lopez (Darnell Garcia), a matador who lost his sight in a bullfight. Fred Williamson features in a late-arriving, over-promoted cameo as Private Investigator Jesse Crowder.

Flashbacks (which show how each of the main characters lost their sight), a realistic-looking 747 explosion, and a meticulously choreographed robbery/rehearsal segment make up for tired one-liners like, "Luck ain't got nothin' to do with it," and "Let's stop the talk and get down to business." Clever and unexpectedly satisfying.

BLUE COLLAR

1978, USA
R (25126), Drama, 114m.
Universal Pictures.
D: Paul Schrader; P: Don Guest; S: Paul and Leonard Schrader.

Cast: Richard Pryor, Harvey Keitel, Yaphet Kotto, Ed Begley Jr.

In an attempt to right past injustices, three auto workers rob their employer, only to discover that they can do little to change the established order.

Downbeat film filled with great performances, realistic dialogue and believable situations. Paul Schrader (in his directorial debut) turns in a compelling picture that seems more like investigative reporting than Hollywood entertainment.

Richard Pryor as Zeke Brown, a struggling African-American assembly line worker, is simply wonderful. The actor/comedian seems at one with a film character whose backstory so closely parallels his own life. (The most noteworthy of these segments depicts Zeke lost in the relish of snorting cocaine from the top of a friend's coffee table – a segment that foreshadows the infamous true incident in which Pryor managed to set himself on fire while taking crack-cocaine.)

Yaphet (*Bone*) Kotto as Smokey James, a sensible-minded plant worker, is also outstanding, conveying both his character's outsize ambition and self-pity. Always dependable Harvey (*Fingers*) Keitel plays Jerry Bartowski, a Polish American plant worker who is trying his best to raise the living conditions of his working class family. (The on-screen chemistry displayed between the three principals is dynamic.)

One of *Blue Collar's* most emotionally charged scenes comes when Zeke (Richard Pryor) addresses a union meeting:

Zeke (to official): *Plant my ass! That's all you talk about, is the needs of the plant. Everyone who works here knows that 'plant' is just short for 'plantation!'*

A serious, politically-minded look at corruption in America's unions, *Blue Collar*, short on flash and heavy with a message, was a bit too steeped in working-life reality to be a hit with its target audience.

"The picture... is graced with a beautiful performance by Kotto... and an unusual one by Pryor."
(Pauline Kael, The New Yorker)

BONE

1972, USA
Alternative Titles: *Housewife*; *Beverly Hills Nightmare*; *Dial Rat for Terror*
R (589), Comedy/Drama, 95m.
Jack H. Harris Enterprises.
D: Larry Cohen; P: Larry Cohen; S: Larry Cohen.
Cast: Yaphet Kotto, Jeannie Berlin, Joyce Van Patten, Andrew Duggan.

"Love Bone... before he loves you."

An unstable African-American criminal invades a Beverly Hills home.

Shrill, teary and overwrought, *Bone* is a black comedy that critics loved but audiences just didn't quite get.

Yaphet Kotto embodies America's longstanding fears of the big black brute in the role of Bone, a criminal bent on robbing and then raping any female in "the biggest house on the block". Playing Bernadette, a self-centred alcoholic housewife, Joyce Van Patten intelligently taps into her character's frustrations and neuroses. Also in the cast are Andrew Duggan as Bill, a semi-famous used car salesman, and Jeannie Berlin as The Girl, a young woman in need of love, affection and a bit of psychotherapy.

Intelligent but tiresome, *Bone* takes a look at everything from child molestation to the public's inclination to become financially over-extended. Flashbacks and fantasy segments are more disorienting than informative. Larry Cohen also directed *Black Caesar* and *Hell Up in Harlem*. See *Q & A: Ten Directors Discuss Their Films*.

above: **Bone** (1972) was re-titled **Housewife** and marketed to the predominantly white Drive-In market.

BOOK OF NUMBERS

1973, USA
R (23572), Action/Adventure, 81m.
Avco Embassy Pictures.
D: Raymond St. Jacques; P: Raymond St. Jacques; S: Larry Spiegel from a novel by Robert Deane Pharr.
Cast: Raymond St. Jacques, Philip [Michael] Thomas, Freda Payne, D'Urville Martin, Gilbert Greene.

"The black king of the numbers game. Blue Boy's got the man's number... and takes it at 600 to 1."

In depression era Arkansas, two competing black numbers racketeers discover that in order to deal with the mob, they must unite.

This story of an older man, his younger protégé and their misadventures has, it seems, been told one too many times.

In the lead as the older, wiser waiter turned illegal numbers king Blueboy Harris, Raymond St. Jacques (who also produced and directed the film) is the regal embodiment of an erudite, well-spoken black man who, nevertheless, can only find decent paying work by operating outside of the law. His eager-to-learn friend and partner in crime is Dave Green (Philip Michael Thomas), an ambitious young upstart who is ready to take over the reins. Rounding things out of course is a pretty young girl, Kelly Simms (played by Freda Payne – best known for her Top Ten radio hit 'Band of Gold'), along with a kooky numbers runner named Billy Bowlegs (D'Urville Martin) and Luis Antoine, an envious white crime lord (Gilbert Greene.)

Over-praised at the time of its release (perhaps because it is so ostentatiously set in the 1920s), *Book of Numbers* is an uneven collection of not very exciting scenes and situations.

"Its spirit comes from its music – rather than from the requirements of plotting."
(Roger Greenspun, New York Times)

BOSS NIGGER

1974, USA
Alternative Titles: *The Black Bounty Killer*
PG (1211), Action/Adventure, 92m.
Dimension Pictures.
D: Jack Arnold; P: Jack Arnold, Fred Williamson; S: Fred Williamson.
Cast: Fred Williamson, D'Urville Martin, William Smith, Carmen Hayworth, R.G. Armstrong.

"White man's town... black man's law!"

In the 1870s, two black bounty hunters become involved in small town politics.

Clever and peppered with interesting characters, *Boss Nigger* is better than average – an alternately fun and solemn look at African Americans in the Old West.

As Boss Nigger a bounty hunter turned sheriff in the sleepy town of San Miguel, California, Fred Williamson does what he does best – project an easy going, amiable, and patently comfortable-with-himself demeanour that puts everyone else in the film, friends and foes alike, at ease. His sidekick is Amos (D'Urville Martin), a jovial, fun-spirited man who, though it's not expected of him, always manages to come through at the last minute. Also impressive are William Smith as Jed Clayton, the head of a gang of racist backwoods town folk, and Carmen Hayworth as Clara Mae, Boss's lady friend.

Filled with a little bit of everything – comedy, romance, betrayal, subjugation and murder – critics loved *Boss Nigger* but audiences were not very interested, perhaps because by this point Fred Williamson had starred in three like-titled and like-themed films: *The Legend of Nigger Charley*, *The Soul of Nigger Charley*, and now, *Boss Nigger*.

"'Boss Nigger' is proof of the enduring strength of the western movie. It's a passel of clichés, but that's exactly what makes it tolerable."
(Jerry Oster, N.Y. Daily News)

BROTHER JOHN

1971, USA
GP (22661), Drama, 95m.
Columbia Pictures.
D: James Goldstone; P: Joel Glickman; S: Ernest Kinoy.
Cast: Sidney Poitier, Will Geer, Beverly Todd, Paul Winfield, Lincoln Kilpatrick, Zara Cully, Bradford Dillman.

A well-travelled and mysterious young man returns home just prior to the death of each of his family members.

Filled with a bevy of good character actors doing their best with extremely vague and often cryptic material, this well-intentioned, inspirational tale came and went without much notice.

Sidney Poitier projects a mystery and self-confidence that serve his character well in the lead role. Is John Kane – a man who, at sixteen, left the impoverished small town of Hackley, Alabama to discover both himself and the world – the Messiah?

Doc Thomas (Will Geer, best known as Grandpa Walton on TV's *The Waltons*) is also very good as the open-minded smalltown doctor who brought Kane into the world and somehow seems to know more about him than anyone else. Also strong in the cast is Beverly Todd as Louisa MacGill, a schoolteacher who has, throughout the years, longed for Kane to return. Beautiful, sensitive, effectively evoking the desire to rise above meagre beginnings, Todd's performance, though small, is a stunner. Of note in cameos are a very young Paul (*Gordon's War*) Winfield, Lincoln (*Together Brothers*) Kilpatrick, and Zara (*Sugar Hill*) Cully.

Filmed in soft shades of light brown, orange and beige and scored by Quincy Jones, *Brother John* is a film that, along with its pointed presentation of man's inhumanity to man, examines Southern racism, union strikes and spirituality. One of blaxploitation's gentler, more disciplined entries.

"Poitier is trapped in a role that encourages a lot of inscrutable, self-righteous pose-striking."
(Gary Arnold, Washington Post)

BROTHER ON THE RUN

1973, USA
Alternative Titles: *Man on the Run*; *Soul Brothers Die Hard*; *"Boots" Turner*
R (773), Action/Adventure, 90m.
Southern Star.
D: Herbert L. Strock; P: Fred Williams; S: Herbert L. Strock.
Cast: Terry Carter, Gwenn Mitchell, Kyle Johnson, James B. Sikking.

"When he stops running... watch out!"

A college professor steps in to help find his former girlfriend's runaway teenage son.

This low-budget crime melodrama attempts to make a social commentary on contemporary race relations in Los Angeles, while at the same time remaining 'hip', 'happening' and realistic.

Surprisingly realistic (given the film's sensational title and poster art), *Brotherhood of Death* is a genuinely suspenseful revenge drama whose cast of characters include: a fair-minded local bar owner named Ace (Michael Hodge); a Ku Klux Klan Grand Dragon named Harold Turner (Rick Ellis); and a tough-talking, pro-action Vietnam War officer named Captain Quinn (Mike Bass).

The idea of returning Vietnam Vets using their army tactics to fight inner city injustices was a popular blaxploitation theme (*Gordon's War*, *The Black Six*) and *Brotherhood of Death*, too, contained many moments that accurately reflected the militant mood of the day:

> Junior (to Klan member): *Do you actually believe that you can put on 'evil spirit' costumes and call yourselves 'dragons', and burn crosses, and **all** the 'darkies' will shake in their shoes? Well **these** darkies are about to do you in!*

A sobering reminder of the way things used to be comes with the film's use of a vintage, real-life, roadside billboard that reads: "Join and support the United Klan of America, Inc. The KKK welcomes you to Smithfield, Alabama." A church burning, a clandestine plan by neighbourhood domestics, a rousing get-out-and-vote church sermon, and a Vietnam training session (in which we are introduced to the many different ways men are captured and/or killed by the enemy) combine to keep viewers interested.

The great movie theme song 'High Horse' is performed by Revelation.

As 'Boots' Turner, a college professor who comes to the aid of an old girlfriend, Terry (*Abby*) Carter is a triple threat: well-spoken; striking to look at; and emotionally committed to character. Gwenn Mitchell is equally credible as Maude, his 'good pay and short hours' ex-girlfriend, a prostitute who is trying to change her life. Both actors deliver performances that seem leaps and bounds above the slim material at hand. Surprisingly miscast is the 'Brother on the Run' himself, Billy Cooper (Kyle Johnson), an 18-year-old kid who took part in a bungled "Hi-Fi Store" hold up. Shrill, distant, obviously untrained, his forced anguish and squeezed out 'tears'

contain all the strong points found in a middle school theatrical production.

Clever dialogue-less segments involving driving, running, chasing, fighting and secretly observing others, as well as a few sexy bedroom scenes, serve the production well. There's also humour:

> Boots (to Maude): *Brother John is a pagan.*
> Maude: *You mean he's a fag?!*

The animated opening and closing credits, and the fantastic soundtrack by Johnny Pate, fill in nicely. Hard to find, but worth a look.

BROTHERHOOD OF DEATH

1976, USA
NR (R), Action/Adventure, 77m.
Downtown Distribution.
D: Bill Berry; P: Richard Barker, Bill Berry; S: Bill Berry from a story by Ronald K. Goldman.
Cast: Roy Jefferson, Le Tari, Haskell V. Anderson III, Mike Bass, Michael Hodge, Rick Ellis.

"Vietnam was a picnic compared to the war they were about to fight!"

When an African-American woman is raped by two members of the Ku Klux Klan, a group of recently returned Vietnam Veterans take action.

above: **Brother on the Run** (1973) was also distributed as **Soul Brothers Die Hard.**

"...an ambitious film that tries to have more of a message than the 'let's kill whitey' films of the era..."
(David Walker, BadAzz MoFo magazine issue #6)

BROTHERS

1977, USA
R (24780), Action/Adventure, 104m.
Warner Bros.
D: Arthur Barron; P: Edward & Mildred Lewis; S: Edward & Mildred Lewis.
Cast: Bernie Casey, Vonetta McGee, Ron O'Neal, Renny Roker.

"He was a nobody; a black man in a white man's prison. She was a somebody; a notorious, beautiful, radical black professor. Their love story shocked the nation. This film is that story."

The story of the unconsummated romance between an African-American political activist and an incarcerated black militant.

Gritty, well done, and loosely based on the real life relationship between teacher/activist Angela Davis and convicted felon George Jackson, *Brothers* is a film that has all the blaxploitation elements in place, but still, perhaps because it came out after the genre's sell-by date, could not entice audiences into theatres.

In the George Jackson role (here named David Thomas), Bernie (*Hit Man*) Casey does a very good job of conveying the unbearable helplessness that one feels when incarcerated. Charged as an accessory to an armed robbery – and sentenced to "one year to life" – Casey's frustration and ongoing disgust with the way African Americans are treated behind bars, is palpable. As the Angela Davis character (here named Paula Jones) Vonetta (*Thomasine & Bushrod*) McGee, a college professor and civil rights champion, captures both the passion and dedication of a woman who is not only in love, but also determined to change the discriminatory policies at her boyfriend's jail.

A surprise, in a small role, is Ron (*Super Fly*) O'Neal as Walter Nance, George's politically-minded cellmate. Strikingly real (*Newsweek* called his "...the most memorable performance in the film..."), O'Neal reminds the viewer that he is an accomplished actor, not just a time-capsule film personality. The film also features Renny (*Deliver Us from Evil*) Roker as Lewis, a tough-as-nails inmate.

The requisite prison indignities are all chronicled here – strip searches, segregated areas, rape – but what one remembers most when the film is finished is the sad, crushing chronicle of two people who never seem to have had a chance to change their particular circumstances.

Note: John (*Black Shampoo*) Daniels turned down the lead role of David Thomas.

"With all of its good ingredients, it's a shame that a quality effort like this... still falls back on 'Get Whitey' as its only lasting message."
(Variety)

BRUBAKER

1980, USA
R (25372), Drama, 130m.
20th Century Fox.
D: Stuart Rosenberg; P: Ron Silverman, Ted Mann; S: Arthur A. Ross, W.D. Richter.
Cast: Robert Redford, Yaphet Kotto, Jane Alexander, Linda Haynes, Morgan Freeman.

"The new inmate in Wakefield prison is the warden."

A newly assigned prison warden goes undercover to expose the corruption and inhumanity that exists in a notorious Arkansas prison.

In the lead as Henry Brubaker, a Governor-assigned warden chosen to expose corruption in an Arkansas penal institution, Robert Redford does an admirable job of submerging his romantic leading man persona and blending into a crowd of ordinary-looking inmates, most of whom are African Americans. Though one wishes his hair was a little less perfect (and a little less highlighted) Redford convincingly plays against his good looks and, instead, puts forward an emotionally charged, intelligent performance. His behind-bars adversary is Richard 'Dickie' Coombes (Yaphet Kotto), a hostile prison trustee who, after a lengthy period of adjustment, comes to believe in and respect Brubaker's desire to affect positive change. Also noteworthy in the cast are: Jane Alexander as Lillian, Brubaker's reporter friend; Linda Haynes

as a desperate sex industry worker named Carol (Haynes also played a prostitute in *Coffy*); and, almost unrecognisable in a bit part, Morgan Freeman as Walter, a deadly and delusional inmate.

Beautifully photographed (in mostly blues and greys), atmospheric (it always seems to be raining), and realistically presenting the unpleasant details of prison life (rape; worm-infested food; routine beatings; slave labour), *Brubaker* is a fully realised film project – a critical examination of the complicated politics and inner workings of the American penal system.

Note: The picture's original director, Bob Rafelson (*Five Easy Pieces*), was replaced by Stuart Rosenberg.

BUCK AND THE PREACHER

1972, USA
PG (23023), Western, 103m.
Columbia Pictures.
D: Sidney Poitier; P: Joel Glickman; S: Ernest Kinoy from a story by Drake Walker.
Cast: Sidney Poitier, Harry Belafonte, Ruby Dee, Cameron Mitchell.

"The fight was against the raiders... but the feud was between themselves!"

An African-American wagon-master helps a band of recently freed slaves establish themselves independently.

Sidney Poitier (in his directorial debut) is Buck, a black wagon-master who is helping a recently freed group of slaves set up new lives for themselves.

Laidback, stoic, at times austere, Poitier's film characterisation (like so many of his others) is the type fashioned to inspire and uplift. As his charlatan preacher friend Reverend Willard Oakes Rutherford, Harry Belafonte adds an uncontained energy and fun-spiritedness that would be lacking otherwise. Also on hand are Ruby Dee as Ruth, Buck's always dependable woman friend, and Cameron Mitchell as Deshay, a white bounty hunter hired to return the freed slaves to their former owners.

Longer than it needs to be, but nonetheless compelling, filled with positive role models and good intentions, and dedicated, "...to those whose graves are as unmarked as their place in history," *Buck and the Preacher* is both entertaining and enlightening. Poitier also directed *A Warm December*, *Uptown Saturday Night*, *Let's Do It Again*, *A Piece of the Action* and *Stir Crazy*.

"...amiable western with a firm though not especially severe black conscience."
(Vincent Canby, New York Times)

BUCKTOWN

1975, USA
R (24329), Action/Adventure, 94m.
American International Pictures.
D: Arthur Marks; P: Bernard Schwartz; S: Bob Ellison.
Cast: Fred Williamson, Pam Grier, Thalmus Rasulala, Tony King, Bernie Hamilton, Carl Weathers.

"Whatever you want they've got... and Bucktown is where you'll find it!"

When a Northerner opens a bar in a small corrupt Southern town, he is met with resistance from both the townspeople and the local police.

Upscale, and featuring blaxploitation's most profitable and photogenic stars (Pam Grier and Fred Williamson), many believed *Bucktown* would take the black action genre to a new level; it did – a lower one!

As Duke Johnson, a Northerner who has inherited his dead brother's saloon, Fred Williamson provides everything he was hired for – good looks, brawn, and a name known to fans of the genre. Pam Grier, too, offers her highly marketable name, but the actress seems absent from the proceedings at hand. Flat-voiced, blank-faced and totally unconnected to the lines she is reading, the fact that she is, additionally, overdressed, over made-up and affecting a southern accent, makes things worse. Overshadowing everyone is Thalmus (*Cool Breeze*) Rasulala as Roy, a local syndicate leader. Other performers include: Tony King as T.J., a cocky strong-arm man; Bernie Hamilton as Harley, the big-hearted (and big bellied) town drunk; and Oakland Raiders football star-turned-actor Carl Weathers (*Rocky*'s Apollo Creed) as 'Hambone.'

Filmed in Platte City and Kansas City, Missouri, *Bucktown* ends with a prolonged knock-down-drag-out fight in which, "the winner takes all and the looser gets out of town." The soundtrack is by Soul favourite Johnny Pate. Arthur Marks's other films include *Detroit 9000*, *Friday Foster*, *J.D.'s Revenge* and *Monkey Hustle*. See *Q & A: Ten Directors Discuss Their Films*.

"Not only does the film demonstrate how low Hollywood will stoop to make a buck, but it luridly displays the capitalist system in its seeming death-throes."
(Todd McCarthy, Hollywood Reporter)

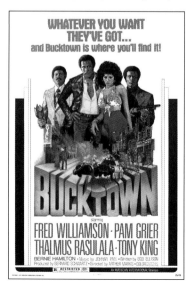

THE BUS IS COMING

1971, USA
GP (409), Action/Drama, 102m.
William Thompson Productions.
D: Wendell J. Franklin; P: Horace Jackson; S: Horace Jackson.
Cast: Mike Sims, Stephanie Faulkner, Burl Bullock, Tony Sweeting, Sandra Reed, Jack Stillman.

"The 'Man' can't stop it... don't miss it!"

A returning Vietnam Veteran works to uncover the truth about his political activist brother's death.

Well-intentioned but terribly slow moving and uneventful, *The Bus Is Coming* features a cast that is being 'introduced' to audiences, and the introduction is not a memorable one.

In the lead as returning Vietnam Vet Billy Mitchell, Mike Sims is the most competent performer in the cast. The breathtakingly incompetent supporting players include: Billy's girlfriend Tanya (Stephanie Faulkner); Billy's fair-minded white Vietnam buddy John (Jack Stillman – also known as Jack Wrangler, under which name he worked as a porn actor); Billy's militant minded friend Michael (Burl Bullock); and Miss Nickerson (Sandra Reed), an African-American schoolteacher who is a major participant in a cover-up.

Behind the times (Quentin Tarantino told the Independent Film Channel that when he saw the film at the time of its release the audience heckled and derided everything on screen), *The Bus Is Coming* is a terribly tiresome blaxploitation-movie-with-a-message whose on-screen coda: "But they that wait upon the lord shall renew their strength..." does not redeem its inexcusable dullness. Director Wendell Franklin and producer/writer Horace Jackson are both African American.

BUSH MAMA

1977, USA
NR, Drama, 97m.
Tricontinental Film Center.
D: Hailé Gerima; P: Hailé Gerima; S: Hailé Gerima.
Cast: Barbara O. Jones, Ben Collins, Charles Brooks, Cora Lee Day.

In the Los Angeles ghetto of Watts, a young African-American woman struggles to keep her life in order.

This black & white art-house film (subsidised by the National Endowment for the Arts) is a stark drama that's so realistic it isn't until a character talks directly into the camera (about thirty minutes into the movie) that viewers are absolutely sure the film is not a documentary.

As Dorothy, an African-American woman who is struggling to keep her head above water during tumultuous times, Barbara O. Jones is simply magnificent. At one with her character, able to convey both reticence and grandiosity, sometimes tender and then furiously angry, hers is the type of 'real life' portrayal that frightens, confounds and has the unmistakable ring of truth about it.

Superior supporting characters include: Ben Collins as Ben, Dorothy's downtrodden companion; Charles Brooks as a knowing family friend; and Cora Lee Day as Molly, Dorothy's much-loved, but confused and always questioning young daughter.

Created with respect for African Americans who struggle beneath the poverty line in America, not afraid to broach politically-charged topics, and reproducing (sometimes expanding on – but never exploiting) the harsh realities of inner-city ghetto life, *Bush Mama* is an unsettling film that, though at times a bit confusing, is an undeniably powerful and highly personal cinematic endeavour by African director/producer/writer Hailé Gerima.

"The sense of the character's imprisonment and frustration is the film's most vivid message. 'Bush Mama' is fiery and furious..."
(Janet Maslin, New York Times)

THE CANDY TANGERINE MAN

1975, USA
Alternative Title: *The Tangerine Man*
R (1274), Action/Adventure, 88m.
Moonstone.
D: Matt Cimber; P: Matt Cimber; S: George Theakos.
Cast: John Daniels, Eli Haines, Pat Wright, Tracy King [Marilyn Joi].

"Git back Jack – give him no jive... he is the baaadest cat in '75."

A ruthless Los Angeles pimp actually leads a double life; pimp by day, upstanding suburban citizen by night.

above: Violent justice in 1975's **The Candy Tangerine Man**. Here, a drug peddler is disposed of in a most expedient way – out the window!

Brutal and obscene, designed both to shock and titillate, *The Candy Tangerine Man*, which features "the actual 'hookers' and 'blades' of the Sunset Strip in Hollywood" tells the raw and sordid tale of a successful Los Angeles pimp.

In the lead as the Black Baron, John (*Black Shampoo*) Daniels does a fine job of conveying the ugly, vulgar and inhumane things that an everyday man (he has a wife and two kids in the suburbs) will and can do – all in the name of capitalism. A game-for-anything performance is also provided by Marilyn (*Black Samurai*) Joi as Clarice, the Black Baron's unknowing wife.

Filled with a disturbing amount of violence and mutilation (one female character gets her breast cut off with a switchblade; another unfortunate victim has his hand forced into a kitchen garbage disposal unit), *The Candy Tangerine Man* is, without question, one of blaxploitation's most relentless and gory pictures. Moments of levity are few and far between, and consequently, when they arrive, they are greatly appreciated. There's a transvestite cop whose charade doesn't quite go over as planned; a shrill, and 'square' elderly neighbour who loves her roses; and a fat lady who recognises the Black Baron from her suburban neighbourhood – but can't quite be sure because she's preoccupied with getting something to eat! Shootouts, car chases, bludgeonings, blush-making diatribes and lewd sexcapades are all part of the mix. Not for the easily offended. See *Q & A: Ten Directors Discuss Their Films.*

"There is much that is crude and amateurish in this low-budget production, but it has a sly sense of humour which dresses up the tawdry tale nicely."
(Parish/Hill, Black Action Films, 1989)

CAR WASH

1976, USA
PG (24617), Comedy, 97m.
Universal Pictures.
D: Michael Schultz; P: Art Linson, Gary Stromberg; S: Joel Schumacher.
Cast: Richard Pryor, Ivan Dixon, Antonio Fargas, Franklin Ajaye, George Carlin, Clarence Muse, Darrow Igus, DeWayne Jessie, Bill Duke, Tracy Reed.

A day in the life of the workers and neighbourhood residents who live in the vicinity of a Los Angeles Car Wash.

Though this film spawned a No.1 hit record (the title cut performed by Rose Royce), and there is no doubt that it must have offered moviegoers a refreshing break from the action/adventure films that were being offered up at the time, today *Car Wash* seems like little more than a dated, not very sophisticated, novelty.

The hodgepodge of cinematic stereotypes include: an ostentatiously and, yes, sometimes genuinely funny gay character named Lindy (Antonio Fargas); an ageing shoeshine boy, Snapper (Clarence Muse); Floyd & Lloyd, a pair of talented young men who have dreams of becoming soul singing stars, played by Darrow Igus and DeWayne Jessie; a radical Muslim known by the names Duane and Abdullah (Bill Duke); a 'high yellow' hard-to-get African-American female named Mona (Tracy Reed); an opportunistic televangelist named Daddy Rich (Richard Pryor); a black stud (actually a skinny geek who just thinks he is) called T.C. (Franklin Ajaye); and a just-dropping-by black female singing group called the Wilson Sisters (The Pointer Sisters).

If anyone in the cast stands out (other than Pryor in his over the top role as the head of the Church of Divine Economics), it must be Lonnie (Ivan Dixon), a reformed felon trying to get his life back together. World-weary, imbuing his clichéd character with a rich and varied inner-life, Dixon is so good and so real that when he is on screen you think you're watching a totally different film.

Silly, episodic and slight, *Car Wash* is a colourful period piece; a summer film release that entertained inner city audiences who were on the lookout for some relief from the stifling heat.

Note: Screenwriter Joel Schumacher also wrote *Sparkle* and *The Wiz*. African-American director Michael Schultz's other films include *Together for Days*, *Honeybaby, Honeybaby, Cooley High*, *Greased Lightning* and *Which Way Is Up?*

"Nothing is fully thought out in this picture. Instead of some comic truth that would unify the episodes, 'Car Wash' settles for leaning back, lying low, and meandering over familiar terrain..."
(Donald Bogle, Blacks in American Films and Television, 1988)

CHARLEY-ONE-EYE

1973, UK
R (23593), Action/Adventure, 96m.
Paramount Pictures.
D: Don Chaffey; P: James Swan; S: Keith Leonard.
Cast: Richard Roundtree, Roy Thinnes, Nigel Davenport, Jill Pearson.

An African-American union army deserter travels to Mexico and joins forces with a renegade Indian.

In the midst of making his super successful trio of *Shaft* pictures, Richard Roundtree starred in this seldom-seen movie-with-a-message (that blacks and Indians have something in common when it comes to discrimination and subjugation in America.)

As The Black Man, Roundtree is both engaging and believable – realistically projecting both the contemporary black man's fears (here cloaked in the trappings of the Old West) as well as his reluctant acceptance of the compromised position he holds in American society. The Black

Man's American Indian comrade, The Indian, a mixed-heritage village outcast, is sensitively played by Roy Thinnes. Also along for the ride is Nigel (*Black Trash*) Davenport as The Bounty Hunter, a brutal man who always seems to be just one step behind the men he is engaged to pursue.

Gunfights, a stoning, and a lengthy tour of the American wilderness (actually a small town in Spain), are all part of the well-intentioned, but generally unexciting proceedings at hand.

"May be well made but holds little popular interest..."
(Variety)

CINDERELLA LIBERTY

1973, USA
R (23734), Drama, 117m. 20th Century Fox.
D: Mark Rydell; P: Mark Rydell; S: Darryl Ponicsan, based on his novel.
Cast: Marsha Mason, James Caan, Kirk Calloway, Sally Kirkland, Eli Wallach.

"What's about to happen to this young woman doesn't happen in the movies. It only happens in life."

A white prostitute struggles to cope with her sailor boyfriend and her illegitimate African-American son.

Super ambitious project that was seen by next to no one, this alternately depressing and uplifting portrait of a woman and her unusual life choices is noteworthy if only for its frank look at the rarely examined challenges that white parents with black children face.

Marsha Mason, in the lead as Maggie Paul, a generally unsympathetic pool hall prostitute, gives what is perhaps the best screen performance of her career. The shrill, studied affectations that would later become her trademarks are absent here. In their place is a relaxed, wholly committed performance that has the uncomfortable ring of truth about it (Mason was nominated for a Best Actress Oscar the following year). James Caan is also superb; as John Baggs Jr., a soldier on 24-hour leave, he is both warm and believable. In fact, his on-screen connection with young actor Kirk Calloway, who plays Doug, Maggie's illegitimate black son, is remarkable for both its nuance and intensity. Calloway, who would later co-star with Yaphet Kotto in *Monkey Hustle*, is perfectly cast too, bringing to vivid life the special challenges that biracial children must face in a racist society. Notable support is provided by Sally Kirkland as Fleet Chick, a homely, overwrought, yet still painfully boring guttersnipe, and Eli Wallach as Forshay, a rootless and embittered former sailor.

Grittier than expected, and a bit tiresome in its unrelenting bleakness, *Cinderella Liberty* offers a twisted take on Hollywood's standard boy-meets-prostitute-with-a-heart-of-gold narrative.

Note: the film's title is navy lingo for a pass that runs out at midnight.

"Sentimental, hokey, old-fashioned, tear-jerky, yet worth seeing..."
(Donald Bogle, Blacks in American Films and Television, 1988)

CLAUDINE

1974, USA
PG (23912), Comedy/Drama, 92m.
20th Century Fox.
D: John Berry; P: Hannah Weinstein; S: Tina and Lester Pine.
Cast: Diahann Carroll, James Earl Jones, Lawrence Hilton-Jacobs, David Kruger, Tamu [Blackwell].

"A heart and soul comedy. Can you dig it?"

A single black mother of six living in the ghetto struggles to keep her family together.

Strong performances, a good script and an outstanding music score (featuring everyone from Gladys Knight & the Pips to Millie Jackson) make this upscale blaxploitation entry worth a look.

In the lead as Claudine Price, Diahann Carroll is everything she needs to be. Beautiful, witty, hip to what's going on. She is the kind of strong African-American female lead that inner-city women recognised and could relate to. Claudine's not-ready-to-get-married-yet garbage collector boyfriend Roop is competently, if not interestingly, portrayed by James Earl Jones. The supporting cast is outstanding. There's hard-to-manage Charles (Lawrence Hilton-Jacobs), Claudine's teenage son; well-meaning but on the wrong path Paul (David Kruger), Claudine's younger militant-minded son; and most memorable of all Charlene (Tamu), Claudine's searching-for-herself teenage daughter. She is so good in fact

JAMES EARL JONES   DIAHANN CARROLL

"CLAUDINE"

that a tearful scene in which Charlene argues with her mother is so potent and real you feel like you should turn away.

Memorable performances (Carroll was nominated for an Oscar the following year), superior music and exciting photography elevate a familiar narrative.

"A joyful, earthy, honest movie, and that's rare."
(Kevin Sanders, WABC TV)

CLEOPATRA JONES

1973, USA
PG (23650), Action/Adventure, 89m.
Warner Bros.
D: Jack Starrett; P: William Tennant; S: Max Julien, Sheldon Keller.
Cast: Tamara Dobson, Bernie Casey, Brenda Sykes, Antonio Fargas, Shelley Winters, Esther Rolle.

"She's 'ten miles of bad road' for every hood in town! 6 feet 2 and all of it dynamite!"

A US narcotics agent destroys a poppy field worth $30,000,000, and becomes the target of an embittered drug queen.

Cleopatra Jones is the embodiment of the liberated '70s woman who can, and does, take care of herself. An expert in foreign affairs (and karate) she is a slick, regal and wholesome super-hero fashioned to appeal to a broad general audience.

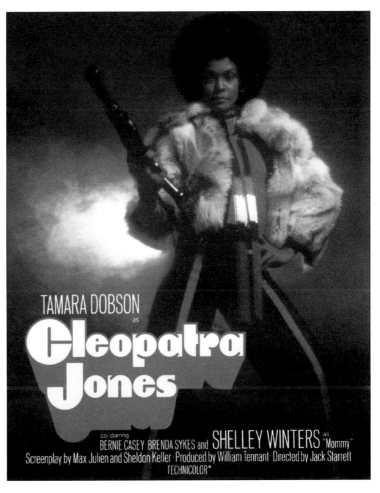

TAMARA DOBSON as **Cleopatra Jones**

co-starring BERNIE CASEY · BRENDA SYKES and SHELLEY WINTERS as "Mommy"
Screenplay by Max Julien and Sheldon Keller · Produced by William Tennant · Directed by Jack Starrett
TECHNICOLOR®

Model turned actress Tamara Dobson is everything she should be in the title role. Attractive, hip, natural on screen, she is the type of woman that any inner-city little girl would want to grow up to be – a woman whose many material possessions, including a gleaming sports car, expensive wardrobe, and meticulously decorated apartment – have come from working *inside* the law. Cleopatra Jones's arch-rival is drug queen Mommy (Shelley Winters), a rotund, loudmouthed, man-hating lesbian! Cleo's community-minded boyfriend Reuben Masters is played authoritatively by Bernie Casey. Other cast members of note include: Antonio Fargas as Doodlebug, Mommy's best inner-city dope pusher; Brenda Sykes as Tiffany, Doodlebug's well-meaning but ill-advised girlfriend; and Esther (of TV's *Good Times*) Rolle as Mrs. Johnson, a small time numbers runner.

Splashy, over the top, filled with great dialogue, great visuals and great music (Millie Jackson's 'Love Doctor' and 'Hurts So Good' were big radio hits) *Cleopatra Jones* was, and still is, the perfect female hero, suitable-for-all-family-members blaxploitation film. Followed by the sequel *Cleopatra Jones and the Casino of Gold*. Jack Starrett also directed *Slaughter*.

"Tamara Dobson makes a smart starring debut..."
(Variety)

CLEOPATRA JONES AND THE CASINO OF GOLD

1975, Hong Kong/USA
R (24128), Action/Adventure, 96m.
Warner Bros.
D: Chuck Bail; P: William Tennant;
S: William Tennant.
Cast: Tamara Dobson, Tanny [Tien Ni], Stella Stevens, Albert Popwell, Caro Kenyatta.

"6ft. 2in. of dynamite explodes into action."

Undercover narcotics agent Cleopatra Jones returns to the screen and takes a trip to the Orient in search of two missing fellow agents.

Spectacularly misguided (but enjoyable for this very reason), *Cleopatra Jones and the Casino of Gold* is noteworthy, not for the script or photography, but for model/actress Tamara Dobson's freakish visual presentation. Shimmery-faced (Dobson is 'credited' with doing her own makeup), objectified and overdressed (at least eight high-fashion costume changes which feature rhinestones, turbans and flowing scarves), Tamara Dobson as Cleopatra Jones is a towering grotesquerie – a futuristic space princess crossed with a wax figurine. Even so, and quite commendably, the actress does possess a strong on-screen personality, one that does not seem too far removed from that of the bawdy Mae West:

Dobson (to an admirer): *Don't race your motor baby. It's not leaving the garage!*
Dobson (to a friend): *The way I feel tonight, Muhammad Ali would have his hands full!*

This misadventure also features: Stella Stevens as Bianca Javin (aka the Dragon Lady), a beautiful and very butch underground drug lord; Tanny as Mi Ling, an undercover police agent posing as a motorcycle moll; and Matthew (Albert Popwell) and Melvin (Caro Kenyatta), two hip, oversexed kidnapped government agents.

above and opposite: Tall and slender, Tamara Dobson's background as a model gave her the poise to confidently strut through her role in **Cleopatra Jones** (1973).

Cartoonish, but undeniably filled with action (the final shootout in the Dragon Lady's casino is, alone, worth the price of the rental) *Cleopatra Jones and the Casino of Gold* is a high-style, high-kicking and high-spirited fun-fest.

"Miss Dobson is a large, beautiful overwhelming presence whose sexuality is denied by her movie role and by costumes that seem to have been designed for a female impersonator."
(Vincent Canby, New York Times)

COFFY

1973, USA
R (23655), Action/Adventure, 90m.
American International Pictures.
D: Jack Hill; P: Robert A. Papazian;
S: Jack Hill.
Cast: Pam Grier, Booker Bradshaw, Robert DoQui, William Elliott, Carol Lawson, Linda Haynes.

"She's the 'Godmother' of them all... the baddest one-chick hit squad that ever hit town!... Coffy. She'll cream you."

A nurse goes on a killing rampage when her 11-year-old sister gets hooked on heroin.

The best of the many 'female hero' blaxploitation entries (director Quentin Tarantino called it, "one of the most entertaining movies ever made"), *Coffy* is a shockingly violent and unapologetically gory revenge fantasy; one of only six blaxploitation films to take the No.1 spot on *Variety*'s 50 Top Grossing Films list.

Pam Grier is a larger-than-life, badder-than-bad, visually stunning superwoman in the titular role of Coffy (Flowerchild Coffin); nurse by day, vigilante murderess by night. At once soft, naive and kittenish, then, suddenly, terrifyingly ruthless, unpredictable and brutal, Grier's Coffy character continually goes way beyond what one expects even a merciless man to do in an action fantasy film. Capable of extreme acts of violence, torture and murder, Coffy speaks to the underground world of pimps and drug pushers in a language they clearly understand.

Coffy's supporting players include: Coffy's sensible and sensitive former boyfriend Carter Brown (William Elliott); her man of the moment, a corrupt politician named Howard Brunswick (Booker Bradshaw); and an outlandishly dressed pimp – who, not too surprisingly, also happens to think he's God's gift to women – King George (Robert DoQui). Also carving out their own place in this lurid little tale are Carol Lawson as Priscilla, King George's drug-addicted ex prostitute/girlfriend (he slashed her face with a razor after she called him "nigger"), and George's current lady Meg (Linda Haynes), a jealous woman who is willing to fight to keep her man.

Coffy is a must-see film filled with gratuitous nudity, blushingly vulgar diatribes and explicitly detailed violence that is, thankfully, offset by a large dose of humour (the multi-cast catfight is a highlight). Trendsetting, raucous and raunchy, *Coffy* also features a top-selling soundtrack by Roy Ayers. See *Q & A: Ten Directors Discuss Their Films*.

"... funny, campy, and engaging."
(Donald Bogle, Blacks in American Films and Television, 1988)

COME BACK CHARLESTON BLUE

1972, USA
PG (23317), Comedy/Adventure, 100m.
Warner Bros.
D: Mark Warren; P: Samuel Goldwyn Jr.;
S: Bontche Schweig and Peggy Elliott, based on the novel by Chester Himes.
Cast: Raymond St. Jacques, Godfrey Cambridge, Jonelle Allen, Adam Wade, Minnie Gentry.

"A ghost has come back to Harlem – and started the wildest gang war ever."

Two New York City detectives try to locate a serial killer.

This 'murder-mystery' follow-up to the super successful *Cotton Comes to Harlem* is not that bad, but not that good either. Returning to their roles as

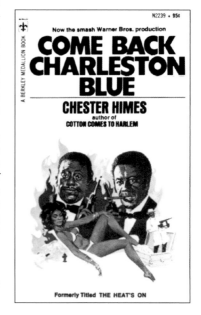

above and top right: Pam Grier set new standards for violence and glamour in the 1973 hit **Coffy**.

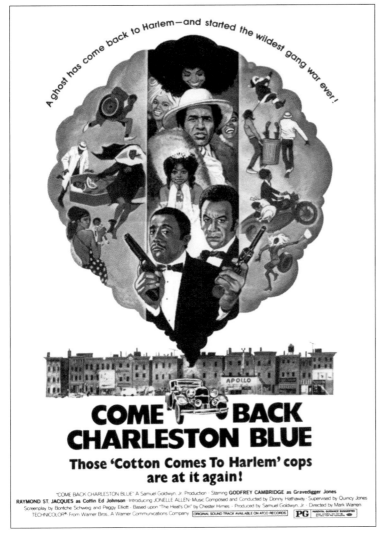

"3 million goes off! The most sensational robbery in crime history."

A just-released convict gathers together a group of highly skilled thieves to plan and execute a major jewellery heist.

A crime *doesn't* pay story, this black remake of *The Asphalt Jungle* (1950) has a lot going on – all at once.

Thalmus Rasulala is wonderful in the lead role of Sidney Lord Jones, a recently released convict. Always engaging to watch, totally in synch with his film character's motives, Rasulala turns in what one can only call a true star performance. Other featured performers include: Raymond St. Jacques as Bill Mercer, a well-to-do businessman; Rudy Challenger as Roy Harris, a dubious minister; Sam Laws as Stretch Finian, an alcoholic bookie; Lincoln Kilpatrick as Lt. Brian Knowles, a put-upon detective; and Jim Watkins as Travis Battle, a Vietnam Vet muscleman.

The female roles are just as plentiful and equally engaging. They include: Paula Kelly as Martha Harris, a sexy preacher's wife; Pam Grier (in a cameo) as Mona, an abused hooker; Margaret Avery (doing her best Marilyn Monroe imitation) as Lark, a feather-brained kept woman; Royce Wallace as Emma Mercer, a foul-mouthed wheelchair-bound harridan (who revels in exclamations about her husband's "shrivelled up little thing!"); Judy Pace as Obalese Eaton, a well-intentioned and stunningly beautiful massage therapist; and an uncredited Colostine Boatwright in a small but memorable role as a sassy, tough-talking, police station-bound hooker.

Cool Breeze's theme, the belief that the black man has to create his own destiny, is set up at the very beginning of the film:

Jones: *I need $50,000.*
Finian: *Holy moly! Ain't nobody else talked to me about that kind of money before. Only white boys play that kind of shit.*
Jones: *You're playing yourself cheap. Brothers got to think bigger than that.*
Finian: *I don't know. That's whitey's kind of job.*
Jones: *Whitey's too busy worrying about when China's going to drop the bomb. I'm gonna get over now – are you ready for me or not?*

Gravedigger Jones (the level-headed one) and Coffin Ed Johnson, (the hot headed one), Godfrey Cambridge and Raymond St. Jacques are game for the proceedings at hand, but don't quite seem to know what the proceedings are, exactly. Neither does first-time director Mark Warren. Some scenes go on for too long (the car chases), some are too short (a meeting with a clairvoyant named Her Majesty (Minnie Gentry), and some seem to convey nothing at all (kitchen table chatter).

Along with the requisite violence and sex, there is an attempt at humour and a notable emphasis on contemporary black slang. More than anything, *Come Back Charleston Blue* is a good example of Hollywood's penchant for producing quick, cheap and easy sequels – poorly conceived projects which were created to capitalise on a previous movie's already established success. Director Warren is African American.

"A tepid, jaded, sluggish picture."
(Donald Bogle, Blacks in American Films and Television, 1988)

COOL BREEZE

1972, USA
R (23261), Action/Adventure, 102m.
Metro Goldwyn Mayer.
D: Barry Pollack; P: Gene Corman; S: Barry Pollack, based on the novel 'The Asphalt Jungle' by W.R. Burnett.
Cast: Thalmus Rasulala, Judy Pace, Lincoln Kilpatrick, Raymond St. Jacques, Pamela [Pam] Grier, Paula Kelly, Colostine Boatwright, Rudy Challenger, Sam Laws, Jim Watkins, Margaret Avery, Royce Wallace.

above: Essentially a black-cast **American Graffiti**, **Cooley High** (1975) was the kind of good-natured, inoffensive blaxploitation entry that critics happily embraced. Glynn Turman *(left)* as "Preach" and Lawrence Hilton-Jacobs *(right)* as "Cochise" discuss their upcoming evening out on the town with two pretty classmates.
opposite: Stand by your man: Bank robber Sidney Lord Jones (Thalmus Rasulala) is flanked by two admiring beauties in this studio promotional shot for 1972's **Cool Breeze** – a black take on **The Asphalt Jungle** (1950). (J. Howard Collection)

The superb soul soundtrack is by Solomon Burke, whose briefly played 'We're Almost Home' will send chills up your spine. *Cool Breeze* is a well-done black take on a film classic. Highly recommended.

COOLEY HIGH

1975, USA
PG (24258), Comedy/Drama, 107m.
American International Pictures.
D: Michael Schultz; P: Steve Krantz;
S: Eric Monte.
Cast: Glynn Turman, Lawrence Hilton-Jacobs, Garrett Morris, Cynthia Davis.

"Where the Student Body was a chick named Veronica... the Senior Prom was a 'belly rub' and the class of '64 ran a permanent craps game in the Men's Room!"

In 1964, a group of seniors attending a Chicago high school learn about life and love in the streets.

Cooley High, a black answer to *American Graffiti*, was that rare blaxploitation film that critics seemed to uniformly single out for praise, but it is in truth somewhat overrated.

Glynn Turman ('Preach') and Lawrence Hilton-Jacobs ('Cochise') give it their all in the leads as two good-time-seeking young men who play hooky from school and are preoccupied with sex. Young, attractive and natural on screen, the two performers – who would later headline in their own blaxploitation features (*Youngblood* and *J.D.'s Revenge* respectively) – imbue their over-familiar film characters with a kinetic energy that is, admittedly, remarkable. Solid support is provided by Cynthia Davis as Brenda, a snooty, light-skinned black beauty that everyone covets, and Garrett Morris (of TV's original *Saturday Night Live* line-up) as Mr. Mason, a passionate-about-his-students high school teacher.

Dance parties, crap games, smoking in the boys room, heavy petting, curbside brawls, and, of course, street-corner singing are all part of the mix.

Preach's speech to his friends about getting out of the ghetto (which in this particular film does not seem all that unpleasant) is a good example of what the filmmakers believe is a 'poignant' moment:

> Preach (to his friends): *You guys think it's so funny because I want to be something besides a factory worker or a football player. That's because you're all a bunch of stupid niggers that don't know shit.*

Cooley High's only *real* poignant moment comes too late, when G.C. Cameron's heartbreaking 'Its So Hard to Say Goodbye to Yesterday' plays during a funeral sequence near the film's end, as Preach's hopes and dreams are put aside and adulthood is ushered in. Genuinely moving, the scene will touch your emotions on a level that the film as a whole never rises to.

"'Cooley High' comes across like a series of TV skits and gags that are skilfully stitched together but that ultimately lack real insight, even cohesion."
(Donald Bogle, Blacks in American Films and Television, 1988)

COONSKIN

1974, USA
Alternative Title: *Streetfight*
R (24026), Animation, 86m.
Paramount Pictures/Bryanston Pictures.
D: Ralph Bakshi; P: Albert S. Ruddy;
S: Ralph Bakshi.
Cast: Barry White, Scat Man [Scatman]
Crothers, Philip [Michael] Thomas,
Charles Gordone.

"This is it folks!"

A convict, who has escaped prison and is waiting to be picked up, listens to the stories of an elderly inmate.

Coonskin is an extremely engaging combination of live action and animation.

Funny, poignant, insulting, politically incorrect, this film pokes just as much fun at gays, Italians and women as it does blacks. *Coonskin* was banned from some inner-city theatres because of protests from the black community, prompting original distributors Paramount to sell the rights to Bryanston Pictures, who continued to profitably distribute the film despite, or maybe even because of, the continued furore it provoked.

Ostensibly the story of a black rabbit named Randy/'Brother Rabbit' (voiced by Philip Michael Thomas) who has travelled north from the rural South, this is a truly daring endeavour that is unlike anything else in the blaxploitation canon.

There's a big, clumsy, oversexed but lovable bear named Sampson/'Brother Bear' (voice provided by Barry White), a scheming, back-stabbing, charlatan fox named Preacherman/'Preacher Fox' (voice provided by Charles Gordone), and an old but feisty storyteller (in the 'Uncle Tom' mould) named Pappy/'Old Man Bone' (voice provide by Scatman Crothers). The 'American Dream' is embodied by a bosomy, blonde, flag-draped female character, who kicks all the black characters to the curb.

The sexual innuendo, foul language and blood-thirsty violence, surprisingly, serve the story well, providing the animated characters with a rich inner life. Highly recommended.

"The most likely candidates to be offended by 'Coonskin' are actually white women and gays. These characters, more than the film's blacks, seem to take us to the bottom of Bakshi's personal obsessions."
(Frank Rich, *New York Post*)

CORNBREAD, EARL AND ME

1975, USA
PG (24254), Drama, 95m.
American International Pictures.
D: Joe Manduke; P: Joe Manduke;
S: Leonard Lamensdorf, from a story by Ronald Fair.
Cast: Keith [Jamaal] Wilkes, Rosalind Cash, Moses Gunn, Thalmus Rasulala, Madge Sinclair, Bernie Casey, Tierre Turner, Laurence Fishburne III, Antonio Fargas.

"We're gonna lick the world!"

When an inner-city youth is mistaken for a criminal, his experience changes the lives of all that knew him.

Grandly compared to both *Sounder* and *The Learning Tree* in its theatrical trailer, *Cornbread, Earl and Me* is a suitable-for-all-family-members blaxploitation entry that doesn't quite deliver everything it promises.

Keith Wilkes is both convincing and endearing as Nathanial 'Cornbread' Hamilton. Always looking out for others, good natured and poised for success, his is the kind of film character that seems expressly designed to uplift and inspire. Madge Sinclair, in the role of his mother Leona, turns in an impassioned performance that goes far beyond the parameters of her sketchily written role. Holding their own in supporting parts are: Moses Gunn as Ben Blackwell, a kindly neighbourhood lawyer; Rosalind Cash as Sarah Robinson, a single

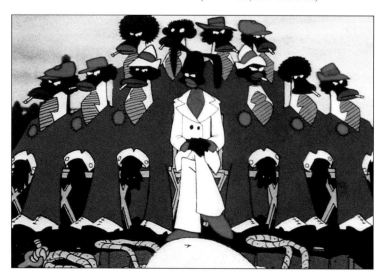

above: **Coonskin** (1974) combines live action and animation. The film is merciless towards everyone... blacks, gays, women, Italians, fat people, the poor, substance abusers and the capitalist American way of life.

above: Caped and ready to preach: Reverend Deke O'Malley (Calvin Lockhart) thrills a crowd in 1970's **Cotton Comes to Harlem**. (J. Howard Collection)

welfare-collecting mother who is trying to teach her son 'how to be a man'; Bernie Casey as Police Detective Atkins, a man who has second thoughts about a tragic shooting; and Tierre Turner (Earl) and Laurence Fishburne III (Wilford), two young boys who idolize Cornbread and play a major part in a pivotal court room scene. Also appearing, in notable cameos, are Thalmus Rasulala as Charlie, Sarah's over-amorous male companion and Antonio Fargas as One Eye, a see-nothing-know-nothing pimp and numbers runner.

Pat, predictable and pointedly avoiding the trappings of the typical blaxploitation film, *Cornbread, Earl and Me* contains much that will appeal to the juvenile viewer. Joe Manduke also directed *Kid Vengeance*.

"Made with a fine cast and the best intentions... the picture turns into a lumbering TV-style courtroom drama..." (Variety)

COTTON COMES TO HARLEM

1970, USA
R (22520), Action/Adventure, 97m.
United Artists.
D: Ossie Davis; P: Samuel Goldwyn Jr.; S: Arnold Perl and Ossie Davis, based on a novel by Chester Himes.
Cast: Godfrey Cambridge, Raymond St. Jacques, Redd Foxx, Calvin Lockhart, Helen Martin, Judy Pace.

"It's cops and robbers with a shade of difference."

When $87,000 in donations is stolen, two policemen believe there is more to the theft than meets the eye.

It's easy to understand why *Cotton Comes to Harlem* thrilled audiences. At the time the film was released, there really had never been anything else quite like it. Incorporating comedy, action and drama,

and colourfully telling the story of a diverse group of African Americans living and working in Harlem, USA, everything about the film seemed novel and forward-thinking. Even so, today, the film does not play nearly as well as one would like it to.

In the dual leading roles of two (rather dull) New York City police detectives, Godfrey Cambridge (as 'Gravedigger' Jones) and Raymond St. Jacques (as 'Coffin' Ed Johnson) give it their all, but do not possess the means to rise above the episodic, laboured, talky and convoluted material. Also of note are: Calvin (*Halls of Anger*) Lockhart as the charming, yet patently corrupt, preacher Reverend Deke O'Malley; Redd (*Norman... Is That You?*) Foxx as Uncle Bud, "an old geezer who goes around picking up junk"; Helen Martin as Church Sister, an elderly woman who is mugged by an opportunistic team of street-smart men; and the breathtakingly poised and beautiful Judy (*Cool Breeze*) Pace, as Iris, a hip-talking, foxy mama who eventually outwits a white police officer.

Well-meaning but tiresome, (you'll hear "am I black enough for you?" and "what would a bale of cotton be doing in Harlem?" about ten times), today, *Cotton Comes to Harlem* remains noteworthy because it made clear, once and for all, that urban-centred black-cast films could make money at the box office. Followed by a sequel, *Come Back Charleston Blue*.

Note: Director Ossie Davis wrote the picture's theme song 'Ain't Now But It's Gonna Be (Black Enough for Me),' performed by Melba Moore.

"Contemporary audiences will wonder what the fuss was all about and may frown at the profusion of stereotypes."
(Donald Bogle, Blacks in American Films and Television, 1988)

COUNTDOWN AT KUSINI

1976, Nigeria/USA
Alternative Title: *Cool Red*
PG (24508), Drama, 99m.
Columbia Pictures.
D: Ossie Davis; P: Ladi Ladebo; S: Ossie Davis, Ladi Ladebo and Al Freeman Jr., from a story by John Storm Roberts.
Cast: Ossie Davis, Ruby Dee, Greg Morris, Tom Aldredge.

"A dynamite story of African revolution."

In Lagos, a government supporter finds himself at odds with the local syndicate.

This super-ambitious film may have been a bit too highbrow and serious-minded for mainstream audiences to connect with.

Ossie Davis, as Ernest Motapo, a crusader whose high hopes for an unnamed African country are in danger of being squashed, is convincing but not quite compelling. Ruby Dee (the actor/director's wife) plays Leah Matanzima, Motapo's helpmate. Most engaging of the film's characters is Greg Morris as Red Salter, an African-American musician who comes to support Motapo's progressive philosophies.

Striving to impress rather than entertain, *Countdown at Kusini*, financed by Delta Sigma Theta (America's largest all-black sorority) was a bomb with both audiences and critics.

"The script is burdened with lamentable lines that require the best efforts of its cast... the film emerges as a sub par adventure with a less than lucid ideology."
(Lawrence Van Gelder, New York Times)

CRAZY JOE

1974, Italy/USA
R (23811), Action/Adventure, 100m.
Columbia Pictures.
D: Carlo Lizzani; P: Dino De Laurentiis; S: Lewis John Carlino, based on a story by Nicholas Gage.
Cast: Peter Boyle, Fred Williamson, Eli Wallach, Paula Prentiss, Henry Winkler, Herve Villechaize.

"No killer of the streets ever gave it or got it like Crazy Joe."

The fictionalised biography of '70s mobster Joseph 'Crazy Joe' Gallo.

Created to appeal to fans of *The Godfather*, *Crazy Joe* is a superior film that examines the ongoing struggle for power in the Italian-controlled New York City underworld. Cleverly written, nicely paced, excitingly photographed and filled with good performances, this seldom-seen film does everything that it is supposed to and does it well.

Peter Boyle embodies his Crazy Joe character, capturing both the ruthlessness and charm that made Joseph 'Crazy Joe' Gallo something of a folk hero. Fred Williamson plays Willy, a minor African-American underground figure who, nevertheless, introduces Joe to the Harlem underworld. Williamson, too, is superb, turning in one of his best (and least swarthy) screen performances. Henry 'The Fonz' Winkler, in a pre-*Happy Days* performance, is featured in a small role as Mannie, an impressionable mob henchman, and Herve (*Fantasy Island*) Villechaize makes an appearance as Samson, a small but very intimidating mob spokesperson. The dialogue between black Willy and his Italian cohort Joe is spot-on:

Willy (to Joe): *This is what you should be getting your head into* (referring to a girlie magazine).
Crazy Joe: *You see that's the trouble with you people, you spend too much time with your animal instincts instead of developing your mind.*
Willy: *Yeah, well when you're in the jungle baby, I figured your animal instincts could count.*

Another clever exchange occurs on the day that Joe is released from jail:

Crazy Joe (to Willy): *You're the product of capitalist, racist*

exploitation, which makes you an incorrigible sociological liability.
Willy: *Yeah, I know just what you mean, man. My momma used to say that to me all the time!*

There's a severed hand, a death by fresh cement, and a timely 'now-we-don't-have-to-do-it-ourselves' heart attack. Also noteworthy is a realistic looking jailhouse riot (started when an Italian barber refuses to cut black Willy's hair), and an Italian American political rally set up on the streets of New York City. Highly recommended.

"...boasts an awareness that few Mafia films have."
(Chris Petit, Time Out Film Guide)

above: **Darktown Strutters** (1975), a funk blaxploitation acid trip that must be seen to be believed.

DARKTOWN STRUTTERS

1975, USA
Alternative Title: *Get Down and Boogie*
PG (24069), Comedy, 84m.
New World Pictures.
D: William Witney; P: Gene Corman;
S: George Armitage.
Cast: Trina Parks, Roger E. Mosley,
Shirley Washington, Bettye Sweet.

"Super sisters on cycles... better move your butt when these ladies strut!"

A female motorcycle gang embarks on a search for a missing family member.

A series of outlandish, highly stylised comedy vignettes performed on sets that look like they were borrowed from TV's *Pee-wee's Playhouse*.

Trina Parks is Syreena, an African-American motorcycle mama who is desperately searching for her kidnapped mother. Roger E. Mosley is Mellow, the ineffectual leader of a rival all male biker gang. The rest of this semi-psychedelic endeavour is filled with 'funny' supporting players along with speeded up photography, kooky sound effects and an endless series of racially charged sight gags (a "nigger alert"; a sign that says "free watermelon with your bone sucking good spare ribs"; and a five man minstrel show performed in blackface).

The shenanigans include: extras walking around in bunny suits; a kung-fu session in which a house is completely demolished; and an entire song, 'Whatcha See Is Whatcha Get,' performed by the soul group The Dramatics (from behind the bars of a jail cell). Choice dialogue:

> White Lady: *You have lovely things in your shop, where do you get them?*
> Black Shop Owner: *I buys them from folks.*
> White Lady: *And where do **they** get them?*
> Black Shop Owner: *They steals them from you folks.*
> White Lady: *And?*
> Black Shop Owner: *I sells them back to you folks!*

Note: the nightclub featured in the film is Maverick's Flat, also seen in *Bare Knuckles* and *Coffy*. William Witney also directed *I Escaped from Devil's Island*.

*"The sight gags and raunchy quips are **not** rib ticklers..."*
(A.H. Weiler, New York Times)

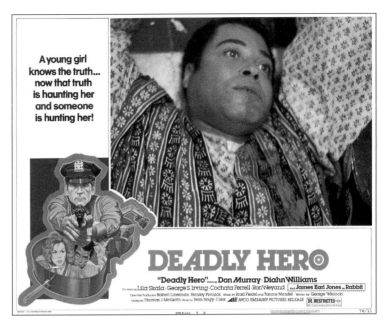

DEADLY HERO

1975, USA
R (24479), Action/Adventure, 101m.
Avco Embassy Pictures.
D: Ivan Nagy; P: Thomas J. McGrath;
S: George Wislocki
Cast: Don Murray, James Earl Jones, Diahn Williams, Treat Williams, Danny DeVito, Beverly Johnson.

"Hero cop or psychotic killer? Not since 'The French Connection' and 'Death Wish' has a movie been so intense!"

A criminal investigation ensues after an unarmed assailant is gunned down by a NYC police officer.

Put together and presented like a 1970s television crime drama (think *Kojak*), *Deadly Hero* would be better titled *Deadening Hero*.

In the lead as Ed Lacy, an over-emotional, bigoted and very violent New York City police officer, Don Murray (best known for his role opposite Marilyn Monroe in *Bus Stop*) looks more like an insurance salesman than a heavy-drinking, working class cop with fifteen years on the force. Operating within the limited parameters of a sketchily written role, the actor (who has to shout, bug his eyes, tremble and stalk a witness) is, at his best, spirited. Diahn Williams (who has a Mary Tyler Moore-like quality about her) plays Sally Devereaux, a musician who teaches school by day and performs with a bizarre rock/ballet/mime theatre group at night. Subtle though she is, there's not much Williams has to do but carefully walk (and peer) around corners, talk in a tentative voice, and occasionally scream. James Earl Jones plays Rabbit, a slightly 'off' mugger/kidnapper/extortionist who recites Shakespeare one moment and spouts profanity the next. Too self satisfied, too ostentatiously cultured and grand, Jones is an unpleasant distraction, a character that is more fake than anyone else in this already very false film.

If there is a moment of levity (not including the orange, purple and green afros and multicolour polka-dot outfits that the theatre group wears), it must be a scene in which an overweight, and obviously hungry, hit man reviews the contents of a grocery bag. "Salami, pork chops, Oreos, oh boy! Hey! You forgot the Fig Newtons!"

Painfully predictable (there is a gory final plot twist that is alluded to one too many times throughout the film), slow moving and filled with one dimensional characters, the only thing to recommend *Deadly Hero* is the on-location filming in several real (cramped, worn, awkwardly laid out) New York City apartments. Look for actor Danny DeVito and model Beverly Johnson (the first African American to make the cover of *Vogue*) in bit parts.

"...thin, commonplace... superficial tale and action."
(A.H. Weiler, New York Times)

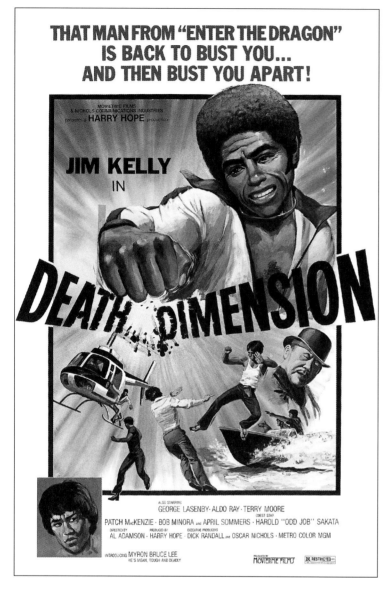

observe having a microchip surgically implanted into her forehead.

Along with the too-long, obviously-filmed-out-of-synch, action sequences (which include karate fights in the woods, in the desert, on a boat and in a hotel room), there are the standard car chases, prostitutes, and double-crosses. The 'explosive' helicopter/sky-car finale sounds good on paper but is poorly realised on the screen.

"...actors fallen on hard times being non-directed by Al Adamson in a mishmash."
(Parish/Hill, Black Action Films, 1989)

DEATH DRUG

1979, USA
Alternative Title: *Angel Dust: The Wack Attack*
PG-13 (28409), Action/Adventure, 73m.
Vistar International.
D: Oscar Williams; P: Demetris Johnson; S: Roland S. Jefferson M.D.
Cast: Philip Michael Thomas, Vernee Watson, Rosalind Cash, Frankie Crocker.

"The first hit didn't cost him anything."

A Los Angeles based singer/songwriter makes it big and then succumbs to drug addiction.

This bargain basement movie-with-a-message features Philip Michael Thomas as an Angel Dust addict named Jesse Thomas. Thomas gives it his all, but is unconvincing in a role that requires subtlety and introspection, not bombast. Lending a helping hand are Vernee (*Trick Baby*) Watson as Carolyn, Jesse's faithful live-in girlfriend, and Rosalind (*The Omega Man*) Cash as Dr. Harry, a concerned physician who works at the Watts Medical Center in Los Angeles.

Filmed in 1978 as an anti-drug TV movie, with an original running time of only 50 minutes, it was released on video in 1986 with the addition of bookending sequences featuring *Miami Vice* star Philip Michael Thomas, and the surprisingly good music video for his song 'Just the Way I Planned It,' from his debut album.

Major incidents include: a tour of a PCP treatment centre; a mad hullucinogenic rampage in a supermarket; and a visit to a local discothèque where The Gap Band just happen to be playing. African-American director Oscar Williams's other films include *The Final Comedown*, *Five on the Black Hand Side* and *Hot Potato*.

DEATH DIMENSION

1978, USA
Alternative Titles: *Black Eliminator*; *Freeze Bomb*; *The Kill Factor*; *Icy Death*
R (25179), Action/Adventure, 88m.
Movietime.
D: Al Adamson; P: Harry Hope; S: Harry Hope.
Cast: Jim Kelly, Terry Moore, Harold Sakata, Aldo Ray.

"He's deadly with his hands, his feet and all available weapons!"

A police detective tries to solve a case involving a maniac in possession of a bomb.

Even though critics liked to harp on the fact that Jim Kelly often appeared 'stiff and expressionless' in his film vehicles, there is no doubt that the karate champion turned actor was useful as a 'star.' In fact, Kelly's star status is never more apparent than in this tedious late-to-market blaxploitation entry that would never have been made were it not for him.

Jim Kelly plays L.A. police detective John Ash, a karate expert who is out to locate a Buddha-like maniac called 'The Pig' (Harold Sakata), a man who is planning to use a freeze bomb to bring humankind to a below zero degree standstill. Terry Moore plays Joan Mason, a woman who we are forced to

DEATH FORCE

1977, Philippines/USA
Alternative Titles: *Force of Death*;
Fighting Mad; *Fierce*
R (24900), Action/Adventure, 92m.
21st Century Film Corp.
D: Cirio H. Santiago; P: Robert E. Waters;
S: Howard R. Cohen.
Cast: James Inglehart, Leon Isaac
[Kennedy], Jayne Kennedy, Carmen
Argenziano.

"Beaten, betrayed and bustin' loose."

**Betrayed by his two closest army
buddies, a Vietnam Veteran returns to
Los Angeles bent on revenge.**

As returning Vietnam Veteran Douglas
Russell (who was beaten, pushed
overboard and left for dead – but was
then befriended by a pair of renegade
Japanese countrymen who taught him the
ancient arts of the Samurai!) James
Inglehart is a bit too large and football
player-like to be convincing in the many
high-kicking fight sequences he is
required to perform in. Maria (Jayne
Kennedy) is Doug's faithful nightclub
performer wife. Soft spoken, pretty, in
possession of a competent but unexciting
singing voice (she does a solo number
called 'I Hear the Rain Whispering Your
Name'), Kennedy and her real life
husband Leon Isaac (here a successful
L.A. mobster named McGee) offer their
attractive faces to a generally unattractive film. Morelli, McGee's tough-
talking partner in crime, is played by
Carmen Argenziano.
  Terribly contrived and protracted,
derivative and generally uninteresting,
Death Force's 'memorable' moments
include a gift-wrapped severed head and a
climactic I'm-going-to-lift-you-off-the-
ground-with-my-samurai-sword 'knock-
'em-dead' finale. Cirio H. Santiago's
other films include *Savage!*, *TNT Jackson*,

Ebony, Ivory & Jade and *The Muthers*.
See *Q & A: Ten Directors Discuss Their
Films*.

DEATH JOURNEY

1975, USA
R (1421), Action/Adventure, 76m.
Atlas Films.
D: Fred Williamson; P: Fred Williamson;
S: Abel Jones.
Cast: Fred Williamson, D'Urville Martin,
Bernard Kuby, Heidi Dobbs.

*"Assignment: Bring in the informer... 3000
miles in 48 hours... alive. The mob says 'No
Way!' Crowder says 'Try and stop me!'"*

**A Private Investigator is hired to escort
a mob-marked witness from Los
Angeles to New York City.**

Death Journey suffers from poor
direction, poor acting, a ridiculous script
and a cheat ending. What's more, you
won't want to hear Kenneth Gamble &
Leon Huff's song 'Do It Any Way You
Wanna' ever again, as it plays as
background music (sans lyrics) throughout the entire length of the film.
  The always tight-panted and/or
shirtless Fred Williamson is fine, such as
he is, in the role of Jesse Crowder, a
Private Investigator who is as quick with
the ladies as he is with a karate chop.

Along for the crawl are Bernard Kuby as
Finley, Crowder's greasy-faced 'fat boy'
charge, and in a lightning fast (unusually
subdued) cameo, D'Urville Martin as
Lockjaw Sampson, a doomed gas station
attendant. The following exchange
reveals just how tiresome and uninventive
the script is:

  Detective One (on learning that Jesse
  Crowder is going to take the case):
  Crowder? That bum? That ex-cop?
  Detective Two: *Just because his
  methods are unorthodox, that doesn't
  make him a bad cop.*
  Detective One: *Wherever he goes,
  there's always trouble and a few
  dead bodies left behind – shoot first,
  ask questions later. Like a page out
  of the old west.*
  Detective Two: *You're right! And
  you've just described the one man
  that can get the witness to us alive –
  Jesse Crowder!*

It plays like a student film; filled with
lengthy dialogue-free chase scenes (in the
desert, on the road, in an airport), it's
juvenile (foggy, purposely out of focus
'romantic' scenes), and carelessly
presented (actors talking in the foreground
while passers-by stop and observe them in
the background). There is no question that
if there had been a home video market in
1975, *Death Journey* would have never
made it into theatres at all.

DELIVER US FROM EVIL

1975, USA
Alternative Title: *Joey*
PG (24343), Drama, 95m.
Dimension Pictures.
D: Horace Jackson; P: Horace Jackson;
S: Horace Jackson.
Cast: Danny Martin, Marie O'Henry,
Renny Roker, Juanita Moore, Kandi
Keith, Cal Haynes.

"Our streets... nightmares! Our neighborhoods... execution chambers! Look what we're doing to ourselves!"

The residents of a Los Angeles neighbourhood take action against a group of thugs who are selling drugs to schoolchildren.

Dull, preachy and striving too hard to distance itself from the standard blaxploitation pictures of the day (in particular *The Bus Is Coming* and *Tough!*, the other two films of African-American director/producer/writer Horace Jackson), *Deliver Us from Evil* is the kind of good-natured, well-meaning movie that might turn up in the schedules as part of a PBS Saturday afternoon TV special for kids.

In the role of hot-headed drifter Chris Townes, actor Renny Roker is merely adequate. Kind, fair-minded and a bit goofy, his quiet turn is nevertheless a welcome respite from the shrill, one-note, and generally unpleasant Marie O'Henry, who takes the role of Mindy, an inner city Recreational Director. Other notable characters include: Michelle (Kandi Keith), a 'confused' aspiring actress; 'Little Joe' (Danny Martin), a wheelchair-bound boy; and Roy (Cal Haynes), Mindy's good-natured husband. Also appearing in a cameo is Juanita (*The Mack*) Moore.

This film's highlights include a schoolyard battle, a clever segment presented as reality (but is actually just a scene from a play), and an unusual coda in which the main character, Chris, talks directly to the film's viewer:

Chris: *Our neighbourhoods are execution chambers. We're just killing one another for nothing. No wonder some people think we're animals with a gullibility for vice that's endless. Our women are afraid to walk the streets and when the sun goes down, it's a nightmare... when will it end?*

The catchy 'Think About What You're Doing to Me (And Know What You're Doing to Yourself)' is performed by the group Enchantment.

DETROIT 9000

1973, USA
Alternative Titles: *Detroit Heat*; *Police Call 9000*
R (875), Action/Adventure, 106m.
General Film Corporation.
D: Arthur Marks; P: Arthur Marks; S: Orville H. Hampton.
Cast: Alex Rocco, Hari Rhodes, Vonetta McGee, Scatman Crothers, Rudy Challenger, Laura Lee [uncredited].

"It's the murder capital of the world. And the biggest black rip-off of the decade. It's gonna get solved or the town's gonna explode."

Two Detroit police detectives combine forces to locate the four masked men who robbed a group of partygoers.

This film enjoys a cult following among police-drama fans. Even so, the narrative, filled with action sequences, shootouts and car chases, remains a generic, uninvolving 'caper' – a word used again and again throughout the film itself.

As Lieutenant Danny Bassett, a Chicago police veteran who is looking for a way to subsidise his (racist) invalid wife's medical care, Alex Rocco is very good, but not good enough to transcend the rudimentary material. Falling into the same unremarkable category of just-good-enough performers is Hari Rhodes as Jesse Williams, Bassett's righteous partner. More interesting than the leads are supporting players Rudy Challenger as corrupt Chicago Mayoral candidate Aubrey Hale Clayton, and Vonetta McGee as Ruby Harris, a prostitute whose unexpected flashback turns out to be the centrepiece of the movie. A noteworthy cameo is provided by Scatman Crothers as conspiratorial fundraiser Reverend Markham.

The best scene in *Detroit 9000* occurs when 200 elegantly clad guests are robbed at gunpoint and told to kneel on the floor with their hands on their heads. With a gun pointed at her temple and tears streaming down her face, uncredited African-American singer Laura Lee performs a heart-stopping a cappella rendition of 'Look for the Answer (You'll Find It in Him).' Lee's brief but magnificent turn is reason enough to recommend this film.

Note: *Detroit 9000* is the Chicago police code for 'Officer Needs Assistance.' See *Q & A: Ten Directors Discuss Their Films.*

"For a change in black exploits, the whites and blacks come out about even in good and evil."
(Variety)

DEVIL'S EXPRESS

1976, USA
Alternative Title: *Gang Wars*
R (1623), Horror, 82m.
Howard Mahler Films.
D: Barry Rosen; P: Niki Patton, Steve Madoff; S: Barry Rosen, Niki Patton, Pascual Vaquer, Ceotis Robinson, Bobbi Sappertein.
Cast: Sam De Fazio, Warhawk Tanzania, Larry Fleischman, Wilfredo Roldan.

"50,000 years of death stalks the subways!!! Take the express train to terror!!!"

After a Chinese burial ground is disturbed, a demon makes its way to the States in search of the man who stole a sacred medallion.

Devil's Express is built upon a great idea – that of a Chinese monster travelling from Hong Kong to America and taking up residence in the dark, dank tunnels of New York's City's subway system – but unfortunately the premise is totally wasted.

In the lead as Luke, a kung-fu master and karate teacher, Warhawk Tanzania is as false and out of place as everything else in the film. His con-man friend Rodan (Wilfredo Roldan) is even worse. Both performers are artificial in both voice and demeanour, uncomfortable in front of the camera, and so stilted one is hard-pressed to figure out just how these two were ever cast.

The film's major incidents include: two very poorly executed 'gang wars' between the (not-too-creatively-named) African American 'Black Spades' and the Chinese 'Red Dragons'; a 'flashback' to 2000 BC; and a romantic interlude accompanied by a song entitled 'That's Why You and I Believe in Each Other' by a group called Rising Sun. (The tune is so bad you'll think it's a joke).

The five screenwriters (perhaps that was the problem) and the film distributor did come up with one good thing – a colourful and terribly misleading poster, which features a King Kong-sized mummy-like creature with a subway car in one hand and a screaming girl in the other!

DIAMONDS

1975, Israel/USA
Alternative Title: *Diamond Shaft*
PG (24437), Action/Adventure, 108m.
Avco Embassy Pictures.
D: Menahem Golan; P: Menahem Golan; S: David Paulsen, Menahem Golan.
Cast: Robert Shaw, Richard Roundtree, Barbara Seagull [Hershey], Shelley Winters.

"Diamonds were forever!"

A London merchant hires an ex-con to rob the Diamond Exchange building in Tel Aviv.

Little-known, but filled with top-of-the-line performances, *Diamonds* is a picture that's beautiful to look at and filled with many interesting twists and turns.

Robert Shaw is fantastic in his dual role of competing twin brothers Charles and Earl Hodgson. The actor's resonant speaking voice combined with his screen presence and good looks serve his spoiled, bored, rich boy character very well indeed. As Archie, Richard Roundtree (often a bit overdressed) is also very effective. Playing a recently-released con looking to make some money in a foreign land, the actor displays none of the swagger or bravado so much associated with his celebrated John Shaft character. Support is provided by Barbara Hershey as Sally, Archie's part-time girlfriend, and Shelley Winters as Zelda Shapiro, a kooky, rotund, always flustered, stereotypical Jewish woman.

Zelda (to Hodgson): *Are you Jewish?*
Hodgson: *No, I'm afraid I'm not.*
Zelda (sympathetic): *Oh, I'm sorry!*

Unusual locations (Jerusalem, Tel Aviv, Israel and London), a good script, sharp editing and creative photography make *Diamonds* a pleasure to watch (though the bombastic soundtrack does sometimes distract).

"A caper movie to end all caper movies..."
(Lawrence Van Gelder, New York Times)

DISCO GODFATHER

1979, USA
Alternative Title: *Avenging Disco Godfather*
R (25782), Action/Adventure, 93m.
Generation International Pictures.
D: J. Robert Wagoner; P: Rudy Ray Moore, Theadore Toney; S: J. Robert Wagoner, Cliff Roquemore.
Cast: Rudy Ray Moore, Carol Speed, Julius J. Carry III, Lady Reed.

After learning that his nephew is hooked on Angel Dust, a former policeman turned popular club DJ takes to the streets.

This strange combination of social commentary and disco craziness is worth a look, if only because it is raunchy comedian Rudy Ray (*Dolemite*) Moore's final starring vehicle.

As Tucker Williams, a popular club DJ/rapper who wants to rid his neighbourhood of PCP (Angel Dust), Moore is a bit more serious here than in his other films. Even so, he still, thankfully, mugs, raps, jives and 'carries on' like there's no tomorrow. His main lady friend is Noel (Carol Speed), a serious-minded woman who also wants to stop the flow of drugs into her community. Others in the cast are Julius J. Carry III as Bucky, Williams's drug-addicted nephew, and Lady Reed (a staple in Moore's films) as Mrs. Edwards, a concerned friend.

Outrageous costumes, kung-fu fighting, disco dancing, stop-action photography, and a wild drug hallucination are all part of the eclectic mix.

"A feast of outrageously ugly mid-'70s fashions, but a step down from the 'Dolemite' pictures."
(Schwartz/Olenski, VideoHound's Cult Flicks & Trash Picks, 2002)

DOLEMITE

1975, USA
R (24139), Action/Adventure, 90m.
Dimension Pictures.
D: D'Urville Martin; P: Rudy Ray Moore, T. [Theodore] Toney; S: Jerry Jones.
Cast: Rudy Ray Moore, D'Urville Martin, Lady Reed, Jerry Jones.

"Bone-crushing, skull-splitting, brain-blasting action!"

A nightclub performer is framed on a bogus drug charge and sent to prison – only to be let out so that he can prove himself innocent.

Rudy Ray Moore brings his nightclub character Dolemite (a man who tells raunchy stories in rhyme) to the screen. Very entertaining in spite of its breathtakingly poor performances, direction, editing, sound, lighting and story, *Dolemite*, a $90,000 production, has become a cult classic and favourite of bad movie lovers around the globe.

As Dolemite, Rudy Ray Moore envelops himself in his tried and true rhymes and embellishes them with outlandish costumes, slapstick situations, karate fight sequences, and a bevy of beautiful women. Moore is not afraid to make a fool of himself, and his debut is a generally satisfying series of disjointed, yet highly entertaining comedy vignettes. The ubiquitous D'Urville Martin (who also directs) stars as Willie Green, a competing nightclub owner, and Lady Reed takes the role of Queen Bee, Dolemite's glamorous I-can-take-care-of-myself-thank-you nightclub manager friend.

Dolemite's shining moments include Moore's recitation of two of his most popular rhyming routines – 'Shine and the Titanic' and 'The Signifying Monkey.'

A hit with audiences, *Dolemite* was followed by the equally outrageous *The Human Tornado*. African-American director D'Urville Martin also directed *Fass Black*. Screenwriter Jerry Jones is also African American.

"With its cheap (if paid at all) actors, stiff action, shaky script and almost inaudible sound 'Dolemite' has to be seen to be believed!"
(Mason Storm, Encyclopedia of Cinematic Trash Vol. 2)

DON'T PLAY US CHEAP

1973, USA
NR (PG), Comedy/Musical, 90m.
Yeah, Inc.
D: Melvin Van Peebles; P: Melvin Van Peebles; S: Melvin Van Peebles.
Cast: Esther Rolle, Mabel King, Joshie Jo Armstead, Joe Keyes Jr., Rhetta Hughes.

In order to earn their horns, two devils are dispatched to disrupt a Harlem birthday party.

Shrill, claustrophobic and stage-bound, *Don't Play Us Cheap* is only noteworthy today because it is director Melvin Van Peebles's follow-up to his super successful *Sweet Sweetback's Baadasssss Song*.

In the lead as Miss Maybell, Esther Rolle (best known for her work on TV's *Good Times*) is superb. Endowed with a wonderful speaking voice, committed to her character, Afrocentric in her visual presentation and her highly ethnic speech patterns, hers is the glue that would have held this ramshackle production together – had it been a bit more fully realised. Other cast members include: Mabel King as Diane, a rotund, bewigged and only marginally entertaining party guest; Joe Keyes Jr. as Trinity, an impish and very impressionable devil; and Rhetta Hughes as Earnestine, a naive twenty-year-old woman who is desperate for love.

Ambitious and fashioned to uplift, but too noisy and too superficial, *Don't Play Us Cheap* is worth a look for a single performance early in the film by former Ikette (of The Ike & Tina Turner Review) Joshie Jo Armstead, who steps forward during the party and gives an impassioned, soulful performance of "You Cut Up the Clothes in the Closet of My Dreams" a riveting love lament. Writer/producer/director Melvin Van Peebles's other films include *Watermelon Man*.

DR. BLACK, MR. HYDE

1975, USA
Alternative Titles: *The Watts Monster*; *Serum: Test-Tube Terror*
R (24473), Horror, 87m. Dimension Pictures.
D: William Crain; P: Charles Walker; S: Larry LeBron.
Cast: Bernie Casey, Rosalind Cash, Marie O'Henry, Ji-Tu Cumbuka, Sam Laws.

"A monster he can't control has taken over his very soul! The fear of the year is here!"

Attempting to find a cure for cirrhosis of the liver, a Los Angeles Doctor unwittingly uses himself as a guinea pig for his new experimental serum.

Director William (*Blacula*) Crain returns to the genre and does a workman-like job of re-telling Robert Louis Stevenson's classic 'The Strange Case of Dr. Jekyll and Mr. Hyde.'

Bernie (*Hit Man*) Casey plays Dr. Pride, a prize-winning physician who has an axe to grind (because his cleaning woman mother was mistreated by prostitutes). Often subtle, but at times off-putting and overwrought, Casey's large, football player frame serves him well but does not make up for the script's terrible lack of invention. The supporting cast is comprised of Rosalind (*Omega Man*) Cash as Dr. Billie North, Dr. Pride's sensitive and sensible research partner, and Marie (*Deliver Us from Evil*) O'Henry as prostitute Linda Monte, a manic, fidgety and totally unlikeable character who dominates the second half of the film. Actor Sam Laws (so good in his role of the beleaguered bookie in *Cool Breeze*) has a cameo as the Moonlight Lounge's know it all bartender.

A well-done back alley chase, an elderly hospital patient who goes through a brief but miraculous transformation, and a King Kong-like finale that takes place atop Los Angeles's famous Watts Towers are all semi-engaging distractions. An attempt at horror that is more silly than scary.

DRUM

1976, USA
R (24466), Action/Drama, 100m.
United Artists.
D: Steve Carver; P: Ralph B. Serpe; S: Norman Wexler, based on the novel by Kyle Onstott.
Cast: Ken Norton, Warren Oates, Yaphet Kotto, Pam Grier, Paula Kelly, Brenda Sykes, Lillian Hayman, Isela Vega, John Colicos.

"'Mandingo' lit the fuse... 'Drum' is the explosion!"

Drum, a slave living on a Southern plantation, leads a revolt after his friend is killed.

Even with a great slogan and successful ad campaign, this eagerly anticipated sequel to *Mandingo* can't hold a candle to its predecessor.

Ken Norton makes the desired impression as Drum, a handsome, well-built and fair-minded slave (though he does speak in a distinctly contemporary voice devoid of the southern inflections the rest of the cast members have adopted). Warren Oates as Hammond Maxwell, a brutal slave-owner with a conscience, is equally competent. Yaphet Kotto plays Blaise, a slave bent on revolt, and he offers, as is customary, a performance that is far superior to the material at hand.

Also in the cast (in a return performance) are: Lillian Hayman as Lucretia Borgia, the Maxwell's housekeeper; Isela Vega as Marianna, a prim and proper former whore – now

above: The stunning Brenda Sykes added depth to her role as slave girl Calinda in 1976's **Drum**. 131

lady of the house; and John Colicos as Bernard DeMarigny, a homosexual slave-owner who, like all the ladies in this film, has a hankering for Drum.

Drum's smaller roles are a virtual who's who of blaxploitation females: Brenda (*Honky*) Sykes plays Calinda, a beautiful, soft-voiced slave girl 'raised for a white master;' Paula (*Trouble Man*) Kelly is Rachel, keeper of her mistresses sordid secrets; and 'Pamela' (*Coffy*) Grier is Regine, a shrewd, scheming 'bed wench'.

Along with a lot of dialogue that seems specifically written for hoots and hollers, there are several poignant moments.

Drum (to Mother): *I want to be free.*
Mother: *What a man wants, and what a man gets, ain't always the same thing – especially if he's a* **black** *man.*

The overly hyped 'fiery revolt' at the end of the film ("It out-Mandingos Mandingo!") is lacklustre, too dark and too long; a disappointing conclusion to a disjointed and melodramatic tale that had been told better and more colourfully the year before.

"One big, elaborate, historically distorted de Sade orgy about as pleasant as a whiplash."
(Donald Bogle, Blacks in American Films & Television, 1988)

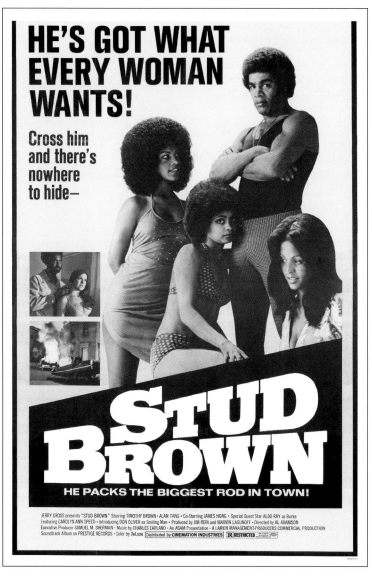

THE DYNAMITE BROTHERS

1974, USA
Alternative Title: *Stud Brown*
R (1097), Action/Adventure, 90m.
Cinemation Industries.
D: Al Adamson; P: Jim Rein, Marvin Lagunoff; S: John R. D'Amato, from a story by Marvin Lagunoff and Jim Rein. Cast: Alan Tang, Timothy Brown, Carol Speed, Aldo Ray.

"The Black cat from Watts... the kung fu cat from Hong Kong... even chained... together nobody can handle them!"

Two fugitives, one African American, one Chinese, join forces to combat a Los Angeles drug lord.

Clever script, good performances, exciting fight sequences and fun opening credits make this low-budget entry much more entertaining than might be expected.

Timothy Brown stars as Stud Brown, a 'man from Watts,' who is on a crusade to keep illegal drugs out of his neighbourhood. Alan Tang plays his do-good partner Larry Chin, a recently-arrived Chinese immigrant who is searching for his missing brother. The two performers compliment one another: Brown offering his good looks, confidence and machismo; Tang providing the agile, high-kicking hijinks that are a staple of the martial arts/blaxploitation hybrid. Carol (*Abby*) Speed plays Sarah, a big-hearted, well-intentioned mute who ends up rather shockingly disfigured.

above: **Drum** featured boxer Ken Norton doing what he was so good at in real life – winning a fight!

Directed with signature economy by Al Adamson, rife with pat quotables like "Hell has no fury like a woman scorned – especially if she's a black one!", and featuring the expected shootouts, karate fights and, yes, the money shot – a car over a cliff, *The Dynamite Brothers* is worth a cursory viewing.

DYNAMITE CHICKEN

1970, USA
R (26781), Comedy, 75m. EYR Programs.
D: Ernest Pintoff; P: Ernest Pintoff; S: Ernest Pintoff.
Cast: Richard Pryor, Joan Baez, Yoko Ono, Ace Trucking Company, John Lennon.

"Finger lickin' funny!"

A politically-minded social satire documentary featuring the most popular comedians of the day.

Funky, dated, but fast-moving and thoroughly entertaining, *Dynamite Chicken* uses everything from magazine clippings to nude dancers to get its anti-establishment point across.

It's all here, from Nixon-era jokes, drop-outs and racists to American flag-toting liberals. Add street corner interviews, old movie clips, newsreel footage, a strip tease, and several comedy vignettes (superbly performed by the Ace Trucking Company) and you have a highly visual, sometimes biting, hodgepodge that covers all the bases. A strikingly young-looking Richard Pryor is memorable as the picture's racy, story-telling Master of Ceremonies.

above: Richard Pryor is a jive-talking Master of Ceremonies in 1970's **Dynamite Chicken**.

EBONY, IVORY & JADE

1976, Philippines/USA
Alternative Titles: *Fox Force*; *She Devils in Chains*; *American Beauty Hostages*
PG (24556), Action/Adventure, 80m. Dimension Pictures.
D: Cirio H. Santiago; P: Cirio H. Santiago; S: Henry Barnes.
Cast: Rosanne Katon, Colleen Camp, Christie Mayuga, Sylvia Anderson.

"Three foxy mamas turned loose... they call 'em Ebony, Ivory & Jade. They can lick any man ever made!"

Three popular American track stars attending the Hong Kong Olympic games are abducted and held for ransom.

Filmed in the Philippines but set in Hong Kong, this economy feature (often confused with the 1979 CBS TV movie of the same name) is not only poor, it's also a cheat. The poster art and title for the film suggest that the three main characters are white, black and Asian. Not so. The story, such as it is, centres around two African Americans and an American white girl.

The titular triumvirate are: Ginger Douglas, aka 'Ivory' (Colleen Camp), a supermarket heiress who has excelled in the sports arena in an attempt to impress her disapproving father; Pam Rogers, aka 'Ebony' (Rosanne Katon), an inner-city girl who is as good at karate as she is on the track; and in a don't-blink-or-you'll-miss-her cameo, Jackie 'Jade' Wau (Christie Mayuga), Pam's high-kicking Asian friend and help mate. Sylvia Anderson provides sterling support as Casey Barnes, the other African American athlete in the movie; despite not being part of the headlining gang, she actually has much more screen time than Mayuga.

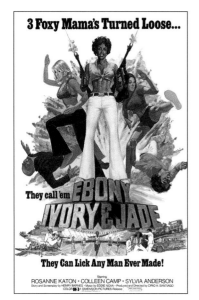

3 Foxy Mama's Turned Loose...

They call 'em **EBONY IVORY & JADE**

They Can Lick Any Man Ever Made!

Starring
ROSANNE KATON • COLLEEN CAMP • SYLVIA ANDERSON
Story and Screenplay by HENRY BARNES • Music by EDDIE NOVA • Produced and Directed by CIRIO H. SANTIAGO
COLOR ■■ A DIMENSION PICTURES Release

Poor lighting, poor sound recording, poor writing, poor acting, inexcusably poor 'sets', more than anything else, *Ebony, Ivory & Jade* confirms Dimension Pictures' reputation as the least discriminating blaxploitation picture distributor. As Fred Williamson said in a 2000 interview with the Independent Film Channel, "Dimension Pictures picked up all the films that no one else wanted." *Ebony, Ivory & Jade*, most certainly, fits the bill. See *Q & A: Ten Directors Discuss Their Films*.

"...filmmaking of the highest ineptitude..." (David Walker, BadAzz MoFo magazine issue #5)

THE EDUCATION OF SONNY CARSON

1974, USA
R (24013), Drama, 104m.
Paramount Pictures.
D: Michael Campus; P: Irwin Yablans;
S: Fred Hudson.
Cast: Rony Clanton, Don Gordon, Joyce Walker, Paul Benjamin.

"You learn a lot in the streets."

A rebellious black youth comes of age in 1950s and 1960s Brooklyn.

Political activist Sonny Carson's inspiring story is brought to vivid, frightening life in one of the most realistically acted blaxploitation films of the 1970s.

In the lead role of Sonny Carson, the felon turned activist, actor Rony

Clanton (who would later change his name to Iwina Lmiri Abubadika) is beyond good. Never hitting a false note (in fact, with his slobbering, trembling, and disfiguring grimaces he seems to be going way beyond the parameters of his role), Clanton offers a disturbing presentation of concentrated anguish and agony. His heroin-addicted girlfriend Virginia (Joyce [*Willie Dynamite*] Walker) also turns in a committed performance that makes it clear she is not present in the narrative just to serve as window dressing. Carson's hard working father is movingly portrayed by Paul Benjamin.

Some of the topics covered include a behind-the-scenes look at two real Brooklyn gangs (the Lords and the Hawks), prison indignities, and the unrelenting racism a black man must face every day, both on and off the harsh ghetto streets.

By no means perfect (many scenes go on much longer than is warranted, thus diluting their impact), *The Education of Sonny Carson*'s violent realism and protracted images of suffering will, nevertheless, stay with you long after the film is finished. Highly recommended. Michael Campus also directed *The Mack*.

"When the historical dust settles on the first wave of black-oriented films, 'The Education of Sonny Carson' should stand up as one of the most outstanding in the genre." (Variety)

"The education of sonny carson"

EL CONDOR

1970, USA
R (22665), Western, 102m.
National General Pictures.
D: John Guillermin; P: Andre de Toth;
S: Larry Cohen and Steven Carabatsos, from a story by Steven Carabatsos.
Cast: Jim Brown, Lee Van Cleef, Patrick O'Neal, Marianna Hill, Iron Eyes Cody.

"It takes the two biggest wall-busters to break through the fortress."

Two adventurers, one white, one African American, along with a band of Apache Indians, besiege a Mexican Fortress in search of gold.

This spectacular Western with a twist is one of the first major American films (predating *Sweet Sweet-back's Baadasssss Song* by a full year) to present a violent, sexualised, unrepentant African-American male in a leading role.

Jim Brown plays Luke, an escaped convict who is fast on the trail of a stash of gold. Tough, handsome, agile, intelligent, and the only film character still standing at the end of the movie, Brown's screen presence was a cause for young black militant-minded audiences to celebrate. Luke's partner in crime is the bumbling, emotional, hard-drinking Jaroo (Lee Van Cleef). This briskly paced adventure also features: Patrick O'Neal as Chavez, the commandant of El Condor, a Mexican fort; Marianna Hill as Claudine, Chavez's semi-faithful wife; and Iron Eyes Cody as Santana, head of a tribe of Apache Indians.

Shootouts, wagon chases (in which a distractingly large number of stunt horses take a tumble), and mass nudity from most of the female characters, are all part of the mix. Beautifully photographed, with deft editing and superior sound, and a cast of who carry their roles admirably, make this a fully realised creative endeavour. John Guillermin also directed *Shaft in Africa*.

EMBASSY

1972, UK
Alternative Title: *Target: Embassy*
PG (631), Action/Adventure, 90m.
K-tel International.
D: Gordon Hessler; P: Mel Ferrer;
S: William Fairchild.
Cast: Richard Roundtree, Max von Sydow, Chuck Connors, Ray Milland, Marie-José Nat.

Wages an
ice-cold war on your
nerves

EMBASSY

Richard Roundtree
the superstar
from Shaft is Back

K-TEL
presents a   Mel Ferrer production

Starring   and
Richard   Chuck   Marie-José Ray   Broderick   Max von Sydow
Roundtree   Connors   Nat   Milland Crawford   as Gorenko

"Richard Roundtree, the superstar from 'Shaft', is back."

Two American embassy employees stationed in Beirut come to the aid of a mysterious Russian defector.

A slipshod and underwhelming look at the dubious roles of politically-minded American employees abroad.

In the lead as Dick Shannon, an African-American political speechwriter from Peoria, Illinois, top-billed Richard Roundtree gives it his all, but is helplessly adrift in a meandering story filled with highly improbable twists and turns. On hand in this mediocre, ugly endeavour are Chuck Connors as Colonel Kesten, a man who is not what he seems to be; Ray (*Slavers*) Milland as a power-crazed Ambassador; and Max von Sydow as Gorenko, a know-it-all Russian spy.

Claustrophobic (almost the entire film takes place within the white-walled confines of several offices) and preposterous (a political refugee is allowed to get drunk and then wrestle a gun from a guard), *Embassy* is a testament to the star power of Richard Roundtree, without whose name this film would never have been financed. Carl 'Kung Fu Fighting' Douglas sings 'Embassy', the picture's equally lacklustre theme song.

EMMA MAE

1976, USA
Alternative Title: *Black Sister's Revenge*
R (24797), Drama, 100m. Pro International.
D: Jamaa Fanaka; P: Jamaa Fanaka;
S: Jamaa Fanaka.
Cast: Jerri Hayes, Ernest Williams II,
Charles D. Brooks III, Malik Carter.

"She's rough 'n' tough don't take no stuff – what ya say she's... Emma Mae!"

An unsophisticated young African-American woman from the South teaches her Northern relatives a thing or two about life and living.

Emma Mae is an outstanding movie that very few people have seen; had it originally been released under its 1980s video title *Black Sister's Revenge*, the film might have enjoyed much greater success.

Newcomer Jerri Hayes is superb in the lead as Emma Mae. Blessed with a wonderful speaking voice and a genuinely uncomplicated and shy demeanour, she is a refreshing change from the over confident superwomen who populate most 'female-hero' blaxploitation pictures. Emma's manipulative 'boyfriend' Jesse (Ernest Williams II) is also very good. Rounding out the cast is Malik (*Black Belt Jones*) Carter who holds his own as a sage, disturbed older man named Big Daddy. Carter's monologues are memorable:

Big Daddy (to a group of young people): *Y'all got the nerve to be talkin' about worrying about facing time* [in prison]. *Nigger, you facing time every day you live and breathe. Why you doin' time right now and don't even know it! You are all jiving at me about my mumbling. You see, what you don't know is that I mumble to forget. That's right, when I mumble I forget that I'm ashamed to be as old as I am and still walking around. Why, if I was anybody at all I'd be dead. I ain't shit and I know it.*

Incorporating many seldom-seen details of inner city black life (kitchen table gossip, the preoccupation with skin colour and hair texture), *Emma Mae* is a sometimes preachy, sometimes stilted, but always engaging cinematic experience whose final act will leave you cheering.

Note: Keisa Brown's theme song 'Long to Be Back Home' (played at the film's start and end) is uncredited. African-American director/producer/screen-writer Jamaa Fanaka's other films include *Welcome Home Brother Charles* and *Penitentiary*. See *Q & A: Ten Directors Discuss their Films*.

"A tribute to the strength and resiliency of black womanhood... one of the most positive female images in recent American pix."
(Variety)

ENTER THE DRAGON

1973, Hong Kong/USA
R (23684), Action/Adventure, 99m.
Warner Bros.
D: Robert Clouse; P: Fred Weintraub, Paul Heller; S: Michael Allin.
Cast: Bruce Lee, Jim Kelly, John Saxon, Shih Kien.

"Their deadly mission: To crack the forbidden Island of Han!"

A martial arts expert enters an unusual tournament hosted by a wealthy eccentric on his far-away island.

Exciting choreography, interesting characters and a fast-moving script are just a few of the elements that come together to make this cult favourite (Bruce Lee's most famous film, and Jim Kelly's breakthrough – as a last-minute replacement for Rockne Tarkington) one of the most exciting action movies of all time.

Martial arts expert Lee is brilliant as he goes undercover to crack a drug and prostitution ring. Comfortable and confident in front of the camera, Lee projects a luminous, otherworldly quality that is, no doubt, one of the reasons he remains a relentlessly discussed pop culture icon to this very day. Also on the side of good are Williams (Jim Kelly), and Roper (John Saxon), two men who are equally adept at martial arts. All are up against Han (Shih Kien) a mysterious Fu-Manchu-like underworld drug king.

A hit with both audiences and critics, the highly influential *Enter the Dragon* raked in $11,500,000 at the box-office.

"Reminiscent of James Bond's 'Dr. No', it moves like lightning and brims with colour."
(Howard Thompson, New York Times)

FAREWELL UNCLE TOM

1971, Italy
Alternative Titles: *Addio zio Tom*; *Goodbye Uncle Tom*
X (833), Drama, 118m. Cannon Group.
D: Gualtiero Jacopetti, Franco Prosperi;
P: Gualtiero Jacopetti, Franco Prosperi;
S: Gualtiero Jacopetti, Franco Prosperi.
Cast: Uncredited.

"It was part of the birth of a nation."

A brutally frank examination of America's role in the slave trade.

Unrelentingly degrading, brutal and genuinely disquieting, this Italian-made 'shockumentary' from the directors of *Mondo Cane* is the kind of movie that has to be seen to be believed.

The characters in this film include a British investigative reporter, an educated black slave who speaks about the *positive* side of being a slave, a mad doctor who performs horrendous experiments on children, a preacher who argues for the moral and spiritual necessity of slavery, and an all-knowing midget slave trader/tour guide.

Some of the film's more disturbing images include hot iron branding of human beings, the rape of a thirteen-year-old girl, masses of people (many deformed) eating cornmeal from an animal trough, and a visit to a slave-breeding farm. Undeniably fascinating, *Farewell Uncle Tom* blurs the lines of social commentary and pure exploitation. It is a film whose discourteous content and truly repulsive imagery will stay with you for a very, very long time.

"Shocking... a film that will please no one..."
(Mark Deming, All Movie Guide)

FASS BLACK

1977, USA
Alternative Titles: *Disco 9000*; *Black Disco*
PG (24855), Action/Adventure, 96m.
Choice Inc./Cosmo Inc.
D: D'Urville Martin; P: Demetris Johnson, Robert Paul Ross, D'Urville Martin; S: Dr. Roland Jefferson.
Cast: John Poole, Jeanie [Jean] Bell, Nicholas Lewis, Johnnie Taylor, Beverly Ann, Harold Nicholas, Sidney Bagby, D'Urville Martin.

"When he's in the groove... the mob better move!"

A successful Los Angeles nightclub owner is pressured to abide by local mob rules.

This late to market, music-centred entry, originally released as *Disco 9000* and re-titled *Fass Black* on video, is one of the genre's most shamelessly padded.

John Poole provides just the right amount of pretension in the lead role of Fass Black, a successful Los Angeles nightclub owner who has cornered sales in the disco market by forming his own label and selling the resultant records in his popular Disco 9000 discothèque. His wife Denise (Beverly Ann) is also believably portrayed; both faithful and ready to take on the challenges that life presents. Notable supporting players include: Fass's girlfriend Karen, played by Jean (*TNT Jackson*) Bell (here lovelier than in any of her other films); Midget (Harold Nicholas), Fass's faithful friend and confidant; Manny (Sidney Bagby), a popular Los Angeles DJ who is in debt to the mob; and Gene 'Music Man' Edwards (pop star Johnnie Taylor in his only fictional film role) as an influential promo man/performer. (Look out for director D'Urville Martin in a cameo).

Terribly stretched (filler includes a disco fashion show, a disco dance contest and a sepia-coloured romp along a beach) and lacking in major incident, *Fass Black*'s music soundtrack does, nonetheless, contain several outstanding Johnnie Taylor tunes including 'The Lord Is Standing,' 'Round and Round,' and, of course, the No.1 pop hit 'Disco Lady.'

above: Blaxploitation superstar Jim Kelly (*seated*) talks to John Saxon in **Enter the Dragon** (1973).

above: 1977's **Fight for Your Life** remains one of blaxploitation's most controversial films. Here escaped convict Jessie Lee Kane (William Sanderson) holds the righteous Ted Turner (Robert Judd) and his family hostage. (Soul Images)

"Borrowing plot elements and themes from other blaxploitation films, 'Disco 9000' comes across as a weird rip-off of 'Super Fly' (with a touch of 'The Mack')." (David Walker, BadAzz MoFo magazine issue #7)

FIGHT FOR YOUR LIFE

1977, USA
Alternative Titles: *Staying Alive*; *Getting Even*; *Held Hostage*
R (25134), Drama, 86m.
William Mishkin Motion Pictures, Inc.
D: Robert A. Endelson; P: William Mishkin, Robert A. Endelson; S: Straw Weisman.
Cast: William Sanderson, Robert Judd, Reginald Bythewood, Lela Small, Daniel Faraldo, Peter Yoshida.

"There is no greater violence than a father's revenge for the rape of his daughter."

Three sadistic escaped convicts terrorize a suburban black preacher and his family.

Breathtakingly base, vulgar and obscene, made to provoke and offend, *Fight for Your Life* is, without a doubt, the most inflammatory blaxploitation film ever made.

As murderer/rapist Jessie Lee Kane, William Sanderson gives a tour de force performance that will leave your mouth agape. Greasy-haired, bullish, ignorant and convincingly relishing in the humiliation of others, his is an over-the-top screen performance that lingers long after the film has finished. Kane's partners in crime are Chino (Daniel Faraldo) a macho Mexican accomplice who idolises Kane and is eager to do his bidding, and Ling (Peter Yoshida), a dim-witted and sadistic prankster.

Kane's gang terrorize the Turners, an African-American family which includes: the family patriarch Ted (Robert Judd), a righteous man who does not believe in violence; his more militant-minded young son Floyd (Reginald Bythewood); and an impulsive, tart-tongued and fearless invalid, Grandma Turner (Lela Small).

Grandma Turner (to Jessie Kane): *I've had it with you Kane, you dung heap. You're nothing but a two-bit cork-poppin' rear end of a sow! You two-legged yellow dog. Go on, shoot me. Shoot me! But I'll tell you something Mr. Poor White Trash. You ain't nothin' but what you got in your hand* [a gun]. *And your pappy should've thought about that before he stuck it in your mammy!*

Along with a relentless barrage of racial epithets ("tar-baby," "darkie," "spade," "jungle-bunny," "wool-head," et al.), the film's 'lowlights' include: three vividly depicted shootings; a death by glass impalement; a gang rape; a character sexually abused and thrown off a cliff; a child bludgeoned to death with a rock; and a man beaten unconscious – with a bible!

Rarely seen upon its original release (many theatres refused to run it for fear of rioting) and banned outright in Great Britain, *Fight for Your Life* is resplendently trashy, filthy, slimy, discomforting, controversial and unapologetically audacious. An unequalled bad-taste success. See *Q & A: Ten Directors Discuss Their Films.*

THE FINAL COMEDOWN

1972, USA
Alternative Title: *Blast*
R (23244), Action/Adventure, 84m.
New World Pictures.
D: Oscar Williams; P: Oscar Williams;
S: Oscar Williams.
Cast: Billy Dee Williams, Raymond St.
Jacques, D'Urville Martin, Celia Kaye,
Maidie Norman.

"It's the people against the law in a violent street battle."

An African-American man 'wronged' by society recruits a group of friends to battle the police.

The Final Comedown is an unrelenting tirade against racism and injustice.

Billy Dee Williams is young, attractive and energetic in the lead role of Johnny Johnson – too bad he's stuck playing a one note character whose angry, militant point of view makes him difficult to like, especially as he despises both his parents, mistreats his girlfriend and thinks he is better than the impoverished black community that he continually says he wants to help. Also in the cast are Raymond St. Jacques as Imir, Johnny's more level-headed friend, and Maidie Norman as Johnny's mother, a woman who speaks for the audience when she tells her son, "I ain't got time to be blamin' white folks for all my troubles."

The major incidents, such as they are, include a surprisingly detailed sex scene and a deadening ten-minute shootout with the police. A low-budget claustrophobic film that audiences wisely ignored, even when it was re-released in 1976 as *Blast*. Director Oscar Williams had his name removed from the project on its re-release.

"Wholly exploitative of both its dramatic form and its social situation."
(Roger Greenspun, New York Times)

FINGERS

1977, USA
R (25010), Drama, 90m. Brut Productions.
D: James Toback; P: George Barrie;
S: James Toback.
Cast: Harvey Keitel, Jim Brown, Tisa Farrow, Michael V. Gazzo, Tanya Roberts, Danny Aiello.

"He has the hands of an artist... and the mind of a madman."

An aspiring concert pianist struggles with his personal obsessions.

Fingers is a heartfelt, realistically presented film that is too oddball to be appreciated by general audiences and never quite hits its mark.

Harvey Keitel turns in a natural and wholly believable performance as frustrated piano player/sexually confused mob debt-collector Jimmy Angelelli. Vulgar, streetwise, but aspiring to more in life, his is a multidimensional character written and performed with great conviction and attention to detail. Jim Brown plays Dreems, an ex-boxer turned nightclub owner who has a stable of young (white) women under his spell and at his beck and call. Quiet voiced, seductive, able to perceive people's hidden neuroses, Brown, too, realistically captures his character's skills at manipulation. Also outstanding as Ben, Jimmy's fading, somewhat desperate, father is Michael V. Gazzo. Of note in minuscule film roles are Tanya (of TV's *Charlie's Angels*) Roberts, and Danny (*Moonstruck*) Aiello.

Filled with life's many frustrations, challenges and disappointments, *Fingers* is a bit too complex and a bit too personal; the film is jam-packed with problems (sex addiction, sexual dysfunction, obsessive compulsive disorder, dashed dreams) whose main objective seems to be to exorcise demons rather than to entertain audiences.

Note: Director James Toback had previously written a best-selling biography of Jim Brown.

"An existential jaunt into the underworld... a very literary film that often falls apart."
(Donald Bogle, Blacks in American Films and Television, 1988)

THE FISH THAT SAVED PITTSBURGH

1979, USA
PG (25812), Comedy, 104m. United Artists.
D: Gilbert Moses; P: David Dashev;
S: Jaison Starkes, Edmond Stevens.
Cast: Julius 'Dr. J' Erving, Jonathan Winters, Meadowlark Lemon, Stockard Channing, Flip Wilson, Kareem Abdul-Jabbar, James Bond III, Margaret Avery, Flip Wilson.

"As jocks they were jokes... The twelve nuttiest, goofiest, spoofiest, singin'est, dancin'est characters to ever call themselves a team."

A losing Pennsylvania basketball team hopes that astrology will reveal the secret to regaining their previous success.

This formula film with a title that confused many prospective theatregoers (it refers to the astrological sign Pisces) is

THE MAN GOT DOWN...
THE BROTHERS WERE READY...

The Final Comedown

starring BILLY DEE WILLIAMS

YOU MUST SEE IT!..
IT'S A MOTHER!

METROCOLOR
A New World Pictures Release · R

filled with a bevy of light, airy performances and contemporary sports stars.

Child actor James Bond III is particularly good as the brains behind the team's success. In possession of that rare quality among young actors (the ability to use one's voice with appropriate nuance and inflection), he is quite amazing to watch and listen to. Stockard Channing is also outstanding as the Python's 'team astrologist' Mona Mondieu. A cameo by Flip Wilson and a dual role by Jonathan Winters are also noteworthy. Margaret Avery as Toby Millman (Tyrone's older sister) delivers the film's only poignant message – that *all* black kids won't grow up to be sports stars. Also appearing in the cast are (top billed) Julius 'Dr. J' Erving and his basketball star cohorts Meadowlark Lemon and Kareem Abdul-Jabbar.

Fashioned to appeal to the younger viewer (think *Thank God It's Friday*), the soundtrack is filled with catchy, self-explanatory songs like 'You Can Make It Happen,' 'Listen to Your Heart,' and 'Chance of a Lifetime' by soul music veteran Thom Bell. The Sylvers perform an elaborate musical number called 'Mighty, Mighty Pisces' during halftime and a rousing gospel turn is provided by The Spinners, who perform 'Jesus, Won't You Walk with Me.' African-American director Gilbert Moses also directed *Willie Dynamite*.

"It's cheerfully inoffensive entertainment designed for the crowd that liked 'Car Wash'..."
(Janet Maslin, New York Times)

As jocks they were jokes...
the twelve nuttiest, goofiest, spoofiest, singin'est, dancin'est characters to ever call themselves a team!

THE FISH THAT SAVED PITTSBURGH

You've been coffy-tized, blacula-rized and super-flied – but now you're gonna be glorified, unified and filled-with-pride...
when you see
"FIVE on the BLACK HAND SIDE"

FIVE ON THE BLACK HAND SIDE

1973, USA
PG (23683), Comedy, 96m. United Artists.
D: Oscar Williams; P: Brock Peters, Michael Tolan; S: Charlie L. Russell.
Cast: Leonard Jackson, Glynn Turman, D'Urville Martin, Godfrey Cambridge, Clarice Taylor, Virginia Capers, Philomena Nowlin.

"You've been Coffy-tized, Blacula-rized and Super-flied – but now you're gonna be glorified, unified, and filled-with-pride... when you see... Five on the Black Hand Side"

A barber shop owner struggles to cope with his unsatisfied wife, militant son and daughter's impending marriage.

This is a foolish suitable-for-all-family-members comedy that misses its mark at every turn.

In the lead as John Henry Brooks, a beleaguered middle class husband and father, Leonard Jackson turns in an obnoxious, totally unlikeable, one-dimensional performance that is, at best, grating. Clarice Taylor plays his wife Gladys, a long-suffering matriarch who goes through a dramatic transformation, with a bit more subtlety. Various cardboard character roles are taken by:

Glynn Turman as Gideon, the family's rebellious young son; D'Urville Martin as Booker T., the older, more level-headed son; and Virginia Capers as Ruby, a young woman who has found an escape route from her dysfunctional home. Also of note is a brief appearance by Philomena (*Miss Melody Jones*) Nowlin.

Burdened by overlong shots, dead dialogue and flat lighting, the only reason to recommend *Five on the Black Hand Side* is the fact that TV's Soul Train Dancers participate in the picture's afro-centric final wedding sequence. Producer Brock Peters and screenwriter Charlie L. Russell are African American.

FORCE FOUR

1975, USA
Alternative Title: *Black Force*
R (1262) , Action/Adventure, 89m.
Howard Mahler Films.
D: Michael Fink; P: Michael Fink, Marvin Schild, Joel Schild; S: Leonard Michaels, Janice Weber.
Cast: Owen Wat-son, Warhawk Tanzania, Malachi Lee, Judie Soriano.

"When things get rough – we get bad!"

Four karate experts are called in to retrieve a priceless stolen artefact.

"All the martial arts sequences in this film are authentic. No attempt has been made to enhance or alter actual fights by the use of special effects or trick photography."

So we are told at the opening of this atrocious super-low-budget entry. *Force Four* is essentially a series of karate sequences strung together (each of the four headliners gets their own fight scene), accompanied by a series of 'montages' (shots of street signs, fire escapes, garbage trucks). The major exposition of the film is delivered to the viewer in a static long shot of the four main characters – three men and one woman – who remain seated around a coffee table in an unidentified, under-lit living room.

Threadbare, padded and dull, the only praiseworthy thing about this movie are three relatively good songs, 'Jesus Is Lurking There,' 'Loving You Is So Beautiful' and, best of all, 'Lock Up Time,' performed by the group Life USA. Michael Fink also directed *Velvet Smooth*.

FOX STYLE

1973, USA
R (819), Drama, 84m.
Presidio Productions Incorporated.
D: Clyde Houston; P: Paul R. Picard; S: Michael Fox.
Cast: Chuck Daniel, Juanita Moore, Richard Lawson, Denise Denise, Hank Rolike.

"They call him the Black Fox... he cleans the scene and makes his name in the money game. A positive black film."

A wealthy Los Angeles nightclub owner returns to his Midwestern hometown to help keep a local factory from closing.

Not just bad, but genuinely awful, and for Juanita Moore (co-star with Lana Turner in *Imitation of Life*) embarrassing.

Chuck Daniel is competent but uniformly uninteresting in the lead as Arthur 'A.J.' Fox, owner of a trendy New York City nightclub called Fox's Lair (and owner/pilot of a snazzy private jet, as well as a few gushing Texas oil wells). Juanita Moore (as his backwoods 'Mama') turns in a mammy-like performance, filled with poor grammar, good intentions and sanctimony. (In a 1970s 'positive-minded' blaxploitation film, she is wholly out of place). As Fox's lovely but neglected girlfriend Cindy, the only thing memorable about Denise Denise is her unusual name.

The best performance in the film comes from Hank Rolike as the Reverend Everett L. Rambo. In possession of a wonderfully theatrical speaking voice, he delivers the picture's only real moment, an impassioned plea (more like a sermon) for the rights of a large factory's employees.

Poorly presented (almost every scene is filmed in full shot with next to no close-ups); poorly performed; poorly scripted, *Fox Style* is in the top ten of the worst of the worst blaxploitation films. Barbara Lynn's soulful theme song 'Fox Style' is the picture's only praiseworthy point. Director Clyde Houston is African American.

"First, 'How did this get made?', second, 'Why did this get made?' The answer: 'This should've never been made!'"
(David Walker, BadAzz MoFo magazine issue #7)

FOXY BROWN

1974, USA
R (23883), Action/Adventure, 91m.
American International Pictures.
D: Jack Hill; P: Buzz Feitshans; S: Jack Hill.
Cast: Pam Grier, Antonio Fargas, Terry Carter, Kathryn Loder, Juanita Brown.

"Don't mess aroun' with... Foxy Brown. She's the meanest chick in town! She's brown sugar and spice but if you don't treat her nice she'll put you on ice!"

A young woman, out to avenge her brother's death, poses as a prostitute to infiltrate a drug ring.

This 'female hero' revenge fantasy is, today, one of blaxploitation's most popular films. From the very beginning of the picture it is clear that Pam Grier, fresh from her success with *Coffy*, has ascended into that rarefied category of black superstar. Evidence for this comes in the form of what seems like a never-ending litany of screen credits for services rendered directly to, and for, 'Ms. Grier.' The performer, who had only three costume changes in *Coffy*, here has at least ten – complete with different wigs to match. The movie's glamorous opening credit sequence borrows much from the 1969 Raquel Welch vehicle *Flareup* (Grier has been called 'the black Raquel Welch'), and features a top notch theme song, 'Theme from Foxy Brown,' performed by popular soul artist Willie Hutch.

As Foxy Brown, a woman who lives lavishly but whose profession is never really clear, Pam Grier is as lovely to look at as she is comfortable with her new semi-sumptuous moviestar surroundings. Supporting the colourful main performer are: Antonio (*Car Wash*) Fargas as Link, Foxy's small-time dope-peddling brother; Terry (*Brother on the Run*) Carter as Michael Anderson/Dalton Ford, Foxy's 'reassigned' boyfriend; Juanita (*Black Starlet*) Brown as Claudia, a well-meaning but drug addled prostitute; and Kathryn (*The Big Doll House*) Loder as Katherine Wall, a pretentious, oversexed and ruthless drug lord.

Entertaining and shamelessly trashy, *Foxy Brown* features an all-female barroom brawl (set in a lesbian nightclub), a backwoods sugar shack filled with 'white trash' dope peddlers, and several raunchy and authentically funny segments involving penis size (or lack thereof). Sarcasm is also at a premium:

Foxy (to corrupt judge): *Danny is such a good person. He just has really bad luck. Like the time he was found in that alley with that nine-year-old girl. He wasn't molesting her; she was loving every minute of it. And those ropes didn't mean a thing!*

A man set on fire, a throat slitting, a beheading, a coat hanger beating, and even a castration, are all part of the over-the-top proceedings. Thoroughly entertaining pulp. See *Q & A: Ten Directors Discuss Their Films*.

"...trashy, lurid and, exploitative..."
(Donald Bogle, Blacks in American Films and Television, 1988)

above: 1974's **Foxy Brown** was Pam Grier's follow up to the the previous year's **Coffy**. (Soul Images)

FRIDAY FOSTER

1975, USA
R (24442), Action/Adventure, 90m.
American International Pictures.
D: Arthur Marks; P: Arthur Marks; S: Orville Hampton, Arthur Marks.
Cast: Pam Grier, Yaphet Kotto, Godfrey Cambridge, Thalmus Rasulala, Eartha Kitt, Carl Weathers, Julius Harris.

"Wham! Bam! Here comes Pam! Pam Grier in 'Friday Foster'."

Fashion photographer Friday Foster foils an assassination attempt on a group of African-American politicians.

This is a thoroughly mundane TV-movie-like adaptation of the adventures of popular comic strip character Friday Foster.

Pam Grier, in the lead as *Glance* magazine's premier fashion photographer, is a cleaned up, feminised, thoroughly ingratiating woman who unwittingly becomes involved in an assassination plot. Yaphet Kotto is Colt Hawkins, her supportive and very witty boyfriend. Other performers include: a Martian-like Eartha Kitt as fashion designer Madame Rena; Carl (*Bucktown*) Weathers as Yarbro, a strong-arm man; Thalmus (*Cool Breeze*) Rasulala as Blake Tarr, an African-American tycoon; Godfrey (*Cotton Comes to Harlem*) Cambridge as Ford Malotte, an effeminate dress designer;

and Julius (*Black Caesar*) Harris as the self-serving Monk Riley.

A poolside fashion show, a firefight on a rooftop, and a clandestine plot entitled 'Black Widow' are the main events in this overpopulated, far too slick, film that signalled an end for Pam Grier's superstar status. See *Q & A: Ten Directors Discuss Their Films*.

"This is one of those films where everyone and everything looks a little too good to be believed..."
(Lawrence Van Gelder, New York Times)

GANJA & HESS

1973, USA
Alternative Titles: *Black Vampire*; *Blood Couple*; *Double Possession*; *Black Out*; *Black Devil*
R (806), Horror, 110m.
Kelly-Jordan Enterprises.
D: Bill Gunn; P: Chiz Schultz; S: Bill Gunn.
Cast: Duane Jones, Marlene Clark, Mabel King, Leonard Jackson.

"Some marriages are made in heaven... others are made in hell!"

A black anthropologist develops an insatiable desire for human blood after accidentally puncturing himself with an ancient African artefact.

A very personal and highly conceptual 'vampire tale' by African-American writer/director Bill Gunn, *Ganja & Hess* is marred by poor production values, sloppy editing and an abundance of fantasy/dream sequences.

Duane (*Night of the Living Dead*) Jones is quiet, dignified and persuasive in the lead role of Dr. Hess Green. Marlene (*Night of the Cobra Woman*) Clark is Ganja, Dr. Green's new girlfriend. Haughty, stunning, passionate and utterly convincing, Clark seems a bit out of place in this student film level production.

Along with the recurring appearance of a dancing, feather-head-dressed, Mabel King as the 'Queen of Myrthia,' and Leonard (*Five on the Black Hand Side*) Jackson as Archie, Dr. Green's obliging manservant, the film also features a suicide in a bathroom, a corpse in a wine cellar, and an absolution in a church. The picture's 'poetic' voiceovers appear to have been added after the fact to explain what would otherwise be incomprehensible.

Uncomfortably juxtaposing surprisingly explicit sex scenes with gore, this box office dud (despite being a hit at the 1973 Cannes Film Festival) is a movie that seems to have been made to appeal to critics and film students rather than general audiences.

"Some very handsome people are given such ridiculous roles that laughter in the wrong places is their only due."
(Variety)

GEORGIA, GEORGIA

1972, USA
R (23278), Drama, 91m.
Cinerama Releasing.
D: Stig Björkman; P: Quentin Kelly, Jack Jordan; S: Maya Angelou.
Cast: Diana Sands, Dirk Benedict, Minnie Gentry, Terry Whitmore.

"They sacrificed Georgia to save her soul."

The dramatic experiences of a world famous African-American singing star.

Diana Sands is an always-entertaining distraction here in the role of Georgia Martin, an African-American singer who is beset by the pressures of fame. At times highly believable, at times affected and patently artificial, hers is a star performance that, at times, feels self-referential. Dirk Benedict sensitively brings to life Georgia's white photographer boyfriend Michael Winters. Equally visible, and perhaps more memorable than the star herself, is Georgia's assistant, Alberta Anderson (played by Minnie Gentry), an extremely verbose presence who plays a major role in the picture's politically-minded final scene.

Discussed extensively by film critics (perhaps because it was written by Pulitzer Prize winning poet Maya Angelou), but seen by very few, *Georgia, Georgia* is a wildly uneven examination of sexism, racism, greed, envy, and the highly complicated role that African-American celebrities must play for their fans, their race, and finally, themselves.

"The characters speak with passion... but their emotion is, sadly enough, too often projected in rhetoric and surface histrionics rather than drama."
(A.H. Weiler, New York Times)

GET CHRISTIE LOVE!

1974, USA
NR, Action/Adventure, 73m.
Wolper Pictures.
D: William A. Graham; P: Peter Nelson; S: George Kirgo, from the novel 'The Ledger' by Dorothy Uhnak.
Cast: Teresa Graves, Harry Guardino, Louise Sorel, Lynne Holmes, Paul Stevens.

An undercover Los Angeles police-woman attempts to crack a drug ring.

Though *Get Christie Love!* did not receive a theatrical release, this popular blaxploitation movie, which was originally made for TV, has enjoyed success on home video. Originally shown as a pilot for a short-lived series (22 episodes), it remains a favourite with both older and newer audiences and is referenced in director Quentin Tarantino's 1992 film *Reservoir Dogs*.

Teresa Graves is simply fantastic as undercover officer Christie Love. No other African-American female performer in the genre possesses such a likeable, can't-wait-to-see-them-again-on-screen persona. Confident (she says a pleasant "hi" to admiring strangers, both male and female), intelligent (she devises a plan to crack an important drug case), shrewd (she coos, bats her eyes and sashays when it serves her own purposes), nonplussed (when a 'john' calls her "nigger" she nonchalantly retorts "nigger lover!"), and admirably unguarded (she intentionally uses bad grammar to make her point), Graves's blaxploitation hero is what both Pam Grier's and Tamara Dobson's are not – refreshingly natural and recognisable from real life.

Forced to perform their parts in the dark shadow cast by the dazzling light that is Graves are: Harry Guardino as Captain Casey Reardon, Christie's frustrated supervisor; Louise Sorel as Helena Varga, a 'trampy' mob girlfriend with a secret; and Lynne Holmes as Celia Jackson, an alcoholic (we meet her at an AA meeting) former friend-turned informant.

Fast-paced, engaging and suitable for all family members, *Get Christie Love!* is unsullied, thoroughly engaging escapist entertainment. Highly recommended. William A. Graham's other films include *Honky* and *Together Brothers*.

above: 1980's **Getting Over** starred John (**Black Shampoo**) Daniels as Mike Barnett, a well-meaning disco music producer. Daniels also produced the film and collaborated on the screenplay.

GETTING OVER

1980, USA
PG (26002), Drama/Musical, 108m.
Maverick Pictures International.
D: Bernie Rollins; P: John Daniels;
S: Bernie Rollins, John Daniels.
Cast: John Daniels, Gwen Brisco, Bernice Givens, Mary Hopkins, Floyd Chatman.

After putting together a successful female singing group, a Los Angeles record producer discovers the ugly truth about the behind-the-scenes machinations of the recording industry.

Created on a shoe string budget and utilising only a handful of different interior locations, *Getting Over* is a 'kooky' disco-themed blaxploitation entry that is as insipid to watch as it is to listen to.

John (*Black Shampoo*) Daniels is, at best, forgettable in the lead as Mike Barnett, a music producer/manger from Ohio who is now in Los Angeles promoting his singing group The Heavenly Sisters. His office cleaner/singer girlfriend Gwen (Gwen Brisco) is no better. The only memorable person in the entire film is Floyd (*Penitentiary*) Chatman in a cameo as Noble, a skirt-chasing dirty old man.

'Major incidents' include: a record company board meeting in which it is decided that the Tremendous Music Corporation should underwrite a black-owned record label ("let's add some pepper to our corporate profile!"); a tacky fashion/slide show; several Sister Sledge-like choreographed disco dance routines; and as a finale, a half-hour Citizens Choice Music Awards talent contest.

Unfunny, overlong, burdened by a number of uninspired songs, and featuring one-dimensional characters that no one cares about, *Getting Over* plays both like a poorly conceived TV-movie, and a last ditch effort to resurrect star/producer John Daniels's stagnant film career. Director Bernie Rollins is African American.

"Really nothing more than a silly movie with terrible acting and almost no production values."
(David Walker, BadAzz MoFo magazine issue #7)

GHETTO FREAKS

1970, USA
Alternative Titles: *Love Commune*; *Sign of Aquarius*
R (22568), Drama, 92m. Cinar Productions.
D: Robert J. Emery; P: George Roberts;
S: Robert J. Emery.
Cast: Paul Elliot, Mickey Shift, Gabe Lewis, Jim Coursar.

"Every white society chick wanted to join his soul family to get in on the integrated action!"

A disillusioned young man takes to the road in search of the meaning of life.

This is a youth-oriented film, whose main character, a "draft-dodger, bum & pervert," named Sonny (Paul Elliot), travels from one Cleveland, Ohio hangout to the next, and eventually ends up living in a commune with 15 other lost souls.

Featuring an acid trip (in which a young woman believes she is giving birth), a shootout and a longwinded (and nonsensical) sermon by a black hippie in a robe, *Ghetto Freaks* is a film whose main characters are long-haired young people who constantly talk about their 'hang ups,' and desperately try to avoid being 'square.' A '70s film with a distinctly '60s air about it.

"There is no real plot – at least not one that can be comprehended without the help of hallucinogenics."
(David Walker, BadAzz MoFo magazine issue #6)

above: Poster art for **Ghetto Freaks** (1970) under its "flower power" alternative title, **Sign of Aquarius**.

GIRLS ARE FOR LOVING

1973, USA
R (920), Action/Adventure, 95m.
Continental Distributing.
D: Don Schain; P: Ralph T. Desiderio;
S: Don Schain.
Cast: Cheri Caffaro, Timothy Brown,
Jocelyn Peters, William Grannell.

"Ginger... the way you like her... with a new way of loving... and a new way of killing!"

The CIA hires a gun-toting female spy in an attempt to stop an unfair American trade agreement with China.

In the starring role of Ginger McAllister, a young woman who is "single, wealthy and goes where the action is," Cheri (*Savage Sisters*) Caffaro (director Schain's wife) is authoritative and admirably comfortable in her many nude scenes (a nude swim scene, a nude tied-to-a-board sex scene, a nude beachfront karate fight, and a nude seduction in a hotel room). Lovely to look at and possessed with a refreshing natural air, Caffaro's only misstep is her on-screen performance of two full songs, neither of which presents her in a flattering light. As Clay Bowers, a fellow CIA agent who is on hand to help Ginger crack the case, Timothy (*Dynamite Brothers*) Brown turns in an articulate, businesslike, yet still seductive performance that is one of the finest in the film. Also noteworthy is the Barbara Eden-like Jocelyn Peters as Ronnie St. Claire, a memorably distant and repressed character in the process of working out her many complicated emotions.

Girls Are for Loving's fun features include bitchy dialogue, split screen photography, beautiful St. Thomas U.S. Virgin Islands locations, and several fantastic helicopter and speedboat escapes. (Sorely missing in this 'action feature' are the requisite sound effects that should have accompanied the many whacks, slaps, kicks and punches that are thrown hither and yonder). Don Schain also directed *A Place Called Today*. See *Q & A: Ten Directors Discuss Their Films*.

WANTED
DEAD
NOT
ALIVE

William B. Silberkleit Presents
JOHN SAXON ROSEY GRIER JOANNA CASSIDY in
THE GLOVE
With JOAN BLONDELL JACK CARTER ALDO RAY KEENAN WYNN
Produced by JULIAN ROFFMAN • Directed by ROSS HAGEN

THE GLOVE

1979, USA
Alternative Title: *Blood Mad*
R (25630), Action/Adventure, 92m.
Pro International.
D: Ross Hagen; P: Julian Roffman;
S: Hubert Smith, Julian Roffman.
Cast: John Saxon, Rosey Grier, Joanna Cassidy, Joan Blondell, Marie O'Henry.

"Wanted dead not alive!"

A recently released convict embarks on a vengeful killing spree, his target the guards who tortured him while he was in prison.

John (*Enter the Dragon*) Saxon turns in a performance filled with surprising nuance as Los Angeles bounty hunter Sam Kellog. Swaggering and cocky, but by turns sad and vulnerable, his multi-dimensional display elevates the material at hand. Former football player Rosey (*The Thing with Two Heads*) Grier plays Victor Hale, a teddybear-like man with a $20,000 price on his head. Amiable and fair-minded, but still a believer in 'an eye for an eye,' he is a super-violent anti-hero whose desire to right wrongs is intended to endear him to the audience. The supporting players include: Joanna Cassidy as Sheila Michaels, an over-ambitious realtor's girlfriend; Joan (*The Baron*) Blondell as Mrs. Fitzgerald, a thieving "sixty-five-year-old" book-keeper; and, in a non-speaking cameo, Marie (*Deliver Us from Evil*) O'Henry as Cathy, Hale's traumatised sister.

Good locations, a clever script and several deftly choreographed fight scenes make this late-arriving box office bomb worth a quick peek.

GOLDEN NEEDLES

1974, USA
Alternative Title: *The Chase for the Golden Needles*
PG (23986), Action/Adventure, 92m.
American International Pictures.
D: Robert Clouse; P: Fred Weintraub; S: Lee Pogostin, Sylvia Schneble.
Cast: Joe Don Baker, Jim Kelly, Burgess Meredith, Ann Sothern, Elizabeth Ashley.

"From the mansions of Beverly Hills and the vice hells of Kowloon they swarmed... searching for the ancient statue with the golden acupuncture needles that hold the power to rule the world!"

An international hunt begins when it is discovered that an ancient Chinese artefact has the power to restore youth.

Among blaxploitation's most notably miscast films, *Golden Needles* is little more than a hastily concocted follow-up vehicle for Joe Don Baker, star of the previous year's super successful *Walking Tall*.

Joe Don Baker is distractingly uncomfortable as Dan, a wanderer-for-hire who is assigned to locate an ancient Chinese statue that has been "stolen, hidden, lost and rediscovered throughout the centuries." Puffy, sweaty-faced, overweight and clumsy-looking, Baker is breathtakingly unbelievable both as a man who can easily move without being noticed and as an agile 'high-kicking' karate expert. The supporting players, many equally off the mark, include: Jim Kelly as Jeff, a tough guy for hire who not only appears bored but also – with his ill-fitting afro wig – ridiculous; Elizabeth Ashley as Felicity, a cold-hearted swindler; Ann Sothern as Fenzie, a feathered, sequined and perpetually tipsy bar proprietress; and Burgess Meredith as Winters, a kooky, very verbose man who is searching for the fountain of youth.

A barroom brawl, a chase through the cluttered streets of Hong Kong, and a robbery, complete with space suits and fire-shooting guns, are a few of this picture's many distractions. (Incidentally, it would appear that the filmmakers managed to get a bargain on breakaway glass, as there are at least five scenes of actors being hurled through glass windows).

"A combination of tedious Far Eastern intrigue, a soupçon of kung-fu, and a healthy dose of sex – all of which add up to a very dull movie…""
(TV Radio Mirror)

GORDON'S WAR

1973, USA
R (23689), Action/Adventure, 90m.
20th Century Fox.
D: Ossie Davis; P: Robert L. Schaffel; S: Howard Friedlander, Ed Spielman.
Cast: Paul Winfield, Carl Lee, David Downing, Tony King, Grace Jones.

"They said it would take an army to get the mob out of Harlem. This is the army! This is Gordon's War!"

A Vietnam Veteran assembles a group of former army buddies to fight corruption in Harlem.

Straightforwardly presented and professionally, if not inventively, photographed, *Gordon's War* (touted in ads as "The Black 'French Connection'") is a violent and fanciful tale that attempts to examine the downfall of America's inner cities.

Paul (*Trouble Man*) Winfield is refreshingly realistic in the lead as Gordon Hudson. No flashy clothes, no hip lingo, no extravagantly ornamented car, he is an everyday man who puts to good use the combat tactics he learned while in Vietnam. His anti-crime force partners include Bee Bishop, a highly persuasive accomplice played by Carl (*Super Fly*) Lee, and Tony (*Bucktown*) King as Roy Green, a doomed ladies man. Singer Grace Jones makes a cameo as Mary, a foxy, foul-mouthed drug carrier.

Curiously, *Gordon's War* bombed at the box office, despite good performances, a good script, and several deftly choreographed action sequences.

"...tough, fast... vividly jabs the crime underbelly of Harlem."
(Howard Thompson, New York Times)

THE GRASSHOPPER

1970, USA
Alternative Titles: *The Passing of Evil*; *Passions*
R (182), Drama, 95m.
National General Pictures.
D: Jerry Paris; P: Jerry Belson, Garry Marshall; S: Jerry Belson and Garry Marshall, from the novel 'The Passing of Evil' by Mark McShane.
Cast: Jacqueline Bisset, Jim Brown, Joseph Cotten, Corbett Monica.

"Today's child sheds no tears, has no regrets, knows no tomorrows. Today's child is Christine."

A beautiful young woman leaves her parents' comfortable suburban home and travels to Las Vegas to 'find herself'.

Jacqueline Bisset is a wooden doll in the role of Christine Adams, a beautiful but unsatisfied young woman from a well-to-do home in British Columbia. Her open-minded, restless call girl character is true to life, but, strangely, neither sympathetic nor interesting. Former Cleveland Browns

football star Jim Brown plays Tommy Marcott, Christine's African-American former-athlete boyfriend who is desperately trying to hold on to his self-confidence and self-esteem.

Essentially a series of vignettes that chronicle Christine's trials and travails, even as the 'satire' it purports to be, *The Grasshopper* is unbearably poor; it's episodic, patently implausible and painfully predictable.

"In a strange way this is one of Jim Brown's most effective roles. He understands the plight of a black man ill-at-ease in a high-powered world that sees him as a symbol of former glory..."
(Donald Bogle, Blacks in American Films and Television, 1988)

GREASED LIGHTNING

1977, USA
PG (24964), Drama, 96m. Warner Bros.
D: Michael Schultz; P: Hannah Weinstein; S: Kenneth Vose, Melvin Van Peebles, Lawrence Du Kore, Leon Capetanos.
Cast: Richard Pryor, Pam Grier, Beau Bridges, Cleavon Little, Maynard Jackson, Julian Bond, Richie Havens.

"In 1950, somebody had the crazy notion to put Wendell Scott, a black taxi driver-bootlegger, on a racetrack and... he drove 'em wild!"

The fictionalised life and times of Wendell Scott, America's first black motor sport champion.

146

Released just three weeks after another Richard Pryor film (*Silver Streak*), *Greased Lightning*, an examination of NASCAR champion Wendell Scott's life and career (Wendell Scott himself served as a technical advisor), was a hit with critics but a flop with audiences. The trouble is not Pryor – he is surprisingly good – but rather the over-written script.

Richard Pryor, in the lead as Scott, turns in an understated performance that almost makes you forget his raunchy renown. Pam Grier (his real life love interest at the time) plays his wife Mary and, though it must have been satisfying for the actress to play against type, it seems like a waste to have such a visual and energetic performer placed so inconspicuously in the cast. Also along for the ride are Beau Bridges as Hutch, Scott's mechanic and friend, and Cleavon Little (who ironically replaced Pryor in 1974's *Blazing Saddles*) as Peewee, Scott's personal manager and confidant. Atlanta mayor Maynard Jackson, congressman Julian Bond, and folk singer Richie Havens appear in cameos.

Reportedly started by Melvin Van Peebles and finished by Michael Schultz, *Greased Lightning* is a jumbled, uneven, overly nostalgic and well-intentioned picture that may have sounded good on paper, but just doesn't come off on film. It is also too similar in theme, time and place to the previous *The Bingo Long Traveling All-Stars & Motor Kings*.

"A sluggish picture without a director or scriptwriter in the driver's seat."
(Donald Bogle, Blacks in American Films and Television, 1988)

THE GREAT WHITE HOPE

1970, USA
GP (22547), Drama, 103m.
20th Century Fox.
D: Martin Ritt; P: Lawrence Turman; S: Howard Sackler, based on his play.
Cast: James Earl Jones, Jane Alexander, Beah Richards, Moses Gunn, Marlene Warfield, Lou Gilbert, Rockne Tarkington.

"He could beat any white man in the world. He just couldn't beat all of them."

The story of an African-American boxer's struggles.

A movie that begins with the words "much of what follows is true," *The Great White Hope* is the film adaptation of the super-successful Broadway play based on the life of boxing champion Jack Johnson.

Reprising his stage role for the screen, James Earl Jones is 'The Great Black Hope' Jack Jefferson, a quick-to-smile, yet unpredictable and often volatile boxer (who looks more than a little like Dr. Seuss's famous Mr. Grinch). With his loud voice and arrogant posturing, Jones, it must be said, more than adequately displays all the bluster that one might expect from a self-made American icon. Jane Alexander (also reprising her stage role) plays Jefferson's white mistress, Eleanor. Lacking in any sort of discernable charisma, Alexander is, at least, believable as a faithful liberal who, we are informed again and again, is genuinely in love. Other substantial characters include: Clara (Marlene Warfield), Jack's very hostile and very jealous ex-wife (a woman who, nevertheless, seems much more interesting than the dull, blindly supportive Eleanor); Goldie (Lou Gilbert), Jack's diminutive, compassionate manager; Rudy Sims, played by Rockne (*Black Samson*) Tarkington, head of the 'coloured' baseball club The Blue Jays; and Moses (*Shaft*) Gunn, as Scipio, a homeless man who, with his diatribe about Jefferson being a "white man's nigger," brings a festive gathering to a complete standstill.

Packed with an impressive number of extras in period clothing and containing several expansively photographed sequences including a Main Street Parade, a prize fight 'weigh in,' and a raucous African-American get together outside an inner-city nightclub, *The Great White Hope* is worth a look just for its unusually lavish (for a black film) visual presentation.

Note: His performance earned James Earl Jones a nomination for a Best Actor Oscar the following year. Martin Ritt also directed *Sounder*.

"Too smug... and too full of stereotypes to be provocative."
(Vincent Canby, New York Times)

THE GREATEST

1977, UK/USA
PG (24851), Drama, 101m.
Columbia Pictures.
D: Tom Gries; P: John Marshall; S: Ring Lardner Jr., based on a book by Muhammad Ali, Herbert Muhammad and Richard Durham.

Cast: Muhammad Ali, Paul Winfield, Ernest Borgnine, James Earl Jones, Roger E. Mosley, Robert Duvall, Phillip McAllister, Mira Waters, Annazette Chase.

"The story you only <u>think</u> you know."

The life story of African-American boxing champion Muhammad Ali.

Playing himself, African-American boxing champion Muhammad Ali is, surprisingly, not up to the task at hand. Somnambulant, tired-looking and lumbering, the way he appears in this picture it's hard to imagine him summing up the energy to do much of anything – much less become the heavyweight boxing champion of the world. Other characters in the film, with their formal acting training, fare better, but also seem a bit lost in the cursory narrative.

The film also features: Roger E. (*Leadbelly*) Mosley as boxer Sonny Liston, who Ali is hankering to fight; Ernest Borgnine as Angelo Dundee, Ali's long-time boxing trainer; Paul (*Gordon's War*) Winfield as Mr. Eskridge, Ali's attorney; James Earl (*Claudine*) Jones as Nation of Islam leader Malcolm X; and Robert Duvall in a seated-behind-a-desk cameo as a cantankerous fight organiser.

If this film has an outstanding performance, it must be that of newcomer Phillip 'Chip' McAllister as 18-year-old Cassius Clay/Ali. Though his braggadocio is a bit tiring, McAllister captures the assured, unrelenting self-belief (at eighteen he already calls himself "The Greatest") that seems to be so much a part

147

of the personality of sports stars. The women in Ali's life include Ruby Sanderson (Mira Waters) a beautiful young lady who Ali wants to make over and then marry, and Belinda Ali (Annazette Chase), his doting, loyal and super sensitive wife.

The picture's most poignant moment is a speech Ali gives in defence of his refusal to serve in the US military:

Ali: *Everybody knows where I stand. I'm against the war in Vietnam. I've said on many occasions in the past that I don't think black people should go over and fight in Vietnam and battle Asians and yellow people who never lynched us, raped us, called us 'nigger,' deprived us of our freedom, justice and equality – why should we fight for the same white man that's not freeing us right here in our own country?*

Actual Muhammad Ali fight footage adds a measure of excitement to a generally lacklustre film.

THE GUY FROM HARLEM

1977, USA
Alternative Title: *The Good Guy from Harlem*
R (24868), Action/Adventure, 88m.
International Cinema, Inc.
D: Rene Martinez Jr.; P: International Cinema, Inc.; S: Gardenia Martinez.
Cast: Loye Hawkins, Cathy Davis, Patricia Fulton, Wanda Starr, Scott Lawrence.

"He's clean... mean... A fighting machine!"

The CIA call on a street-smart Miami private detective to help them protect a visiting African princess.

Awful – but wonderfully so! Blaxploitation's *Plan 9 from Outer Space* is so breathtakingly messed-up that you can't help but love it.

Loye Hawkins plays Al Conners, a former New York City policeman-turned Miami private detective. Tall, good-looking, 'suave,' yet wooden, Hawkins has a Philip Michael Thomas quality

about him that adds to this film's unintentional kitsch value. Other memorable characters include: a dead-voiced secretary named Sue (Wanda Starr); a buff, over-tanned, white villain named Big Daddy (Scott Lawrence); and, most enjoyable of all, Cathy Davis as Wanda De Bauld, an unrelentingly hostile woman who is being held for ransom.

The Guy from Harlem's many unforgettable moments include a ridiculous 'fight' in which a character is supposedly knocked unconscious after being pushed gently to the ground, a litany of flubbed, forgotten or hastily rearranged lines ("what is... what... what might that be?"), and a scene in which a character delivers an obviously empty legal-sized envelope (that is supposed to contain five thousand dollars in cash) – "it's all there, count it!"

Shoddy photography, tinny music, poor sound effects and a makeshift plot make *The Guy from Harlem* a jaw dropping fiasco – an absolute must for trash film fans. Rene Martinez Jr. also directed *The Six Thousand Dollar Nigger*.

above: Guilty Pleasures: 1977's **The Guy from Harlem** may be nonsensical and inept, but you still can't help but love it. Here, private detective Al Conners (Loye Hawkins) gets the best of an adversary named Big Daddy (Scott Lawrence).

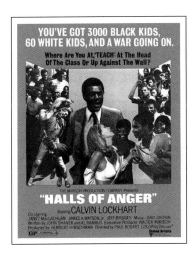

above: **Halls of Anger** (1970) looked at the special challenges that white students faced when attending a predominantly black inner-city high school.

HALLS OF ANGER

1970, USA
GP (22204), Drama, 100m. United Artists.
D: Paul Bogart; P: Herbert Hirschman;
S: John Shaner, Al Ramrus.
Cast: Calvin Lockhart, Janet MacLachlan, Jeff Bridges, James A. Watson Jr., DeWayne Jessie, Edward Asner, Rob Reiner, Michael Warren.

"You've got 3000 black kids, 60 white kids, and a war going on."

A suburban African-American high school teacher is asked to repeat his classroom success in an urban setting.

This film has a fantastic title; too bad the script is strictly paint-by-numbers.

In his role as teacher-turned Vice Principal Quincy Davis, Calvin Lockhart is both charismatic and persuasive. Handsome, eloquent, but still able to relate to his students (he drives a cool green Mustang, and uses phrases like "I'm hip," "you're cool man," and "give me a blast when you're done"), Lockhart turns in a performance filled with both authority and conviction. Unfortunately however, because he is rather diminutive, he is not quite believable as a former professional basketball player! The supporting characters include: Davis's eager-to-move-on-to-a-better-job co-worker Lorraine Nash (Janet [*The Man*] MacLachlan); class clown Lerone Johnson (DeWayne Jessie); militant yet still sensitive J.T. Watson

(James A. Watson Jr.); and the new white kid in the class, Doug (Jeff Bridges). Cameos are provided by Edward Asner, Rob Reiner, and in a non-speaking role as a high school basketball instructor, Michael (*Norman... Is That You?*) Warren.

A locker room strip, a schoolyard fight, and a student 'strike'/riot are all part of the activity in this borrowed-from-contemporary-headlines, issue-oriented production. Paul Bogart also directed *Skin Game* and *Mr. Ricco*. See *Q & A: Ten Directors Discuss Their Films*.

"...occasionally purposeful... but the resolution is predictable a mile away."
(Howard Thompson, New York Times)

HAMMER

1972, USA
R (23414), Action/Adventure, 92m.
United Artists.
D: Bruce Clark; P: Al Adamson;
S: Charles Johnson.
Cast: Fred Williamson, Bernie Hamilton, Vonetta McGee, D'Urville Martin, Mel Stewart, Nawana Davis, Leon Isaac [Kennedy], Marilyn Joi, Elizabeth Harding.

"Hammer is a black explosion!"

A boxer rises through the ranks, only to discover that his career is controlled by the mob.

Superior and highly entertaining, this audience favourite turned former San Francisco 49ers football star Fred Williamson into a highly popular film star.

Fred Williamson is utterly convincing in the lead as B.J. Hammer (a co-opting of Williamson's professional football nickname 'The Hammer'), a dock worker-turned prize-winning fighter. Not yet burdened by film stardom, he turns in an earnest performance that is lacking in the winking, mugging and showboating that would later become his trademarks. Other characters include: Hammer's secretary/girlfriend Lois (Vonetta [*Brothers*] McGee); a failed boxer-turned-trainer played by Mel Stewart; and most striking of all, a shrill-voiced, frighteningly realistic (and likeable) prostitute, Mary (Nawana Davis). A years-later exchange between Mary and Hammer is poignant:

Mary: *I don't want your money black boy. You sold out nigger. You can't buy no soul down here* [in the ghetto]. *They* [corrupt whites] *made you dance and now you tryin' to give they money away. Well I don't want it. Jive sucka!* [She walks away].

Cameos are provided by Leon (*Penitentiary*) Isaac and Marilyn (*Nurse Sherri*) Joi.

A well executed car chase, an underground garage shootout, an authentically harrowing beating (of a beloved, well-meaning character), and several genuinely exciting fight sequences make *Hammer* a knockout. The superior soundtrack is by Solomon Burke.

"The ring scenes are all outstanding and well handled... active and fairly intricate appreciation of lowlife types and stereotypes."
(Roger Greenspun, New York Times)

above: A recurring theme in blaxploitation films: Black anti-establishment hero beds white establishment female. Pictured above are Fred Williamson and Elizabeth Harding in 1972's **Hammer**. (Soul Images)

THE HARDER THEY COME

1973, Jamaica
R (757), Action/Adventure, 103m.
New World Pictures.
D: Perry Henzell; P: Perry Henzell;
S: Perry Henzell, Trevor D. Rhone.
Cast: Jimmy Cliff, Janet Bartley, Carl Bradshaw, Basil Keane, The Maytals.

"He makes women and the charts... and is on top with both."

The minor rise and total fall of a Jamaican musician.

This show business story, starring popular singer Jimmy Cliff, is a fast and furious look at the lowest levels of inner-city Jamaican life.

In the lead as Ivanhoe ('Ivan') Martin, an ambitious singer/songwriter, Jimmy Cliff is simply fantastic – so comfortable in front of the camera that it often feels as if you're watching a documentary. On hand in supporting roles are: Basil Keane as the preacher who is sceptical of Ivan's chances of making it as a singer; Janet Bartley as Elsa, Ivan's lovely and committed girlfriend; and Carl Bradshaw as Jose, the highly successful local ganja dealer.

Above all a revealing look at the discrepancy between Jamaica's highly touted tourist industry and the country's breathtakingly squalid ghettos, subplots involving recording industry corruption, politics and drug dealing are all part of this superior, outlaw-becomes-folk-hero movie. The Jimmy Cliff soundtrack, showcasing 'You Can Get It If You Really Want It,' 'Many Rivers to Cross,' and 'The Harder They Come (The Harder They Fall)' is a classic.

"...a hard-edged story of poverty, crime and outlaw culture that plays like a West Indian corollary to the classic gangster films of the '30s and '40s."
(Mark Deming, All Movie Guide)

HELL UP IN HARLEM

1973, USA
R (23822), Action/Adventure, 94m.
American International Pictures.
D: Larry Cohen; P: Larry Cohen, Janelle Cohen; S: Larry Cohen.
Cast: Fred Williamson, Julius W. Harris, Gloria Hendry, D'Urville Martin.

"Black Godfather is back... and there's gonna be Hell Up in Harlem."

Two mob factions, one black, one white, compete for turf in New York City.

This astonishingly poor sequel to *Black Caesar* is a shamelessly padded, incoherent and relentlessly over-hyped bore.

In the lead as Harlem drug lord Tommy Gibbs, Fred Williamson is confident, natural and self-sufficient, but his contribution has a quickie-repeat-performance feeling about it that is, ultimately, unsatisfactory. Faring a bit better is Julius Harris as Papa Gibbs, Tommy's long-lost father (who in *Black Caesar* was a righteous man but here has discovered the many perks that a life of crime has to offer). Gloria Hendry is also worth mentioning as Helen Bradley, a well-kept black Mafioso widow; and D'Urville Martin stands out as Reverend Rufus, a small-time con artist who, nevertheless, wants to help clean up his neighbourhood.

More engaging than the 40 or more killings, protracted car chases and explicitly depicted violence, are the picture's large assortment of vintage New York City locations, which include Times Square, Coney Island and Kennedy Airport. See *Q & A: Ten Directors Discuss Their Films*.

"The key problem is the script, which manages to be underwritten and over-plotted all at once... ultimately unsatisfying."
(Donald Guarisco, All Movie Guide)

A HERO AIN'T NOTHIN' BUT A SANDWICH

1977, USA
PG (24877), Drama, 105m.
New World Pictures.
D: Ralph Nelson; P: Robert Radnitz;
S: Alice Childress, from her novel.
Cast: Cicely Tyson, Paul Winfield, Glynn Turman, Larry B. Scott, David Groh.

A young boy discovers the path out of drug addiction.

Banal, but well acted and with good intentions, *A Hero Ain't Nothin' But a Sandwich* is a formula family drama whose uplifting message might mean a great deal to a juvenile viewer.

As Benjie, a 13-year-old boy who becomes addicted to heroin, Larry B. Scott is affecting, but hemmed in by an overly predictable script. His mother Sweets (Cicely Tyson) and step father Butler (Paul Winfield) also seem like overqualified actors trying to add depth and nuance to shallow one-note film roles. Glynn Turman makes an impression as Nigeria, a school teacher bent on making his students aware of their potential and inner beauty.

Poignant moments are sprinkled throughout; a step father telling his son a personal story about his childhood; a mother trying to, literally, wash away her son's indiscretions. Even so, this TV-movie-style film, with its sepia toned 'rehabilitation' sequence and ambiguous ending, never really hits the mark. Ralph Nelson also directed *...tick...tick...tick...*

above: **Hell Up in Harlem** (1973) pales in comparison to its predecessor **Black Caesar** (also 1973).

HICKEY & BOGGS

1972, USA
PG (23287), Comedy, 111m. United Artists.
D: Robert Culp; P: Joel Reisner; S: Walter
Hill.
Cast: Bill Cosby, Robert Culp, Rosalind
Cash, Isabel Sanford.

"They're not cool slick heroes. They're worn, tough men and that's why they're so dangerous!"

Two inactive private detectives take on a case involving a missing girl.

This overly familiar comedy-action film reunited the 'I Spy' detective television team of Bill Cosby and Robert Culp.

As Al Hickey, a down-on-his-luck private detective who comes to life challenged to find a missing girl, Bill Cosby is, as expected, a laid-back, perpetually amiable everyday man. Robert Culp, as Frank Boggs, a man who drinks a bit too much and still pines for his ex-wife, is also, if not particularly engaging, at least believable. Hickey's frustrated wife Nyona is played by Rosalind Cash.

Double crosses, double entendres and a pull-out-all-the-stops multi-cast finale contribute towards a credible picture that, energetic though it may be, feels like it's been made one too many times.

HIT!

1973, USA
R (23681), Action/Adventure, 134m.
Paramount Pictures.
D: Sidney J. Furie; P: Harry Korshak;
S: Alan R. Trustman.
Cast: Billy Dee Williams, Richard Pryor,
Paul Hampton, Gwen Welles, Sid Melton,
Janet Brandt, Warren Kemmerling.

"To pull off a job no one would ever dare, you need a team that no one would ever believe!"

A US narcotics agent, whose ten-year-old daughter overdosed on heroin, seeks revenge on drug kingpins in Marseilles.

Billy Dee Williams is authoritative, yet oddly uninteresting, as Nick Allen, a federal agent who is determined to kill all nine members of the dope ring responsible for supplying the drugs that killed his daughter. The diverse assemblage of like-minded characters (all of whom have also suffered life-changing personal tragedy) are an engaging bunch; most interesting of Allen's vengeance-seeking helpmates is Mike Willmer (Richard Pryor), an engineer whose wife was raped and violently murdered by a junkie. Playing it straight, Pryor is refreshingly unguarded. Also taking part in this misguided adventure are: Herman and Ida (Sid Melton and Janet Brandt), a married couple con artist team; Sherry Nielson (Gwen Welles), a drug-addicted prostitute; Barry Strong (Paul Hampton), a Vietnam Vet who is skilled in commando tactics; and Dutch Schiller (Warren Kemmerling), a disgruntled government narcotics agent.

Sidney J. Furie also directed *Lady Sings the Blues*.

"Implausible, incoherent and even immoral..."
(Variety)

above: Suave but ineffective: Billy Dee Williams in 1973's ironically titled box office flop **Hit!** (J. Howard Collection)

HIT MAN

1972, USA
R (23533), Action/Adventure, 90m.
Metro Goldwyn Mayer.
D: George Armitage; P: Gene Corman;
S: George Armitage, based on a novel by
Ted Lewis.
Cast: Bernie Casey, Pam Grier, Sam
Laws, Don Diamond, Roger E. Mosley,
Christopher Joy, Diane Sommerfield,
Tracy Ann King [Marilyn Joi].

"He aims to please!"

**A small-time hood resolves to violently
avenge his brother's murder.**

This is a colourfully photographed,
briskly paced entry that is particularly
notable for featuring a mind-boggling
number of unique location shoots. As
was pointed out by the *New York Times*
writer Roger Greenspun at the time,
"There have been very few recent
movies quite so pleasantly involved with
their locations... and very few movies so
aware of the kinds of unpretentious
entertainment that merely being on
location can provide."

San Francisco 49ers football star-
turned actor Bernie (*Dr. Black, Mr. Hyde*)
Casey plays Tyrone Tackett, a small-time
criminal who has come to town to bury his
brother. Studly, streetwise and refreshingly real, Casey's single-minded determination and quest for righteousness is
arresting. 'Pamela' Grier plays a prostitute
named Gozelda (in one of her pre-
superstar supporting roles), and here she
effortlessly enhances her legendary status
as a walking, talking cinematic goddess.
She is so striking to behold that the sheer
force of her visual magnetism obliterates
her distractingly minimal acting skills.
Rounding out the cast is Sam (*Cool
Breeze*) Laws, in great form as usual, as
Sherwood, a foul-mouthed, drink-loving
used car salesman. Roger E. (*Sweet Jesus*

The stars of "SUPERFLY" are back in

THE HITTER

RON O'NEAL in "THE HITTER"
Starring SHEILA FRAZIER Also Starring ADOLPH CAESAR

Preacher Man) Mosley, Christopher (*Big
Time*) Joy, Diane (*The Black Godfather*)
Sommerfield and Marilyn (*Black
Samurai*) Joi appear in cameos.

Borrowing much from the previous
year's white-cast *Get Carter*, the ultra-
violent *Hit Man* was a smash hit with
audiences and, today, retains much of its
ability to dazzle, surprise and elicit a
visceral response from the spectator.

*"Its interest is lifestyle rather than
literary style, and as it turns out, that is
interest enough."*
(Roger Greenspun, New York Times)

THE HITTER

1978, USA
R (25438), Action/Adventure, 94m.
Peppercorn-Wormser, Inc.
D: Christopher Leitch; P: Gary Herman,
Christopher Leitch; S: Christopher Leitch,
Ben Harris.
Cast: Ron O'Neal, Sheila Frazier, Adolph
Caesar, Bill Cobbs.

*"In a world of sharp hustlers, fast women,
and bloodthirsty crowds... look out for
The Hitter."*

**A former prizefighter and a former
Louisiana pimp stage a series of
profitable back-alley fist fights.**

This seldom-seen third teaming of Ron
O'Neal and Sheila Frazier (*Super Fly*
and *Super Fly T.N.T.*) is much better
than might be expected.

As Otis, a one time pro boxer, Ron
O'Neal turns in a strong and convincing
performance that both moves and
dazzles the viewer. Adolph Caesar is
equally good in the role of Nathan, "a
washed up, strung out pimp with
somebody else's money in his pocket."
Least effective in the cast, and it is
unfortunate as she throws several scenes
off, is Sheila Frazier as Lola, Otis's just-
happy-to-tag-along girlfriend. Lovely to
look at, yet consistently overwrought
(she puts her hand over her mouth and
bursts into tears on three occasions),
Frazier's performance comes across like
little more than a stagy, much too-broad
and patently manipulative series of
parlour tricks.

Good photography, a good script,
and a melancholy country-flavoured
soundtrack by Garfeel Ruff are all part
of the mix. Uneven, but worthy of note;
had anyone gone to see it, *The Hitter*
might have returned Ron O'Neal to his
fleeting position as a blaxploitation
headliner.

Note: Adolph Caesar had a second
career as a voiceover artist; his distinct
gravely voice was used for many
blaxploitation movie trailers and radio
spots, including those for *Super Fly*.

HIT MAN
He aims
to please.
Starring BERNIE CASEY
RESTRICTED   METROCOLOR   MGM

HONEYBABY, HONEYBABY

1974, USA
Alternative Title: *Honeybaby*
PG (23950), Action/Adventure, 94m.
Kelly Jordan Enterprises.
D: Michael Schultz; P: Jack Jordan; S: Brian Phelan, from a story by Leonard Kantor.
Cast: Calvin Lockhart, Diana Sands, Seth Allen, J. Eric Bell, Brian Phelan.

"She's after your money... honey!"

On a trip to the Middle East, an African-American interpreter becomes the unwitting pawn in a political plot.

This frankly awful movie is so complicated and difficult to follow (while at the same time lacking in any major incident) that the picture begins with one of the film characters walking into frame, sitting down, and explaining to the audience what they are about to see.

In the lead as interpreter Laura 'Honeybaby' Lewis, Diana (*Willie Dynamite*) Sands is elegant, refined and lovely to behold, but a bit too stilted, mannered and wrapped up in self-display to be likable. Looking very much like Diana Ross in *Mahogany*, hers is a star turn (she has a separate wardrobe credit) that is out of synch with the rest of the film. Always-elegant Calvin (*Melinda*) Lockhart, playing a confused mercenary named Liv, also comes off as stiff, stuffy and out of place. The 'comic relief,' such as it is, is provided by Skiggy (J. Eric Bell), Laura's energetic young nephew, and Harry (Brian Phelan), a travelling television producer.

There's a frantic chase through the back streets of Beirut, a quarry of attack dogs that are sidetracked by a bag of marshmallows (!), and a sleep-inducing finale that takes place in a museum after closing time.

Note: Both *Honeybaby, Honeybaby* and *Willie Dynamite* were released posthumously (Diana Sands died prematurely, at the age of 39, from breast cancer).

"Banal, not funny, tedious... Diana Sands is a vibrant presence undermined by a highly confusing script."
(Variety)

HONKY

1971, USA
R (22750), Drama, 89m.
Jack H. Harris Enterprises.
D: William A. Graham; P: Will Chaney, Ron Roth; S: Will Chaney, based on the novel *Shelia* by Gunard Solberg.
Cast: Brenda Sykes, John Neilson, William Marshall, Marion Ross, Lincoln Kilpatrick.

"A love story of hate."

When two high school students, one black, one white, become romantically involved, both their lives undergo a dramatic change.

A frighteningly good film; visceral, unconventional and sensational, *Honky* is a provocative and unapologetic picture that will leave you genuinely unsettled.

Brenda Sykes is both touching and magnificent to look at in the role of Sheila Smith, an African-American high school student who loves to smoke pot and have a good time. Her highly impressionable blonde-haired, blue-eyed boyfriend Wayne Divine (John Neilson) is also attractive, comfortable in front of the camera and eager to impress. Both actors convincingly embody their particular generation's disenchantment with the old guard represented by their parents. Support is provided by William (*Blacula*) Marshall as Dr. Craig Smith, Sheila's bourgeois father, and Marion (of TV's *Happy Days*) Ross as Mrs. Divine,

HONEY BABY

Starring Calvin Lockhart

Political Dynamite in the Middle East. Fast moving and hair-raising escapades in an incredible plot.

IVER FILM SERVICES
THE PROFESSIONALS AT PINEWOOD

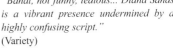

above: Lincoln Kilpatrick, Brenda Sykes and John Neilson in 1971's serious-minded but sensationally titled interracial love story **Honky**. (J. Howard Collection)

Wayne's racist mother. Lincoln (*Together Brothers*) Kilpatrick appears in a cameo.

Set in America's Midwest and accompanied by an outstanding Quincy Jones soundtrack, *Honky* is dated (many references to 'dropping out' and hitchhiking across the country), preachy and a bit over-familiar, however it is still a satisfying look at the special challenges presented by interracial dating during the early 1970s.

THE HOT BOX

1972, Philippines/USA
Alternative Title: *Hell Cats*
R (534), Action/Adventure, 85m.
New World Pictures.
D: Joe Viola; P: Cirio H. Santiago, Jonathan Demme; S: Joe Viola, Jonathan Demme.

Cast: Margaret Markov, Andrea Cagan, Rickey Richardson, Laurie Rose, Carmen Argenziano.

"Their guns are hot and their bodies hard!"

After suffering a string of abuses behind bars, four kidnapped nurses join a cult of Pacific Island revolutionaries.

Terribly scripted and poorly produced, *The Hot Box* is a blaxploitation film whose most outstanding feature is its sensational poster art.

In the lead as Lynn Forrest, the 'intelligent' one, Margaret (*The Arena*) Markov does her best with a dull, uninspired role. Further clichéd characters include: Bunny Kincaid (Andrea Cagan) – the dumb one; Sue Pennwright (Laurie

Rose) – the frightened one; and Flavio (Carmen Argenziano) – the butch one.

Derivative, stretched and wholly uninteresting, *The Hot Box*'s high nudity and sex quotient is overshadowed by a relentless barrage of arch and unconvincing conversations that are not even satisfying on a camp level.

Note: Jonathan Demme (later to direct the Oscar-winning *The Silence of the Lambs*) co-wrote and co-produced the film.

HOT POTATO

1975, USA
PG (24391), Action/Adventure, 87m.
Warner Bros.
D: Oscar Williams; P: Fred Weintraub, Paul Heller; S: Oscar Williams.
Cast: Jim Kelly, George Memmoli, Geoffrey Binney, Irene Tsu.

RAVAGED...SAVAGED...Licked by the fiery tongues of

THE HOT BOX

A tropical torture chamber where anything can happen.

THEIR GUNS ARE HOT AND THEIR BODIES HARD.

Starring
ANDREA CAGAN · MARGARET MARKOV
RICKEY RICHARDSON · LAURIE ROSE
CARMEN ARGENZIANO · CHARLES DIERKOP

METROCOLOR

Written by JOE VIOLA and JONATHAN DEMME · Produced by JONATHAN DEMME · Directed by JOE VIOLA · A NEW WORLD PICTURES RELEASE

JIM KELLY is back
as 'Black Belt' Jones

HOT
POTATO

A WEINTRAUB-HELLER PRODUCTION · JIM KELLY · GEORGE MEMMOLI
in "HOT POTATO" Starring GEOFFREY BINNEY · IRENE TSU and JUDITH BROWN as Leslie
Produced by FRED WEINTRAUB and PAUL HELLER · Written and directed by OSCAR WILLIAMS

above and bottom right: **Hot Potato** (1975) was too many things all at once; even the poster art contained mixed messages that left audiences in the dark about exactly what kind of movie they had paid to see.

"The adventure movie to end them all."

A martial arts expert and his two friends are hired to rescue a kidnapped American senator's daughter who is missing in Thailand.

This film could almost have been designed to disappoint audiences; it was promoted as an action/adventure film "from the producers of *Enter the Dragon*" when in truth it plays like a not-so-funny screwball comedy.

A year after his success with *Black Belt Jones*, middleweight karate champion Jim Kelly was recast as 'Jones,' the leader of a trio of American mercenaries who have travelled to Thailand in search of a kidnapped American woman. Kelly struggles to impose himself on this thinly scripted film, which has not-so-subtly been fashioned around several elaborately staged fight sequences. On hand as

Jones's two 'playful' cohorts are the rotund Rhino, aka 'Piggy' (George Memmoli) – the butt of the film's many fat jokes – and Johnny Chicago (Geoffrey Binney), a perpetually horny young man who can't get a date. Irene Tsu provides strong support in the form of a high

kicking, I-don't-need-any-help Taiwanese investigator named Pam.

The karate fight scenes (all choreographed by Kelly) take place in the jungle, around a lagoon, on the steps of an ancient monument, in the streets of Taiwan and in the ornately adorned courtyard of an Asian multi-millionaire. Complete with kooky sound effects (belches, farts and whooshing sounds), manic music (which is occasionally patriotic, sometimes cartoonish), and Laurel & Hardy-like pratfalls (people stepping on each others toes; a running joke about the sanctity of one's hat), *Hot Potato* is not quite a total bomb, but it's no great rib tickler either.

THE HOUSE ON SKULL MOUNTAIN

1974, USA
PG (24075), Horror, 85m.
20th Century Fox.
D: Ron Honthaner; P: Ray Storey;
S: Mildred Pares.
Cast: Victor French, Janee Michelle, Mike Evans, Jean Durand, Xernona Clayton.

"Every room is a living tomb."

When a wealthy elderly woman dies, her friends and family are summoned to her secluded rural estate for the reading of her will.

A rehash of a tale told countless times before, *The House on Skull Mountain* has little value, even on a camp level. The great idea of having a diverse group of people meet in a deserted mansion for the reading of a will, had been used very effectively with the Vincent Price vehicle *House on Haunted Hill*. Here the well-established formula is cluttered with a ridiculous, and much protracted, voodoo subplot.

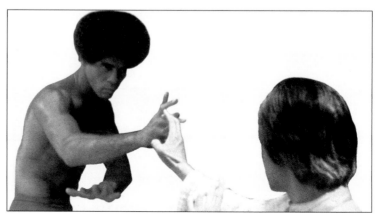

EVERY ROOM
IS A LIVING TOMB
IN

THE HOUSE ON SKULL MOUNTAIN

Which of these five will come down alive?

Momma to Jethro: *Looky yonder, something's going on up there at that big house.*
Jethro: *You're right! Them people up there is havin' a party.*
Momma: *Damn it Jethro, them ain't people, them's niggers!*
Jethro: *Well, by God thems is niggers! Well they got to be niggers 'cause it ain't Halloween is it?!*

So begins *The Human Tornado*, an unofficial sequel to the previous year's *Dolemite*.

A considerable improvement on the film that preceded it, *The Human Tornado* has a refreshingly clever script, wonderfully realised supporting performances, and a nightclub segment that showcases Moore doing what he does best – regaling audiences with his raunchy, rhyming stories.

Rudy Ray Moore is simply fantastic in the role of Dolemite, a charismatic club owner/pimp/popular entertainer. Appropriately comical, "able to leap tall buildings at a single bound," vulgar (every other word is 'motherfucker'), and oversexed (we see him three separate times nude in bed making love to different women), Dolemite is an indestructible populist hero; an average looking, rather portly film character who is at one with the young black audience that has come to see him. The most notable support in this camp carnival comes from the Christmas-tree-like Queen Bee (Lady Reed), proprietor of Miss Bee's nightclub.

Rapping, cursing and general noisemaking (along with a large dose of toilet humour) are all script-defining pluses.

The assembled guests at this run-down, rain-soaked estate include: the rakish, jive-talking Phillippe (Mike Evans – best known as Lionel on the TV's *The Jeffersons*); the beautiful but overly mannered Lorena (Janee Michelle); a matronly church-going housekeeper, Harriet (Xernona Clayton); and a confused-about-his-racial-origins white anthropologist named Andrew (Victor French).

Over-lit, uninventively photographed and incorporating no atmospheric elements whatsoever (save the 'foggy' matte shot of a miniature house on the side of a skull-carved cliff), the best thing about *The House on Skull Mountain* is the poster art.

"An anthology of horror-film clichés."
(Variety)

THE HUMAN TORNADO

1976, USA
Alternative Title: *Dolemite II*
R (24653), Action/Adventure, 96m.
Dimension Pictures.
D: Cliff Roquemore; P: Rudy Ray Moore,
T. [Theadore] Toney; S: Jerry Jones.
Cast: Rudy Ray Moore, Lady Reed,
Jimmy Lynch, Howard Jackson.

"Watch out mister... here comes the twister. Nerve shattering... brain battering... mind splattering... a one man disaster!"

A popular comedian helps his nightclub-owner friends in their battle against the mob.

Popular comedian Rudy Ray Moore starred as a fast talking performer and ladies man in several raucous low-budget productions, including **Dolemite** (1975), **The Human Tornado** (1976) *(above)*, and **Disco Godfather** (1979). (Soul Images)

You either love or hate Rudy Ray Moore and his films. African-American director Cliff Roquemore also directed *Petey Wheatstraw...* Screenwriter Jerry Jones is also African American.

"A crude tasteless film... somebody put a lot of effort into making something so revolting."
(Danielle Spencer, Los Angeles Free Press)

I ESCAPED FROM DEVIL'S ISLAND

1973, USA/Mexico
R (23722), Action/Adventure, 87m.
United Artists.
D: William Witney; P: Roger and Gene Corman; S: Richard L. Adams.
Cast: Jim Brown, Christopher George, Rick Ely, Paul Richards.

"He's the devil they named the island for! No man ever broke this prison! No prison ever broke this man!"

In 1918, two French penal colony inmates lead a revolt against prison inhumanities.

This low budget Philippine-shot escape-from-prison film came and went without much notice.

Jim Brown stars as Le Bras, a battered and abused inmate at the notoriously brutal French Guiana penal colony known as Devil's Island, which was also chronicled in the successful mainstream Hollywood film *Papillon*. Intimidating, macho, and determined to do whatever he wants to do, Brown offers up what is essentially a repeat performance of his role in the same year's similarly themed *The Slams*. His equally fed up and eager to escape cellmate, Davert, is played by Christopher George.

Sadistic prison guards, indifferent wardens, ostentatiously gay inmates, an encounter with lepers, a romp with a native Indian girl, and a surprisingly gory shark attack are highlights amongst the generally rather laboured and predictable proceedings.

"...a slovenly, gamy potboiler."
(Variety)

above: Have gun will travel: Jim Brown (*right*) as Le Bras, and Christopher George as Davert, two desperate inmates in 1973's **I Escaped from Devil's Island**.

J.D.'S REVENGE

1976, USA
R (24601), Mystery/Horror, 95m.
American International Pictures.
D: Arthur Marks; P: Arthur Marks;
S: Jaison Starkes.
Cast: Glynn Turman, Joan Pringle, Louis
Gossett Jr., Carl Crudup.

"He came back from the dead to possess a man's soul, make love to his woman, and get the vengeance he craved!"

A student is possessed by the spirit of a man who was murdered in the 1940s.

Glynn Turman is credible and engaging as Isaac/Ike, a law student who may or may not be the reincarnation of razor-toting pimp J.D. Walker. Too bad his more-than-adequate performance is lost in the dismal murk of this film. Future Oscar winner Louis Gossett Jr. is terribly miscast as Reverend Bliss, a corrupt Baptist minister; his performance here is unbelievable, conveying a just-passing-through aura. Much more effective in a diminutive role is Joan Pringle as Christella, Ike's young, pretty and very understanding wife.

Derivative, tired, and missing its mark on both the dramatic and occult levels (*New York Times* writer Lawrence Van Gelder accurately observed its failure was "...mistaking repulsive effects for frightening ones"), *J.D.'s Revenge* is a blaxploitation oddity, which is literally more interesting on paper (the poster art is fantastic) than it is as a film. Screenwriter Jaison Starkes is African American. See *Q & A: Ten Directors Discuss Their Films.*

"...so poorly shot and so jumbled that the best moment comes when it's finally over." (Donald Bogle, Blacks in American Films and Television, 1988)

KID VENGEANCE

1977, USA/Italy/Israel
Alternative Title: *Vendetta*
NR (R), Western, 90m. Irwin Yablans Co.
D: Joe Manduke; P: Menahem Golan;
S: Bud Robbins, Jay Telfer, Ken Globus.
Cast: Lee Van Cleef, Jim Brown, Glynnis O'Connor, Leif Garrett.

"You're never too young for vengeance!"

A teenage boy sets out to avenge the murder of his pioneer parents.

A quickie, super-low-budget, Middle Eastern-shot follow-up to the fantastic *Take a Hard Ride*, this little-known (and for good reason) sequel is embarrassingly lame in comparison to its predecessor.

Essentially reprising their roles (but this time using different names) are Lee Van Cleef as McClain, a ruthless travelling gang leader, and Jim Brown as Isaac, a fair-minded, hardworking man who seems to have no roots and no connections. Leif Garrett stars as Tom, the teenager bent on revenge, and Glynnis O'Connor provides support as Lisa, his tart-mouthed sister.

The bad guys in this picture are killed off in a variety of ways – one gets beaten to death with a shovel, another gets hanged from a cliffside, another gets shot through the heart with a bow and arrow –

but these are mere moments of levity in a rather dull whole. The best line in the film comes when belligerent carriage-bound Lisa wards off a would-be rapist: "Get away from me! I can't stand the smell of you. I can't stand the smell of any of the men here. I can't even stand the smell of myself!"

KILLER OF SHEEP

1977, USA
NR (R), Drama, 83m.
Mypheduh Films, Inc.
D: Charles Burnett; P: Charles Burnett; S: Charles Burnett.
Cast: Henry G. Sanders, Angela Burnett, Kaycee Moore, Charles Bracy.

The day-to-day struggles of an African-American slaughterhouse worker.

Killer of Sheep is an ambitious, well-intentioned and unflinching look at the many challenges and unique frustrations that must be faced by an inner city black family living in the Watts ghetto of Los Angeles. One of fewer than a hundred films designated a 'National Treasure' by the film registry of the Library of Congress (1990), and written, produced and directed by an African American, this low budget ($15,000) slice-of-life family portrait does not follow Hollywood's traditional narrative structures, but instead tells its story through a series of open-ended incidents that are never fully resolved.

Film characters include Stan (Henry G. Sanders) a father struggling to keep his family together and keep his dignity, and Stan's wife (Kaycee Moore), a troubled woman whose emotional support of her husband and family is fleeting.

Chillingly oppressive and bleak, documentary-like, and filled with more questions than answers, *Killer of Sheep* is, in the end, a highly-personal vision that director/producer/screenwriter Charles Burnett has invested with respect, sensitivity and loving attention to detail.

Note: Director Burnett served as cinematographer on the previous year's similarly stark and disquieting *Bush Mama*.

THE KLANSMAN

1974, USA
Alternative Titles: *The Burning Cross*; *KKK*
R (24074), Drama, 112m.
Paramount Pictures.
D: Terence Young; P: William Alexander; S: Samuel Fuller, Millard Kaufman.
Cast: Lee Marvin, O.J. Simpson, Richard Burton, Linda Evans, Lola Falana, Cameron Mitchell, Luciana Paluzzi, Jeanie [Jean] Bell.

"Welcome to scenic Atoka County, population 10,000. Cross burnings. Rape. Murder. Arson. It's a great place to live... if they let you!"

A Southern sheriff and a local landowner become involved in a dispute with the Ku Klux Klan.

The colourful cast of this absurd, trashy and lurid Southern Town melodrama includes: Richard Burton (in a dramatic career drop) as Breck Stancill, a sympathetic Southern land owner; sports star O.J. Simpson (long before his 'Trial of the Century' infamy) as Garth, a militant-minded thief and murderer; TV commercial queen Linda Evans (not yet known for her late-career 'comeback' on the night-time TV soap opera *Dynasty*) as Nancy Poteet, an ostracised small-town damsel in distress; *Playboy* bunny Jean (*TNT Jackson*) Bell as a young woman who is brutalised by a gang of white thugs; and Lola (*Lady Cocoa*) Falana as Loretta Sykes, an educated woman who has returned to her backward-thinking home-town to care for her ailing grandmother. Add to this a confused but fair-minded town official, Sheriff 'Big Track' Bascomb (Lee Marvin), and the racist Assistant Deputy 'Butt Cut' Cates (Cameron Mitchell), and you've got a convoluted hodgepodge of cookie-cutter film characters, none of whom are particularly engaging.

Tiresome and uninventive, *The Klansman*, with its over-long shots, clichéd dialogue and predictable script, is not even fun on a camp level. Producer William Alexander is African American.

"...there's not a shred of quality, dignity, relevance or impact in this yahoo-oriented bunk..."
(Variety)

LADY COCOA

1975, USA
Alternative Title: *Pop Goes the Weasel*
R (1272), Action/Adventure, 93m.
Moonstone.
D: Matt Cimber; P: Matt Cimber; S: George Theakos.
Cast: Lola Falana, Gene Washington, Alex Dreier, 'Mean' Joe Greene, James A. Watson Jr.

"Lady Cocoa, Miss Lady Luck, took a gamble and got stuck... 'Cause 'Mean' Joe Greene ain't playin' when he goes slayin'."

A young woman is pursued by the mob after agreeing to testify against her drug dealer boyfriend.

High-pitched, one-note, and ugly to look at, but no less fascinating because of it, *Lady Cocoa* is a base, foul and violent little film that serves as a showcase for Lola Falana, 'The Queen of Las Vegas.'

Falana is, along with Teresa (*Get Christie Love!*) Graves, one blaxploitation's most underrated female performers. As Cocoa DeLange, a gangster's moll with a heart of gold (or at least glitter), she is a sheer delight; admirably comfortable with herself in front of the camera, she is sometimes quietly coquettish, sometimes shrill and

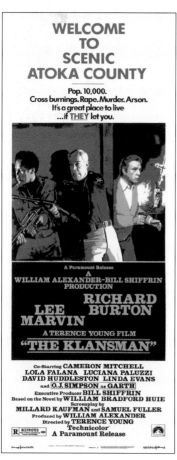

"Diana Ross is Billie Holiday in Lady Sings the Blues."

The fictionalised life story of African-American jazz singer Billie Holiday.

This lavish bio-pic is one of only six blaxploitation films to take the top spot on *Variety*'s Top 50 Grossing Films list.

Diana Ross is simply magnificent as Billie Holiday. Embodying Holiday's well-documented and wildly uneven mood swings, as well as her flair for reinvention, Ross offers a vivid and memorable tour-de-force that exceeded the expectations of both audience and critics. Billy Dee Williams plays Louis McKay, the one man in Holiday's life who really seemed to care about her, with an ease and naturalness that still plays well today. On hand in memorable roles are Richard (*Greased Lightning*) Pryor as

off-putting, sometimes overcome with what appears to be genuine emotion.

Also in the cast are: Alex Dreier as Ramsey, an overweight, always wheezing, cane-wielding white Lieutenant; Gene (*The Black Six*) Washington as Doug, a handsome and cultured police detective who, not surprisingly, falls in love with Cocoa; James A. Watson Jr. as Eddie, Cocoa's two-timing pimp boyfriend; and, in a cameo, football star 'Mean' Joe Greene as Big Joe, a murderer for hire.

A nude bedroom scene, a car chase in which an automobile travels right through the front doors of a casino, and a hotel room ambush are all part of the low budget, primitive, but undeniably engaging proceedings at hand. Cocoa's opinion of a painting in her hotel suite is typical of the film's vulgar tone:

> Cocoa: *I've seen better art on a used Kotex!*

Lola Falana's theme song 'Pop Goes the Weasel' is superb. See *Q & A: Ten Directors Discuss Their Films*.

LADY SINGS THE BLUES

1972, USA
R (23290) , Drama, 144m.
Paramount Pictures.
D: Sidney J. Furie; P: Berry Gordy Jr., Jay Weston, James S. White; S: Terence McCloy, Chris Clark and Suzanne de Passe.
Cast: Diana Ross, Billy Dee Williams, Richard Pryor, Isabel Sanford, Scatman Crothers.

top right: Diana Ross in her motion picture debut as legendary jazz singer Billie Holiday
in 1972's appropriately titled **Lady Sings the Blues**.

Holiday's troubled, drug-addicted but well-intentioned piano-playing friend, and Isabel Sanford (of TV's *The Jeffersons*) as a fast-talking whorehouse owner who gives Holiday her first job.

The film's outstanding moments include a chillingly real opening sequence in an insane asylum, a bathroom razor fight over drugs, Holiday's rape as a young girl, and a rare look at the indignities black performers had to suffer in the 1930s and '40s.

"Vastly entertaining... The screen's first full-fledged black romantic melodrama." (Donald Bogle, Toms, Coons, Mulattoes, Mammies & Bucks, 1973)

THE LANDLORD

1970, USA
R (22202), Drama, 110m. United Artists.
D: Hal Ashby; P: Norman Jewison;
S: Bill Gunn, based on the novel by Kristin Hunter.
Cast: Beau Bridges, Diana Sands, Louis Gossett Jr., Pearl Bailey, Lee Grant, Marki Bey, Marlene Clark, Gloria Hendry.

"Watch the landlord get his."

A wealthy white man buys a tenement building and then becomes involved in his tenant's lives.

This over-long, seldom-seen comedy/melodrama contains a little bit of everything.

Beau Bridges is exceptional in this film's lead role of Elgar Enders, a blond-haired, blue-eyed rich white boy in search of himself. Appropriately confused, frightened and out of his depth, he conveys the liberal naiveté so often seen in the coming-of-age movies of the late 1960s and early '70s. Lee Grant is also outstanding in the role of his equally 'liberal' Barbie doll mother Joyce Enders. As Francine/Fanny ('Miss Sepia of 1965'), Enders's disenfranchised but street savvy one night stand, Diana (*Willie Dynamite*) Sands turns in a delicate, multi-dimensional performance that is both inspiring and at the same time, heartbreaking.

Other players of note include: Fanny's militant minded live-in boyfriend Copee (Louis Gossett Jr.); a sassy non-rent-paying clairvoyant, Marge, played by Pearl (*Norman... Is That You?*) Bailey; and, most memorable of all, Marki (*Sugar Hill*) Bey as Lanie, Elgar's sensitive bi-racial girlfriend. Featured in non-speaking cameos are Marlene (*Ganja & Hess*) Clark and Gloria (*Black Belt Jones*) Hendry.

A rich-white-man-meets-poor-black-woman fairy tale, *The Landlord* is a film that critics loved but audiences almost totally ignored. Screenwriter Bill Gunn is African American.

"Delightful comic touches combined with perceptive sidelights on the black experience... a vibrant comedy-drama." (Leonard Maltin, Movie & Video Guide, 1999)

LEADBELLY

1976, USA
PG (24174), Drama, 126m.
Paramount Pictures.
D: Gordon Parks Sr.; P: Marc Merson;
S: Ernest Kinoy.
Cast: Roger E. Mosley, Madge Sinclair, Paul Benjamin, Loretta Green, Dana Manno, Art Evans.

"Meet Leadbelly... a real man who's a winner!"

The life and times of African-American folk singer Huddie Ledbetter.

Leadbelly is a well meaning but terribly protracted bio-pic that romanticises the very difficult life of an African-American singer/songwriter.

Roger E. Mosley is superb in the lead as Huddie 'Leadbelly' Ledbetter. Convincing as a man whose early circumstances have made life unnecessarily difficult, and competently lip-synching Ledbetter's most popular tunes – such as 'Goodnight Irene,' 'The Midnight Special' and 'Green Corn' among others – Mosley's performance is, nevertheless, overwhelmed by a narrowly written, largely stereotypical role. Doing slightly better in an equally uncomplicated part is Madge (*Cornbread, Earl and Me*) Sinclair as Miss Eula, a prostitute who is at first beautiful, but becomes ravaged by time as the film progresses; she heartbreakingly sums herself up toward the film's end: "There's

above: Who's been sleeping in my bed? In **The Landlord** (1970), Copee (Louis Gossett Jr.) is not too happy with the fact that his white landlord, Elgar (Beau Bridges), is sleeping with his girlfriend.

nothing sadder than a broke whore." Also in the cast are Dana Manno as Margaret Judd, Leadbelly's one true love (and mother of his child), and Art Evans as Blind Lemon Jefferson, a friend and fellow musician.

Self-indulgent, and preoccupied with being a serious and sophisticated 'biography,' *Leadbelly* is a largely joyless picture whose message of ongoing strength and endurance – "seven years [in prison] and you ain't broke my mind, you ain't broke my body and you ain't broke my spirit" – does not come through as clearly as the filmmakers no doubt wanted it to. African-American director Gordon Parks Sr.'s other films include *Shaft* and *Shaft's Big Score!*

"Gordon Parks can't disguise the fact that the details of the black folk-hero's life have been laundered for the widest possible audience."
(John Pym, Time Out Film Guide)

THE LEGEND OF NIGGER CHARLEY

1972, USA
PG (23171), Western, 100m.
Paramount Pictures.
D: Martin Goldman; P: Larry G. Spangler;
S: Martin Goldman, Larry G. Spangler.
Cast: Fred Williamson, D'Urville Martin, Don Pedro Colley, Gertrude Jeanette.

"Somebody warn the West. Nigger Charley ain't running no more!"

A recently freed slave is pursued by a relentless bounty hunter.

This film is totally engaging, and what a pleasant change it is to see empowered African-American cowboys riding horses and wearing mid-century clothing in a western setting.

As Nigger Charley ("I called it 'Nigger Charley' because it was contro-versial," admitted Williamson in a 2001 interview), a recently freed slave who is on the run because he killed his master, Fred Williamson is charming, believable and engaging; his natural screen presence elevates and excuses a string of increas-ingly implausible situations. D'Urville Martin plays Charley's best friend Toby, a sometimes comical, sometimes intro-spective helpmate. Along for the ride is a third 'buddy,' Joshua (Don Pedro Colley).

After becoming a hit with audiences and critics, *The Legend of Nigger Charley*

was followed by a quickie sequel (*The Soul of Nigger Charley*) and a slew of other 'blacks in the west' action/ melodramas.

"...structured to appeal to the black community, providing onscreen role models (of sorts) in a fantasy tale they can empathize with or just plain enjoy."
(Parish/Hill, Black Action Films, 1989)

LET'S DO IT AGAIN

1975, USA
PG (24286), Comedy, 113m. Warner Bros.
D: Sidney Poitier; P: Melville Tucker;
S: Richard Wesley.
Cast: Sidney Poitier, Bill Cosby, Calvin Lockhart, Jimmie Walker, John Amos, Ossie Davis, Denise Nicholas, Mel Stewart, Julius Harris, Jayne Kennedy.

"It's the same two dudes from 'Uptown Saturday Night'... but this time they're back with kid dyn-o-mite!"

During a trip to New Orleans, two friends devise a scheme that they hope will raise money to keep their lodge from going under.

For a time, actor/director Sidney Poitier had a free hand at Warner Bros. Sadly, it seems that no one had the courage to tell him that his trio of movies with Bill Cosby would be much more satisfying (and entertaining) if they were substantially shortened; at almost two hours, *Let's Do It Again* is at least a half an hour too long.

Playing two lodge brothers who get involved in a complicated 'fun-spirited' chain of events, Sidney Poitier (Clyde Williams – a milkman) and Bill Cosby

above: Bill Cosby (*left*) and Sidney Poitier (*right*) play two hapless lodge brothers in the not-too-subtly titled sequel to 1974's **Uptown Saturday Night**, **Let's Do It Again** (1975).

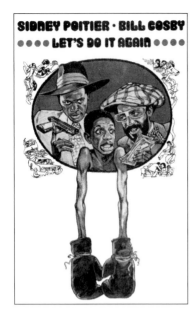

(Billy Foster – a factory worker) do their best, and despite the film's lethargic editing, at least the performers themselves are energetic. Support is provided by: Calvin Lockhart as Biggie Smalls (not to be confused with the rap artist who incidentally uses the same name!), a bookie looking to expand his territory; Beth (Denise Nicholas), Clyde's self-sufficient wife; Bootney Farnsworth (Jimmie Walker, of TV's *Good Times*), a skinny, timid but highly impressionable boxer; and Kansas City Mack (John '*Good Times*' Amos). Mel Stewart, Julius Harris and Jayne Kennedy all put in cameo appearances.

Despite its faults, *Let's Do It Again* was a hit; the other Cosby/Poitier comedies were *Uptown Saturday Night* and *A Piece of the Action*. Screenwriter Richard Wesley is African American.

"...a broad comedy filled with basic visual slapstick rather than clever verbal wit."
(Parish/Hill, Black Action Films, 1989)

THE LIBERATION OF L.B. JONES

1970, USA
R (22285), Drama, 102m.
Columbia Pictures.
D: William Wyler; P: Ronald Lubin; S: Stirling Silliphant and Jesse Hill Ford, based on a novel by Ford.
Cast: Roscoe Lee Browne, Lee J. Cobb, Lola Falana, Yaphet Kotto, Anthony Zerbe, Lee Majors, Barbara Hershey, Zara Cully, Brenda Sykes.

"Some of his best friends are black. Some of her best friends are white. A story of Southern hospitality!"

An intimate portrait of the inhabitants of Sundown, an off-the-beaten-track Southern town.

This initially controversial movie stars Roscoe Lee Browne as wealthy black funeral parlour owner Lord Byron Jones; Browne's portrayal of a middle aged man who is desperately in love is regal, cultured and believable. The object of Jones's affection is his much younger wife Emma (Lola Falana); she too is superb, conveying with great naturalness the power a worldly woman can wield simply due to her beauty. Other characters include: Emma's white lover Willie Jo Worth (Anthony [*The Omega Man*] Zerbe); a bigoted white lawyer, Oman Hedgepath (Lee J. Cobb); and a militant-minded out-of-towner bent on revenge, Sonny Boy Mosby (Yaphet Kotto). Lee Majors, Barbara Hershey, Zara Cully and Brenda Sykes all appear in cameos.

Well-meaning but overlong, politically-minded but somehow always missing its mark, *The Liberation of L.B. Jones* is a competent yet tired retread of material better covered elsewhere.

Note: This was veteran director William (*Wuthering Heights*, *The Heiress*) Wyler's final film.

"There is a pervading commercial patness to the script... many another film has made the ground covered almost stereotyped and cliché herein."
(Variety)

THE LIMIT

1972, USA
PG (23288), Action/Adventure, 90m.
Cannon Group.
D: Yaphet Kotto; P: Yaphet Kotto; S: Sean Cameron, from a story by Yaphet Kotto.
Cast: Yaphet Kotto, Pamela Jones, Richard Kennedy, Ted Cassidy, Quinn K. Redeker.

"How far will a black man go for his woman?"

A Los Angeles policeman enters into delicate negotiations with a violent and unpredictable biker gang.

As L.A. cop Mark Johnson, a black man who is sympathetic to a local black biker gang, and then gets caught up in the drama surrounding them, Yaphet Kotto is totally believable and engaging. His fellow cop and friend, Jeff McMillan (Quinn K. Redeker), also rises above the level of the material at hand.

Despite being filled with all the necessary blaxploitation ingredients (car chases, sexual situations, crime and violence) *The Limit* was poorly promoted. Kotto is a great actor whose name, nevertheless, meant nothing on a theatre marquee at that time; and unfortunately this film did not achieve what it set out to do – elevate him to the position of blaxploitation superstar. Sadly forgettable.

THE LONG NIGHT

1976, USA
PG (1549), Drama, 85m.
Howard Mahler Films.
D: Woodie King Jr.; P: Woodie King Jr., St. Claire Bourne; S: Julian Mayfield, adapted from his novel.
Cast: Woodie King Jr., Dick Anthony Williams, Peggy Kilpatrick.

"One of the most positive black films ever made."

An African-American teenager takes to the streets in search of the meaning of life.

Misdirected advertising (the black & white poster shows a collage of a preacher, an African tribesman and a woman lying face up in what appears to be a trance) destroyed any chances this low-budget but atmospheric film might have had at the box office.

The story of Jenny (Marlene Clark) and her teenage daughter Billie (Avis McCarther), and their relationship with a man named Memphis (Wally Taylor), who may or may not be the reincarnation of a Yoruban priest named Jabo (Lawrence Cook), is well performed by all but a bit confusing. *Lord Shango* is a modern-minded-African-Christians against primal African superstitions tale that, ultimately, misses its mark

THE MACK

1973, USA
Alternative Title: *The Mack and His Pack*
R (23404), Action/Adventure, 110m.
Cinerama Releasing.
D: Michael Campus; P: Harvey Bernhard;
S: Robert Poole.
Cast: Max Julien, Richard Pryor, Roger E. Mosley, Carol Speed, Juanita Moore.

"Now that you've seen all the rest... make way for The Mack... the biggest and the best."

A petty Los Angeles criminal transforms himself into the city's most financially successful pimp.

Though it does not play as well today, at the time of its release *The Mack* (slang for pimp) was a huge success that, like *Sweet Sweetback's Baadasssss Song* before it, dared to present an African-American outlaw as a folk hero.

As John 'Goldie' Mickens, a young man who has just spent five years in prison and is now refashioning his life as Oakland, California's most successful pimp, Max Julien is an unusually charming, considerate and tolerant film character. Likening his relationship with his 'girls' to that of a large, prosperous organisation of which he is "the president, director and teacher," his glossy rise to the top (shown in a slow motion montage) is the stuff of fantasy. Slim (played by Richard Pryor) is Goldie's best friend; twitchy, only occasionally dependable, but always entertaining. Also appearing in the cast are: Roger E. (*Leadbelly*) Mosley as

One of several 'lost' blaxploitation films, this never-seen-since-it-was-initially-theatrically-released family picture was a well-meaning attempt (by all accounts very similar to *Tough!*) at making a blaxploitation film minus nudity, drugs, profanity and sexual situations.

The stock film characters include: Paul Brown (Dick Anthony Williams), a troubled teenager who runs away from home; Steely (played by director Woodie King Jr.), an embittered, confused and physically abusive returning Vietnam Veteran father; and Mae (Peggy Kilpatrick), Paul's loving mother.

LORD SHANGO

1975, USA
Alternative Titles: *Soulmates of Shango*; *The Color of Love*
R (24272), Drama/Horror, 91m.
Bryanston Pictures.
D: Raymond Marsh; P: Steve Bono, Ryan Hobbs; S: Paul Carter Harrison.
Cast: Lawrence Cook, Marlene Clark, Wally Taylor, Avis McArthur.

"Sacrifice your soul to Shango in the blood ritual of life and death!"

A tribal priest is reincarnated to avenge his murder.

MAHOGANY

1975, USA
PG (24373), Drama, 109m.
Paramount Pictures.
D: Berry Gordy Jr.; P: Rob Cohen; S: John Byrum.
Cast: Diana Ross, Billy Dee Williams, Anthony Perkins, Beah Richards, Jean-Pierre Aumont.

"Success is nothing without someone you love to share it with."

A young female fashion student in Chicago becomes an internationally celebrated model.

Mahogany still fascinates because it speaks directly to the dreams and fantasies in all of us – women and men alike.

Diana Ross as Tracy Chambers, a single woman living in the Chicago ghetto, is nothing short of mesmerising. Convincingly embodying the ongoing struggles and frustrations of life in a racist, sexist and class-structured society but, at the same time, still indefatigable, she is a film heroine who everyone wants to see succeed – and her on-screen success is a dazzling spectacle.

Billy Dee Williams is also rigorously engaging as Tracy's politically-minded boyfriend Brian, a man who is unable to understand Tracy's need for independence. Attractive, suave and street-smart, he, too, appears to have all the qualities needed to realise *his* dreams. There is a problem, of course. If Tracy and Brian are to build a life together, one of these two super ambitious individuals is going to have to subvert their inclinations for the sake of the other. The supporting roles are filled out by: Anthony (*Psycho*) Perkins as Sean McAvoy, a quirky and controlling world-famous photographer; Jean-Pierre Aumont as Christian Rosetti, Tracy's unexpected benefactor; and Beah Richards as Florence, Tracy's seamstress, friend and personal champion.

Mahogany had immense popular appeal, especially with urban audiences; in New York City's Times Square the demand to see it [and see it again] was so great that the Paramount Theater played it 24 hours a day for a full two weeks! This success came about because of several converging factors: Ross and Williams had already proved to be an engaging on-screen pair in 1972's *Lady Sings the Blues*; black audiences were becoming

Olinga, Goldie's militant-minded brother; Carol (*Abby*) Speed as Lulu, Goldie's former girlfriend (now his most prized prostitute); and Juanita (*Fox Style*) Moore, Goldie's devout, highly sceptical mother.

Notable moments in *The Mack* include: trips to the annual 'Players' picnic and ball (events where successful pimps and their 'families' get together); several violent murders (including one character whose fate is to be injected with battery acid, and another who is placed in the trunk of a car which is filled with rats); and a classroom-setting

demonstration on how to steal clothing and jewellery from retailers.

Poorly directed, carelessly edited (almost all the scenes go on for too long) and sketchily written (the whole production feels improvised), this vastly overrated film's redeeming feature is the constant parade of patently outrageous 1970s fashions.

"...inept, so confused that occasionally it seems unreal... plot elements bump into each other like air bubbles in an empty stomach."
(Vincent Canby, New York Times)

bored with the over-saturation of pimps and players in blaxploitation's most heavily promoted pictures; the movie contained the No.1 pop hit 'Theme from Mahogany (Do You Know Where You're Going To)'; and, perhaps most important of all, Diana Ross's triumph as a fashion model seemed to be an on-screen confirmation of the 'Black Is Beautiful' slogan so often repeated at the time.

Note: *Mahogany*'s original director Tony Richardson was replaced by African-American Motown Records president Berry Gordy Jr. Highly recommended.

"...it remains one of the very few American features that has ever attempted telling a story about a black woman, her dreams, her hopes and her fears."
(Donald Bogle, Blacks in American Films and Television, 1988)

Mahogany-the woman every woman wants to be- and every man wants to have.

A Berry Gordy Film
Diana Ross in Mahogany

The man who knew what Mahogany was and where she came from and still loved her

The fashion photographer who created the most beautiful model in the world and then tried to destroy her

The rich count who owned everything... and now he wanted to own Mahogany

THE MAN

1972, USA
G (23293), Drama, 93m.
Paramount Pictures.
D: Joseph Sargent; P: Lee Rich; S: Rod Serling, based on a novel by Irving Wallace.
Cast: James Earl Jones, Janet MacLachlan, Burgess Meredith, Martin Balsam, Robert DoQui, Georg Stanford Brown, Barbara Rush.

"The first black president of the Unites States. First they swore him in. Then they swore to get him!"

When a freak accident kills the president of the United States and the vice president declines to take office due to ill health, the African-American head of the Senate becomes the acting president.

Ambitious but confusing, *The Man* takes a cursory (and somewhat fantastic) look at the unlikely chain of events that follow the killing of the president of the United States.

James Earl (*Claudine*) Jones is well cast as Douglass Dilman, the newly elected leader of the free world. Authoritative, professional looking and eager to please, this is a star turn that, unfortunately, very few people bothered to see. The supporting cast is impressive, including Burgess (*Golden Needles*) Meredith, Martin Balsam, Barbara Rush, Janet (*Halls of Anger*) MacLachlan, Robert (*Coffy*) DoQui, and Georg Stanford (*Stir Crazy*) Brown, but none of the actors are able to transcend the mediocre material at hand. Well intentioned but ill advised, *The Man* is one of those films that, played today, seems like little more than a mediocre TV-movie. (In fact *The Man* was filmed as a TV-movie and only theatrically released after network sponsors refused to air it – citing the picture's 'controversial' subject matter.)

"The dullness of the drama and the fuzziness of its thinking evoke the magic of the Eisenhower years."
(Vincent Canby, New York Times)

MAN AND BOY

1971, USA
G (22934), Western, 98m.
Columbia Pictures.
D: E.W. Swackhamer; P: Marvin Miller; S: Harry Essex, Oscar Saul.
Cast: Bill Cosby, Henry Silva, Yaphet Kotto, Leif Erickson, George Spell, Gloria Foster, Shelly Morrison, Douglas Turner Ward.

"Bill Cosby makes a stunning switch from his comedy to a startlingly dramatic role."

An African-American father and son set out on a journey to locate a stolen horse.

Creatively photographed, well acted and cleverly presented, *Man and Boy* is a warm-hearted, lesson-filled saga that is suitable for all family members.

Bill Cosby is, as always, charismatic and methodically engaging as Caleb Revers, a land-owning African-American war veteran who embarks on a search for his stolen horse. Comfortable with himself (and the inoffensive material), attractive, and possessed with a highly developed on-screen persona, Cosby is a well-intentioned African-American actor who is obviously (and admirably) concerned with the fair and accurate representation of blacks in American films. As his quick-to-cry son Billy, George Spell (who also played Sidney Poitier's son in both *They Call Me Mister Tibbs!* and *The Organization*) is equally attractive and competent in this film about men, their dreams and their fantasies. Gloria Foster, as Caleb's wife Ivy, adds the knowing-female touch that balances the film. Other notable perform-ances come from: Shelly Morrison as Rosita, a lonely Mexican widow; Yaphet Kotto as Nate Hodges, Ivy's not too secret admirer; and Douglas Turner Ward as Lee

Christmas, a desperate outlaw who is not above kidnapping a little boy.

Man and Boy is a valuable film, in that it is one of very few blaxploitation pictures to responsibly place African Americans in pivotal turn-of-the century western roles.

"The plight of a black man in the frontier west is a wonderfully provocative film theme..."
(Howard Thompson, New York Times)

MAN FRIDAY

1975, UK
PG (24262), Drama, 115m.
Avco Embassy Pictures.
D: Jack Gold; P: David Korda; S: Adrian Mitchell.
Cast: Peter O'Toole, Richard Roundtree, Peter Cellier, Christopher Cabot.

"The motion picture adventure of the year. The emotional experience of a lifetime."

A contemporary retelling of Daniel Defoe's literary classic *Robinson Crusoe*.

Peter O'Toole is authoritative, believable and often very funny as Robinson Crusoe, one of two men stranded on a desert island. Richard Roundtree is also exceptional as Crusoe's companion/servant Friday; he is single-minded and markedly different in appearance and temperament to his master.

Sometimes intense (a struggle for power and domination), but often light-hearted (a talking parrot; a misguided attempt to create a flying machine), this predictable but generally entertaining film lacked the inner-city trappings necessary to appeal to the action-hungry young black audience to whom it was marketed.

"Roundtree shows himself to be much more than a stud; he is an actor of incredible skill and talent."
(Rana Arons, Photoplay)

MANDINGA

1976, Italy
NR, Action/Adventure, 92m.
S.E.F.I. Cinematografica.
D: Mario Pinzauti; P: Mario Pinzauti; S: Mario Pinzauti.
Cast: Antonio Gismondo, Maria Rosaria Riuzzi, Rita Manna, Serafino Profumo, Paola D'Egidio.

"Goes beyond Mandingo... the lust of slave owners for Black flesh!!"

A Southern plantation slave gives birth to a daughter who mysteriously disappears.

Tired yet still titillating quickie follow-up to *Mandingo* (the title graphics are an exact copy of *Mandingo*'s) this Italian-made, English-dubbed exploitation flick remains true to formula. There's a nymphomaniac visiting cousin, Miss Rhonda (Paola D'Egidio), an elderly not-too-evil plantation owner, Mr. Hunter (Serafino Profumo), a cultured son just home from Britain, Clarence (Antonio Gismondo), and a goody-two-shoes minister's daughter, Mary Foster (Maria Rosaria Riuzzi).

Rape, beatings, sadomasochism, miscegenation; all the lurid plantation staples are here, and they are aided and abetted by a steady parade of attractive young performers (with an apparent sense of humour) who are comfortable with their nudity and nonchalantly perform in gratuitous, often debased, sexual situations. Perversely enjoyable. Mario Pinzauti also directed *Passion Plantation*.

MANDINGO

1975, USA
R (24251), Drama, 126m.
Paramount Pictures.
D: Richard Fleischer; P: Dino De Laurentiis; S: Norman Wexler, based on the novel by Kyle Onstott and the play by Jack Kirkland.
Cast: James Mason, Perry King, Susan George, Ken Norton, Brenda Sykes, Lillian Hayman, Ben Masters.

above: 1975's **Mandingo** was one of the first films to invert Hollywood's popular presentation of contented slaves and their fair-minded masters. Here white plantation heir Hammond Maxwell (Perry King) enjoys a fringe benefit – Ellen (Brenda Sykes), a young black slave girl. (J. Howard Collection)
bottom right: White master and black slave: Perry King *(left)* and prize fighter-turned actor Ken Norton *(right)* as Mede – **Mandingo**'s celebrated warrior-in-residence.

"From the shocking bestseller that told the truth... the <u>real</u> truth about the old South!"

Life on a formerly-grand Southern plantation turns sour when the master of the house's son falls in love with a slave.

A year before producing the re-make of *King Kong*, Dino De Laurentiis produced a film version of Kyle Onstott's tawdry 1960s bestseller (ten million copies sold) *Mandingo*.

James Mason is chillingly effective as run-down Falconhurst plantation owner Warren Maxwell. Foul-mouthed, hostile, racist and terribly ignorant, he presents a fascinating and almost too-realistic portrait of a man desperately trying to validate his life and the very harmful choices he has made. Perry King, too, is superb as his handsome, compassionate and curiously shy son Hammond (he fell off of a horse when he was young and has a 'bad leg'). Placed in the hands of another actor his sketchily written role might fall flat. Instead King (who is as comfortable with full-frontal nudity as he is with shedding tears of frustration) underlines the duplicitous roles that fair-minded whites had to play in the turn of the century, racist South. His new bride, Blanche (Susan George), is also fascinating. Trashy, but trying not to be; desperate to escape her dysfunctional family; the victim of early sexual abuse, she is at turns, coquettish, needy and sadistic – a complex character who has no empathy whatsoever with anyone else's plight.

The always-lovely Brenda (*Honky*) Sykes plays Ellen, Hammond's black 'bed wench,' who is everything that her master's wife isn't. Soft, sincere, sane and sober, she challenges Hammond (and the viewer) to consider her not only as a beautiful black woman, but also as a living, breathing human being. Champion prize fighter Ken Norton is also noteworthy; though he is undeniably stiff (especially in his nude seduction scene), as Mede, a 'pure bred' hard-fighting 'Mandingo' (the top of the line as far as African slaves go), he is most certainly a tall dark and handsome man with an undeniably well maintained (and, as it turns out, highly desirable) physique.

The superior supporting cast includes Lillian Hayman as Lucrezia Borgia, the rotund, knows-what's-really-going-on mammy, and Ben Masters as Charles, a faithful servant who objects to Mede's violent fights, but also cares and understands the trickery and deceit necessary to move forward in the role of slave on a large plantation.

Mandingo lushly presents a dramatic inversion of Hollywood's antiseptic vision of Southern plantation life and mores. Deft direction, beautiful lighting, inventive photography, a sweeping musical score (including a theme song by soul legend Muddy Waters), and true-to-life costumes (and lack of them) all engage the viewer and compliment the story. Violence, incest, rape, beatings, interracial sex, sado-masochism, infanticide, murder, torture and a host of other 'unmentionable' goings-on are all part of the heady stew. A Hollywood film unlike any other, *Mandingo* was followed by a sequel, *Drum*. Highly recommended.

"A pulpy, lurid, antebellum potboiler that turns the fantasy world of a romanticized film like 'Gone with the Wind' inside out."
(Donald Bogle, Blacks in American Films and Television, 1988)

MAURIE

1973, USA
Alternative Title: *Big Mo*
G (23688), Drama, 110m.
National General Pictures.
D: Daniel Mann; P: Frank Ross, Douglas Morrow; S: Douglas Morrow.
Cast: Bernie Casey, Bo Svenson, Janet MacLachlan, Stephanie Edwards.

"Maurie is an unforgettable man. Maurie is an unforgettable picture."

When an African-American basketball star suffers sudden paralysis, his white friend and teammate assists in his rehabilitation.

The true story of black Cincinnati basketball player Maurice Stokes (who lapsed into a coma following a head injury) and his white best friend and teammate Jack Twyman, *Maurie* is burdened by an overly-familiar plot, clichéd dialogue and a gushing, full-orchestra soundtrack.

Bernie Casey (looking more attractive here than in any of his other films) delivers a thrilling tour-de-force as Maurice Stokes. Be it frustration, sadness, fleeting glee, or quiet resignation, the actor turns in a performance that succeeds on a level far above that of the

unimpressive material at hand. Stokes's best friend and most ardent champion Jack Twyman is played by Bo Svenson (who hit his stride two years later playing a super-violent, revenge-seeking sheriff in *Walking Tall Part 2*). Not as good in this more subdued role, Svenson is, at least, predictably amiable. His long-suffering, always understanding, wife Carole is played by Stephanie Edwards. Also in the cast is Janet (*Halls of Anger*) MacLachlan as Dorothy Parsons, a woman bound by conflicting emotions concerning her boyfriend's sudden incapacity.

Not terrible, yet terribly predictable, *Maurie* is a well-intentioned family film; a 'true story' picture that offers a cursory 'uplifting' look at a star athlete's personal misfortune.

Note: *Maurie* was released for just 4 weeks in 1973, before being pulled from theatres due to its poor performance. It was re-released as *Big Mo* in 1975.

"Hard as everyone works to keep this from being just a weepy soap opera, it's no more than that..."
(Donald Bogle, Blacks in American Films and Television, 1988)

THE McMASTERS

1970, USA
Alternative Title: *The Blood Crowd*
GP (22232), Action/Adventure, 89m.
Chevron Films.
D: Alf Kjellin; P: Monroe Sachson;
S: Harold Jacob Smith.
Cast: Brock Peters, Burl Ives, Jack Palance, Nancy Kwan, John Carradine, David Carradine.

"Bigotry! Violence! Southern Vengeance in the Old West!"

This post-Civil War melodrama is one of blaxploitation's very first western-themed pictures.

Brock Peters turns in a performance filled with both subtlety and nuance as recently released Union soldier Benjie. Even more engaging is Burl Ives as McMasters, Benjie's big-hearted, big-bellied former owner. Equally impressive in supporting roles are: Nancy Kwan as Robin, Benjie's Indian wife; Jack Palance as Kolby, the town bigot and rebel-rouser; and David Carradine as White Feather, an Indian tribesman who struggles to understand Benjie's unwavering sense of entitlement.

Creative photography, picturesque locations, and an unresolved final act make this a film of note.

Note: The stunning opening title sequence was created by artist Sandy Dvore, who would later create the memorable titles for *Blacula*.

MEAN JOHNNY BARROWS

1975, USA
Alternative Titles: *Street Warrior*; *The Hit Man*
R (24352), Action/Adventure, 85m.
Atlas Films.
D: Fred Williamson; P: Fred Williamson;
S: Charles Walker, Jolivett Cato.
Cast: Fred Williamson, Roddy McDowall, Jenny Sherman, Elliott Gould, Stuart Whitman.

"Brutal! Blasting! Blazing! Fred Williamson is Mean Johnny Barrows."

A discharged Army Officer puts his combat tactics to work for the mob.

In the lead as former football star (and returning Vietnam Veteran) Johnny Barrows, Fred Williamson seems to be

present in physical form only. Flat-voiced, uninvolved, coasting on facial expressions and antics that have worked elsewhere, the actor comes across like anything but the star he is – more like just another face in the crowd. Similarly, Jenny Sherman is merely adequate as Nancy, a bosomy mob girlfriend. Others in the cast include: Stuart Whitman as Mario Racconi, a mob boss with a conscience (he won't get involved in the drug trade); Roddy McDowall as Tony DaVinci, a flower shop-owning double-crosser; and Elliott Gould as Theodore Rasputin Waterhouse, a 'kooky' homeless man. A good example of the breathtakingly clichéd dialogue comes when Johnny tells mob girlfriend Nancy about his dreams.

Johnny: *How do you measure a man's worth? Is it by what he owns? His dreams? Or what he wants from life? My dreams are small. A home, some land, something I can own that nobody can ever take away from me.*

Sub-par performances, tinny music, inadequate lighting, unconvincing 'fight' sequences and a general lack of incident (at least fifteen minutes of the main character aimlessly walking around the streets of Hollywood, for example) make *Mean Johnny Barrows* not just inferior, but actually embarrassing.

Note: The film was originally due to be called *Peace Is Hell* – this title is shown on *Hollywood Reporter* trade ads published literally weeks before it was released.

"...a claustrophobic downer..."
(Linda Gross, Los Angeles Times)

MEAN MOTHER

1973, Spain/Italy/USA
Alternative Titles: *Run for Your Life*; *El hombre que vino del odio*; *Quello sporco disertore*
R (837), Action/Adventure, 87m.
Independent-International Pictures Corp.
D: Al Adamson, León Klimovsky; P: Sam Sherman; S: Charles Johnson, Joy Garrison.
Cast: Clifton Brown [Dobie Gray], Dennis Safren, Luciana Paluzzi, Lang Jeffries.

"Super cool & wild! Smashing the man and the mob for his women!"

Two Vietnam deserters, one black, one white, go their separate ways. One becomes unjustly implicated in a jewellery heist; the other becomes a messenger of stolen goods.

Mean Mother is one of the least enjoyable entries among the entire blaxploitation catalogue. Ostensibly the story of two Vietnam deserters – black Beauregard Jones (Dobie Gray – credited here as Clifton Brown – best known for his 1973 number 5 hit 'Drift Away') and white Joe (Dennis Safren), this meandering, nonsensical mess of a film came about by taking footage from a 1971 Spanish/Italian film and stitching it together with a few new scenes. The unexplained discrepancy in fashions, hairstyles and language is breathtaking. Nothing works. Wooden performances, poorly chosen location shooting, a ridiculous script and two directors whose 'visions' don't match, make this an entirely joyless endeavour.

MELINDA

1972, USA
R (23321), Action/Melodrama, 109m.
Metro Goldwyn Mayer.
D: Hugh A. Robertson; P: Pervis Atkins; S: Lonne Elder III.
Cast: Calvin Lockhart, Vonetta McGee, Rosalind Cash, Jim Kelly, Rockne Tarkington.

"Your kind of black film"

When a mysterious young woman is murdered, her DJ boyfriend turns detective and tries to find out why.

Melinda is one of the very few blaxploitation pictures that was written, produced and directed by three *different* African Americans.

In the lead as narcissistic Los Angeles DJ Frankie J. Parker, Calvin Lockhart turns in a performance that seems to play on his reputation for being self-absorbed, outspoken and difficult to deal with (his on-set tirades while making *Halls of Anger* were chronicled in *Life* magazine). Vonetta McGee plays the beautiful and mysterious Melinda Lewis. Comfortable with herself, engaging and charming yet still elusive, it must be said that the onscreen chemistry between McGee and Lockhart

above: 1972's **Melinda**, promoted as "Your kind of black film," purported to be much more than just another black-cast action-adventure movie. Here Melinda Lewis (Vonetta McGee) and popular DJ Frankie J. Parker (Calvin Lockhart) discuss their lives in a scene that the picture's director had to fight to keep. (Soul Images)

is nothing short of mesmerising. Other characters include: Frankie's sensible-minded ex-girlfriend Terry Davis, played by Rosalind (*Dr. Black, Mr. Hyde*) Cash; Rockne (*Black Samson*) Tarkington as Tank, a former football player turned nightclub owner; and Jim (*Black Belt Jones*) Kelly as Atkins, Frankie's karate instructor best friend.

Filled with committed performances and realistic, sometimes strikingly vulgar, dialogue, and offering an unusual triangular plot that is centred around a dead woman, *Melinda* was a hit with critics, but unfortunately did not quite connect with the young black audiences it was made for.

"A blistering suspense melodrama framed with a whodunit format."
(Vincent Canby, New York Times)

MISS MELODY JONES

1973, USA
Alternative Titles: *Ebony Dreams*; *The Gauntlet*
PG (807), Drama, 86m.
American Films Ltd.
D: Bill Brame; P: Bill Brame; S: Bill Brame.
Cast: Philomena Nowlin, Ron Warden, Peter Jacob, Jacqueline Dalya, Garth Howard, John Kimbro.

"She gladly paid the price for stardom... but was black beautiful enough?"

A naive young girl ventures to Hollywood in pursuit of motion picture stardom, only to find out that the road is littered with people eager to exploit her.

Very far from "the shattering portrait of a black woman sucked into a cruel vortex" (tagline on the video box), *Miss Melody Jones* is, instead, a miniature exercise in wish fulfilment.

In the lead, bunny-faced Philomina Nowlin plays the just-arrived-in-town, wide-eyed, over-eager and very confused Melody. Off putting, and a nag, Ms. Nowlin is not a character that we come to care much about.

The supporting roles are filled out by Tim (Ron Warden), Melody's well-intentioned UCLA grad student boyfriend, and Helen (Jacqueline Dalya), Melody's husky-voiced lesbian agent. Other cardboard characters include: a swishy, kaftan-wearing gay roommate Jack (Peter Jacob); a lecherous older movie producer, Scott (Garth Howard); and a rotund, greasy-faced 'Money Man' (John Kimbro). A good example of the embarrassing dialogue comes when Melody's boyfriend tries to explain his reason for choosing filmmaking as a career.

> Tim: *I just see film as a means of informing people that need to be informed about the human pain and suffering that is going on around them.*
> (Ironically, earlier in the film, Tim admonished Melody, saying, "I hate clichés!")

Filled with flubbed lines, boom mikes that are visible within the frame, and poor post-dubbing, Melody's agent sounds like she talking about *this* film when she says "Nobody's gonna want it. Nobody's gonna buy it. And nobody's gonna see it."

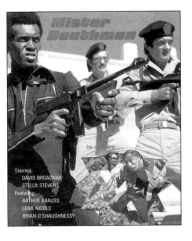

MISTER DEATHMAN

1977, South Africa
NR, Action/Adventure, 90m.
Karat Films International.
D: Michael Moore; P: Hans Kuhle, Raymond R. Homer; S: Emmett Murphy, based on a story by David Broadnax.
Cast: David Broadnax, Stella Stevens, Arthur Brauss, Lena Nicols.

"He delivers..."

An African-American Private Investigator is hired to locate stolen NASA documents.

Mister Deathman's ambitious plot and exotic locations (South Africa) don't make up for its relentlessly threadbare production values and breathtakingly poor performances.

David Broadnax is just plain bad as Private Investigator Geoffrey Graves. Wooden, unconvincing and not especially

above: 1977's **Mister Deathman** (not to be confused with the same year's **Mr. Mean**) was an ambitious South African picture that came and went without much notice.

above: **Monkey Hustle** (1976) was an audience-pleasing PG-rated confection. Baby D. (Kirk Calloway, *left*) is not always keen on taking orders from his sly but amiable "boss," Daddy Fox (Yaphet Kotto, *right*).

photogenic, his casting is presumably a direct concession to the fact that the script is based on his original story idea. Stella Stevens as Liz, a lesbian extortionist, is a bit more engaging in what is essentially a repeat performance of the shrill lesbian drug lord the actress played in 1975's *Cleopatra Jones and the Casino of Gold*. Other performers include Arthur Brauss as Vince Napier, Graves's partner, and Lena Nicols as Pamela, Liz's lesbian-lover sidekick.

MONKEY HUSTLE

1976, USA
PG (24731), Comedy, 90m.
American International Pictures.
D: Arthur Marks; P: Arthur Marks;
S: Charles Johnson.
Cast: Yaphet Kotto, Rudy Ray Moore, Rosalind Cash, Kirk Calloway, Randy Brooks, Thomas Carter, Donn Harper.

"Meet Daddy Fox, Baby D. and Goldie. They gonna do the Monkey Hustle!

It ain't legal an' it ain't safe... but it do seem worthwhile!"

Residents of a Chicago neighbourhood combine forces to block the construction of a freeway that will cut through their neighbourhood.

This entertaining romp is, in essence, a black version of the Paul Newman-Robert Redford vehicle *The Sting*. Mimicking elements of that film's basic storyline and its advertising campaign (and casting young Kirk Calloway, who with his strong jaw and bright blue eyes looks like a sepia-tinted Paul Newman), *Monkey Hustle* is a nicely photographed, sometimes funny, look at inner-city hustlers, pimps and con men.

Yaphet (*Across 110th Street*) Kotto is nothing less than superb as ringleader Daddy Fox. Delivering his lines with a charming tell-tale wink in his eye and a cigar dangling from his mouth, his Daddy Fox is a highly likeable character whose mantra, "getting down means getting

over," is eventually adopted by the rest of the cast. As his pint-sized student and partner in crime Baby D., Kirk (*Cinderella Liberty*) Calloway, too, turns in a thoroughly enjoyable performance. Also in the cast are Rudy Ray (*Dolemite*) Moore as Goldie, a quick-tongued, outlandishly dressed pimp, Rosalind Cash as Mama, a Soul Food restaurant owner, and Randy Brooks as Win, Baby D.'s wandering drum-playing brother. Thomas Carter and Donn Harper are Player & Tiny, Daddy Fox's newest 'film flam' students.

A wig-flying catfight between two competing young women, a visit to Roller Skate City (an African-American disco roller rink), and a block party finale are all part of the shenanigans. Screenwriter Charles Johnson is African American. See *Q & A: Ten Directors Discuss Their Films.*

"...crossover possibilities are nil since white audiences probably won't relate to any of it and probably can't understand most of the lingo spoken."
(Variety)

they don't call them that for nothing!

MOTHER, JUGS & SPEED

1976, USA
PG (24559), Comedy/Drama, 98m.
20th Century Fox.
D: Peter Yates; P: Tom Mankiewicz, Peter
Yates; S: Tom Mankiewicz, from a story
by Mankiewicz and Stephen Manes.
Cast: Bill Cosby, Raquel Welch, Harvey
Keitel, Larry Hagman.

"They don't call them that for nothing!"

The adventures and personal discoveries of a group of employees at an L.A. ambulance company.

Mother, Jugs & Speed is a jumbled, misguided, over-populated, socio-political 'comedy' that misses its mark at every turn.

   In the role of Mother, the F & B Ambulance Company's most knowledgeable and life-worn driver, Bill Cosby provides his usual shtick but gets lost in the murk of a script that wants to be too many different things – all at the same time. Raquel Welch plays Jennifer (she's also known as 'Jugs,' for reasons that are rather obvious), an ambulance company dispatcher who wants to move up to being a certified driver. Failing to live up to the hoopla and excitement that her name evokes, Welch gives a forced, insincere, self-conscious performance. Harvey Keitel plays Tony Malatesta (also known as Speed, because he was accused of selling drugs at his former job), the most believable and sympathetic character in

this film. Soap opera superstar Larry Hagman stars as John Murdoch, Speed's perpetually horny ambulance partner.

   Corruption, unfair competition, politics, shotgun murders, sexual romps, car chases, and the 'kooky' insertion of fast-paced (very dated-sounding) disco music, all come together to make *Mother, Jugs & Speed* a hard-on-the-ears, disjointed, unfunny and ultimately insulting film.

"Typical of so many post 'M*A*S*H' comedies that assume that a lunatic juxtaposition of slapstick, brutal realism, obscenities, romance and bad humour automatically make an important statement about the world we live in." (Vincent Canby, New York Times)

MR. MEAN

1977, USA
NR (R), Action/Adventure, 81m.
Lone Star Pictures/Po' Boy Distributions.
D: Fred Williamson; P: Fred Williamson;
S: Fred Williamson.
Cast: Fred Williamson, Crippy Yocard,
Lou Castel, Raimund Harmstorf, Stelio
Candelli, Anthony Maimone, Rita Silva.

"If the price is right, the job is right!"

A former police officer turned hit man accepts an offer to fly to Rome and assassinate a corrupt mob associate.

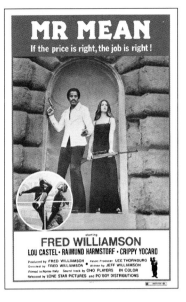

There are many things that distinguish Fred Williamson from the rest of blaxploitation's leading men. Perhaps his most noteworthy accomplishment is that he is the only genre performer to write, produce and direct several of his own starring vehicles. It's a shame then that many of the actor's entrepreneurial endeavours are so shoddy, smarmy and poorly put together.

   As Mr. Mean (that's his real name throughout the film!), a gun-for-hire, Williamson does all that he is supposed to but seems a little too comfortable and a little too detached to be believable. Matching Williamson's indifference are a

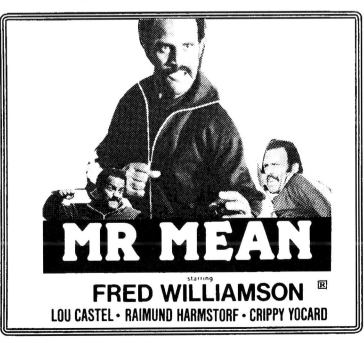

bevy of Italian non-actors (and beautiful female models) who have been forced to make the concentrated effort to speak their lines phonetically – totally obliterating any emotional impact their scenes might have. The cast includes: Lou Castel as Huberto, a dull-faced Italian 'trouble-maker'; Stelio Candelli as a Chuck Norris-like Italian hit-man named Ranati; Anthony Maimone as a lying, disgruntled mobster called Rico; and Rita Silva in the role of Carla, a beautiful Italian girl who is not what she appears to be.

Filled with street-corner camera setups (with passers-by looking on curiously in the background), and containing a thankless performance by the Ohio Players, *Mr. Mean*'s preposterous 'surprise' ending is the cherry that sits atop this stale, bitter-tasting cake.

"Often the only distinction and dimension [Williamson's] screen personae have are their unique surnames."
(Parish/Hill, Black Action Films, 1989)

MR. RICCO

1975, USA
PG (24078), Action/Adventure, 98m.
Metro Goldwyn Mayer.
D: Paul Bogart; P: Douglas Netter; S: Robert Hoban, from a story by Ed Harvey and Francis Kiernan.
Cast: Dean Martin, Thalmus Rasulala, Denise Nicholas, Cindy Williams, Philip [Michael] Thomas.

"The only thing that people hate more than a cop killer is the lawyer who gets him off!"

A white San Francisco lawyer begins to question his black client's innocence.

Seen by next to no one, this late-career, TV-movie style Dean Martin vehicle, with its creative photography and involved African-American subplot, offers a few nice surprises.

Martin is successfully nonchalant as widowed lawyer Joe Ricco, an amiable man who has a special relationship with his dog Hank. Ricco's client is Frankie Steele (Thalmus Rasulala), a member of the black militant group The Black Serpents. Also in the cast are Philip Michael (*Black Fist*) Thomas as Purvis Mapes, Steele's jive-talking, pot smoking, gang member friend; and Denise (*A Piece of the Action*) Nicholas as Irene, Purvis's suspicious but still sympathetic sister.

Along with the requisite car chases, shootouts and police station in-fighting, *Mr. Ricco* takes the viewer on a visit to an underground African-American nightclub, and concludes in grand style with an art gallery ambush. Look for Cindy (of TV's *Laverne & Shirley*) Williams as Jamison, Ricco's over-eager secretary. See *Q & A: Ten Directors Discuss Their Films*.

THE MUTHERS

1976, USA
R (24711), Action/Adventure, 82m.
Dimension Pictures.
D: Cirio H. Santiago; P: Cirio H. Santiago; S: Cyril St. James, from a story by Leonard Hermes [Cirio H. Santiago].
Cast: Jeanne [Jean] Bell, Rosanne Katon, Jayne Kennedy, Trina Parks.

"Out of the steaming slave markets come the raging sea-savages... the Muthers!"

Hoping to locate her missing sister, an African-American woman and her friend join an international pirate ship.

Entertaining, quite literally fast moving (everybody is running all the time) and unusual, *The Muthers* is one of just a handful of blaxploitation films in which the starring roles are occupied by four beautiful women.

The cast of lovelies includes: Kelly, the doll-faced (and magnificently built) former *Playboy* bunny Jean (*TNT Jackson*) Bell; Serena, played by Jayne (*Big Time*) Kennedy; Trina (*Darktown Strutters*) Parks as Marcie; and Rosanne (*Ebony, Ivory & Jade*) Katon in the role of Anggie.

The Muthers is a visually arresting, fun-filled, escapist action adventure film whose Santo Domingo locations (and extras) offer a welcome change of scenery. Highlights include: camp fight sequences (in which the male stunt-double is clearly discernable); entertaining one-liners (after being bitten on the breast by a snake, Marcie retorts "Just like every other snake I've ever known, they just can't keep their mouths off my tits!"); and several preposterous machine-gun (and cannon!) shootouts. See *Q & A: Ten Directors Discuss Their Films.*

NIGGER LOVER

1973, USA
Alternative Title: *The Bad Bunch*
NR (R), Action/Adventure, 80m.
Mardi Rustam Film.
D: Greydon Clark; P: Alvin L. Fast;
S: Greydon Clark, Alvin L. Fast.
Cast: Greydon Clark, Tom Johnigarn, Jacqulin [Jacqueline] Cole, Aldo Ray, Pamela Corbett, Bambi Allen.

"The chase that begins with love and ends with violence... the movie they tried to stop!"

After returning from service in Vietnam, a white GI encounters resistance from the friends and family of his lost African-American best friend.

This explosively titled entry (renamed *The Bad Bunch* when re-released in 1976) is, actually, a liberal-minded, painfully earnest 'study' of race, youth and the politics of the day.

As the confused, just-returned-from-Vietnam Vet Jim, Greydon Clark (who also directs) turns in a performance that can best be called subtle. With a never changing disengaged look on his face, he is a poor choice to represent the youth generation's angst, restlessness and problems. Other characters include Makimba (Tom Johnigarn), the militant brother of Jim's deceased Army buddy, and Lieutenant Stans (Aldo Ray), a violent and racist police officer. There are also three sensitively written (though not particularly well acted) female supporting roles: Nancy (Jacqueline Cole), a dull but 'safe' choice for a wife; Tina (Pamela Corbett), a sassy black prostitute who feels degraded because she has to sell herself to white men; and

HELD OVER! HELD OVER! HELD OVER!
MARDI RUSTAM presents
NIGGER LOVER
SEE THE MAN MEET THE SPADE...
FACE TO FACE
THE MOVIE THEY TRIED TO STOP!
...BUT YOU MADE THEM SHOW IT!
in Color
black and white passions explode!
NOW SHOWING!
LOEWS PALACE   BOOKER T

Bobbi (Bambi Allen), a free-spirited and sexually active young woman who is in search of herself.

An outrageous nude pool-party scene (that genuinely looks like a lot of fun), a violent back yard ambush, and a surprise final act will keep you, if not enthralled, then at least moderately entertained. Greydon Clark also directed *Black Shampoo.*

"The best performers in this would-be gritty urban action drama are the people of Watts, shown going about their daily business."
(Parish/Hill, Black Action Films, 1989)

NIGHT OF THE COBRA WOMAN

1972, Philippines/USA
R (561), Horror, 76m. New World Pictures.
D: Andrew Meyer; P: Kerry Magness, Harvey Marks; S: Andrew Meyer, from a story by Andrew Meyer & Kerry Magness.
Cast: Marlene Clark, Joy Bang, Roger Garrett, Vic Diaz.

"When making love is no longer enough... she sucks the life from the bodies of men!"

After getting bitten by a cobra in the Philippines, an African-American war nurse stays alive by procuring a constant supply of human blood.

"A serpentine seductress struggles to keep eternal youth," screamed the posters to this rarely-seen Philippine-shot atrocity, and you, the viewer, will struggle to stay awake.

In the lead as Lena Aruza, an African-American woman who lives alone on a Philippine mountaintop, Marlene (*Ganja & Hess*) Clark is almost too beautiful to be believed. Comfortable in her many topless scenes, confident and generally convincing as a woman with dubious intentions, she, nevertheless, has a model-turned-actress air about her that undermines the already juvenile proceedings. Stranded with her in this obscure, joyless production are Joy Bang as Joanna, an over-inquisitive college student, Roger Garrett as Stan Duff, Joanna's well-meaning but painfully naive boyfriend, and Vic Diaz as Lope – literally a one-eyed, mute, hunchback!

A cock and snake fight, an in-cave ritual – complete with hot pink smoke – and an out of place, highly disturbing segment that features a real monkey being used in sinister 'lab experiments' are all part of this picture; a film that could have – and should have – been a lot more fun.

NIGHT OF THE STRANGLER

1972, USA
Alternative Titles: *Is the Father Black Enough?*; *Vengeance Is Mine*
R (793), Drama, 89m.
Howco International Pictures.
D: Joy N. Houck Jr.; P: Albert J. Salzer; S: J.J. Milans, Bob Weaver, Jeffrey Newton.
Cast: Chuck Patterson, Micky Dolenz, James Ralston, Michael Anthony, Ann Barrett, Susan McCullough.

"A racist wind blows the dust from a black man's grave to choke the honkies to death!"

An investigation ensues when a wealthy Southern white girl, who is planning to marry an African-American man, is murdered.

Dark, dank and dull, this trek through the backwoods of Louisiana is both poorly put together and a cheat (a genuine trip through the backwoods would be much more entertaining to look at than the endless static shots of people delivering exposition in a series of under-lit rooms). The cast of characters include: Father Jessie (Chuck Patterson), a friendly neighborhood priest; Lt. De Vito

(Michael Anthony), a detective assigned to investigate a string of gruesome murders; and Carol (Ann Barrett), best friend of a recent 'suicide' named Denise (Susan McCullough). Poorer than anyone else in the cast are the film's two feuding brothers – Vance (played by Micky Dolenz of The Monkees TV show and pop group), the sympathetic one, and Dan (James Ralston) the racist one. Both give hollow, artificial performances that distract from what there is of the narrative.

This film's convoluted script, sub-par acting and uninventive photography combine to make for a tiresome viewing experience.

NO WAY BACK

1976, USA
Alternative Title: *Tracer*
R (1524) , Action/Adventure, 91m.
Atlas Films.
D: Fred Williamson; P: Fred Williamson;
S: Fred Williamson.
Cast: Fred Williamson, Charles Woolf, Tracy Reed, Virginia Gregg.

"Never trust a woman with her clothes off!"

A private detective is hired to locate a missing person.

Not particularly good, but still better than most of Fred Williamson's independently

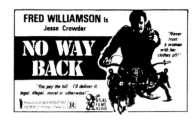

produced pictures, *No Way Back* is a relatively fast-moving tour of L.A.'s Watts ghetto.

Fred Williamson is his amiable, I'm-just-having-a-good-time, best as Private Investigator Jesse Crowder. Whether he is violently beating up the bad guys or tenderly making love to any number of attractive females, he is, at least, always busy. Also appearing in the cast are Charles Woolf as Pickens, an embezzling bank clerk, Virginia Gregg as Mrs. Pickens, his scheming, double-crossing wife, and Tracy (*The Take*) Reed as Candy, Pickens's lovely accomplice.

"Toward the end I only did pictures in which I won the girl, got the bad guys and came away alive" said Fred Williamson in a 2002 interview with the BET cable network. *No Way Back* is one of these films.

"...whites and women should stay away because the picture revels in contempt for both categories."
(Variety)

NORMAN... IS THAT YOU?

1976, USA
PG (24642), Comedy, 91m.
Metro Goldwyn Mayer/United Artists.
D: George Schlatter; P: George Schlatter;
S: Ron Clark and Sam Bobrick, based on their play.
Cast: Redd Foxx, Pearl Bailey, Dennis Dugan, Michael Warren, Tamara Dobson, Wayland Flowers.

"There's a sexual revolution going on... and all the leaders are in my family."

A conservative father devises a plan to 'straighten out' his gay son.

"Cream puff," "fag," "homo," "pansy," "fairy," "Tinkerbelle," "AC-DC," "sissy," "fruitcake," "bitch"... it's all here!

Redd Foxx is perfectly cast as Ben Chambers, a grumpy, old, confused (but loveable) father. In this, his only starring film role, Foxx pulls out all the stops.

*above: 1972's tepid mystery **Night of the Strangler** was swiftly re-released under the much more contentious title, **Is the Father Black Enough?***

The bugged eyes, sideward glances, double entendres (all familiar from his popular TV series *Sanford and Son*) serve his character, and the film, very well indeed. Michael Warren turns in an intelligent and understated performance as Norman Chambers, the homosexual son who is not 'out' to his parents. His on-screen partner, Garson Hobart (Dennis Dugan), is saddled with the swishy, lisping, over-effeminate 'homo' role so common in Hollywood films. Other featured players include: Pearl (*The Landlord*) Bailey as Beatrice, Norman's charming, distinctly ethnic (lots of "honey child"s and "sugar"s) mother; and the spectacularly miss-cast Tamara (*Cleopatra Jones*) Dobson as Audrey, a prostitute with a heart of gold. (Brittle, awkward and detached, the best that can be said about Dobson is that she is, at times, energetic.) Stealing the show is comedian/puppeteer Wayland Flowers (with his two marionettes, Madame and Jiffy), as Larry, a flamboyant nightclub performer. The dialogue is often genuinely funny:

Ben (upon learning his son is gay): *Tell me it isn't true. Tell me you're on drugs. That's it, you're on drugs! Thank God! My son is on drugs! You're a dope fiend, that's all. Now I can sleep nights!*

And during an exchange in his son's kitchen:

Ben (to Norman): *You got any orange juice?*
Norman: *Yeah.*
Ben: *You got any vodka?*
Norman: *Yeah.*
Ben: *Well give me the vodka and hold the orange juice!*

Norman's kitsch gay bachelor pad (complete with purple drapes, shag rugs and a waterbed), along with some nice location shooting (Rodeo Drive; Los Angeles International Airport; trendy North Hollywood) all make for good eye candy. Sometimes stage bound and often exceedingly chatterish, *Norman... Is That You?* is still very much worth a look.

NURSE SHERRI

1977, USA
Alternative Titles: *Black Voodoo*; *Killer's Curse*; *Hospital of Terror*
R (25038), Horror, 88m.
Independent-International Pictures Corp.
D: Al Adamson; P: Mark Sherwood; S: Michael Bockman, Gregg Tittinger.
Cast: Jill Jacobson, Geoffrey Land, Marilyn Joi, Prentiss Moulden, Mary Kay Pass.

"Meet Sherri... for an evening of pleasure and terror!"

A nurse becomes possessed by the evil spirit of a religious fanatic who died while in her care.

This late genre entry is much more fun than it ever should have been. Jill Jacobson plays Sherri Martin, a nurse who becomes possessed by one of her recently departed patients. She gives a detached, uninvolved performance that is so relentlessly flat it's comical. Her other two nurse friends are Beth Dillon (Mary Kay Pass), a practical minded intern, and Tara Williams, played by Marilyn (*The Candy Tangerine Man*) Joi, a sexy African-American woman who knows that you can catch more flies with honey than you can with vinegar (accordingly she provides the picture's only topless scene). Also in the cast are Geoffrey (*Black Heat*) Land as Peter Desmond, a 'dead' yet still vindictive spiritualist, and Prentiss Moulden as Marcus Washington, a recently-blinded professional football player (whose mother happens to be a voodoo priestess!)

Nurse Sherri is the only film in the entire blaxploitation genre to feature a hand-painted green mist (credited to Optical Systems Unlimited) that envelops, glitters and 'makes love' to the film's main character! Add to this some flying beer cans (obviously attached to fishing wire), slamming doors and windows, and a sinister incessant echoing laugh, and you have a movie that you can't take too seriously and you can't really hate either. Good parallel editing (between two women digging up a corpse in a graveyard, and a blood-spattered apartment that may or may not be empty) makes for a semi-engaging finale.

THE OBSESSED ONE

1979, Suriname
NR (R), Action/Adventure, 76m.
Euro-American Pictures/
21st Century Film Corporation
D: Ramdjan Abdoelrahman; P: R. Sookrat,
M. Abdoelrazak, F. Ch. Ganpat; S: Ramdjan
Abdoelrahman.
Cast: Malc Panday. Sally Savalas, Tracy
Parrish. Ronald Jones.

**A newlywed exacts vengeance on the
men who raped and murdered his wife.**

Lost for years, *The Obsessed One* is an
ultra-violent vigilante film with a mystical
bent. Marc Panday is Tyrone, a man whose
blissful nuptials are haunted by the murder
of his new wife Gina (Sally Savalas). Don't
worry though, he, at first accused of his
own wife's murder, will catch up with her
sadistic assailants and make them pay: and
good. Flashbacks, soul music, "fight"
sequences, unintentionally humorous
dubbing, car chases, female nudity, and a
castration make for a dizzying experience!
Look for Ronald Jones as Sugarcane, the
neighborhood's sassy/flashy pimp.

OLD DRACULA

1974, UK
Alternative Title: *Vampira*
PG (23804), Comedy, 88m.
American International Pictures.
D: Clive Donner; P: Jack H. Wiener;
S: Jeremy Lloyd.
Cast: David Niven, Teresa Graves, Jennie
Linden, Nicky Henson, Peter Bayliss.

*"That old blood sucker is back and this
time he's biting off more than he can
chew!"*

**The legendary vampire Count Dracula
tries to resurrect his long-dead wife.**

A half-baked knockoff of the same year's
Young Frankenstein (which is itself
overrated), *Old Dracula* (most well-
known under its re-release title *Vampira*)
paid 'homage' to the former film in both
its title and poster art.

In the lead as (Old) Count Dracula,
David Niven is adequate but given little
room in which to do anything but show his
fangs and, occasionally, mug for the
camera. Flashier, but no more successful
at transcending the painfully unfunny

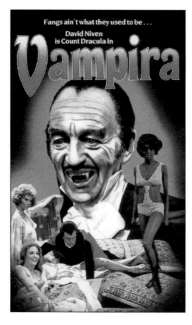

script is Teresa (*Get Christie Love!*)
Graves as Vampira, Count Dracula's
recently resurrected (but because of a
mixed up blood transfusion, now black)
dearly departed wife. On hand in thankless
supporting roles are Peter Bayliss as
Maltravers, Dracula's trusty manservant,
and Nicky Henson as Marc Williams, an
investigative reporter for *Playboy*
magazine.

A tour of mod downtown London, a
visit to an ornate theatre that is showing
another blaxploitation film (*Black Gunn*),
and a 'madcap' costume party don't do
anything to elevate this miserable little
nothing of a film that, sadly, given the cast
and the ripe-for-parody source material,
could have been so much more.

*"Director Donner... and the rest of the
cast... don't seem to have a clue as to why
they're making this movie, or how they
want us to respond."*
(Roger Ebert, Chicago Sun Times)

THE OMEGA MAN

1971, USA
GP (22866), Science Fiction, 98m.
Warner Bros.
D: Boris Sagal; P: Walter Seltzer; S: John
W. Corrington and Joyce H. Corrington,
based on the novel 'I Am Legend' by
Richard Matheson.
Cast: Charlton Heston, Anthony Zerbe,
Rosalind Cash, Paul Koslo, Lincoln
Kilpatrick.

"The last man alive is not alone."

**Following a worldwide catastrophe, a
Los Angeles doctor finds that he is the
only man alive – or so it seems**.

This big-budget, heavily promoted oddity
is a film worth seeing, if only for the
spectacle of witnessing Hollywood screen
legend Charlton Heston keep a straight
face while looking at a bunch of albino
zombies wearing hooded cloaks and
sunglasses!

Heston plays Robert Neville, a doctor
whose experimental vaccine has saved
him from an apocalyptic nightmare. Soon
enough, Neville hooks up with Lisa,
another nuclear holocaust survivor, who
becomes his romantic companion.
Rosalind Cash is hip, jive-talking and
contemporary-looking as Lisa, and her
on-screen romance with Neville feels
fresh and genuinely new.

Other characters include Matthias
(Anthony [*The Liberation of L.B. Jones*]
Zerbe), a half-blind mutant, and Zachary
(Lincoln [*Together Brothers*] Kilpatrick),
spokesperson for the nocturnal mutant
tribe laying siege to Neville's fortified
home.

Ambitious, visually exciting, and
containing an unconventional final act,
The Omega Man (the second screen
adaptation of Richard Matheson's novel 'I
Am Legend', the first being 1964's *The
Last Man on Earth*, and the most recent
being 2007's *I Am Legend*) is a thoroughly
engaging novelty; the kind of film whose
anti-war/anti-technology theme still
resonates today.

*"...reminds us just how thought provoking
the best science-fiction can be."*
(Kevin N. Laforest, Montreal Film Journal)

above: Charlton Heston and Rosalind Cash
in **The Omega Man** (1971).

THE ORGANIZATION

1971, USA
GP (22954), Action/Adventure, 107m.
United Artists.
D: Don Medford; P: Walter Mirisch;
S: James R. Webb.
Cast: Sidney Poitier, Barbara McNair, Ron O'Neal, Sheree North, Raul Julia, George Spell, Demond Wilson, Lani Miyazaki, James A. Watson Jr., Billy Green Bush.

"One honest cop has the guts to take on 'The Organization'."

A San Francisco detective joins forces with a group of anti-drug vigilantes to crack a mob case.

Sidney Poitier's third (and final) appearance in the role of detective Virgil Tibbs (preceded by *They Call Me Mister Tibbs!* and *In the Heat of the Night*) is beautifully photographed, cleverly scripted and filled with a cast of actors who are giving it their all. This box-office dud is a fast-paced, genuinely exciting crime drama that is not only satisfying to watch, but also totally believable.

Sidney Poitier does not stray very far from the familiar in the role of detective Virgil Tibbs. Well-educated, erudite and sensitive (in particular when interacting with his curious son Andy [George Spell]), this role fits Poitier like a glove. Tibbs's dutiful, always-supportive, wife Valerie is played by Barbara McNair. Not as convincing as Poitier, McNair has an overly cultivated air about her that seems out of synch with her practical-minded, stay-at-home-mom film character.

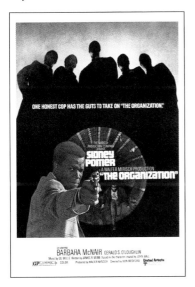

Shining as bright as this film's two headline stars is the large cast of supporting characters, including: Charlie Blossom (Demond Wilson), an expert pole-vaulter; Annie Sekido (Lani Miyazaki), a champion runner; Joe Peralez (Ron [*Super Fly*] O'Neal), a hot-headed Latin; Stacey Baker (James A. Watson Jr. from *Lady Cocoa*), a salesman by day, law student by night; Juan Mendoza (Raul Julia), a former U.S. Marine; and Dave Thomas (Billy Green Bush), head of a neighbourhood community centre.

Attractive San Francisco locations, imaginative plot details, and elaborately choreographed opening and closing segments make this overlooked gem worthy of rediscovery.

"Effectively bridges the gap between the high-minded, race-conscious films of the late 1960s and the new wave of cheekier, more visceral blaxploitation films..."
(Michael Hasting, All Movie Guide)

PACIFIC INFERNO

1978, Philippines/USA
NR, Action/Adventure, 89m.
Euro London Films Ltd.
D: Rolf Bayer; P: Spencer Jourdain, Cassius V. Weathersby; S: Rolf Bayer.
Cast: Jim Brown, Richard Jaeckel, Rik Van Nutter, Tim [Timothy] Brown, Wilma Reading, Tad Horino.

"The prize was $16,000,000... the price was death!"

After the fall of the Philippines, two American POWs are engaged to recover a stash of 'lost' silver coins.

Not quite the "epic battle of World War II" that it promises to be, *Pacific Inferno* is, instead, a stock footage-heavy collection of military training exercises, combat films, air strikes (and in flashbacks) an inner-city race riot, a 'sit-in,' and a depression era dance party.

Jim Brown looks good and is relatively convincing as Clyde Preston, a Michigan-born US Navy officer who also happens to be an expert 'search & destroy' diver. Amiable, athletic and 'cool,' the actor (also credited as Executive Producer) is the vessel around which this meandering, under-lit sea-bound tale has been constructed.

Richard Jaeckel provides support as Robert "Dealer" Fletcher, Preston's helpmate (the two spearhead a plan that involves using sheepskins as air tanks!), along with: Rik Van Nutter as Dennis, a racist turncoat; Timothy (*Dynamite Brothers*) Brown playing Preston's just-go-with-the-flow friend Zoe Dawson; and Wilma Reading as Tita, a willing participant in more than just Preston's plot to escape.

A point blank range execution, a few treks through the jungle, and lots of underwater photography do little to help make this movie particularly engaging.

PASSION PLANTATION

1976, Italy
Alternative Titles: *Emanuelle bianca e nera*; *Emmanuelle Black and White*
R (25282), Action/Melodrama, 85m.
Howard Mahler Films.
D: Mario Pinzauti; P: Mario Pinzauti;
S: Mario Pinzauti.
Cast: Antonio Gismondo, Maria Luisa Longo, Rita Manna, Serafino Profumo.

"A shocking story filled with love... lust... hate and above all passion!"

When a black slave saves her white master's life, a romance begins.

Passion Plantation may be quite easily confused with the similarly-themed *Mandinga* – and there's a good reason why; the two pictures were filmed simultaneously by the same director, utilising the exact same sets, locations, costumes, music and leading players.

Maria Luisa Longo plays Emanuelle, the oversexed daughter of a wealthy plantation owner. Blonde, bosomy, and comfortable being photographed in the nude, Longo's performance is as obnoxious as it is humourless. Antonio Gismondo as Lawrence, an opportunistic slave-owner who goes through a dramatic personal transformation, and Rita Manna as Judith, his beautiful mulatto mistress, fare a bit better in cardboard roles that don't offer much space in which to move. The standard plantation scenarios are all here – rape, torture, miscegenation – but, in the context of this particular movie, they don't amount to much. A 'Dirty ol' South' movie with a message, whose most memorable moments occur during the imaginatively-designed opening credit sequence.

PENITENTIARY

1979, USA
R (25885), Drama, 99m.
Jerry Gross Organization.
D: Jamaa Fanaka; P: Jamaa Fanaka;
S: Jamaa Fanaka.
Cast: Leon Isaac Kennedy, Thommy Pollard, Hazel Spears, Donovan Womack, Floyd Chatman, Chuck Mitchell, Gloria Delaney, Badja Djola.

"A brutal masterpiece of violent prison life."

A wrongly accused man comes away from his imprisonment with experiences that help set him on a new life path.

This unsettling look at life behind the walls of a brutal prison was a hit with both audiences and critics. Leon Isaac Kennedy plays Martel 'Too Sweet' Gordone, a drifter who, while defending a woman in a diner brawl becomes wrongly implicated

in a murder. Slender, agile, and always displaying a curious look in his eyes, 'Too Sweet's' most important behind-bars challenge is to avoid being 'broken in.' Other characters include: Eugene 'Genie' Lawson (Thommy Pollard), a young and naive inmate who finds himself the 'property' of his larger cellmate Jesse 'The Bull' Amos (Donovan Womack); Hezzikia 'Seldom Seen' Jackson (Floyd Chatman), a wise old institutionalised fight trainer; and Lt. Arnsworth (Chuck Mitchell), a rotund Italian prison supervisor who genuinely likes his charges and wants to help position them for success in the boxing ring. Also of note are two small but memorable female roles: Linda (Hazel Spears), a straight-talking, straight-shooting prostitute/drug dealer; and Peaches (Gloria Delaney), a visiting female inmate who finds a way to have a few much-needed sexual trysts in the ladies room.

Penitentiary is superbly acted and photographed, written with an eye for realism in both situations and dialogue, sensitive, bloody, violent, and moving:

'Seldom Seen': *You know don't you? You know I'm afraid of the streets. It scares me to think about going back out there and being a nobody. Who wants me? Who would want to even be an attendant to an old, out-of-date fool like me? Nobody. In here* [prison] *at least I mean something. I've got respect.*
'Too Sweet': *There's only one thing wrong with what you say – you ain't got no hope.*

Penitentiary offers a rare and unflinching look at the seldom examined, very complicated roles that all inmates must play in order to simply survive.

Note: Followed by *Penitentiary II* (1982) and *Penitentiary III* (1987). See *Q & A: Ten Directors Discuss Their Films*

"...one of the most expressive American movies of the year..."
(Tom Allen, Village Voice)

PETEY WHEATSTRAW: THE DEVIL'S SON-IN-LAW

1977, USA
R (25115), Action/Comedy, 95m.
Generation International Pictures.
D: Cliff Roquemore; P: Theodore Toney;
S: Cliff Roquemore.

Cast: Rudy Ray Moore, Jimmy Lynch, Leroy & Skillet, Ebony Wright, Wildman Steve [Steve Gallon], G. Tito Shaw.

"Have no fear it's the comedy smash of the year!"

A stand-up comic makes a pact with the devil to return to life and exact his revenge on the rival nightclub owners who have murdered him.

This third feature starring comedian/rapper Rudy Ray Moore is a bit tiresome; even though it's only 93 minutes, it seems way too long.

In the lead as popular stand-up comic Petey Wheatstraw, Moore is, as always, manic, verbose and extremely likeable. His rhyming soliloquies are as entertaining as his questionable status as 'the world's greatest lover.' Supporting players include: the rotund and slightly oafish comedy team of Leroy & Skillet (Leroy Daniels and Ernest Mayhand); a bearded professor-like Satan (G. Tito Shaw); and a lovely, always-trying-to-get-her-man-to-make-love-to-her, personal assistant, Nell (Ebony Wright).

Laden with overly familiar sight gags (including a fat woman who can't get herself into a lawn chair, a frightened character who defecates and urinates on himself, and a group of horned, caped, red tights-wearing 'devils'), *Petey Wheatstraw* is a juvenile, tired and stretched film that will only appeal to die-hard Rudy Ray Moore fans.

above: Denise Nicholas and Bill Cosby in 1977's PG-rated comedy **A Piece of the Action**. (J. Howard Collection)

PIPE DREAMS

1976, USA
PG (24723), Drama, 89m.
Avco Embassy Pictures.
D: Stephen Verona; P: Stephen Verona; S: Stephen Verona.
Cast: Gladys Knight, Barry Hankerson, Altovise Davis, Sally Kirkland, Bruce French, Sherry Bain, Arnold Johnson.

"When Gladys Knight sings... you feel good! When Gladys Knight stars in the most romantic movie of the year... you feel even better!"

An African-American woman travels to Alaska to meet up with her boyfriend and work on their troubled relationship.

Terribly slow and inexcusably contrived, the only thing to recommend about *Pipe Dreams* is the superior soundtrack by Gladys Knight and The Pips.

More of a travelogue than a movie. For what it's worth, *Pipe Dreams* does feature several spectacular visual tours, including the Alaskan Pipeline and 'snow forests,' and an aerial view of what seems like an endless snow-capped mountainous vista.

A PIECE OF THE ACTION

1977, USA
PG (24989), Comedy, 135m. Warner Bros.
D: Sidney Poitier; P: Melville Tucker; S: Charles Blackwell, from a story by Timothy March.
Cast: Sidney Poitier, Bill Cosby, James Earl Jones, Denise Nicholas, Hope Clark, Ja'net DuBois.

"Two clever cons go from doing well... to doing good."

Two successful African-American con men must submit to an unusual form of blackmail.

Too Many Pieces of the Action would be a more accurate title. Along with Sidney Poitier as Manny Durell, an always immaculately dressed con man, and Bill Cosby as Dave Anderson, a laid back yet totally self aware safe cracker, the cast of characters in this disjointed mess of a film

include: a petulant, yet well-meaning retired police captain, Joshua Burke (James Earl Jones); a frustrated, always searching-for-the-right-answer school-teacher, Sarah Thomas (Hope Clark); a tipsy visiting relative, Aunt Nellie (played by Ja'net DuBois of TV's *Good Times*); and an intelligent, attractive, yet still curiously single project coordinator, Lila French (Denise Nicholas).

Stunning Chicago locations, a segment including a performance by The Dance Theater of Harlem, a back-alley ambush, a kidnapping, and a light-hearted visit to a discotheque are pleasant enough distractions, but don't excuse this overlong, overloaded and overpopulated effort. (Soul singer Mavis Staples's 'A Piece of the Action' theme song is superb.)

"...a few genuinely touching moments struggle to hold their own against soggy social commentary."
(People)

top: Gladys Knight and Barry Hankerson in **Pipe Dreams** (1976).

A PLACE CALLED TODAY

1972, USA
Alternative Title: *City in Fear*
X (718), Drama, 103m.
Avco Embassy Pictures.
D: Don Schain; P: Ralph T. Desiderio;
S: Don Schain.
Cast: J. Herbert Kerr Jr., Cheri Caffaro,
Lana Wood, Richard Smedley.

"Fear is power! You want your city... fight for it!"

An African-American mayoral candidate is suspected to be the culprit behind a series of inner city bombings.

J. Herbert Kerr Jr. is impressive as corrupt lawyer turned mayoral candidate Randy Johnson. Modern-looking, authoritative and emotionally involved, the actor is also convincing when delivering the picture's many politically and racially charged diatribes and public speeches. Other characters include: Ron Carton (Richard Smedley), head of a local TV news division; Carolyn Schneider (Lana Wood), a well-meaning student/activist; and Cindy Cartwright, a self-involved, sexually liberated young woman who also happens to be the residing Mayor's daughter, played by Cheri (*Girls Are for Loving*) Caffaro.

Shrill, overwrought and talky, but strangely compelling, *A Place Called Today* is a highly quotable look at politics, corruption and indifference: "One day you're going to have to choose between what makes you happy and what you believe in." Newark, N.J. location shooting, creative framing (characters often talk directly to the camera) and committed performances are a plus. See *Q & A: Ten Directors Discuss Their Films.*

POOR PRETTY EDDIE

1974, USA
Alternative Titles: *Black Vengeance*;
Heartbreak Motel; *Redneck County*
R (24248), Drama, 82m. Westamerica.
D: Richard Robinson; P: Richard Robinson; S: B.W. Sandefur from a story by Sandefur and Richard Robinson.
Cast: Leslie Uggams, Shelley Winters, Michael Christian, Dub Taylor, Slim Pickens, Ted Cassidy.

"The nightmare thriller of the year!"

A popular African-American singer is kidnapped by a psychotic backwoods murderer after her car breaks down.

A sad tale of people whose dreams will never come true, *Poor Pretty Eddie* is a sordid, trashy and violent picture made memorable by some laudable, if sometimes misdirected, performances.

The lead role is taken by Leslie Uggams, who plays Elizabeth Wetherly, a popular African-American singer whose car lets her down, leading her to encounter a frightening bunch of crude and racist country hicks. Forced to stay at a dilapidated motel while she waits for her car to get fixed, she becomes a pawn in the lives of Eddie Collins (Michael Christian), a buff, swarthy and manipulative would-be country music singer, and Bertha (Shelley Winters), a shrill, overweight and drunken former actress who is now way past the prime of both her career and life. Other characters include an illiterate, over-sized and big-hearted caretaker named Keno (Ted Cassidy – best known for his role as Lurch on TV's *The Addams Family*), and a

lecherous, foul-mouthed county sheriff named Orville (Slim Pickens). An example of Orville's cruelly funny vulgarity comes when Elizabeth travels to the 'station house' to report that she has been raped:

> Orville: *Did he bite you on your titties?*
> Elizabeth: *What?!*
> Orville: *Well, did he put his suck marks on you?*

A major problem with this simple film is the casting of Leslie Uggams as the picture's victim. Rich, bitchy and above it all, her Elizabeth is an unlikeable woman who is always looking down her nose at these pathetic backwoods people and their shabby little lives. Consequently, in a twist probably not intended by the filmmakers, it is rapist Eddie, a man who is forced to live off the scraps provided for him by others, who garners the spectator's sympathy.

Two scenes in *Poor Pretty Eddie* are fashioned specifically to shock. One is a rape scene that is edited together with shots of two dogs copulating (as two confused children look on); the other is a breakfast party scene in which the delicious main dish (supposedly rabbit) turns out to be something very different.

Making liberal use of slow motion photography, and heavy on fantasy segments, *Poor Pretty Eddie* is a truly sick, shamelessly exploitative film that will, nevertheless, keep you wondering how it's all going to wind up. An unsung trash classic.

QUADROON

1971, USA
Alternative Title: *Black Agony*
R (389), Drama, 88m. Starline Pictures.
D: Jack Weis; P: Jack Weis; S: Sarah Riggs, from a story by R.B. McGowen Jr.
Cast: Kathrine McKee, Madelyn Sanders, Tim Kincaid, George Lupo.

"Now... the shocking truth about the passion slaves of 1835 New Orleans!"

In 18th Century New Orleans a 'Quadroon' woman prepares for her presentation to wealthy Creole society.

Quadroon is an extremely slow moving and super-low-budget look at the unique challenges that people of mixed black and white backgrounds faced in old New Orleans.

above: J. Herbert Kerr Jr. as mayoral candidate Randy Johnson in **A Place Called Today** (1972).

The characters in this excruciatingly dull endeavour include a light-eyed and light-skinned Creole woman named Coral (played by Kathrine McKee, incidentally Lonette [*Sparkle*] McKee's sister), and Celeste (Madelyn Sanders), Coral's willing-to-sell-her-daughter-to-the-highest-bidder mother. Tim Kincaid plays the part of Caleb, a big-hearted, ready to buck the system visiting Northerner, and George Lupo is Dupree, a sadistic, wealthy old patron of young black beauty.

Photographed for the most part in long shot and featuring flat lighting, cardboard sets and zombie-like line readings, *Quadroon* is a film that attempts to seriously examine seldom-discussed subject matter (The rigid caste system of New Orleans – and, for that matter America), but what with its whippings, lynchings and to-the-death fencing matches, it ends up being little more than sensationalist claptrap.

REPORT TO THE COMMISSIONER

1975, USA
Alternative Title: *Operation Undercover*
PG (24120), Action/Adventure, 112m.
United Artists.
D: Milton Katselas; P: M.J. Frankovich; S: Abby Mann, Ernest Tidyman.
Cast: Michael Moriarty, Yaphet Kotto, Tony King, Susan Blakely.

A rookie detective investigating a drug lord finds himself up against policy, procedure and the NYC police department.

In one of the best crime dramas of the 1970s Michael Moriarty plays Bo Lockley, a new to the precinct long-haired undercover detective who passes for a drugged-out hippie. Bo's charged with getting close to heroin dealer Stick Henderson (Tony King), but becomes distracted by his beautiful "girlfriend" Patty (Susan Blakely). Fellow detective Richard Blackstone (Yaphet Kotto) is on hand to make everything run smoothly. Jam packed with action, a showcase for superior acting, decorated with extended, elaborately staged segments filmed on the streets of NYC, and modern in its depiction of an illicit interracial relationship, *Report to the Commissioner* is a seldom-referenced gem. A legless man's harrowing skateboard ride and the climactic showdown in an elevator are leaps and bounds above other procedurals. Essential viewing.

RIGHT ON!

1970, USA
NR, Poetry, 80m. Leacock-Pennebaker.
D: Herbert Danska; P: Woodie King; S: Gylan Kain, Felipe Luciano, David Nelson.
Cast: Gylan Kain, Felipe Luciano, David Nelson.

Three African-American poets recite their original work.

This highly political documentary film has a distinct 1960s college campus feel to it. Sometimes moving, but more often than not just noisy, the hip-titled *Right On!* is a collection of emotionally charged 'dramatisations' that cover everything from slavery to the women's movement.

Cleverly photographed (on street corners, in alleys, on rooftops) and occasionally blessed with performances filled with what looks like genuine emotion, *Right On!* was a hit with the black intelligentsia but a flop with the inner-city audiences it was made to appeal to.

THE RIVER NIGER

1976, USA
R (1455), Drama, 105m.
Cine Artists Pictures.
D: Krishna Shah; P: Sidney Beckerman, Isaac L. Jones; S: Joseph A. Walker.
Cast: Cicely Tyson, James Earl Jones, Louis Gossett Jr., Glynn Turman, Roger E. Mosley, Hilda Haynes.

"The story of a black family… that couldn't be dammed and wouldn't be broken."

An African-American family copes with the world and themselves.

The River Niger is a well-intentioned picture that totally misses its mark, due to the seen-it-all-before script, and the wildly uneven and unconnected performances.

The story revolves around a family that includes: a poetry-writing house painter father named John Williams (James Earl Jones); his cancer-stricken wife Mattie (Cicely [*Sounder*] Tyson); the Williams' son Jeff (Glynn Turman), an Air Force dropout; and John's devout mother, Wilhelmina Geneva Brown (Hilda Haynes). Other characters include cynical physician/family friend Dr. Dudley Stanton (Louis Gossett Jr.), and a black-empowerment group leader named Big Moe Hayes (Roger E. Mosley.)

The River Niger is convoluted and populated by isolated acting performances.

"…an almost completely oblique collage of… unmotivated comings and goings." (Frank Rich, New York Post)

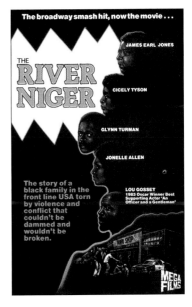

top: Michael Moriarty and Tony King in **Report to the Commissioner** (1975).

185

above: All the necessary element of a blaxploitation film are in place on this Mexican lobby card for **Savage!** (1973)... guns, violence, sexy women and an aggressive African American protagonist.

SAVAGE!

1973, Philippines/USA
Alternative Titles: *Black Valor*; *The Technician*
R (722), Action/Adventure, 81m.
New World Pictures.
D: Cirio H. Santiago; P: Cirio H. Santiago; S: Ed Medard.
Cast: James Iglehart [Inglehart], Lada Edmund Jr., Carol Speed, Sally Jordan.

"He's more than a man, he's a death machine! Men call him Savage... women call him all the time."

Two American performers and an African-American missionary lead a Philippine island revolt.

Ex-Pittsburgh Pirate football star James (*Bamboo Gods & Iron Men*) Inglehart gives it his all in the lead as Jim Haygood, a 'government hired' expatriate missionary who avoided a jail sentence (for stealing a car) by enrolling in the American Army. Impassioned, yet still oddly unremarkable, he is, nevertheless, a perfect match for 'jive' talking African-American gymnast Amanda (Carol Speed), a woman who is comfortable running around the jungles of the Philippines dressed in a yellow leotard with embroidered red flames emanating

from her crotch. Suitably upbeat support is provided by blonde-haired, blue-eyed expert knife thrower/circus performer Vicki (Lada Edmund Jr.).

Savage! is distractingly abusive to women (there is an early – too realistic – rape scene, a torture/'investigation' by electric prod, and a segment in which a female character is ordered to "just shut up and start undressing") and filled with highly unlikely but, nevertheless, well thought out plot twists. With its nude swimming scenes, night-time ambushes, jungle locations and gory murders, Cirio H. Santiago's movie is an, admittedly, action-packed hodgepodge that never quite hits its mark. See *Q & A: Ten Directors Discuss Their Films*.

"...a carry-on, rumble in the jungle, piece of good-natured nonsense."
(Mason Storm, Encyclopedia of Cinematic Trash Vol. 2)

SAVAGE SISTERS

1974, USA
R (24010), Action/Adventure, 86m.
American International Pictures.
D: Eddie Romero; P: Eddie Romero, John Ashley; S: H. Frank Moon, Harry Corner.
Cast: Gloria Hendry, Cheri Caffaro, Rosanna Ortiz, John Ashley, Sid Haig.

"Beware! They are still at large..."

Three diverse women, two of them thieves, one of them a corrections officer, join forces to steal a million dollars in cash.

The least exciting of director Eddie Romero's low budget, Philippine-shot films, this lacklustre tale of vengeance manages to be both vulgar and dull at the same time.

In the lead as sadistic female corrections officer Lynn Jackson (she tortures one prisoner by attaching a gadget to his penis – and then, when asked how the interrogation went, quips "It came off quite nicely!"), Gloria (*Black Belt Jones*) Hendry is pretty-faced, but a bit too diminutive to be the menacing force she is supposed to be. Lynn's compatriot is Jo Turner, played by Cheri (*Girls Are for Loving*) Caffaro, the vengeful widow of a recently murdered militant leader. Rounding out the 'all girl army' is an 'Asian' helpmate, Mei Ling (Rosanna Ortiz). The supporting players include Sid (*Coffy*) Haig as Malavael, a machine-gun-toting, lunatic fortune hunter, and John Ashley (who co-produced the film) as

W.P. Billingsley, a double-crossing man-about-town, whose mantra ("It's just the three of us – you, me and the money!") is repeated, ad nauseam, throughout the film.

Highlights include a 'striptease' in a local bar, and a daring prison escape. Better than the strikingly similar *Ebony, Ivory & Jade*, but not as good as the also-very-similar *The Muthers*.

"Jail is the place for sexual games and no woman can wield a rifle unless her shirt is unbuttoned."
(Nora Sayre, New York Times)

SAVE THE CHILDREN

1973, USA
G (23760), Concert, 123m.
Paramount Pictures.
D: Stan Lathan; P: Matt Robinson; S: Matt Robinson.
Cast: Marvin Gaye, Gladys Knight & The Pips, Curtis Mayfield, The Jackson Five, Sammy Davis Jr., The Staple Singers, Nancy Wilson, Wilson Pickett, The Temptations, Roberta Flack.

"It's a motion picture about emotion and pride and soul and music and gettin' it on."

A big-budget, politically-minded showcase for the era's top musical talent.

This engaging picture, filmed in Chicago at an exposition helmed by the Reverend Jesse Jackson's charitable organisation PUSH (People United to Save Humanity), showcases the most popular black musical artists of the day, while at the

same time making a strong anti-Vietnam war statement. Outstanding musical moments (in particular courtesy of The Staple Singers) are interspersed with well-meaning, but heavy-handed, anti-war speeches.

"A gratifying, varied and persuasive entertainment."
(A.H. Weiler, New York Times)

SCREAM BLACULA SCREAM

1973, USA
PG (23660), Horror, 96m.
American International Pictures.
D: Bob Kelljan; P: Joseph T. Naar; S: Joan Torres, Raymond Koenig, Maurice Jules.
Cast: William Marshall, Pam Grier, Don Mitchell, Richard Lawson, Janee Michelle.

"The black prince of shadows stalks the earth again!"

Los Angeles is terrorized by a blood-sucking fiend once again, when a voodoo ceremony reincarnates a vampire named Mamuwalde (Blacula).

In the lead as the bloodsucking vampire Mamuwalde (aka Blacula), William Marshall is, as always, a pleasure to both watch and listen to. This misguided, quickly produced follow-up to the super successful *Blacula* also features: Pam Grier as Lisa Courtier, a young woman

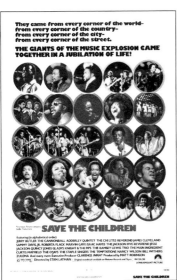

with "exceptional powers in the exceedingly complex science of voodoo"; Richard Lawson as Willis, a cocky jive-talking man bent on revenge; Janee (*House on Skull Mountain*) Michelle as Gloria, a know-it-all African artefact collector; and Don Mitchell as Justin, a highly suspicious police detective.

Yet another blaxploitation film with an overcomplicated voodoo subplot, *Scream Blacula Scream* includes a somnambulant coven of zombie vampires, a man-turns-into-bat sequence, and a wholly unsatisfying cheat ending that suggests AIP hoped to return for yet another instalment. Thank goodness that never happened.

"Fails for lack of incident, weakness of invention, and insufficient story."
(Roger Greenspun, New York Times)

above: William Marshall in **Scream Blacula Scream** (1973), the lacklustre sequel to 1972's **Blacula**. **187**

SHAFT

1971, USA
R (22835), Action/Adventure, 100m.
Metro Goldwyn Mayer.
D: Gordon Parks Sr.; P: Joel Freeman;
S: Ernest Tidyman and John D.F. Black,
based on the novel by Ernest Tidyman.
Cast: Richard Roundtree, Moses Gunn,
Charles Cioffi, Christopher St. John.

"The mob wanted Harlem back. They got Shaft... up to here! Shaft's his name. Shaft's his game."

A New York City police detective is hired to find the kidnapped daughter of a Harlem drug lord.

This standard detective story, featuring a young African-American male in a starring role, is one of blaxploitation's most discussed pictures.

Richard Roundtree plays John Shaft, a hip, jive-talking, streetwise detective, who also happens to be quite the ladies man. Photogenic, comfortable in front of the camera and eager to please, the former model turned actor was a much-needed fresh face who won the coveted role over Fred Williamson, Jim Brown and Paul Winfield, among others. The

equally engaging supporting roles are played by: Moses Gunn as Bumpy Jonas, a wealthy Harlem drug lord; Charles Cioffi as Lieutenant Vic Androzzi, an imposing strong-arm police department supervisor; and Christopher (*Top of the Heap*) St. John as Ben Buford, a militant-minded leader who is not above kidnapping a young girl to further his cause.

Filled with fantastic New York City locations and featuring Isaac Hayes's hit theme song ('Theme from Shaft'), *Shaft* offered audiences a collection of black images that served as a pivotal turning point in the history of African-American representation in the movies. It is also the only blaxploitation film to be followed by *two* sequels (*Shaft's Big Score!* and *Shaft in Africa*), as well as a short-lived (9 episodes) prime time television series.

"The pad, the girls, the clothes... 'Shaft' really is wish fulfilment..."
(Vincent Canby, New York Times)

SHAFT IN AFRICA

1973, USA
R (23566), Action/Adventure, 112m.
Metro Goldwyn Mayer.
D: John Guillermin; P: Roger Lewis;
S: Stirling Silliphant.
Cast: Richard Roundtree, Vonetta McGee, Frank Finlay, Cy Grant.

"The Brotherman in the Motherland. Shaft is stickin' it... all the way!"

above: Everyone loves John Shaft (Richard Roundtree) in the 1971 classic, **Shaft**.

A STIRLING SILLIPHANT ROGER LEWIS Production
Starring RICHARD ROUNDTREE · VONETTA McGEE
Written by STIRLING SILLIPHANT Produced by ROGER LEWIS
Directed by JOHN GUILLERMIN

New York City detective John Shaft is asked to fly to Africa and assist in stopping a modern day slave ring.

With *Shaft* a success and *Shaft's Big Score!* even more exciting than the original, a third instalment was almost inevitable.

Retaining top-billing as John Shaft, Richard Roundtree is, as always, a pleasure to watch and listen to. Even so, in this film, dressed as he is in traditional African robes and sandals, he seems somewhat lost and out of his comfort zone. The other cast members, perhaps because they are less familiar to audiences, seem slightly more at home. There's an Ethiopian dignitary, Emir Ramila (Cy Grant), Ramila's sexy, young and exceedingly well informed daughter Aleme (Vonetta McGee), and an opportunistic slave dealer, Vincent Amafi (Frank Finlay).

Ambitious, well-intentioned, even laudable, *Shaft in Africa*, with its exotic locations (Ethiopia and France), novel fighting methods (stick boxing), and unusual examination of third world injustices, was not quite what fans of the genre wanted to see. Consequently the movie bombed at the box office and brought about a swift end to the *Shaft* motion picture franchise.

"'Shaft in Africa' is less daring, less ethnically sophisticated, more antiseptic and more comfortably middle-class..." (Roger Greenspun, New York Times)

SHAFT'S BIG SCORE!

1972, USA
R (23262), Action/Adventure, 105m.
Metro Goldwyn Mayer.
D: Gordon Parks Sr.; P: Roger Lewis, Ernest Tidyman; S: Ernest Tidyman.
Cast: Richard Roundtree, Moses Gunn, Joseph Mascolo, Drew Bundini Brown, Julius W. Harris.

"You liked it before, so he's back with more. Shaft's back in action!"

New York City detective John Shaft is asked to help find a Harlem number dealer's murderer.

Shaft's Big Score! is that rare sequel that surpasses the quality of the original. Cleverly written (by *Shaft* screenwriter Ernest Tidyman), excitingly directed, beautifully photographed, and featuring a spectacular, big-budget helicopter/boat/automobile finale, John Shaft here has much in common with that high-flying, international sophisticate James Bond.

Richard Roundtree returns in the role of John Shaft, a hip detective who has a way with the ladies. His one-more-time star

above: Moses Gunn reprised his role as egocentric Harlem racketeer Bumpy Jonas in 1972's **Shaft's Big Score!** (J. Howard Collection)

turn surpasses expectations. The supporting cast includes: Moses Gunn as Harlem racketeer Bumpy Jonas; Joseph Mascolo as Gus, an Italian mobster who wants to take control of the numbers racket; and Julius W. Harris as Captain Bollin, a strong-willed black police detective.

A fast moving, genuinely exciting follow-up film, that is as entertaining today as it was twenty five years ago. Recommended.

"...far more ambitious and professional than the original."
(Roger Greenspun, The New York Times)

"This is the movie that 'Shaft' wants to be! It is a better, tighter, and more assured film..."
(Mikel J. Koven, Blaxploitation Films, 2001)

SHEBA BABY

1975, USA
PG (24159), Action/Adventure, 90m.
American International Pictures.
D: William Girdler; P: David Sheldon; S: William Girdler.
Cast: Pam Grier, Austin Stoker, D'Urville Martin, Dick Merrifield, Christopher Joy.

"Hotter n' Coffy, Meaner n' Foxy Brown, Pam Grier is the queen of the private eyes."

Private Investigator Sheba Shayne comes to the aid of her father, whose loan business is being threatened by the mob.

Noteworthy only because this is Pam Grier's final film for the movie studio that made a star out of her, *Sheba Baby* is more than just bad, it's embarrassing. The basic problem is that a cleaned up (no sex, no foul language, no nudity) Pam Grier is not the Pam Grier that her fans have paid to see.

As Sheba Shayne, a former Chicago policewoman turned Private Investigator, Pam Grier is only really believable when she is playing coquettish and dealing with male characters by using her dazzling figure and good looks. Confirming the obvious lack of connection she has with her sanitised role is a truly awful scene in which she is forced to 'emote' at her father's hospital sickbed.

Also inexcusably poor and wholly unconvincing are the 'action' sequences – one of which features Sheba 'strong arming' street thugs and various underground criminal types. A chase through a street fair (in which passers-by continually look into the camera) adds insult to injury.

If there is a standout performance in this lamentable drivel it must be a brief appearance by Christopher (*Big Time*) Joy as Walker, an overdressed and very cowardly purveyor of stolen merchandise. Also in the cast are D'Urville Martin as an obnoxious mob runner, and Austin (*Zebra Killer*) Stoker as Brick Williams, Sheba's new insurance salesman-like lover.

Ridiculous situations, artificial-sounding dialogue, and a conscious effort on the part of everyone involved to *not* give the audience what they have paid to see, make this movie a thoroughly unsatisfying viewing experience.

"Once you get past Grier's dazzling looks... 'Sheba Baby' is a flat suspenser..."
(Variety)

SILVER STREAK

1976, USA
PG (24647), Comedy, 113m.
20th Century Fox.
D: Arthur Hiller; P: Thomas L. Miller, Edward K. Milkis; S: Colin Higgins.
Cast: Gene Wilder, Richard Pryor, Jill Clayburgh, Scatman Crothers, Ned Beatty.

"By train, by plane, by the edge of your seat... it's the most hilarious suspense ride of your life."

A look at the shenanigans and mysteries that surface during an L.A. to Chicago train ride.

Gene Wilder plays George Caldwell, a mild-mannered publisher who is travelling from Los Angeles to Chicago by train. Unconvincing and unfunny (be it his 'frightened' response to a sudden death, or his seduction of a female fellow

passenger), every one of Wilder's actions and interactions are stock, time-tested and tiresome. Jill Clayburgh, playing Hilly Burns, a fellow passenger, is no better. An example of the 'laugh riot' dialogue follows:

> Hilly: *Would you write out my dinner order for me? I can't read my own writing. I also don't do shorthand and I can't type.*
> George: *Oh, what do you do for a living?*
> Hilly: *I'm a secretary.*

Richard Pryor, playing the part of recently-escaped petty criminal Grover Muldoon, is *Silver Streak*'s one and only saving grace. Lively, street-smart, funny and at the same time angry, his is a performance that effortlessly stands out in front – way out in front – of everyone else in the cast. Along for the ride are Scatman (*Black Belt Jones*) Crothers as Ralston, an elderly, eager-to-please railway employee, and Ned Beatty as Bob Sweet, a horny convention-bound salesman.

A plane/train chase, two murders and a beheading are all part of the mix. For what its worth, *Silver Streak*'s most celebrated comic segment involves Richard Pryor trying to teach Gene Wilder how to act 'black.'

Note: An audience favourite double-act, Pryor and Wilder were re-teamed in 1980's *Stir Crazy*.

"A train comedy often derailed."
(Variety)

THE SIX THOUSAND DOLLAR NIGGER

1978, USA
Alternative Title: *Super Soul Brother*
R (25538), Comedy, 80m.
International Cinema Inc.
D: Rene Martinez Jr.; S: Laura S. Diaz, Rene Martinez Jr.
Cast: Wildman Steve [Steve Gallon], Jocelyn Norris, Benny Latimore, Peter Conrad, Wild Savage.

"They made Wildman Steve into a bionic bruiser in the wackiest comedy ever!"

An unsuspecting African-American every-day man is used as a guinea pig in a sinister experiment.

Borrowing much from Rudy Ray Moore and his series of low-budget *Dolemite* films, stand-up comedian Wildman Steve steps into the spotlight with this outrageous vehicle filled with 'naughty' jokes, nudity and sight gags.

As a wino named Steve who is tricked into taking a serum that will give him superpowers for a week but then kill him, Wildman Steve is ingratiating, funny and game; his manic energy and general excitement are reason enough to give this hard-to-find film a one time viewing.

Other characters include: the amusingly named Dr. Dippy (Peter Conrad); a sexy nurse/girlfriend, Peggy (Jocelyn Norris); and an eager-to-make-a-buck con man, Bob (Benny Latimore).

Steve's showy display of his super-powers, and a super-bosomed dominatrix named Monica (played by the suitably named Wild Savage) are hardly the ingredients for a laugh riot, but the movie is entertaining nonetheless. *The Six Thousand Dollar Nigger* concludes with a confident on-screen coda: "This nigger is coming back!" He never did.

"Wildman Steve comes across as a cross between Stepin Fetchit and Jimmie Walker on crack."
(David Walker, BadAzz MoFo magazine issue #6)

SKIN GAME

1971, USA
GP (22960), Drama, 102m. Warner Bros.
D: Paul Bogart; P: Harry Keller; S: Pierre Marton [Peter Stone].
Cast: James Garner, Lou [Louis] Gossett [Jr.], Brenda Sykes, Susan Clark, Edward Asner, Juanita Moore.

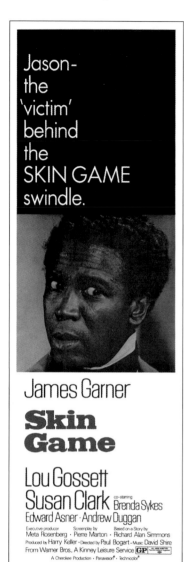

"Would you buy a used slave from this man?"

Two pre Civil War con men, one white, one black, join forces and swindle their way through the Midwest.

Skin Game is a well done, but tiresome, black/white buddy film with a twist. As always, James Garner is solid and dependable. Here he plays con man Quincy Drew (sometimes a Quaker, sometimes a government official, sometimes a slave-owner), and he does so as unfussily and professionally as you would expect. In the more complicated role of Jason O'Rourke, a well-spoken, highly educated, free African-American man (from New Jersey!), Louis Gossett

Jr. has to convey several different emotions at the same time: he must pacify whites by downplaying his sophistication; endure degrading jokes and scams (he is often 'sold' by his 'Master' Drew); and must overlook the atrocities of slavery in the small towns and plantations that he visits. Gossett is up for the challenge at hand, but is ultimately unconvincing – especially in scenes where he has to play 'ignorant.' Rounding things out nicely are Brenda (Honky) Sykes as Naomi, a stunningly beautiful 'bed wench,' and Susan Clark as Ginger, a white con woman who is as savvy, skilled and manipulative as both Drew and O'Rourke.

Predictable, never really funny and only semi-engaging, if Skin Game is to be commended for anything, it is for making black Naomi as prominent in the narrative as white con woman Ginger. Incidentally, Juanita (The Mack) Moore is granted a five-line cameo as Viney, a neighbourhood Mammy! See Q & A: Ten Directors Discuss Their Films.

"'The Skin Game' really does make a mockery of 200 years of terror and agony – but not without scoring many serious points along the way..."
(Maurice Peterson, Essence)

THE SLAMS

1973, USA
R (23761), Action/Adventure, 91m.
Metro Goldwyn Mayer.
D: Jonathan Kaplan; P: Gene Corman; S: Richard L. Adams.
Cast: Jim Brown, Judy Pace, Roland 'Bob' Harris, Frank De Kova.

"Jim Brown goes over the wall to flash – with a million dollars in cash."

After stashing 1.5 million dollars of stolen mob money, an inmate must find a way to escape before the cash is destroyed.

Jim Brown turns in an understated performance as Curtis Hook, a convict with a conscience (before serving his time he dumps a suitcase full of heroin into the Pacific ocean). The supporting characters include: Captain Stambell (Roland 'Bob' Harris), a sloppy, unpleasant looking (and sounding) supervisor; Campiello (Frank De Kova), a well mannered, charismatic, yet still very intimidating Mafia don; and Iris (Judy [Cool Breeze] Pace), Hook's beautiful, always-there-for-her-man girlfriend.

The only moment of levity in The Slams occurs when Hook commandeers a cab to help with a prison escape:

> Nervous Cab Driver (to Hook): I don't keep much money in the cab anymore. I've been robbed before. Last time it was by a big coloured guy... uhm... Negro fellow... uh... black gentleman. Afro-American?!

One-note, tired and stretched, The Slams, with its bevy of characters that the viewer knows nothing about (and therefore doesn't care about), is a too-familiar 'Action/Adventure' film that contains very little from either category. Jonathan Kaplan also directed Truck Turner. See Q & A: Ten Directors Discuss Their Films.

"...a racial prison picture for people who hate people."
(Variety)

above: All you need is a gun: Jim Brown shows just what is needed to break out of **The Slams** (1973).

above: Attractive, uninhibited, eager to please – and deadly: Stella Stevens (*left*) and Jim Brown (*right*) in 1972's **Slaughter**. The picture, along with its sequel **Slaughter's Big Rip-Off** (1973), was one of only a handful of blaxploitation pictures to be filmed in the Todd-AO widescreen process. (Soul Images)

SLAUGHTER

1972, USA/Mexico
R (23371), Action/Adventure, 92m.
American International Pictures.
D: Jack Starrett; P: Monroe Sachson;
S: Mark Hanna, Don Williams.
Cast: Jim Brown, Rip Torn, Stella Stevens, Don Gordon, Marlene Clark.

"Jim Brown is 'Slaughter'. It's not only his name, it's his business and sometimes his pleasure!"

An ex-Green Beret travels to Mexico to avenge his parents' murder.

A violent, yet stylishly photographed, 'comeback' vehicle for Jim Brown (whose early film success had started to diminish during the early '70s, largely due to his widely reported unpredictability), *Slaughter* proved to be a smash hit with audiences.

Brown is superb as Slaughter, a former army captain who has a score to settle. Imposing, handsome and charming, his casual screen presence works well with the material (this man does not need to walk with an exaggerated swagger.) In the much-talked-about supporting role of Ann, a blonde-haired, blue-eyed mob mistress who has a hankering for Slaughter (they have two expansively photographed semi-nude love scenes), Stella Stevens is a performer whose confidence seems to stem from her physical appearance; in addition to her intimate moments with Brown, the actress also performs in a solo nude shower scene that makes clear, once and for all, that she is indeed blessed with a truly magnificent form. As Slaughter's never-can-get-a-date comrade Harry Bastoli, Don Gordon is a bumbling goofball who can be depended on to both provide laughs and commit murder.

A knock-down-drag-out scenery-wrecking fight (in which a casino ends up completely demolished) and at least 25 deaths by point blank shotgun blasts are all part of the mix. Followed by *Slaughter's Big Rip-Off.*

"...Brown is playing what he was meant to play and can play better than anyone else: the black superman with a discernable link to the brother in the ghetto..."
(David Elliott, Chicago Daily News)

SLAUGHTER'S BIG RIP-OFF

1973, USA
Alternative Title: *Slaughter 2*
R (23659), Action/Adventure, 93m.
American International Pictures.
D: Gordon Douglas; P: Monroe Sachson;
S: Charles Johnson.
Cast: Jim Brown, Ed McMahon, Brock Peters, Gloria Hendry, Judy Brown, Scatman Crothers.

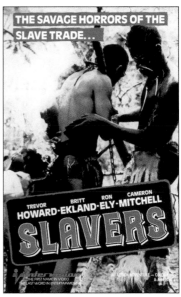

SLAVERS

1977, West Germany
R (25543), Action/Adventure, 102m.
ITM Releasing Corporation.
D: Jürgen Goslar; P: Jürgen Goslar;
S: Nathaniel Kohn, Marcia McDonald,
Henry Morrisson.
Cast: Trevor Howard, Britt Ekland, Ron
Ely, Ray Milland, Ken Gampu.

"...trading human lives for gold and the pleasures of the flesh. God help anyone who fell into their clutches."

Havoc reigns during the final days of Europe's African slave trade.

This incomprehensible jumble of real life footage of Africans performing native rituals, spliced together with an 'all star' European cast dressed in period clothing, neither entertains nor informs.

The stars include: Trevor Howard as Alec Mackenzie, a 'white devil' flesh merchant; Ron Ely as Steven Hamilton, Mackenzie's empathetic nephew; Britt Ekland as Anna von Erken, a Swedish whore; Ray (*Embassy*) Milland as Hassan, an Arab 'businessman,' and Ken (*Black Trash*) Gampu as Masulma, the righteous leader of an African tribe.

No amount of action can disguise the fact that this *Roots* inspired atrocity is a wholly unengaging mess.

"Incoherent narrative, lumpen expository dialogue... Black exploitation at its worst."
(Jennifer Selway, Time Out Film Guide)

"The mob put the finger on slaughter... so he gave them the finger right back... curled around a trigger! The baddest cat that ever walked the Earth."

Ex-Green Beret Slaughter avenges the death of his best friend, victim of a mob hit.

Critics raked *Slaughter's Big Rip-Off* over the coals, but viewed today one has to wonder why, as it is no better or worse than its carnage-filled predecessor.

In the lead as Slaughter (who is now being actively pursued by the mob he so colourfully smashed in *Slaughter*) Jim Brown is tall, dark, handsome, and very deadly. Authoritative, if just a bit too casual, he is, nevertheless, a picture-perfect action hero. The supporting players include: Gloria (*Black Belt Jones*) Hendry as Marcia, Slaughter's overly clingy girlfriend; Judy (*The Big Doll House)* Brown as Norja, Slaughter's clairvoyant ex; and, a surprise in the cast, Johnny Carson's TV side-kick Ed McMahon as Duncan, a mob figure in possession of an incriminating ledger. Cameos roles are provided for Scatman Crothers and Brock Peters.

Engagingly photographed (in the Todd-AO widescreen process) and literally leaving no stone unturned, *Slaughter's Big Rip-Off* is a big budget follow up that did only so-so business at the box office. Gordon Douglas also directed *They Call Me Mister Tibbs!*

Note: Shamelessly cutting corners, AIP uses 'Coffy Is the Color' from *Coffy*, during one of the film's scenes.

SOLOMON KING

1974, USA
R (1176), Action/Adventure, 101m.
Entertainment Pyramid.
D: Jack Bomay, Sal Watts; P: Sal Watts;
S: Sal Watts.
Cast: Sal Watts, Claudia Russo, C.B.
Lyars, Tito Fuentes, Jamie Watts.

"His friends call him 'King'... his enemies call him tough!"

An L.A. police detective heads into the Arabian desert in search of an African Princess's elusive murderer.

Super-low-budget, and seen by very few, *Solomon King* is a revenge fantasy film with a 'black pride' sub-plot. Written, produced and directed by Sal Watts (who, as detective Solomon King, is merely adequate), the only other noteworthy thing about the picture is a cameo appearance by baseball great Tito Fuentes.

One of only a handful of blaxploitation films that have never been seen since their original theatrical release, the characters in this film include: a painfully naïve Princess named Oneeba (Claudia Russo); an outwardly righteous but inwardly corrupt preacher (C.B. Lyars); and King's eager-to-please son Manny (played by 'Little' Jamie Watts, African-American director Watts's real-life son).

SOUL BROTHERS OF KUNG FU

1977, Hong Kong
Alternative Titles: *Kung Fu Avengers*;
The Tiger Strikes Again; *The Last Strike*
NR (R), Action/Adventure, 88m.
Cinema Shares International.
D: Hwa I Hung; P: Pal Ming; S: Lin Chan Wai.
Cast: Bruce Li [Ho Chung Tao], Ku Feng, Carl Scott, Au Yeung Pui San, Kuan Lun [Lo Meng].

"The best fighting team since The Green Hornet and Kato!!!"

A drifter becomes a karate champion, and finds he must prove himself inside and outside of the ring.

This karate-blaxploitation hybrid has the broad-based general appeal of the similarly-themed *Black Dragon*.

Ho Chung Tao stars as Wong Wei-loon, a tall, lean, angular and fantastically agile 'kung fu fighting machine.' Of course all his friends are karate experts too. His high-kicking cohorts include the actor/martial arts experts Ku Feng, Lo Meng, and Au Yeung Pui San. The over-promoted "Soul Brother" in the cast is Tom (Carl Scott), a diminutive and goofy looking African American youngster who, of course, is also an expert in karate.

A silly but fast-moving film, filled with deftly choreographed fight sequences, and containing more female nudity and sexual situations than usual for Chinese-made pictures from this period, *Soul Brothers of Kung Fu* is a titillating and thoroughly enjoyable distraction.

THE SOUL OF NIGGER CHARLEY

1973, USA
R (23666), Western, 110m.
Paramount Pictures.
D: Larry G. Spangler; P: Larry G. Spangler; S: Harold Stone.
Cast: Fred Williamson, D'Urville Martin, Denise Nicholas, Kirk Calloway.

"Nigger Charley is on the loose again. And this time he's got his soul brothers with him! Watch out!"

A recently freed slave attempts to liberate a group of African Americans being held against their will in Mexico.

This sequel to 1972's super-successful *The Legend of Nigger Charley* is a tired, overlong and preposterous effort. Both Fred Williamson (in the role of Nigger Charley) and D'Urville Martin (as Toby, his faithful sidekick) are back, but one has to wonder why. The problem is not that the actors are particularly poor; it's just that the movie's audience have seen and heard it all before. Other film characters include Denise (*Let's Do It Again*) Nicholas as Elena, Charley's sometime love interest, and Kirk (*Monkey Hustle*) Calloway as Marcellus, an orphan.

Stretched, predictable and over-whelmed by an air of 'lets do it once again just because we can,' *The Soul of Nigger Charley* is a film that neither expands upon nor compliments the original.

"Gunfire, not characterization, is the order of the day."
(A.H. Weiler, New York Times)

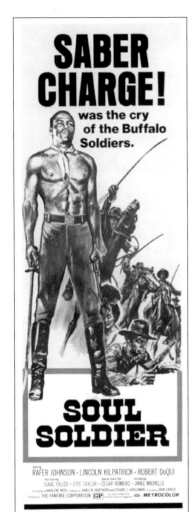

SOUL SOLDIER

1970, USA
Alternative Titles: *The Red, White and Black*; *Black Cavalry*
GP (284), Western, 84m.
The Fanfare Corporation.
D: John Cardos; P: James M. Northern, Stuart Z. Hirschman; S: Marlene Weed.
Cast: Rafer Johnson, Robert DoQui, Lincoln Kilpatrick, Cesar Romero, Isaac Fields.

"They were black troopers who fought and killed the red man for a white government that didn't give a damn about either one!"

The all black Tenth Cavalry faces the problems of day-to-day living while fighting off the Indians.

This standard 'blacks in the west' picture was a flop with both critics and audiences but, nevertheless, served as an early prototype for a string of like-themed films.

The cast of characters includes: Private Armstrong (played by African-American decathlon champion Rafer Johnson); Sergeant Hatch (Lincoln [*Together Brothers*] Kilpatrick); First Sergeant Robertson (Isaac Fields); Eli Brown (Robert DoQui); and, in a small role, Cesar Romero as Colonel Grierson.

Melodramatic but spirited, predictable but well-intentioned; *Soul Soldier* draws a distinct parallel between the indignities and injustices suffered by African Americans and American Indians.

SOUL TO SOUL

1971, USA
G (23042), Concert, 96m.
Cinerama Releasing.
D: Denis Sanders; P: Richard Bock, Tom Mosk.
Cast: Roberta Flack, Ike & Tina Turner, Santana, Wilson Pickett, The Staple Singers, Willie Bobo, Eddie Harris, Les McCann.

"From the place where it all came from... Africa!"

A visual documentation of a 15-hour concert performed in Ghana, Africa to celebrate that nation's independence.

Sub-par production values (and sound) don't seriously undermine this feel-good film, whose main theme and focus is to encourage its audience to become more politically aware, informed and proud of their African ancestry.

Memorable moments include a tour of an African slave dungeon, a rousing version of 'River Deep Mountain High' by Ike and Tina Turner, and an all-dancing, all-singing musical finale headed by Wilson Pickett. *Soul to Soul*'s success at the box office paved the way for the release of two more (bigger budgeted) soul music concert films – *Save the Children* and *Wattstax*.

Note: Singer Roberta Flack (one of the most exciting performers in the film) had her name, images and voice removed from the DVD release.

above: **Soul Soldier** (1970) came out of the gate with a bang.
It was one of the very first films to place African Americans in the old West.

SOUNDER

1972, USA
G (23325), Drama, 105m.
20th Century Fox.
D: Martin Ritt; P: Robert Radnitz;
S: Lonne Elder III, based on the novel by
William H. Armstrong.
Cast: Cicely Tyson, Paul Winfield, Kevin
Hooks, Carmen Mathews.

"At last, a compassionate and loving film about being black in America."

A family of African-American sharecroppers struggle to survive in 1930s depression-era Louisiana.

A lovely film filled with superior performances, *Sounder* is a movie that was, nevertheless, heaped with an inordinate amount of praise simply because it was not a black-cast action-adventure picture set in the ghetto.

Cicely Tyson is both believable and emotionally committed to her role as Rebecca Morgan, a beleaguered young mother of two whose biggest contribution to her family is the love she can give. Her hard-working, but always behind the ball, husband Nathan (Paul [*Gordon's War*] Winfield) is even better. Stoic, intimidating, but worthy of praise and determined to do whatever he has to do to keep his family afloat, his is the kind of cinema hero that's difficult to find fault with (especially considering that he is black). The supporting players include young David (Kevin Hooks, whose real-life father Robert Hooks starred in the same year's *Trouble Man*), and Mrs. Boatwright (Carmen Mathews), a white neighbour and sympathiser.

An intimate, earthy Southern drama that has over the years grown to become something of an African-American cinema classic. *Sounder* was nominated for four Academy Awards – best actress, best actor, best picture and best screenplay based on material from another medium; screenwriter Lonne Elder III became the first African-American man to be nominated for the Academy Award for writing (African-American woman Suzanne de Passe was also nominated that year, for her work on *Lady Sings the Blues*).

"A black revolution in filmmaking... broadens the definition of what a new black movie can be."
(Newsweek)

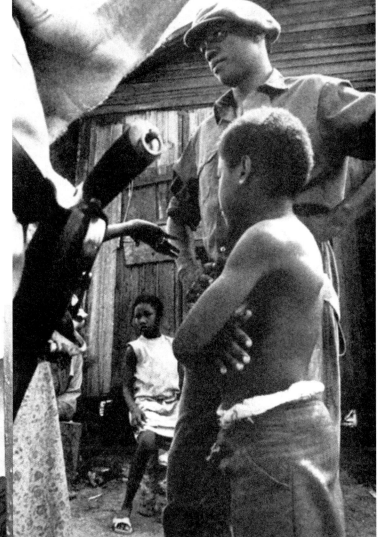

this page: 1972's **Sounder** differentiated itself from the glut of blaxploitation films amidst which it was released. These stills accurately sum up the mood of the film and its characters.

SPACE IS THE PLACE

1974, USA
R (24942), Action/Adventure, 81m.
North American Star System.
D: John Coney; P: James Newman;
S: Joshua Smith, Sun Ra [uncredited].
Cast: Sun Ra, Raymond Johnson,
Christopher Brooks, Barbara Deloney.

**A musical alien comes to Earth with a
plan to free African Americans from
'organised oppression.'**

A colourful theatrical outing for avant-
garde jazz percussionist Sun Ra (as well as
a visual adaptation of his critically
acclaimed album of the same name),
Space Is the Place is a fast-moving arty
film that can be likened to a good episode
of television's *Pee-wee's Playhouse*.

Inflatable spaceships, teleportation
chambers, gambling tables set up in the
desert, and performances by Sun Ra and
his twelve-member Intergalactic Myth-
Science Solar Arkestra are all part of the
space-age mix. Characters include: Sunny
Ray (Sun Ra), a positive minded alien jazz

musician; Overseer (Raymond Johnson), a
rumbustious spiritual guide; and Jimmy
Fey (Christopher Brooks), a frantic young
man who, like the viewer, is trying to
figure out just what is going on.

Highly conceptual and difficult to
follow, but never boring, the best thing
about *Space Is the Place* is not the
bizarre costumes, highly theatrical sets
and rapid-fire editing, but the real-life
tour of Oakland California's bleak and
empty streets.

SPARKLE

1976, USA
PG (24415), Drama, 97m. Warner Bros.
D: Sam O'Steen; P: Howard Rosenman;
S: Joel Schumacher, Howard Rosenman.
Cast: Philip M. Thomas, Lonette McKee,
Irene Cara, Dwan Smith.

"From Ghetto to Superstars."

**Three young singing sisters find success
and then heartache in the entertainment industry.**

This story of three African-American
female singers, 'Sister & the Sisters,'
who grow up in humble surroundings,
only to be discovered and then catapulted
to fame, sounds very much like that of
The Supremes. Even so, this patently
derivative tale about the world of
showbusiness does contain several standout moments.

As Sister, the drug addicted, co-
dependent lead singer of Sister & the
Sisters, Lonette McKee is nothing less
than superb, turning in an emotionally
charged performance that transcends the
boundaries of her sketchily written role.
As Sparkle, Irene Cara (from *Aaron
Loves Angela*) is also engaging.
Emotionally committed, earnest and
highly believable, she is at one with her
ambitious young woman character.
Dwan Smith plays Dolores, the third
sister in the group, and she turns in a
quieter, more introspective, performance
that is nevertheless equally intriguing.
Support for the female leads is provided
by Philip Michael (*Death Drug*) Thomas
as Stix, Sister & the Sisters' over-
anxious manager.

What do these three beautiful ladies have in common? They are all emotionally disturbed!
(above, left to right): Dwan Smith, Lonette McKee and Irene Cara as the singing trio Sister & the Sisters in 1976's **Sparkle**. (Soul Images)

Slow, sloppy, poorly photographed and atrociously edited (emotional scenes run on long after they have reached their natural climax), *Sparkle* is a sometimes glittery, sometimes teary opus whose overrated Curtis Mayfield soundtrack album remains an underground favourite.

Note: Joel Schumacher also wrote 1978's equally uneven 'musical' *The Wiz*.

"...although Irene Cara has a persistent charm and conviction... it's a sob story and a predictable one at that."
(Richard Eder, New York Times)

SPEEDING UP TIME

1971, USA
NR (R), Action/Adventure, 80m.
Cougnar Productions.
D: John Evans; P: John Evans; S: John Evans.
Cast: Winston Thrash, Pamela Donegan, Ellen Brown, Harry Dolan.

"He's the dude and he's out for revenge."

An African-American man searches for his mother's murderer.

In the lead role of Marcus, an out of work, highly intellectual public speaker, Winston Thrash gives an indifferent performance that works in perfect tandem with everything else in the film. In fact, unprofessional performances, poor sound, and a uniformly uninventive visual presentation haunt this production from beginning to end.

If *Speeding Up Time* has a star, it must be Pamela Donegan, who plays Valerie, Marcus's girlfriend. Blessed with a particularly expressive voice, and obviously a trained and genuinely talented actress, Donegan provides the picture's only bright and believable moments. (Though there is just one slightly disconcerting thing about Donegan's usefulness in the context of this picture; it would appear that the director has an obsessive interest in her buttocks – including at least seven nude close-ups.)

A tedious chase set in a shopping centre parking lot, a night-time frolic on the beach, several student film-like flashback scenes, and declarations such as "You have a mind, you don't have to waste it" will have your eyes rolling back in your head.

THE SPOOK WHO SAT BY THE DOOR

1973, USA
Alternative Title: *The Keepers*
PG (23669), Action/Adventure, 102m.
United Artists.
D: Ivan Dixon; P: Ivan Dixon, Sam Greenlee; S: Sam Greenlee and Melvin Clay, based on the novel by Sam Greenlee.
Cast: Lawrence Cook, Paula Kelly, Janet League, J.A. Preston, David Lemieux.

"The controversial best selling novel now becomes a shocking screen reality."

America's first black CIA agent quits and puts his top-secret knowledge of guerrilla warfare to use on the streets of Chicago.

Less sensational and much more serious than its title might suggest, *The Spook Who Sat by the Door* is a bleak, very violent, militant-minded film that, at the time of its release, caused quite a stir.

Lawrence Cook gives a subtle and supple performance in the role of Dan Freeman, an African-American CIA agent hired to fulfil racial quotas. Determined, single-minded, intelligent and exceedingly persuasive, the actor brings to life a character whose unique charm and multidimensional personality make him capable of 'passing muster' for whites, while at the same time appealing to the unique concerns and sensibilities of a group of disenfranchised inner-city blacks. Equally compelling is the always lovely Paula (*Top of the Heap*) Kelly as

Dahomey Queen, a hardened prostitute who is still faithful to the black cause.

Other characters include: Reuben Dawson (J.A. Preston), Freeman's 'ex hoodlum-turned cop' friend; Joy (Janet League), Freeman's upper-middle-class, eager-to-get-married ex; and Pretty Willie (David Lemieux), a light-skinned African-American male who can and does (when it is advantageous) pass for white.

Urban riots, diatribes about the injustices suffered by African Americans, and an unusually candid look at the debilitating mindset of many impoverished blacks, are all conveyed realistically. An exchange between Freeman and an old friend's mother underlines the picture's bleak view:

Freeman: *How's your son Shorty?*
Mrs. Duncan: *He's fine.*
Freeman: *The way I hear it he's running numbers and pushing drugs. I also hear that he's hooked.*
Mrs. Duncan: *Well, he ain't no real junkie. Sure he shoots up every now and then. I don't think he's got no more than a $20 or $30 dollar a week habit. And that ain't no habit at all.*

The Spook Who Sat by the Door is a very busy film that is most definitely worth a look. African-American director Ivan Dixon also directed *Trouble Man*.

"...a mixture of passion, humour, hindsight, prophecy, prejudice, and reaction"
(Walter Burrell, New York Times)

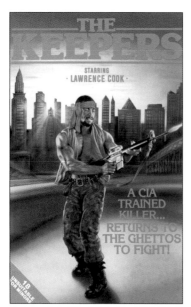

above: 1973's **The Spook Who Sat by the Door** was released on video as **The Keepers**.

STIGMA

1972, USA
R (23401), Drama, 93m.
Cinerama Releasing.
D: David E. Durston; P: Charles B. Moss Jr.; S: David E. Durston.
Cast: Philip M. [Michael] Thomas, Peter H. Clune, Harlan Poe, Josie Johnson.

"The curse that begins with a kiss!"

A young African-American doctor travels to a small town in search of the origins of a mysterious disease.

As Dr. Calvin Crosse, Philip Michael (*Black Fist*) Thomas is the personification of the hip-talking, out of his element, small town visitor. Trying to discover the source of an outbreak of syphilis, he sums up his own dilemma succinctly: "I'm a nigger in a bigoted white community trying to find an epidemic I don't know the first damned thing about." Sheriff Whitehead (Peter H. Clune) is Crosse's not-too-happy-to-have-a-black-man-on-his-'island' nemesis.

Stigma is simultaneously a 'mystery' (which character is spreading the disease without knowing it?), a lecture (all the particulars of the disease, how it's contracted, how it progresses, and its various symptoms are told to the viewer in protracted detail), and a disorienting slide show (actual medical photographs of real patients, their lesions, their rashes – and even a dead baby!) Ultimately, one is never really sure exactly what this film is trying to do or say.

A visit to an on-the-edge-of-town brothel, an 'experimental' make-out party, and a climactic confrontation that takes place in an abandoned light house are all part of this lead-footed production's mix.

STIR CRAZY

1980, USA
R (26114), Comedy, 111m.
Columbia Pictures.
D: Sidney Poitier; P: Hannah Weinstein; S: Bruce Jay Friedman.
Cast: Richard Pryor, Gene Wilder, Georg Stanford Brown, JoBeth Williams, Jonathan Banks.

"Gene Wilder and Richard Pryor dress up as woodpeckers and get framed for robbing a bank... and when they discover that prison life is for the birds they go... Stir Crazy!"

Two friends, one black, one white, are mistaken for bank robbers.

Though it took an impressive $58,000,000 in domestic rentals in 1980, time has revealed *Stir Crazy* to be a terribly unfunny, convoluted and protracted film.

As out of work security guard/screen-writer Skip Donahue, Gene Wilder is even less tolerable than he was in the first Wilder/Pryor pairing, *Silver Streak*. Buffoonish and unpleasant, he has a screen presence that you wish would just go away. Pryor, as Harry Monroe, an out of work waiter/actor is, as always, game for the necessary shenanigans, but the viewer is struck by the feeling that this immensely talented comedian is slumming it – he is, and he deserves much better than the material at hand. The on-screen chemistry between the film's two stars is best summed up by James Parish and George Hill in their 1989 book *Black Action Films*: "With each new movie Gene Wilder has become more hysterical and shrill while Richard Pryor is forced to look on in amazement, scorn, and half-hearted acceptance." The supporting cast includes Georg Stanford Brown as Rory Schultebrand, an inmate with romantic designs on Monroe, and Jonathan Banks as Jack Graham, an overly-verbose cellblock 'spokesman.'

The activity in this laborious endeavour includes Wilder and Pryor getting dressed up in giant feathered woodpecker outfits, a mechanical bull riding contest, and a repeat performance of the 'act black' scene from the previous Wilder/Pryor pairing *Silver Streak*. A chore to sit through.

"A slovenly, loose-jointed movie, with anecdotes that lead to nowhere and minor performances that don't come off."
(David Denby, New York magazine)

SUDDEN DEATH

1977, USA
R (24808), Action/Adventure, 83m.
Topar Films.
D: Eddie Romero; P: J. Skeet Wilson, John Ashley; S: Oscar Williams.
Cast: Robert Conrad, Felton Perry, Don Stroud, John Ashley.

"Two masters with a thousand ways to kill trigger a marathon massacre!"

When a prominent family is murdered, two hired killers try to crack the case.

above: Felton Perry as the improbably named gun-for-hire Wyatt Spain in **Sudden Death** (1977).

Robert Conrad is wholly unconvincing in the lead as Harrison Smith, a man with a dubious past who is summoned to uncover the truth behind an international corporation's clandestine operations. Too diminutive to be threatening, too awkward to be covert, he looks and acts like a down-on-his-luck soap opera star. Felton Perry as Wyatt Spain, Harrison's over-sexed African-American sidekick, is slightly more entertaining. It's not that he's any better than Conrad – just that he appears a bit more comfortable with himself. Also featured are Eddie Garcia, Vic Diaz and co-producer/actor John Ashley, all favourites of director Eddie Romero.

'Major incidents' include a visit to a Philippine brothel, an exploding automobile, and a climactic slow motion fight sequence. Add a cruel tagged-on ending and you have a movie that is unsatisfying on all levels; poorly executed, breathtakingly unimaginative and inexcusably dull.

SUGAR HILL

1974, USA
Alternative Titles: *Voodoo Girl*; *The Zombies of Sugar Hill*
PG (23836), Horror, 91m.
American International Pictures.
D: Paul Maslansky; P: Elliot Schick; S: Tim Kelly.
Cast: Marki Bey, Robert Quarry, Don Pedro Colley, Zara Cully, Betty Anne Rees.

"Meet Sugar Hill and her zombie hit men! Her voodoo powers raised the dead. She's Super-Natural!"

An African-American woman offers her soul in exchange for the power to kill the men who murdered her boyfriend.

Marki Bey (who looks more than a little like Dawn Wells of TV's *Gilligan's Island*)

is outstanding in the lead as Diana 'Sugar' Hill, a fashion photographer turned zombie ringleader. Shapely, glamorous and intimidating, the actress puts forward an intelligent and thoughtful performance that is in stark contrast to her cartoonish surroundings. Don Pedro Colley is also a strong presence as Baron Samedi, the representative of the un-dead. Comical, wry and not afraid to push his scenes over the top, his is a very visual performance filled with a wide variety of highly entertaining interpretations. Other characters include: Mama Maitresse (Zara Cully), an elderly voodoo priestess; Morgan (Robert Quarry), a marked mob henchman; and Celeste (Betty Anne Rees), Morgan's insecure and very racist girlfriend.

Fun touches include: a voodoo ceremony opening segment (which turns out to be a nightclub performance); a wandering (and deadly) severed chicken leg (!); and a transformative costume and hairdo change that takes place whenever Sugar is about to do in her enemies. The dialogue, too, is often genuinely funny:

Celeste (to Sugar): *Don't you get uppity with me!*
Sugar: *Uppity? My dear, talking to you means I look nowhere but down!*

Inexpensively shot, ridiculous, but always entertaining, *Sugar Hill* (like so many *AIP* pictures) is a 'PG'-rated, suitable-for-all-family-members party film that, refreshingly, never over-stretches itself.

"Carries enough novelty and offbeat action... to rate a good response in its intended market."
(Variety)

SUPER DUDE

1974, USA
Alternative Title: *Hangup*
R (23647), Action/Adventure, 93m.
Warner Bros./Dimension Pictures.
D: Henry Hathaway; P: T.W. Sewell; S: John B. Sherry and Lee Lazich, from a novel by Bernard Brunneer.
Cast: William Elliott, Marki Bey, Cliff Potts, Danny 'Big' Black.

"Super Dude... and his Saturday night special... licensed to kill!"

A Los Angeles detective tries to destroy the drug dealer responsible for his girlfriend's addiction.

This hard-to-see action film stars William (*Coffy*) Elliott as Ken, an emotionally involved inner-city detective trying to bring down a network of ruthless drug dealers. Support is provided by Cliff Potts as Lou, Ken's dubious best friend, and Marki (*Sugar Hill*) Bey as Julie, Ken's ever-loving and surprisingly resourceful girlfriend.

Super Dude (also known as *Hangup*) is one of several blaxploitation entries that disappeared after its initial theatrical

His job was busting junkies. His mistake was loving one.

HANGUP

A BRUT PRODUCTION · Starring WILLIAM ELLIOTT · MARKI BEY · CLIFF POTTS · Music by TONY CAMILLO
Screenplay by JOHN B. SHERRY and LEE LAZICH · Based on the novel "The Face Of Night" by BERNARD BRUNNER
Directed by HENRY HATHAWAY · Technicolor® · From Warner Bros. A Warner Communications Company

release – only two prints are known to still exist. It is also a rare example of a film that was immediately bought up by a rival company and redistributed with a new marketing campaign. Low budget and flashy, but fast-moving and consistently entertaining, *Super Dude* was veteran Hollywood director Henry (*Go West Young Man*, *True Grit*) Hathaway's final movie.

SUPER FLY

1972, USA
R (23376), Action/Adventure, 93m.
Warner Bros.
D: Gordon Parks Jr.; P: Sig Shore;
S: Phillip Fenty.
Cast: Ron O'Neal, Carl Lee, Sheila Frazier, Julius Harris, Charles MacGregor [McGregor], Polly Niles.

"Never a dude like this one! He's got a plan to stick it to the man!"

A Harlem cocaine dealer puts together a plan to retire from the drug trade.

Super Fly is the best of the 'male hero' blaxploitation films. Directed by Gordon Parks Jr. (Gordon Parks <u>Senior</u> directed *Shaft*), *Super Fly* is that rare film distinguished by a host of top performances.

Ron O'Neal gives what would turn out to be his signature performance in the lead as the elaborately coiffed, hip dressing, and street-tough dope dealer Priest. Though he was equally impressive in the previous year's *The Organization*, here O'Neal embodies the youthfulness, anxieties, and duplicitous aspirations of the inner-city African-American poor. As Scatter, Priest's father figure and 'main man' (a former dope dealer who now cooks food in a popular nightclub), Julius (*Hell Up in Harlem*) Harris possesses a fascinating mixture of dignity and faded machismo. A man whose own life dreams have yet to come true, Scatter cherishes his former renown as a major dealer in Harlem's drug trade, but has realised that to stay alive, one must get out – and move on.

Other characters include: Eddie (Carl Lee), a practical-minded hustler whose only goal is to maintain and satisfy his white benefactor; Fat Freddie (Charles McGregor), a plain-faced, thoroughly misguided dope runner with a heart of gold; Georgia (Sheila Frazier), Priest's always-supportive female companion ("I just can't be another person that you've got to deal with"); and Cynthia (Polly Niles), an equally lush, rich white woman who is attracted to Priest both because he is a safe drug connection and because he operates in a twilight world very different from her own.

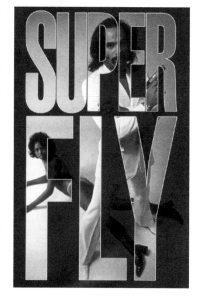

Super Fly has great winter-in-New York City locations (Greenwich Village, Harlem, Central Park), wonderful music (written, produced and performed by Curtis Mayfield, who makes a cameo appearance in a nightclub segment singing 'Pusher Man'), a well-written screenplay by Phillip Fenty (who would later write and direct blaxploitation's *The Baron*), inventive photography (including a split-screen, stop-action-sequence that seems more like a contemporary music video), and an unusually lengthy and very erotic slow motion love scene that takes place in a bubble bath. The movie also contains a great deal of frank, realistic and pointed dialogue:

> Priest: *I'm getting out.*
> Eddie: *Getting out of what?*
> Priest: *The cocaine business.*
> Eddie: *Oh sweet Jesus them junkies must have knocked a hole in your head. You're going to give all this up? You've got an 8-Track stereo, colour TVs in every room, and can snort half a piece of coke every day. That's the American dream!*

Super Fly, a super success at the box office (one of only 6 blaxploitation films to top *Variety*'s Top Grossing films list), was followed by the sequel *Super Fly T.N.T.* Both the film and the music soundtrack are highly recommended.

"A brilliantly idiomatic film. 'Super Fly's gut pleasures are real and there are a lot of them..."
(Roger Greenspun, New York Times)

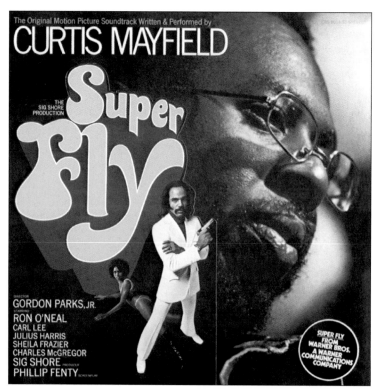

above: Curtis Mayfield's soundtrack album for **Super Fly** showed that blaxploitation films were selling more than just theatre tickets. Other hit albums were produced by Marvin Gaye, James Brown and Isaac Hayes.

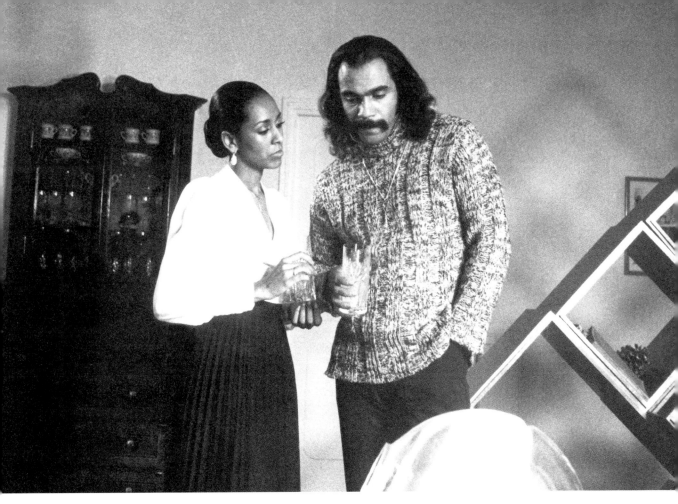

above: Who said quitting the drug trade is a good thing? Stand-by-her-man Georgia (Sheila Frazier, *left*) tries to convince retired coke dealer Priest (Ron O'Neal, *right*) that everything is going to be OK. It wasn't – and neither was the film **Super Fly T.N.T.** (1973), a box office bomb.

SUPER FLY T.N.T.

1973, USA
R (23705), Action/Adventure, 87m.
Paramount Pictures.
D: Ron O'Neal; P: Sig Shore; S: Alex Haley.
Cast: Ron O'Neal, Roscoe Lee Browne, Sheila Frazier, Robert Guillaume.

"Same dude with a different plan... in another country with a different man."

A NYC drug dealer moves to Europe, where he attempts to rebuild his life after outsmarting the mob.

Priest, the former African-American cocaine dealer (who in the first instalment beat the mob out of a million dollars in cash), is now residing in Rome with live-in girlfriend Georgia (Sheila Frazier). Bored with his life (he spends his days and nights gambling) and desperately searching for something to give him a feeling of relevance ("Ain't my nature to sit on my ass"), the floundering retired drug king has a fortuitous hook-up with a politically progressive African named Dr. Lamine Sonko (Roscoe Lee Browne), and is asked to aid in the delivery of a cachet of stolen guns to a group of African revolutionaries who are fighting Colonialism.

Intelligent (the film was co-written by Alex 'Roots' Haley) and fair-minded, *Super Fly T.N.T.* is, nevertheless, an eyecrossingly dull film whose theatrical release, especially given the rich source material, truly does boggle the mind (in fact Warner Bros., *Super Fly*'s distributor, passed on it.)

Long-winded and self-indulgent, this quickly (and cheaply) produced vanity project (O'Neal also directs and contributed to the screenplay) is the archetypal picture that the filmmakers wanted to make, but audiences did not want to see.

"Long on talk and short on action... 'Super Fly T.N.T.' is a wet firecracker."
(Howard Thompson, New York Times)

SWEET JESUS PREACHER MAN

1973, USA
Alt. Title: *Sweet James Preacher Man*
R (23685), Action/Adventure, 103m.
Metro Goldwyn Mayer.
D: Henning Schellerup; P: Daniel B. Cady; S: John Cerullo, M. Stewart Madden, Abby Leitch.
Cast: Roger E. Mosley, William Smith, Sam Laws, Marla Gibbs, Della Thomas.

"Amen, Brother!"

A killer-for-hire posing as a Baptist minister infiltrates a local drug ring.

The slick, graphically-arresting poster art for this film (which features a priest standing in front of a giant cross with a bible in one hand and a gun in the other), is thoroughly misleading. What looks like a big-budget, action-packed, MGM extravaganza is actually a no-budget, poorly scripted, incompetently photographed mess.

Roger E. Mosley

Roger E. (*Terminal Island*) Mosley seems thoroughly out of place in the lead as hit man-turned preacher Holmes/Lee. Loud mouthed, stilted and unconvincing, he is, without question, this picture's least likeable and least believable character.

Providing much-needed balance in supporting roles are: William (*Black Samson*) Smith as Martelli, a hot-tempered mob henchman; Sam (*Cool Breeze*) Laws as Deacon Green, a corrupt church appointee; Marla Gibbs (the sassy talking maid on TV's *The Jeffersons*) as Beverly Soloman, a recently widowed woman desperately in need of some affection; and Della Thomas as Foxey, a lovely, tell-it-like-it-is, cocktail waitress.

The major incidents in this film include a night-time 'riot' (brought on by the police shooting of two youths), an impassioned, topless 'soul dance' in a nightclub, along with several pointedly gruesome murders. A good indicator of *Sweet Jesus Preacher Man*'s wider significance is the fact that the exhaustive 'all inclusive' 1975 coffee table book *The MGM Story* does not even mention it.

"...a glaring testimony to all the negative stereotypes that surround the blaxploitation genre."
(David Walker, BadAzz MoFo magazine issue #6)

SWEET SWEETBACK'S BAADASSSSS SONG

1971, USA
R (1130), Action/Adventure, 97m.
Cinemation Industries.
D: Melvin Van Peebles; P: Melvin Van Peebles; S: Melvin Van Peebles.
Cast: Brer Soul [Melvin Van Peebles], Simon Chuckster, Johnny [John] Amos, John Dullaghan, Mario [Van] Peebles.

"You bled my momma... bled my poppa... but you won't bleed me."

After attacking two police officers who have brutalised a suspect, an African-American 'sexual stud' flees and is pursued by the law.

Originally rated 'X' (as the ads read – "By an all-white jury"), *Sweet Sweetback's Baadasssss Song* is a bombastic, offensive and politically incorrect examination of one black mans journey toward self realisation and self respect.

Melvin Van Peebles is utterly convincing in the lead as 'Sweetback,' an inner-city African-American male who makes his living performing live sex shows in a brothel. Young, arrogant and contemporary looking, his is a black fantasy character that speaks directly to the myths and fears surrounding the African-American male. Other cast members include: John (*Let's Do It Again*) Amos as Biker, a member of a black biker gang; Simon Chuckster as Beetle, Sweetbacks's trusted and highly-quotable friend; and John Dullaghan as a white police detective in relentless pursuit of Sweetback.

Sweet Sweetback's Baadasssss Song is loved and hated, lauded and lambasted, and filled with controversial images (including an underage boy – the director's son Mario Van Peebles – simulating sex with a nude grown

woman, intercourse performed in front of a cheering, leering crowd, and several shots of a bloated dead water-soaked dog). With its sub-par production values, non-linear narrative structure, double exposure and split screen photography, and man on the street interviews, the movie has, in many ways, an avant garde art house feel to it.

A smash hit with audiences, and one of only six blaxploitation films to top *Variety*'s Top Grossing Films list, *Sweetback* is a distinctly personal and extremely confrontational statement film.

Note: The picture's oddly spelled title was created so that newspapers and magazines would not object to printing the word 'Ass.'

"...Van Peebles charts a course through cinematic waters no one else has ever even put a toe in... he lets us see a sector of ourselves we wish, perhaps, he had left alone..."
(Kevin Thomas, New York Times)

THE TAKE

1974, USA
PG (23799), Action/Adventure, 92m.
Columbia Pictures.
D: Robert Hartford-Davis; P: Howard Brandy; S: Del Reisman, Franklin Coen.
Cast: Billy Dee Williams, Eddie Albert, A Martinez, Vic Morrow, Frankie Avalon, Tracy Reed.

"Meet the brother with a badge... on the take. Who takes on the mob and wins both ways!"

A popular police lieutenant, known for his honesty, is secretly taking bribes from the mob.

Billy Dee Williams plays Sneed, a San Francisco cop who is flown out to Paloma, New Mexico to help crack a major drug case, in this regulation police drama. Charming, eager to please and convincing as a man who moves comfortably between the police department and the underground world, Williams is nevertheless unable to transcend the mediocre material at hand. Stock film characters include: Sneed's independent-minded ex-girlfriend, Dr. Nancy Edmonson (Tracy [*Car Wash*] Reed); Sneed's well-meaning but sceptical partner, John Tall Bear (A Martinez); an overworked but fair-minded police chief, Berrigan (Eddie Albert); and a dangerous

Blaxploitation's very first anti-hero, Melvin Van Peebles, as renegade Sweetback in 1971's highly controversial **Sweet Sweetback's Baadasssss Song**. (J. Howard Collection)

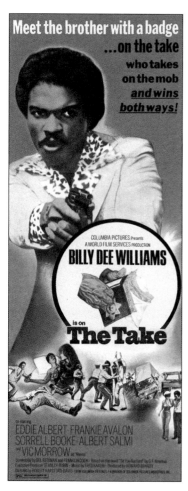

Lee Van Cleef is his turtle-faced best as tough-as-nails bounty hunter Kiefer. Diminutive, but still intimidating, he is a realistic villain who reads people for what they are – not for what they say they are. Jim Brown (who starred with Van Cleef in 1970's *El Condor*) is better than usual as Pike, a wealthy white cattleman's farm hand. Relating honestly to children, comfortable with his righteous screen role (and his co-stars), Brown offers an unusually subdued performance that works well. Fred Williamson is perfectly cast as Tyree, a tall, dark and handsome con-man-drifter. Along for the ride are Jim Kelly as Kashtok, a mute American Indian (who also happens to be a karate expert!), and Catherine Spaak as 'Lady' Catherine, a recently widowed French prostitute.

In addition to gunfights, double crosses and numerous stunts there is a truly harrowing rickety bridge crossing, together with a cross-canyon leap, a visit to a small Mexican town, and a special effects mine-explosion. Add a cameo from 1950s film star Dana Andrews, and you have one of the genre's finest western-themed films.

Note: *Take a Hard Ride* was made by Italian director Antonio Margheriti, using the pseudonym Anthony M. Dawson.

"A solid bit of entertainment."
(David Walker, BadAzz MoFo magazine issue #4)

Italian drug lord, Manso (Vic Morrow). 1950s pop music star Frankie Avalon appears in a cameo.

Shamelessly derivative, unexciting and stretched though it is, *The Take*'s rare appreciation of New Mexico's breathtakingly beautiful sunsets, interiors and landscape, make it worth a quick viewing.

TAKE A HARD RIDE

1975, USA/Italy
PG (24345), Western, 103m.
20th Century Fox.
D: Anthony M. Dawson [Antonio Margheriti]; P: Harry Bernsen; S: Eric Bercovici, Jerry Ludwig.
Cast: Jim Brown, Lee Van Cleef, Fred Williamson, Jim Kelly, Catherine Spaak, Dana Andrews.

"It rides with the great westerns."

An African-American cowboy vows to deliver $86,000 to his dead friend's wife.

THE TATTOO CONNECTION

1978, Hong Kong/USA
Alternative Titles: *E yu tou hei sha xing*; *Black Belt Jones II*; *Hong Kong Connection*
R (26226), Action/Adventure, 90m.
World Northal.
D: Lee Tso Nam; P: Luk Pak Sang; S: Luk Pak Sang.
Cast: Jim Kelly, Chen Sing, Tan Tao Liang, Bolo Yeung, Lee Hoi Gei.

An African-American insurance agent travels to Hong Kong in pursuit of the 'North Pole Star,' a priceless stolen gem.

above: A scene from the superior western **Take a Hard Ride** (1975). The cast included Jim Brown (*far left*) and, beginning third from left: Jim Kelly, Fred Williamson, Lee Van Cleef and Catherine Spaak.

A quick, cheap and *final* starring vehicle for Jim Kelly. Shoddy camera work and sloppy editing do nothing to deter 1971's middleweight karate champion from giving it everything he's got.

As Lucas, an American insurance agent hired to locate a stolen diamond, Kelly is, as ever, photogenic, agile and eager to please; he is, without question, this film's most outstanding player. Excellent support is provided by: Chen Sing as Boss Lok, an all-powerful and exceedingly corrupt underworld figure; Tan Tao Liang as Dong Ho, Lok's high-kicking second in charge; Bolo Yeung as Tan Yu, Boss Lok's thug; and Lee Hoi Gei as Nana, Dong Ho's prostitute girlfriend.

A hot iron branding, an ambush, a topless nightclub dance, and a visit to a Chinese tattoo parlour are all part of the proceedings. A deftly choreographed latecomer that, curiously, holds its own. The disco theme song 'Diamonds' is performed by Anders Nelsson.

"...Kelly exhibits less acting here than usual, but next to the grass roots crew he is a polished pro."
(Linda Gross, Los Angeles Times)

TERMINAL ISLAND

1973, USA
Alternative Title: *Island of No Return*
R (812), Action/Adventure, 88m.
Dimension Pictures.
D: Stephanie Rothman; P: Charles S. Swartz; S: Jim Barnett, Charles S. Swartz and Stephanie Rothman.
Cast: Ena Hartman, Roger E. Mosley, Phyllis Davis, Tom Selleck, Sean Kenney.

"Men and Women... black and white. Taken from death row – condemned to Devil's Island, USA. Where living is worse than dying!"

When the death penalty is outlawed in California, criminals are sent to a deserted island to serve out their time indefinitely.

An ensemble piece, this politically aware film's cast of characters includes: Carmen Sims (Ena Hartman), the island's newest inhabitant; Monk (Roger E. Mosley), the island's resident 'muscleman'; Dr. Milford (Tom Selleck), a doctor accused of a mercy killing; and Bobby (Sean Kenney), a double-crossing murderer who also happens to be afraid of the dark.

Shootings, knifings, poisonous darts, a bloody public whipping and a deadly bee attack make up the recreational activity on *Terminal Island*. So do rapes, food fights and competing island factions.

Note: Stephanie Rothman is the only female blaxploitation movie director.

"The island is apparently furnished with a great beauty salon for the women!"
(Roger Ebert; Chicago Sun-Times)

THANK GOD IT'S FRIDAY

1978, USA
PG (25245), Comedy, 89m.
Columbia Pictures.
D: Robert Klane; P: Rob Cohen; S: Armyan Bernstein.
Cast: Donna Summer, Debra Winger, Jeff Goldblum, Paul Jabara, Ray Vitte, Chick Vennera.

"After 5,000 years of civilisation – we all need a break!"

The misadventures of a disparate group of people, all of whom attend a popular Los Angeles discothèque.

This joint effort by Columbia Pictures and record giants Casablanca and Motown was an attempt to create a music-filled film whose multi-artist (Donna Summer, Diana Ross, The Commodores, Thelma Houston) soundtrack album would rival the phenomenal success of *Saturday Night Fever*. It didn't work.

As (19-year-old!) Nicole Sims, Donna Summer is, at best, lively. Her only shining moment comes when, during the picture's final segment, she is allowed to do what she does best: sing. Her "Last Dance" went on to win both an Oscar and a Grammy.

Debra Winger is superb as Jennifer, a bored young woman who has made the trip to The Zoo discothèque to placate her restless girlfriends. By turns friendly, angry and confused, hers is a multi-faceted, highly-emotional portrayal that is at odds with the trivial material at hand. Paul Jabara, too, seems to be performing in a vacuum. His lonely character Carl is instantly recognisable; a man whose manic energy and chilling desperation can be found on display at any bar or discothèque.

Other characters include: man on the make Tony DiMarco (Jeff Goldblum); popular club DJ Bobby Speed (Ray Vitte); and Marv 'Leather Man' Gomez (Chick Vennera), a highly animated disco dance contest contender (he does his routine on the roofs of several parked cars).

Dull characters, painfully derivative music, and a star (Donna Summer) who is actually only on screen for twenty minutes, all conspire to make this movie a much less than it hoped to be.

"In her role as an aspiring singer Donna Summer is merely an aspiring actress."
(Ben Fong-Torres, Rolling Stone)

THAT MAN BOLT

1973, USA
R (23746), Action/Adventure, 103m.
Universal Pictures.
D: Henry Levin, David Lowell Rich; P: Bernard Schwartz; S: Quentin Werty and Charles Johnson, based on a story by Johnson.
Cast: Fred Williamson, Teresa Graves, Byron Webster, Miko Mayama, Jack Ging, Satoshi Nakamura.

"The highest flyin', slickest, meanest dude you'll ever face is Jefferson Bolt... on the case. That Man Bolt... he's 'Bonded'."

Shine When You're Not Around'), Graves's appearance is noteworthy not just for her remarkable screen presence, but also because this would be one of her final film performances before renouncing her acting career and turning to religion.

Other film characters include Griffiths (Byron Webster), a bumbling British investigator, Connie Mellis (Jack Ging), a well-meaning casino owner, and Kumada (Satoshi Nakamura), a corrupt businessman.

An intricately staged airport men's room brawl, a high-speed car chase through the streets of Hong Kong, a light-hearted scene in a massage parlour where Bolt is affectionately referred to as "Chocolate Man," and a fight-to-the-death karate sequence between Bolt and a very talented Asian adversary, are all part of the mix. *That Man Bolt* is one of only a few blaxploitation films to present its lead African-American performers like genuine Hollywood stars.

"A mixture of James Bond, 'Mission Impossible', and Kung Fu."
(Ann Guarino, N.Y. Daily News)

THAT'S THE WAY OF THE WORLD

1975, USA
Alternative Title: *Shining Star*
PG (24354), Drama/Comedy, 100m.
United Artists.
D: Sig Shore; P: Sig Shore; S: Robert Lipsyte.
Cast: Harvey Keitel, Ed Nelson, Bert Parks, Cynthia Bostick, Jimmy Boyd, Earth Wind & Fire.

"There are two sides to every hit record!"

A music producer learns that a mob-dominated record label has its own ideas about talent and artist promotion.

Harvey (*Fingers*) Keitel plays Coleman Buckmaster, a soul music loving producer/manager who is saddled with an easy listening Carpenters-like band to promote. As always, Keitel gives it his all, but the story is a bit obvious and something of a cheat (the heavily-promoted appearance by Earth Wind & Fire is too brief and much too late in the film). Others characters include: Velour Page (Cynthia Bostick), a Janis Joplin-like white female soul singer; Frank (Bert Parks), Velour's paedophile father; and

An international courier is hired to deliver a million dollars from Hong Kong to Mexico.

Scenic (Hong Kong, Los Angeles, Las Vegas, Macao), well acted, cleverly scripted and boasting a large budget enabling a genuinely 'explosive' ending, *That Man Bolt* is a James Bond-like film filled with everything from sunglasses that are also binoculars, to an action sequence in which a skyscraper is broken into by scaling the building's exterior walls.

In the lead as the indomitable international courier Jefferson Bolt, Fred Williamson is charmingly disarming; in fact 'charming' is his favourite word. Confident and exceedingly athletic

(though too often pictured with his shirt off), Bolt has a Masters degree in physics, is a karate expert, and invests his money wisely (he owns the thirty-storey apartment building in which he lives). Williamson is to be commended for providing exactly the type of larger-than-life super hero that young black audiences wanted, for a time, to see.

Teresa (*Get Christie Love!*) Graves is a wonder to behold as his Las Vegas performer girlfriend Samantha ('Sam') Nightingale. As assured as her globe trotting boyfriend Bolt/Williamson (who she also starred with in the same year's *Black Eye*), and a consummate show-woman (she performs two full songs, 'She's a Lady' and 'The Sun Doesn't

1950s pop music singer Jimmy Boyd plays Gary Page, a hardened junkie.

Convoluted but at times entertaining, *That's the Way of the World* (hastily re-titled *Shining Star* to capitalise on Earth, Wind & Fire's hit single of the same name) was a bomb at the box office – a film that, even today, very few people have seen or even heard of.

THEY CALL ME MISTER TIBBS!

1970, USA
GP (22466) , Drama, 108m. United Artists.
D: Gordon Douglas; P: Herbert Hirschman; S: Alan R. Trustman.
Cast: Sidney Poitier, Martin Landau, Barbara McNair, Edward Asner.

"The last time Virgil Tibbs had a day like this was 'In the Heat of the Night'."

An African-American detective tries to solve a complex case involving the murder of a young prostitute.

This second instalment in the Virgil Tibbs trilogy (preceded by *In the Heat of the Night* and followed by *The Organization*) is the least exciting entry.

Sidney Poitier is just fine as Private Investigator Virgil Tibbs. Committed, and believable, it's too bad that he is forced to act within the confines of a startlingly pedestrian script. Support is provided by: Barbara McNair as Valerie, Tibbs's always-angry-that-he's-late-for-dinner wife; Martin Landau as Rev. Logan Sharpe, a neighbourhood organiser who also enjoys the company of prostitutes; and Edward Asner as Woody Garfield, a shady character with a murky history.

Well done, but generally uninvolving, the most memorable thing about *They Call Me Mister Tibbs!* is the defiant and ultimately misleading film title.

"Poitier establishes another inalienable right, that of a black movie star to make the sort of ordinary, ramshackle, pointless movie that a white movie star like Frank Sinatra has for most of his career..."
(Vincent Canby, New York Times)

THE THING WITH TWO HEADS

1972, USA
PG (583), Horror/Comedy, 91m.
American International Pictures.
D: Lee Frost; P: Wes Bishop; S: Lee Frost, Wes Bishop, James Gordon White.
Cast: Ray Milland, Rosey Grier, Don Marshall, Roger Perry, Chelsea Brown.

"They transplanted a white bigot's head onto a soul brother's body! The doctor blew it – the most fantastic medical experiment of the age. And now, with the fights, the Fuzz, the chicks and the choppers... man, they're really in deeeeep trouble!"

An African-American death-row inmate donates his organs to science, only to wake up and discover that the head of a white bigot has been transplanted onto his body!

Ray (*Slavers*) Milland is, as always, committed and wholly credible here, as

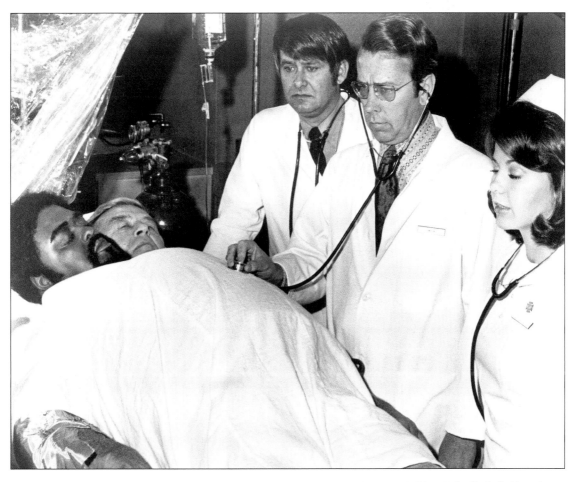

above: A trio of medical staff examine a rather unusual looking patient (Rosey Grier and Ray Milland) in 1972's **The Thing with Two Heads**. (Soul Images)

he plays Dr. Maxwell Kirshner, a medical professional who is dying of cancer, but who has also perfected a surgical technique that will spare him by transplanting his head onto another man's healthy body. In Milland's capable hands, this bizarre plot does not even seem too far-fetched! Former New York Giants football star Rosey (*The Glove*) Grier is both refreshingly natural and quietly amusing in the role of Kirshner's falsely-accused saviour/ nemesis, Jack Moss.

Other characters in the film include Lila (Chelsea Brown), Moss's confused, but oddly not horrified, girlfriend (as she wryly observes, "You're gonna' have to give me some time to deal with this!"); and Dr. Philip Desmond (played by Roger Perry), a celebrated black physician who is hired to do the fantastic surgery.

Lacklustre, poorly conceived and filled with one-dimensional cardboard characters (the viewer patiently waits for the two surgically attached men to learn something from one another – but they never do), *The Thing with Two Heads*, a film with an admittedly fabulous title is, more than anything else, a missed opportunity.

THOMASINE & BUSHROD

1974, USA
PG (23856), Western, 95m.
Columbia Pictures.
D: Gordon Parks Jr.; P: Harvey Bernhard, Max Julien; S: Max Julien.
Cast: Max Julien, Vonetta McGee, Glynn Turman, Juanita Moore.

"Thomasine & Bushrod. Driven by love. And bank robbing. Known to have many friends among Indians, Mexicans, poor whites and other coloured people."

An African-American female bounty hunter joins forces with a much sought after black bank robber.

A hit with critics, but a flop with audiences, *Thomasine & Bushrod* is a tired black-cast retread of 1967's super-successful *Bonnie and Clyde*.

In the lead as Bushrod, a horse breaker turned bank robber, Max (*The Mack*) Julien (who also wrote the script) is authoritative but, oddly, not very interesting. His girlfriend (on-screen and off) is bounty hunter Thomasine, played by Vonetta (*Melinda*) McGee.

Beautiful, liberated and self-sufficient, she too, even when trying to command our attention, fails to deliver a fully rounded performance. Also in the cast are Juanita (*Abby*) Moore as Pecolia, a blind 'Indian' tribeswoman, and Glynn (*J.D.'s Revenge*) Turman as Jomo, a Jamaican drifter.

Repetitive (how many bank robberies, carriage chases, and treks across baron land do we have to see before we get the idea?), uninventive and overly clichéd, *Thomasine & Bushrod* is a stretched and tired misstep – a 'blacks in the Old West' tale that had been done before, and done better.

"Those expecting a rootin' tootin' western will be disappointed."
(David Walker, BadAzz MoFo magazine issue #4)

THREE THE HARD WAY

1974, USA
R (23935), Action/Adventure, 93m.
Allied Artists.
D: Gordon Parks Jr.; P: Harry Bernsen; S: Eric Bercovici, Jerry Ludwig.
Cast: Jim Brown, Fred Williamson, Jim Kelly, Sheila Frazier, Jeannie [Jean] Bell, Richard Angarola.

"It's the bad guys against the bad guys!"

When a neo-Nazi develops a serum that will kill all black people, three African-American men join forces to foil the plot.

They're all here in one picture! Jim (*Black Gunn*) Brown as Jimmy Lait, a Los Angeles-based record promoter, Jim (*Black Belt Jones*) Kelly as Mr. Keyes,

"The black Moses, the Hammer, and the Preacher Man. They've got their own kind of mean game."

A priest and an ex-cop combine forces to locate a gang of ruthless murderers.

Though its title should be *Two Tough Guys and a Brief Cameo by a Third*, this super-violent detective drama is a nicely photographed look at both the world of underworld crime and the driven personalities that keep it flourishing.

Italian-born Lino Ventura is fantastic in the lead role of Father Charlie, a priest who takes a leave of absence from the Church so that he can solve a murder case. Quiet, dignified and bound by his own set of rules (he refuses to shoot anyone!) yet more than willing to beat someone to a bloody "why does it always take a slap to get a conversation rolling?"

pulp, Ventura's ease, naturalness and professionalism are the centrepiece of this production. Isaac (*Truck Turner*) Hayes plays ex-Chicago cop Lee Stevens, a man who joins forces with Father Charlie to crack a case. Hayes is pleasant enough, but his enunciation is strikingly poor (he mumbles almost all of his lines). Fred Williamson – in a role much smaller than the poster art suggests – plays Joe 'Snake' Marshall, a swaggering, deceitful and very deadly underworld leader. Paula (*Trouble Man*) Kelly is also on hand as Fay Collins, the only person alive who knows the whereabouts of a million dollars stolen in a bank heist.

Not quite original, but most definitely intriguing, *Three Tough Guys* – a picture filmed in and around the Chicago area – is a fast-moving, colourful film that is worth a quick look.

Lait's New York-based karate expert friend, and Fred (*Black Caesar*) Williamson as Chicago businessman Jagger Daniels. All three are macho, cool, larger than life super-heroes who can take on all-comers with consummate ease. Notable support players include Sheila (*Super Fly*) Frazier as Wendy Kane, Lait's vulnerable girlfriend, and Richard Angarola as Dr. Fortrero, the deadly serum-creating racist madman.

Filled with action (at least thirty cars are destroyed), several deftly choreographed fight sequences, and splendid Chicago, New York City, Los Angeles and Washington D.C. locations, *Three the Hard Way* is a fast-moving, cleverly produced feature that, though filled with many unanswered questions (how do these three men have access to firearms? And when and where did they learn how to use them so deftly?), is no less entertaining because of it. An action/adventure novelty film that features three blaxploitation superstars in their prime.

Note: The blaxploitation superstar triumvirate of Brown, Williamson and Kelly would be paired again in the following year's *Take a Hard Ride*.

THREE TOUGH GUYS

1974, Italy/France
Alternative Titles: *Tough Guys*; *Uomini duri*; *Les durs*
PG (23864), Action/Adventure, 92m.
Paramount Pictures.
D: Duccio Tessari; P: Dino De Laurentiis; S: Luciano Vincenzoni, Nicola Badalucco.
Cast: Isaac Hayes, Lino Ventura, Fred Williamson, Paula Kelly.

...tick...tick...tick...

1970, USA
G (22213), Action/Adventure, 97m.
Metro Goldwyn Mayer.
D: Ralph Nelson; P: Ralph Nelson, James Lee Barrett; S: James Lee Barrett.
Cast: Jim Brown, George Kennedy, Fredric March, Lynn Carlin, Janet MacLachlan, Bernie Casey.

"Listen boy! Any black man that runs for sheriff down here in Colusa County should have his head examined. Before the coroner does it for him!"

A recently-elected African American sheriff must convince residents of a racist Southern town that he is worthy of the job.

...tedious...tedious...tedious... would have been a more apt title for this, blaxploitation's one and only lower-case-titled picture. As new Sheriff Jimmy Price, former football star Jim Brown offers the laid back on-screen charm and charisma that made him the featured player of several action oriented 1960s films.

Essentially playing himself, Brown is an objectified performer (often photographed with his shirt off) who successfully exploits both his good looks and his renown as a star athlete. As his wife Mary, Janet (*Halls of Anger*) MacLachlan alternates between being fear-stricken and relentlessly determined. Also in the cast are: George Kennedy as John Little, Colusa County's former sheriff; Fredric March as Mayor Jeff Parks, an ineffective sitting official; and Bernie (*Hit Man*) Casey as George Harley, a black man who is charged with raping a fifteen-year-old girl.

A bloody ambush, random references to the Ku Klux Klan, and the arrest of a politically-connected defendant, are all, admirably, underplayed. Even so, the same year's similar but more sensational *The Liberation of L.B. Jones* brings this film's message (that there are better days ahead) home much more succinctly – and much more entertainingly.

"...Mr. Brown saves the picture... this fine-looking giant of a man has a rock-ribbed sincerity and natural dignity that rivet attention..."
(Howard Thompson, New York Times)

TNT JACKSON

1974, USA
R (24039), Action/Adventure, 72m.
New World Pictures.
D: Cirio H. Santiago; P: Cirio H. Santiago; S: Dick Miller, Ken Metcalfe.
Cast: Jeanne [Jean] Bell, Pat Anderson, Stan Shaw, Ken Metcalfe, Chiquito.

"Spine shattering... bone blasting. She's a one mama massacre squad! TNT Jackson... she'll put you in traction."

An African-American woman travels to the Philippines in search of her missing brother.

In the lead as Diana 'TNT' Jackson, a 24-year-old Harlem-born woman who can hold her own in any and all circumstances (one of her early boyfriends – a black belt in karate, taught her how to 'take care of herself'), Jean Bell's flat-voiced, stone-faced and emotionless contribution to this super-low-budget and disjointed but thoroughly entertaining film, is surprisingly effective. Simply magnificent to look at, and quick to use the popular phrases of the day, she is a self-possessed and self-empowered female film character whose main purpose – obliterating her enemies – always remains front and centre.

Charlie (Stan Shaw) is TNT's unexpected mentor and love interest. One dimensional, not given too much to do but complain (he is planning to overthrow a Filipino drug lord), Shaw is at least convincing in the film's many fight sequences. Able support is provided by: Pat Anderson as Elaine, a mobster's girlfriend who also happens to be an undercover FBI agent; Ken Metcalfe as Sid, a super-successful American drug-runner (wait to you see his house!); and Chiquito as Joe, a very friendly and very shy (especially in the presence of beautiful women like TNT) neighbourhood informant.

Surprisingly violent and gory, filled with long, intricately-staged multi-cast karate fight scenes, and making good use of both slow-motion and fast-motion photography, *TNT Jackson*, best known for its lights-on-lights-off topless karate fight (performed by Bell), is a well thought-out fantasy/action/exploitation picture. Recommended – both director Santiago's, and star Bell's, most entertaining work.

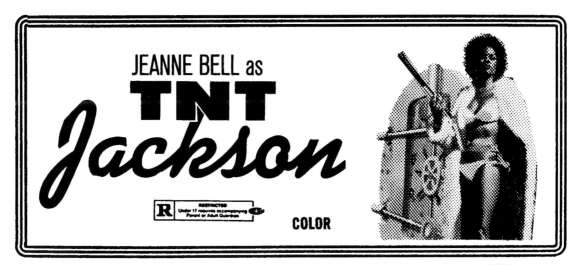

JEANNE BELL as
TNT *Jackson*

R RESTRICTED
Under 17 requires accompanying
Parent or Adult Guardian

COLOR

Note: The motion picture poster art features Bell posed in a bank vault, wearing high heels, a mink coat and diamonds – a scene that has no connection at all to this jungle-bound film. See *Q & A: Ten Directors Discuss Their Films*.

TOGETHER BROTHERS

1974, USA
PG (23813), Action/Adventure, 95m.
20th Century Fox.
D: William A. Graham; P: Robert L. Rosen; S: Jack De Witt and Joe Green, from a story by Jack De Witt.
Cast: Anthony Wilson, Ahmad Nurradin, Lincoln Kilpatrick, Glynn Turman, Richard Yniguez, Ed Bernard, Craig Campfield, Joe Zapata, Bessie Griffin.

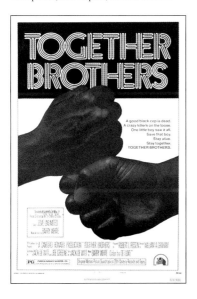

"It's about finding a killer. Saving a little boy. It's about fighting, loving. It's about being a kid in a world where childhood isn't allowed."

Five neighbourhood teenagers join forces to search for a popular policeman's murderer.

Filmed in Galveston, Texas, this engaging, atypical blaxploitation entry has a little bit of everything: there's a good-guy African-American policeman affectionately known as 'Mr. Kool' (Ed Bernard); a teenage sleuth named H.J. (Ahmad Nurradin); an adorable little boy whose life is in danger, Tommy (Anthony Wilson); a white-afroed female impersonator, Maria (Craig Campfield); a Latin gang leader, Chicano (Joe Zapata); a female minister, Reverend Brown (Bessie Griffin); and a psychotic cross-dressing murderer, Billy Most (Lincoln Kilpatrick). What is surprising is that the disparate characters all fit together in this film quite nicely.

Lincoln Kilpatrick is both menacing and sympathetic as the vengeful transvestite murderer. Ed Bernard as H.J., the teenager who solves the case, is both natural and believable in his film debut. What is there to say about Anthony Wilson in the role of Tommy, the winsome little boy? Here Wilson, who is struck temporarily mute by the trauma of witnessing the murder of 'Mr. Kool', conveys an impressive range of emotions and is admirably comfortable interacting with the other adult players.

Though at times it's a bit slow, *Together Brothers* is noteworthy for its presentation of rarely-seen African-

above:
Actors Jean Bell (credited for this film as 'Jeanne' Bell, one of the many variant spellings of her name) and Stan Shaw, in promotional stills from 1974's **TNT Jackson**, one of the very first blaxploitation films to emerge on DVD, and one of the genre's most fully-realised 'zero-budget' entries.

American film characters – not to mention soul artist Barry White's superb soundtrack – *Together Brothers* is most definitely worth a look.

"Preaching cooperation, brotherhood and a sense of obligation... 'Together Brothers' has its heart in the right place." (Lawrence Van Gelder, New York Times)

TOGETHER FOR DAYS

1972, USA
Alternative Title: *Black Cream*
PG (23385), Drama, 84m.
Olas Corporation.
D: Michael Schultz; P: Robert S. Buchanan; S: William B. Branch, from a story by Lindsay Smith.
Cast: Clifton Davis, Samuel L. Jackson, Lois Chiles, Leonard Jackson.

"A brother's struggle for identity!"

A radical black activist and a sympathetic young white woman fall in love during volatile times.

The directorial debut of African-American director Michael Schultz was the first film to feature Academy Award winner Samuel L. Jackson. It's one of blaxploitation's lost pictures: unavailable on VHS or DVD and not seen since the time of its original theatrical release.

Inexpensively filmed in Atlanta, Georgia, and offering a rare look at the black community's displeasure with black/white interracial relationships, *Together for Days* also features Leonard (*Five on the Black Hand Side*) Jackson and Clifton (of TV's *That's My Mama*) Davis.

TOP OF THE HEAP

1972, USA
R (563), Action/Adventure, 84m.
The Fanfare Corporation.
D: Christopher St. John; P: Christopher St. John; S: Christopher St. John.
Cast: Christopher St. John, Paula Kelly, Florence St. Peter, Patrick McVey.

"His rage was the illness of the times! He was a violent man... trouble was he also was a cop."

A black Washington D.C. policeman struggles to come to terms with his family, his job and himself.

Too unusual to have been whole-heartedly embraced by mainstream audiences, this intense look at the struggles that an African-American male faces in a racist society (and a divided home) is filled with flashbacks, flash-forwards and colourfully presented fantasy segments.

As police officer George Lattimer, Christopher (*Shaft*) St. John (who also directed, produced and wrote the screenplay) turns in a performance filled with both bombast and nuance. Unfulfilled, aggravated and perpetually searching, his is a painfully realistic character who, when all is said and done, lacks the courage of his convictions. Florence St. Peter is also startlingly true to life as his wife Viola. Frustrated, misunderstood and shut out, Viola delivers several highly emotional diatribes that give both her husband and the viewer pause for thought:

> George: *You never listen to a word I say.*
> Florence (snarling): *That's because in twelve years of marriage you've never said a word worth listening to.*

Paula (*Trouble Man*) Kelly is as alluring as ever, in a supporting role as George's nightclub singer-girlfriend. Hooked on drugs, sex, and her married man George, she lives in a basement apartment, likes to play the guitar while dancing in the nude, and is not above asking for money when she needs it.

Earnest, political (including several references to then-president Richard Nixon), highly intellectual and arty, *Top of the Heap*'s many fantasy segments include: George and his girlfriend as nude African natives demolishing a watermelon in the African jungle; an encounter with George's recently-deceased mother; a walk on the moon; and an abandoned city street which turns into a festive welcome home ticker tape parade.

opposite: Young Tommy (Anthony Wilson) is rendered speechless after witnessing the murder of a favourite neighbourhood cop in 1974's **Together Brothers**. (J. Howard Collection)

Top of the Heap is ambitious, at times strident and overwrought, but never preachy. Writer/producer/director Christopher St. John turns in a highly conceptual film that speaks directly to those who have not quite realised their life's ambitions. Most definitely worth seeing.

"...manages to break out of the already deadly stereotypes of black-white confrontation films to become ironic, sometimes fantastic, and even comic." (Roger Greenspun, New York Times)

TOUGH!

1974, USA
Alternative Title: *Johnny Tough*
G (1115), Action/Adventure, 87m.
Dimension Pictures.
D: Horace Jackson; P: Horace Jackson; S: Horace B. Jackson.
Cast: Renny Roker, Sandra Reed, Dion Gossett, Richard McCready.

"He's bad. He's black. He's beautiful. He'll steal your heart."

A young boy, whose home life is filled with discord, finds it difficult to connect to his parents, friends and schoolmates.

Though it is a refreshing change to see a blaxploitation film about suburban blacks who are dealing with the same challenges as suburban whites (have-it-all delinquent children), *Tough!*, as well-meaning as it is, is an all-round juvenile disappointment.

In the lead as Phil, a not-so-exciting insurance salesman, Renny (*Deliver Us from Evil*) Roker turns in a ponderous performance devoid of both passion and introspection. As his troubled young son, Johnny 'Tough', Dion Gossett is also much less impressive than you want him to be; a pudgy, poor actor, he is an odd choice to play an active, hard-as-nails youth who smokes, steals, and teases car-bound animals. Sandra (*The Bus Is Coming*) Reed does little more than flail her hands and sigh as she goes through the motions of playing Phil's

self-centred wife Denise. As if the performances in this film are not bad enough, the dialogue is even worse:

Phil (to his wife): *You're not half as good looking as you think you are.* Denise: *You're just afraid I'm going to make it in Hollywood* [as an actress] *and overshadow you!*

With cardboard characters (and sets), and clichéd themes and dialogue, this choppy and incoherent 'movie-with-a-message' ends with the perfunctory, on-screen coda, "Parents, teachers and kids... get it together!" Actors, directors and filmmakers... get it together!

"...superficial surface performances from the adult cast... who seem to be performing, not feeling, their shocks and anguish." (A.H. Weiler, New York Times)

TRICK BABY

1972, USA
Alternative Title: *Double Con*
R (23497), Action/Adventure, 94m.
Universal Pictures.
D: Larry Yust; P: Marshal Backlar; S: Larry Yust, T. Raewyn and A. Neuberg, based on a novel by Iceberg Slim.
Cast: Kiel Martin, Mel Stewart, Dallas Edward Hayes, Vernee Watson, Clebert Ford, Beverly Ballard.

"Shake hands with 'Folks' and 'Blue.' And then count your fingers!"

Two Philadelphia-based con-men find themselves being pursued by the Mafia.

This engaging, well acted, creatively photographed and cleverly written film is a forgotten gem. The story concerns two black con men: a younger one who appears to be white, Johnny 'White Folks' O'Brien (Kiel Martin); and an older father figure named Blue Howard (Mel Stewart). Both performers endow their parts with passion and studied nuance. The supporting players include: Beverly Ballard as Susan, a woman whose loneliness is so vividly portrayed you feel for a moment that you should turn away from the screen; Clebert Ford as Josephus, a chillingly real (and often prophetic) curb-side philosopher; and Vernee (*Death Drug*) Watson as Cleo, Blue's estranged, embittered daughter.

Elaborate schemes, broken promises and cross-town car chases – it's all here. Colourful, inventive, entertaining and filled with a bevy of remarkably believable performances, *Trick Baby* is a thoroughly enjoyable film whose surprise ending makes it all the more memorable.

Note: The movie title refers to the fact that lead character O'Brien is the son of a black hooker and a white 'John.'

TROUBLE MAN

1972, USA
R (23343), Action/Adventure, 99m.
20th Century Fox.
D: Ivan Dixon; P: Joel D. Freeman; S: John D. F. Black.
Cast: Robert Hooks, Paul Winfield, Ralph Waite, Paula Kelly, Julius Harris, Bill Henderson.

"His friends call him 'T'... his enemies call for mercy. One cat that plays like an army"

A gambling ring hires popular underground figure Mr. T to find out who is at the bottom of a string of robberies.

Robert Hooks is superb in the lead as Mr. T, a jack-of-all-trades (in this instance hired as a Private Investigator). Attractive and charismatic (he wears $300 suits), intimidating (he beats up and kills several people), sexually active (he has a number of young, eager girls who can be called on for favours), and informed (he knows exactly what's going on at every crap shoot in town), Mr. T is a macho-fantasy figure for the masses – a take-charge super-hero who, though tough, believes in justice, and has a heart.

In the role of his beautiful nightclub-singer girlfriend Cleo (who is so enamoured with Mr. T that she refuses to take gigs out of town), Paula (*Top of the Heap*) Kelly is, as always, lovely. Sensitive, intelligent, but still bound by emotion, hers is a female character whose life choices are difficult to understand, but at the same time, utterly familiar from real life. Standing out in three smaller roles are: Julius (*Super Fly*) Harris as Mr. Big, the neighbourhood numbers king;

Bill Henderson as Jimmy, Mr. T's pool hall owner best friend; and Paul (*Gordon's War*) Winfield as Chalky Price, a double-crossing numbers organiser.

Deft direction, a clever script, fine actors, good locations (an old movie palace, Century City), and a great Marvin Gaye soundtrack all help make *Trouble Man* a thoroughly enjoyable viewing experience. Recommended.

TRUCK TURNER

1974, USA
R (23892), Action/Adventure, 91m.
American International Pictures.
D: Jonathan Kaplan; P: Paul M. Heller, Fred Weintraub; S: Oscar Williams, Michael Allin and Leigh Chapman, from a story by Jerry Wilkes.
Cast: Isaac Hayes, Yaphet Kotto, Nichelle Nichols, Dick Miller, Alan Weeks, Annazette Chase, Scatman Crothers.

"He's a skip tracer, the last of the bounty hunters. If you jump bail you're his meat!"

After killing a popular Madame's boyfriend, a bounty hunter finds himself being pursued by the mob.

Isaac Hayes as Matt 'Truck' Turner, is a convincing, yet surprisingly dull, film presence in his one and only starring role (he also composed and performed the music soundtrack). Even less engaging is Turner's partner-in-crime, Jerry (played by Alan Weeks). Plain-faced, too much of a follower, and lacking any kind of an edge, Jerry makes a strikingly poor 'action/adventure' partner for 'Truck'.

The pivotal performer, and sole reason for recommending this film, is Nichelle Nichols (best known for her goody-two-shoes African-American female space-travel character on TV's *Star Trek*) as Dorinda, a slutty, filthy mouthed, shrill, gun-toting, merciless, and unrepentantly violent Madame:

Dorinda (to her 'girls'*): All you whores listen to me. Anybody thinking about leaving is gonna find my fucking shoe up their ass. Do you understand me bitches? As for those two whores who left, they better learn to sell pussy in Iceland because if I ever see them again I'm gonna cut their fucking throats. Remember all your asses belong to me! I tell you what you can and can't do with them!*

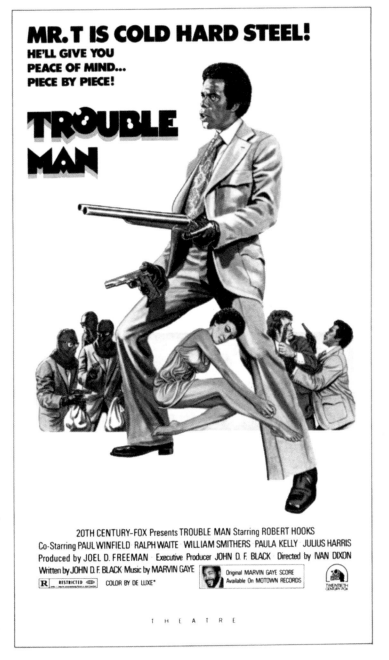

MR. T IS COLD HARD STEEL!
HE'LL GIVE YOU PEACE OF MIND... PIECE BY PIECE!

TROUBLE MAN

20TH CENTURY-FOX Presents TROUBLE MAN Starring ROBERT HOOKS
Co-Starring PAUL WINFIELD RALPH WAITE WILLIAM SMITHERS PAULA KELLY JULIUS HARRIS
Produced by JOEL D. FREEMAN Executive Producer JOHN D. F. BLACK Directed by IVAN DIXON
Written by JOHN D. F. BLACK Music by MARVIN GAYE Original MARVIN GAYE SCORE Available On MOTOWN RECORDS
R RESTRICTED COLOR BY DE LUXE*

THEATRE

Breathtakingly crude (this is only one of two blaxploitation films that features a female character using the word "pussy" – the other is *Melinda*), Dorinda/Nichols's crazed, over-heated verbal assaults are all the more shocking because they are emanating from a simply gorgeous woman who is swathed in an endless array of feather boas, form-fitting satin and velour pantsuits, and strappy gowns.

Much more memorable than the 'stars' of this film are: Yaphet Kotto as Harvard Blue, an opportunistic pimp;

above: Isaac Hayes uses more than his gun when apprehending fugitives in **Truck Turner** (1974).

217

above: Musical giant Isaac Hayes becomes an action hero in the blaxploitation hit **Truck Turner** (1974).

Annazette Chase as Annie, Turner's often-incarcerated sometimes-girlfriend; and Scatman Crothers as The Duke, a know-it-all retired underground figure.

Truck Turner's major incidents include a longer-than-it-needs-to-be car chase, a bloody shootout, and a semi-interesting kidnapping/gun battle that takes place in a hospital! See *Q & A: Ten Directors Discuss Their Films.*

"...its constant barrage of chases, bloody fights and shoot-outs is as unusual as a local 4th of July fireworks display."
(A.H. Weiler, New York Times)

THE TWILIGHT PEOPLE

1972, Philippines/USA
Alternative Title: *Beasts*
PG (539), Horror, 80m.
Dimension Pictures.
D: Eddie Romero; P: John Ashley, Eddie Romero; S: Eddie Romero, Jerome Small.
Cast: John Ashley, Pat Woodell, Charles Macaulay, Pam Grier, Tony Gosalvez, Ken Metcalfe, Mona Morena, Kim Ramos.

"Animal desires... human lust!"

A deranged doctor conducts unspeakable experiments on humans in the Philippines.

Sound familiar? Yet another variation on *The Island of Dr. Moreau*, shot in super-vivid colour, this 'horror' flick is a great, fun-for-the-whole-family, party movie.

The cast of characters includes: Ayesa, the panther woman (Pam Grier) – who snarls, shows her fangs, and, when in

a playful mood, purrs and rolls around on her back in the grass; Darmo, the bat man (Tony Gosalvez) – who, try as he might, can't quite seem to fly; Kuzma, the antelope man (Ken Metcalfe) – who falls in love with Lupa, the wolf woman (Mona Morena); and Primo, the ape man (Kim Ramos) – a creature who is on the lookout for a little romance.

The 'people' characters populating the film include an impressionable drifter, Matt Farrell (John [*Savage Sisters*] Ashley), a mad scientist, Dr. Gordon (Charles Macaulay), and Neva, Gordon's compassionate daughter (Pat Woodell).

Shamelessly peopled with a cast of non-actors, filled with artificial-looking

sets and bad Halloween-like costumes, and featuring several lengthy sojourns into the Filipino jungles, *The Twilight People* is a good-natured, cheaply made, and wholly inoffensive oddity whose beautiful underwater opening credits sequence is, in itself, worth the price of a rental.

"Typically, it had inferior production values, post-dubbing for many of the performers, and yet, despite it all, it was entertaining on a minimal level."
(Parish/Hill, Black Action Films, 1989)

UPTOWN SATURDAY NIGHT

1974, USA
PG (23863), Comedy, 104m. Warner Bros.
D: Sidney Poitier; P: Melville Tucker; S: Richard Wesley.
Cast: Sidney Poitier, Bill Cosby, Harry Belafonte, Richard Pryor, Flip Wilson, Paula Kelly, Calvin Lockhart, Rosalind Cash, Roscoe Lee Browne.

"They get funny when you mess with their money."

Two factory workers enter New York's underworld to locate a missing $50,000 lottery ticket.

Sidney Poitier (who also directs) plays Steve Jackson, a down-to-earth factory worker. His best buddy is good-natured cab driver Wardell Franklin (Bill Cosby). Both actors interact well with one another, and when these two confused, misguided characters meet up with Geechie Dan Beauford (Harry Belafonte – unrecognizable as a

mumbling *Godfather*-like mobster), things really get crazy.

The picture's strong supporting characters include: an impassioned, fast-talking minister played by Flip Wilson; a neighbourhood pimp named Silky Slim (Calvin Lockhart); a self-important public servant, Congressman Lincoln (Roscoe Lee Browne); Lincoln's good time girl wife Leggy Peggy (Paula Kelly); and a down-on-his-luck Private Investigator named Sharp Eye Washington (Richard Pryor).

Filled with a litany of one-liners, sight gags and pranks, *Uptown Saturday Night*'s shining moment takes place in a church. Backed by the soaring voices of a gospel choir singing 'How I Got Over (To the Other Side),' two underworld kingpins meet to exchange stolen goods. (Incredibly the choir – and its magnificent lead singer – do not receive a credit.) A hit at the box-office and with critics, *Uptown Saturday Night* concentrates on entertaining its audience, and it succeeds admirably.

Note: Poitier and Cosby were paired twice more; in *Let's Do It Again* and *A Piece of the Action*.

"...a carnival of fine comic characters."
(Paul D. Zimmermann, Newsweek)

VELVET SMOOTH

1976, USA
R (1505), Action/Adventure, 89m.
Howard Mahler Films.
D: Michael Fink; P: Marvin Schild, Michael Fink, Joel Schild; S: Leonard Michaels, Jan Weber.
Cast: Johnnie Hill, Owen Wat-son, Emerson Boozer, Elsie Roman, René Van Clief, Frank Ruiz.

"Tall, lean and mean! Velvet Smooth, she's smooth as velvet."

'Protection Agency Chief' Velvet Smooth is hired to find out who is trying to put an inner-city numbers syndicate out of business.

This no-budget attempt to jump on blaxploitation's 'female hero' bandwagon is a hoot! Johnnie Hill (in her only film role) plays Velvet Smooth with awkward aplomb. Helping her solve her latest case are Frankie (René Van Clief), an independent woman who makes a point of spending 'quality time' with her man, and Ria (Elsie Roman), a high-kicking Latina who's studying to become a lawyer. Also

"**Velvet Smooth**" Starring **Johnnie Hill** Special Guest Star **Emerson Boozer**
Also starring Owen Wat-son René Van Clief Elsie Roman
Frank Ruiz Moses Iylla   Produced by Marvin Schild
Michael Fink Joel Schild   Directed by Michael Fink
Original score by Media Counterpoint, Inc.

in the cast are Owen Wat-son as King Lathrop, an inner-city gang lord, and Frank Ruiz as Lieutenant Ramos, a macho supervisor who provides a final plot twist. Football star-turned actor Emerson Boozer makes a cameo.

Filled with lengthy fight sequences – in a schoolyard, a warehouse, a back alley, on a rooftop, at an illegal casino, and in a pool hall – *Velvet Smooth*, like its titular main character, just wants to deliver the goods! Kitschy and campy.

"...yet another effort to create a super-cool black heroine, but with such reduced production values that the entertainment possibilities proved to be minimal."
(Parish/Hill, Black Action Films, 1989)

above: Johnnie Hill as **Velvet Smooth** (1976).

above: **A Warm December** was a "throwback" film that audiences responded to accordingly – they threw it back! Catherine (Esther Anderson) and Dr. Younger (Sidney Poitier) are the lovers who didn't stand a chance.

A WARM DECEMBER

1973, UK/USA
PG (23420), Drama, 100m.
National General Pictures.
D: Sidney Poitier; P: Melville Tucker;
S: Lawrence Roman.
Cast: Sidney Poitier, Esther Anderson,
Earl Cameron, Yvette Curtis.

*"His love. Her December. Their story.
Something to remember."*

**On holiday in England, a doctor falls in
love with a mysterious young woman.**

A Warm December is an uninspired and
highly improbable story about a successful
African-American doctor (who also
happens to be a prize-winning race car
driver!), and an English-accented black
beauty (who also happens to be the daughter
of a prominent African Ambassador).

As Dr. Matt Younger, Sidney Poitier
(who also directs) seems to be taking great
pains to promote himself (at the age of 50)
as a desirable and alluringly eligible
bachelor. Though Poitier is undoubtedly
attractive, eloquent and a 'good catch,' the
effort involved in trying to convince the
viewer that he is, additionally, sexy

(numerous scenes that show him *sans* shirt)
don't quite come off. British actress Esther
Anderson plays Catherine, a mysterious
young woman who is always being
followed. Though Anderson appears to be a
competent actress, given so little to do, she
comes across a little more than a decorative
stick figure. Young actress Yvette Curtis
pulls up the slack in a small role as
Stefanie, Dr. Younger's exuberant daughter.
Also of note in the cast is British actor Earl
Cameron (often referred to as the British
Sidney Poitier), as George Oswandu, a
regal but combative African diplomat.

A 'soul' performance in an off-the-
beaten-path nightclub, a trip to the British
Museum of Ethnography, and a tour of an
African embassy are all part of the show.
A Warm December is a scenic 'live, cry &
learn' 1950s melodrama in '70s blackface.

WATERMELON MAN

1970, USA
R (22400), Comedy, 100m.
Columbia Pictures.
D: Melvin Van Peebles; P: John B.
Bennett; S: Herman Raucher.
Cast: Godfrey Cambridge, Estelle
Parsons, Howard Caine, D'Urville Martin.

"The uppity movie!"

**A suburban white bigot wakes up one
morning to discover that he is black!**

Shrill, one-note, and ugly to behold, the
only point of interest about this picture is
that at the time of its release, the subject
matter titillated audiences.

As Jeff Gerber, an insurance salesman who has realised the 'American dream,' Godfrey Cambridge is energetic but lost in a debilitating coat of 'white face' makeup that makes him look like a sweaty-faced marionette. Faring only slightly better is comic character actress Estelle Parsons as Althea, Gerber's tart-tongued, willing to 'work it through' wife. Blaxploitation 'favourite' D'Urville Martin is also in the cast as a sympathetic bus driver.

Set-bound, stilted, and filled with artificial-sounding speeches, this social-commentary film plays like an over-long *Saturday Night Live* comedy sketch.

"Not much of a picture, but as a transient innocuous entertainment it is harmless." (Variety)

WATTSTAX

1973, USA
R (23541), Concert, 102m.
Columbia Pictures.
D: Mel Stuart; P: Larry Shaw, Mel Stuart.
Cast: The Staple Singers, Isaac Hayes, Jesse Jackson, Richard Pryor, Johnnie Taylor, Carla Thomas, Rufus Thomas, Luther Ingram.

"Laugh! Cry! Sing! Hear! Feel! Dance! Shout! Wattstax... A soulful expression of the living word."

A concert film featuring Stax Records' premier musical acts.

Wattstax, filmed at the Memorial Coliseum in Los Angeles during the summer of 1972, is a movie in which the audience (young, beautiful and ethnic) is as memorable as the many performers. Richard Pryor (in a repeat performance of the Master of Ceremonies role he played in *Dynamite Chicken*) provides a very funny, witty and engaging afro-centric running commentary.

The wonderful performances come one right after the other, and serve to remind the viewer that there really was a time when singers had to actually have decent voices. Standouts include: Carla Thomas ('Picking Up the Pieces'); The Staple Singers ('Respect Yourself'); Rufus Thomas ('Breakdown' and 'Funky Chicken'); and Luther Ingram ('If Loving You Is Wrong, I Don't Want to Be Right'). Also impressive is Johnnie Taylor (best known for 'Disco Lady') doing a choir-backed performance of 'Jody'. Sadly, the picture's premier act, the highly touted

above: Isaac Hayes showing off his musical prowess in 1973's concert film **Wattstax**. (Soul Images)

Isaac Hayes (who closes the picture, entering and exiting the stadium like a late-career Elvis Presley) is the film's least exciting performer. Interviews shot on the streets of the Watts ghetto of Los Angeles are sage, on-point and highly quotable. (When an elderly man is asked how he makes ends meet he flatly replies, "If I can't work and make it... I just steal and take it!" Director Mel Stuart and producer Larry Shaw are African American.

"An extraordinary film that has percolated under the public radar. A must for music fans." (Ann Hornaday, Washington Post)

WAY OF THE BLACK DRAGON

1978, Hong Kong
NR (R), Action/Martial Arts, 92m.
Madison World Films.
D: Chan Cho; P: Serafim Karalexis; S: Chan Cho.
Cast: Ron Van Clief, Carter Wong, Cecilia Wong Hang Sau, Charles Bonet.

Two martial arts troubleshooters, one African American, one Chinese, combine forces to crack an international drug-smuggling/slave-trading ring.

Far removed from its two, rather tame, predecessors, this oddly lurid and salacious look at an underground slave ring trafficking in women (who are forced not only to perform sexual acts with strangers, but also must transport drugs stashed in their private parts) is the final installment in the popular *Black Dragon* series.

In the lead as Private Investigator Billy Eden, Ron Van Clief does what he always does; that is, mug, pose, grunt and kick high. Carter Wong plays Hai Chow, the karate expert brother of Allison (Cecilia Wong Hang Sau), a woman who has been kidnapped and sold into slavery, and Charles Bonet – in a don't-blink-or-you'll-miss-him cameo – is Charlie, Eden's exceedingly agile friend.

Overloaded with the requisite car chases (and even a boat chase) and street corner ambushes, *Way of the Black Dragon* is a queasy stew of misogyny that, with its constant focus on women in their underwear, women being beaten, and women having 'cargo' removed from their bodies, just doesn't sit right. (It is perhaps significant that the name of the film's star, Ron Van Clief, is misspelled in the pictures opening credits as 'Ron Van Cliff'.)

WELCOME HOME BROTHER CHARLES

1975, USA
Alternative Title: *Soul Vengeance*
R (24392), Action/Adventure, 99m.
Crown International Pictures.
D: Jamaa Fanaka; P: Jamaa Fanaka; S: Jamaa Fanaka.
Cast: Marlo Monte, Reatha Grey, Ben Bigelow, Ed Sander.

"They tried to take everything... even his manhood. You done the man's time, now you're gonna do ours."

After serving time in prison for a crime he didn't commit, a young African-American male seeks a most peculiar revenge.

As Charles Murray, a recently-released small time pimp and drug dealer, Marlo Monte is both admirably comfortable in front of the camera and believable in the picture's many absurd and far-fetched fantasy segments. Reatha Grey is also praiseworthy in the part of his former

prostitute girlfriend, Carmen. Their paths cross with those of Harry Freeman, a racist cop played by Ben Bigelow, and Ed Sander, in the role of a corrupt court appointee who enjoys the company of prostitutes.

Welcome Home Brother Charles is politically-charged, filled with earnest but off the mark performances, and determinedly controversial. This surreal, sensational and salacious (the film features a segment with a 20 foot long murderous penis!) look at American racism, police brutality and an all consuming quest for vengeance, is a socio-political fantasy film that, even with its circus side show special effects attraction, did not connect with audiences. See *Q & A: Ten Directors Discuss Their Films*.

"One simply has not lived until seeing the black anaconda strangulation scene!"
(David Duncan, Rewinder, Volume 1, Number 2)

WHICH WAY IS UP?

1977, USA
R (24886), Comedy, 94m.
Universal Pictures.
D: Michael Schultz; P: Steve Krantz; S: Carl Gottlieb, Cecil Brown.
Cast: Richard Pryor, Gloria Edwards, Lonette McKee, Margaret Avery.

The story of three diverse African-American men's lives.

Richard Pryor's three much-talked-about characters in this multi-role starring vehicle are: Reverend Lenox Thomas, a pompadoured minister who seduces almost all the women in his congregation; Leroy Jones, a blue collar Southern California orange picker (who can't get his wife to have sex with him); and Rufus Jones, Leroy's cantankerous, vulgar, oversexed and undeniably funny father.

A remake of the 1972 Italian film *The Seduction of Mimi*, *Which Way Is Up?* is an attempt at social satire, but it only occasionally succeeds. Comic segments include a desperate wife donning sado-masochist gear to entice her 'impotent' husband, and a turn-the-tables kitchen brawl that invigorates an entire family. (Not so convincing is Pryor's sermon on the sanctity of the home by "pot-bellied, black, big nosed, ugly, non-preaching nigger" Reverend Thomas).

Poorly scripted, and filled with a cast of characters that are essentially despicable liars, cheats and manipulators, *Which Way Is Up?* is an only occasionally humorous collection of disjointed comedy vignettes.

Note: Stargard's title song 'Which Way Is Up?' became a big hit in discos.

"This ambitious but unfocused vehicle has all the raunchy humour one would expect from Pryor's stand-up material, but none of the warmth or heat."
(Donald Guarisco, All Movie Guide)

WILLIE DYNAMITE

1974, USA
R (23724), Action/Adventure, 102m.
Universal Pictures.
D: Gilbert Moses; P: Richard D. Zanuck, David Brown; S: Ron Cutler.
Cast: Roscoe Orman, Diana Sands, Thalmus Rasulala, Joyce Walker, Royce Wallace.

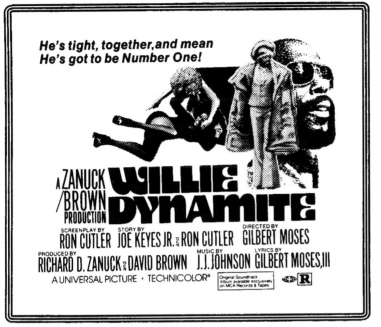

"Ain't no one crosses Willie 'D'. He's tight, together and mean. Chicks, chumps, he uses 'em all. He's got to be Number One."

A New York City pimp and a social worker vie for control of a young prostitute's destiny.

This film's poster art is utterly deceiving. What would appear to be a gritty, hardcore and depressing film is, instead, a jaunty, costume-heavy, inner-city fantasy picture.

Roscoe Orman is only adequate in the titular role of a flamboyantly dressed pimp; he simply does not possess much in the way of screen presence. Supporting players Diana (*Honeybaby, Honeybaby*) Sands as Cora, a sympathetic ghetto social worker, and Joyce (*The Education of Sonny Carson*) Walker as Pashen, a new-to-town prostitute, are both infinitely more interesting. Also in the cast are Thalmus (*Mr. Ricco*) Rasulala as Robert Daniels, a sympathetic assistant district attorney, and Royce (*Cool Breeze*) Wallace as Willie's mother.

Cartoonish and predictable, *Willie Dynamite* plays like a TV movie; it's an over-colourful, patently stagey and artificial looking endeavour whose only recommendation is the smorgasbord of 1970s hairstyles, fashions and fantasy interiors on display. Screenwriter Ron Cutler (along with director Gilbert Moses) is African American.

"The costumes, language, melodrama, performances and soundtrack are so outrageously broad it seems as if the film were putting itself on..."
(A. H. Weiler, New York Times)

THE WIZ

1978, USA
G (25326), Musical, 133m.
Universal Pictures.
D: Sidney Lumet; P: Rob Cohen; S: Joel Schumacher, based on the musical by William F. Brown and Charlie Smalls.

Cast: Diana Ross, Michael Jackson, Richard Pryor, Lena Horne, Nipsey Russell, Ted Ross.

The Wiz! The Stars! The Music! Wow!"

A New York City schoolteacher's most heartfelt hopes and desires are revealed in a dream/fantasy.

This hopelessly misguided film adaptation of the Broadway musical *The Wiz* (which itself was an African-American adaptation of the 1939 film *The Wizard of Oz* – which was a filmed version of the 1900 children's book *The Wonderful Wizard of Oz* by L. Frank Baum) is a failure on every level.

Diana Ross is embarrassingly miscast in the lead as Dorothy, a 30-something Harlem schoolteacher. Too old and too jaded, Ross's performance reads false at every turn. As the timid, eager-to-please scarecrow who only wants a brain, Michael Jackson (in a role that predated both his plastic surgery infamy and his notoriety as the 'king of pop') also seems to lack the vitality and individuality needed to overcome both his unattractive costuming and uncomfortable-looking, clown-like makeup. (His weak-voiced contribution to the soundtrack album is equally disheartening.) The Tin Man, here discovered in an abandoned amusement park, is deftly played by veteran actor/comedian Nipsey Russell – who makes the character not only genuinely funny, but also oddly believable. Last, but not least, is Ted Ross as the cowardly lion who wants courage. Ross, the only actor

above: Ted Ross, Michael Jackson, Diana Ross and Nipsey Russell lost in unflattering costumes and make-up in the dark, dank and thoroughly uninspired musical **The Wiz** (1978).

in the film who was also in the original Broadway production, turns in an I've-seen-and-done-all-this-many-times-before performance that satisfies, but at the same time seems pat and tired. Cameo slots are provided for Richard Pryor as the lying, incompetent 'leader' of Emerald City, and Lena Horne as Glinda the Good Witch.

Overlong, pretentious and over-reaching, this $30,000,000 flop (at the time, the most expensive black-cast film ever made) was a movie that not only played to empty houses, but also arguably gave Hollywood the excuse it needed to cease making black cast and black themed motion pictures altogether.

"Sidney Lumet has worked for two years and employed the talents of hundreds of people only to produce a film that looks rushed and cheap..."
(Pauline Kael, New Yorker)

WOMEN IN CAGES

1971, Philippines/USA
Alternative Titles: *Bamboo Doll House, Women's Penitentiary III*
R (414), Action/Adventure, 78m.
New World Pictures.
D: Gerry De Leon [Gerardo de Leon];
P: Ben Balatbat, Cirio H. Santiago [uncredited], Roger Corman [uncredited];
S: James H. Watkins, David R. Osterhout.
Cast: Pamela [Pam] Grier, Judy Brown, Roberta Collins, Jennifer Gan.

"They've been sexually abused, tortured and beaten, but their will to survive is strong."

A group of women, who are the victims of sadomasochistic rituals behind bars, plot an escape.

The cast of characters in this dull, drab, painfully derivative bore of a film include: Alabama (Pam Grier), a masochistic lesbian head mistress; Jeff (Jennifer Gan), a hulking dim-witted redhead; Stoke (Roberta [*The Big Doll House*] Collins), a tart-tongued trouble-maker; and Sandy (Judy [*Slaughter's Big Rip-Off*] Brown), the gang's sensible leader.

Super-low-budget and filled with bored-looking performers, this film has an admittedly great title, but is itself a laboured, over-stretched and joyless endeavour that, even though it features Pam Grier in an against-type villainess role, is a major disappointment.

above: Gang member Rommel (Lawrence Hilton-Jacobs) shows his shotgun to a mob heavy played by Bernie Weissman, in 1978's **Youngblood**. (J. Howard Collection)
opposite top right: Pam Grier as the sadistic Alabama in 1971's **Women in Cages**.

YOUNGBLOOD

1978, USA
R (24929), Action/Adventure, 90m.
American International Pictures.
D: Noel Nosseck; P: Nick Grillo, Alan Riche; S: Paul Carter Harrison.
Cast: Bryan O'Dell, Lawrence Hilton-Jacobs, Ren Woods, Ann Weldon, David Pendleton, Bernie Weissman.

"If you live through the gang wars, the pushers, the back-alley death traps... you gonna be a star!"

An African-American teenage boy attempts to prove his manhood by joining a local gang.

Bryan O'Dell is outstanding in his big screen debut as 'Youngblood' Gordon, a troubled youth in search of himself. Emotionally involved, subtle and, at times, convincingly mischievous and violent, he is part of a small group of young, exceptionally talented performers who have the ability to breathe fresh new life into familiar film situations. Lawrence Hilton-Jacobs (best known as Freddie Washington on TV's *Welcome Back, Kotter*) is also remarkable as returning Vietnam Vet, Rommel. Arrogant, yet fearful, his is a frustrated black character that, as he awkwardly makes the transition from adolescence to adulthood, is recognisable from real life. Also memorable is Ann Weldon as Mrs. Gordon, 'Youngblood's' matter of fact mom:

Mrs. Gordon (to Principal): *My husband passed on a long time ago.*

Principal: *Oh, I'm sorry – I didn't know.*
Mrs. Gordon: *Ain't nothin' to be sorry about – he just passed on* [abandoned the family].

Other cast members who provide memorable performances include David Pendleton as Reggie, Youngblood's successful 'banker' brother, and Ren Woods as Sybil, Youngblood's drug-addicted girlfriend.

Violent gang wars, a visit to a neighbourhood discothèque (in which several of TV's *Soul Train Dancers* are featured), and a climactic shootout and chase through a lumberyard, are all part of this film's vastly entertaining mix; *Youngblood* is one of blaxploitation's best youth-centred pictures, along with *Aaron Loves Angela*.

THE ZEBRA FORCE

1976, USA
R (1439), Action/Adventure, 90m.
Entertainment International Pictures.
D: Joe Tornatore; P: Joe Tornatore, Larry Price; S: Joe Tornatore.
Cast: Rockne Tarkington, Timothy Brown, Mike Lane, Richard X. Slattery.

"Who are these men of steel? When they strike all hell explodes... and the underground world trembles!"

A gang of 'black' men execute a series of high-stakes robberies of mob-controlled money.

A man's blaxploitation film – literally (there are no females in lead or minor parts) – this little-seen, low-budget entry features an inspired story idea that, unfortunately, does not quite come off.

Mike Lane gives an impassioned and believable performance in the lead as Lt. Johnson, a horribly disfigured, armless and vengeful returning Vietnam Vet. By turns excitable, then melancholy, his is the crafty presentation of a man who has not accepted the heavy price he has had to pay for serving his country. Rockne (*Black*

Samson) Tarkington is also impressive in the role of African-American Mob associate Earl Lovington. Fearless, somewhat arrogant, and tired of having to prove himself to 'whitey,' he is the kind of street smart black man who can, and does, back up everything he says. Also notable are Richard X. Slattery as Carmine Longo, an Italian mob henchman, and, in a surprise final-act cameo, Timothy (*Dynamite Brothers*) Brown.

Filled with slow motion shootouts, car crashes, 'masked' underground heists, and a Vietnam War flashback, *The Zebra Force* is an ambitious but uneven, and ultimately unsatisfying, film. Even so, the peculiar plot twist, along with superior special effects and decent 'transformation' makeup, make it worth a look.

THE ZEBRA KILLER

1974, USA
Alternative Titles: *Combat Cops*; *Panic City*
PG (1142), Action/Adventure, 90m.
General Film Corporation.
D: William Girdler; P: Gordon C. Layne, Mike Henry; S: William Girdler.
Cast: Austin Stoker, James Pickett, Hugh Smith, D'Urville Martin, Valery Rogers.

"No black man ever killed like this!"

A young black man is the main suspect in an investigation into a series of bizarre killings.

In the role of Mac, a marauding racist killer, James Pickett seems to be having a good time. Energetic, quirky, and comfortable spewing a litany of racial epithets, the actor gives his all, and if he is not totally convincing, at least he is thoroughly game as he negotiates this movie's unusual twists and turns with a degree of warped style. Fast on his trail is ultra fastidious detective Frank Savage, played by Austin (*Sheba Baby*) Stoker. Support comes in the shape of Valery Rogers as 'Frank's Lady,' and D'Urville Martin as a loud-mouthed flesh peddler who, in a satisfying turn of events, ends up being beaten up by a group of disgruntled prostitutes in an alley!

Filled with poorly executed scenes of violence (a stabbing, a car bomb, a man pushed down an elevator shaft), and unfortunately laden with a relentlessly tinny soundtrack, *The Zebra Killer* is a meandering film whose novel story idea is never fully realised. (In an apparent attempt at redemption the filmmakers decided to dedicate the picture to "the officers and men of the Louisville, Kentucky Police Department." It's a dedication that the police department can, most definitely, do without.)

"A boring mess with very little action and even less production values."
(David Walker, BadAzz MoFo magazine issue #6)

Bibliography

Albright, Brian. "Hell Up in Harlem: Pushermen, Private Dicks, Pimpmobiles and Baadasss Songs." *Alternative Cinema*, Summer, 1996

Albright, Brian. "Original Gangstas: Superbad Superheroes of the Seventies Save the Hood." *Alternative Cinema*, Summer, 1996

Alexander, Francis. "Stereotyping As a Method of Exploitation in Film." *Black Scholar*, May 1976

Allen, Bonnie. "The Macho Men: Whatever Happened to Them?" *Essence*, February 1979

Ames, Catherine and Smith, Sunde. "Queen of the B's." *Time*, 2 February, 1976

Arkoff, Sam. *Flying Through Hollywood By the Seat of My Pants*. New York: Birch Lane Press, 1992

Bailey, Peter. "A Black Woman with White Fever." *New York Times*, 26 March, 1972

Bennett, Lerone, Jr. "The Emancipation Orgasm: Sweetback in Wonderland." *Ebony*, September 1971

Bogle, Donald. *Blacks in American Films and Television*. New York: Simon & Schuster, 1988

Bogle, Donald. *Toms, Coons, Mulattoes, Mamies & Bucks: An Interpretive History of Blacks in American Films*. New York: Continuum, 1973

Cocks, Jay. "Mothers Day." *Time*, 12 December, 1972

Corman, Roger. *How I Made a Hundred Movies in Hollywood and Never Lost a Dime*. New York: Random House, 1990

Cripps, Thomas. *Black Film As Genre*. Indiana: Indiana University Press, 1979

Cripps, Thomas. *Making Movies Black*. England: Oxford University Press, 1993

Donalson, Melvin. *Black Directors in Hollywood*. University of Texas Press, 2003

Dotson, John. "I Want Freedom to See the Good and the Bad." *Newsweek*, 23 October, 1972

Fraser, Gerald. "An Artist Reminisces" *New York Times*, 3 December, 1975

Freidson, Michael. "Getting the Shaft." *Time Out*, 8 August, 2002

Gardella, Kay. "Cicely Tyson: Actress By Accident, Star By Design." *N.Y. Daily News*, 6 January, 1974

George, Nelson. *Blackface: Reflections on African Americans and the Movies*. New York: Harper Perennial, 1995

Green, Theophilus. "The Black Man As Movie Hero: New Films Offer a Different Male Image." *Ebony*, August 1972

Greenspun, Roger. "Screen: Soul Gumshoe." *New York Times*, 3 July, 1971

Guerrero, Ed. *Framing Blackness: The African-American Image in Film*. Philadelphia: Temple University Press, 1993

Harmetz, Aljean. "The Dime-store Way to Make Movies-and Money." *New York Times*, 4 August, 1974

Harris, Middleton. *The Black Book*. New York: Random House, 1974

Higgins, Chester. "Black Films: Boom Or Bust." *Jet*, 8 June, 1972

Hoberman, Jim. "A Forgotten Black Cinema Surfaces." *Village Voice*, 17 November, 1975

Holly, Ellen. "Where Are the Films About Real Black Men and Women?" *New York Times*, 2 June, 1974

Horton, Lucy. "Battle Among the Beauties: Black Actresses Vie for Top Film Roles." *Ebony*, November 1973

Hyatt, Marshall. *The Afro-American Cinematic Experience*. New Brunswick, New Jersey: Rutgers University Books, 1983

James, Darius. *That's Blaxploitation*. New York: St. Martin's Press, 1995

Klotman, Phyllis Rauch. *Frame By Frame... A Black Filmography*. Indiana University Press, 1979

Koven, Mikel J. *Blaxploitation Films*. Great Britain: Pocket Essentials, 2001

Landay, Eileen. *Black Film Stars*. New York: Drake, 1973

Leab, Daniel J. *From Sambo to Superspade: The Black Experience in Motion Pictures*. Boston: Houghton Mifflin, 1975

MacDonald, J. Fred. *Blacks & White TV*. Chicago: Nelson-Hall Publishers, 1983

Mapp, Edward. *Blacks in American Films: Today and Yesterday*. Metuchen, New Jersey: Scarecrow Press, 1972

Martinez, Gerald, Martinez, Diana and Chavez, Andres. *What It Is... What It Was! The Black Film Explosion of the '70s in Words and Pictures*. New York: Hyperian, 1998

Michener, Charles. "Black Movies: Renaissance Or Rip-off?" *Newsweek*, 23 October, 1972

Murray, James. *To Find an Image: Black Films from Uncle Tom to Super Fly*. Indianapolis: Bobbs-Merrill, 1973

Nederveen Pieterse, Jan. *White on Black: Images of Africa and Blacks in Western Popular Culture*. London, England: Yale University Press, 1992

Null, Gary. *Black Hollywood: The Black Performer in Motion Pictures*. Seacacus, New Jersey: Citadel Press, 1975

Parish, James Robert and Hill, George H. *Black Action Films*. North Carolina: McFarland & Company, 1989

Parks, Gordon. *A Hungry Heart*. New York: Atria Books, 2005

Patterson, Lindsay. *Black Films and Film-makers*. New York: Dodd, Mead, 1975

Poniewozik, James. "Can You Dig It? Right On!" *Time*, 19 August, 2002

Pym, John. *Time Out Film Guide*. London: Penguin Books, 2003

Reid, Mark, A. *Redefining Black Film*. University of California Press, 1993

Richards, Tyson. "Black Films: Culture Or Con Game?" *Ebony*, 12 December, 1972

Riley, Clayton. "What Makes Sweetback Run?" *New York Times*, 9 May, 1971

Schwartz, Carol and Olenski, Jim. *VideoHound's Cult Flicks & Trash Picks*. Michigan: Visible Inc. Press, 1995

Storm, Mason. "Blaxploitation & Spaghetti Westerns." *Encyclopedia of Cinematic Trash Vol. 2*, 1997

Thompson, Howard. "'Super Fly T.N.T.' Continues with His Adventures in Rome and Africa." *New York Times*, 16 June, 1973

Walker, John. *Halliwell's Film & Video Guide*. New York: Harper Collins, 2003

Ward, Renee. "Black Films, White Profits." *The Black Scholar*, May 1976

Weiler, A.H. "'Coffy,' Black Oriented Film Arrives." *New York Times*, 16 June, 1973

Williams, John A., and Williams, Dennis A. *If I Stop I'll Die: The Comedy and Tragedy of Richard Pryor*. Thunder's Mouth Press, 1991

Blaxploitation Admat Gallery

A selection of rare admats for Blaxploitation movies, including alternative variations upon designs shown elsewhere in the book.

GIT BACK JACK — GIVE HIM NO JIVE...
HE IS THE BAAAD'EST CAT IN '75

A MATT CIMBER PRODUCTION

THE CANDY TANGERINE MAN

R

Those 'Cotton Comes To Harlem' cops are at it again!

Coffin Ed and Gravedigger Jones and a ghost that just won't quit!

COME BACK CHARLESTON BLUE

PG

WATCH OUT MISTER... HERE COMES THE TWISTER!

RUDY RAY MOORE is THE HUMAN TORNADO

...Nerve-Shattering
...Brain-Battering
...Mind-Splattering
...A ONE MAN DISASTER!

The Final Comedown

THE MAN GOT DOWN...THE BROTHERS WERE READY...YOU MUST SEE IT!...IT'S A MOTHER!

R METROCOLOR

starring BILLY DEE WILLIAMS
special guest star RAYMOND ST. JACQUES

The stars of "SUPERFLY" are back in

THE HITTER

RON O'NEAL   SHEILA FRAZIER

R

NEVER BEFORE A PICTURE LIKE THIS — HARLEM PRESS

GHETTO FREAKS (GONNA GET YOUR STUFF)

R

Don't call him "Boy" if you want to keep breathing!

GHETTO RAT

...in a town where all the chicks are on the make and all the dudes are on the take...

COLOR

THEIRS:

THIS IS THE MOB. THEY SAID IT WOULD TAKE AN ARMY TO GET THEM OUT OF HARLEM.

OURS:

THIS IS THE ARMY!

IT'S WAR BABY, IT'S GORDON'S WAR!

The battlefield is Harlem.   The enemy is the Mob.   The General is a cat named Gordon.   He's got a four-man army and a foolproof plan.

DESTROY THE PUSHER'S CAR!   HARRASS THE HOSTILES!   CUT THE SUPPLY LINES!   DON'T GET DESTROYED YOURSELF!

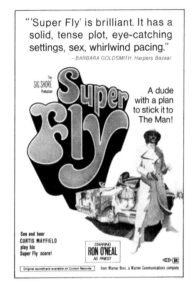

Index

Page references in **bold** refer exclusively to illustrations, though pages referenced as text entries may also feature relevant illustrations.

Blacula

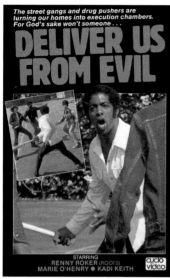

right: Jim Kelly in **Three the Hard Way**

More Quality Books for Cult Connoisseurs from FAB Press

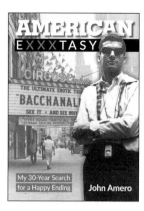

AMERICAN EXXXTASY
My 30-Year Search for a Happy Ending
The Autobiography of John Amero
Paperback
ISBN: 978-1-913051-13-6

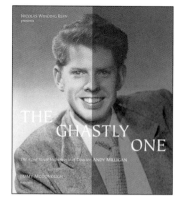

THE GHASTLY ONE
The 42nd Street Netherworld of Director
Andy Milligan by Jimmy McDonough
Paperback
ISBN: 978-1-913051-15-0

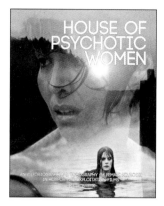

HOUSE OF PSYCHOTIC WOMEN
An Autobiographical Topography of
Female Neurosis in Horror and
Exploitation Films by Kier-La Janisse
ISBN: 978-1-903254-69-1

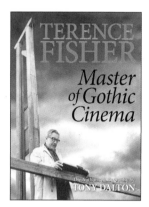

TERENCE FISHER
Master of Gothic Cinema
The Authorised Biography by Tony Dalton
ISBN: 978-1-913051-09-9

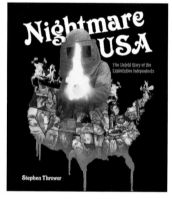

NIGHTMARE USA
The Untold Story of the Exploitation
Independents by Stephen Thrower
ISBN: 978-1-903254-46-2

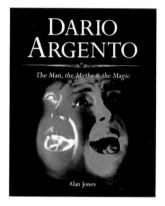

DARIO ARGENTO
The Man, the Myths & the Magic
by Alan Jones
ISBN: 978-1-903254-70-7

RE-AGITATOR
A Decade of Writing on Takashi Miike
by Tom Mes
ISBN: 978-1-903254-71-4

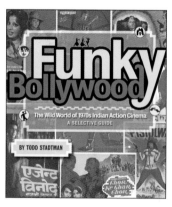

FUNKY BOLLYWOOD
The Wild World of 1970s Indian Action Cinema
A Selective Guide by Todd Stadtman
ISBN: 978-1-903254-77-6

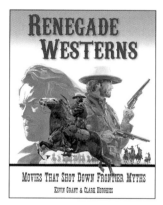

RENEGADE WESTERNS
Movies That Shot Down Frontier Myths
by Kevin Grant & Clark Hodgkiss
ISBN: 978-1-903254-93-6

For further information about these books and many more from the extensive FAB Press range please visit our online store, where you can purchase them at special discounted rates and browse our fine selection of cult movie merchandise from all over the world!

www.fabpress.com